FEDERAL

TAX RESEARCH

GUIDE TO

MATERIALS AND TECHNIQUES

By

GAIL LEVIN RICHMOND

Professor of Law
Nova Southeastern University, Shepard Broad Law Center

—————

EIGHTH EDITION

UNIVERSITY TEXTBOOK SERIES

FOUNDATION PRESS
2010

© 1990, 1997, 2002 FOUNDATION PRESS
© 2007 THOMSON REUTERS/FOUNDATION PRESS
© 2010 By THOMSON REUTERS/FOUNDATION PRESS
195 Broadway, 9th Floor
New York, NY 10007
Phone Toll Free 1–877–888–1330
Fax (212) 367–6799
foundation–press.com
Printed in the United States of America

ISBN 978–1–59941–742–4

Mat #40880270

To

My grandchildren

PREFACE

In 1975 I first offered a Tax Practice Seminar involving current issues in taxation. Students selected issues and presented their findings as ruling requests, audit protest memoranda, and statements before congressional committees. After being deluged with requests for library tours, I consulted the standard legal research texts to compile readings describing the available materials. Much to my surprise, I discovered those texts devoted little, if any, space to materials commonly used for tax research. This text is an outgrowth of my 1975 library tours.

Research techniques are highly personalized. While the format of this text reflects my own preferences, it can be adapted to almost any variation the user may devise. Although I use it most frequently as an instructional guide for students, I know of many practitioners who have used it as an aid to finding materials.

The problems at the end of most chapters cover both historical materials and fairly recent items. Both types have value as teaching tools. Most problems involving recent law can be solved using electronic sources—both government and commercial; those problems enhance or introduce online and CD/DVD research skills. Historical materials appear for a different reason. Although electronic databases continue to add retrospective coverage, some materials are not yet available electronically. In those cases, users must consult print or microform materials. In addition, electronic searches may involve usage fees. Researchers who are familiar with print materials should be able to use them in a cost-effective manner.

Every new edition benefits from suggestions made by numerous tax professors, practitioners, and librarians. Library staff members at my own institution are particularly generous with their time and their budget allocations. I could not describe so many items were they not committed to maintaining an excellent tax collection.

GAIL LEVIN RICHMOND

Davie, Florida
March 2010

v

Summary of Contents

TABLE OF CONTENTS

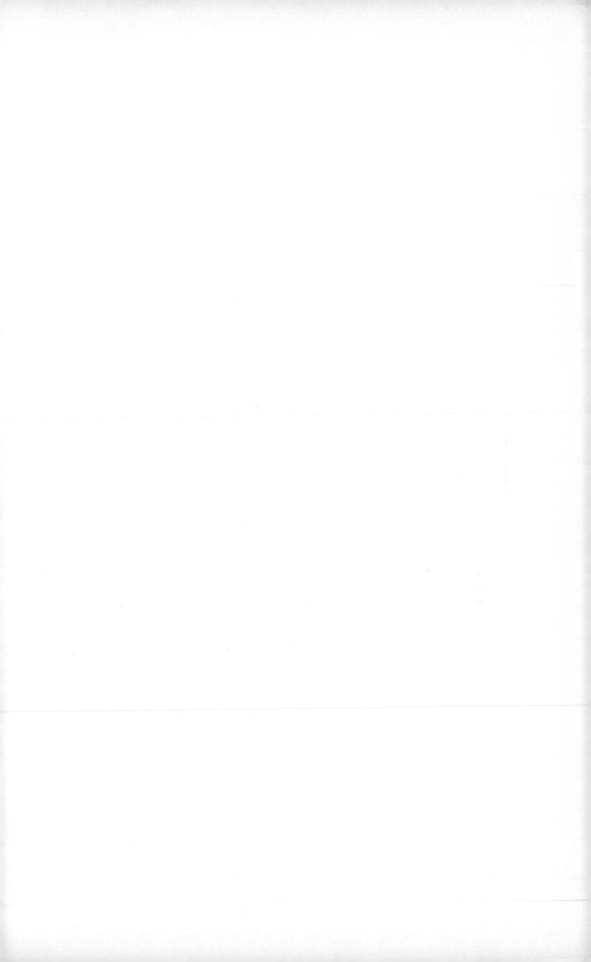

FEDERAL

TAX RESEARCH

GUIDE TO

MATERIALS AND TECHNIQUES

CHAPTER 1. OVERVIEW

SECTION A. INTRODUCTION

This book is about federal tax research. If you covered tax in a general legal research course, you already know that tax research has much in common with other types of legal research. If this is your first experience with tax research, this book will introduce you to those common features.

Common features are a good starting point, but there are complicating factors. Unlike problems in some areas of law, a single tax problem often involves legislation, administrative rulings, and judicial opinions. You may have to plan a transaction rather than litigate a completed event. Planning can require researching alternative structures—and you may still encounter after-the-fact litigation. Because tax law changes rapidly, and some changes are retroactive, keeping current is a time-consuming task. Certain specialties within tax are—to say the least—extraordinarily complex. Given these facts, it is not surprising that many attorneys believe tax research has nothing in common with traditional legal research.

SECTION B. FORMAT OF THIS BOOK

This book has five functions. First, it lists and describes primary and secondary sources of federal tax law. Second, it provides information about finding those materials. Third, it discusses evaluating what you have found. Fourth, it covers methods for updating the results of your research. Fifth, and perhaps most important, it includes problems designed to exercise your tax research skills. In carrying out these functions, this book builds on techniques covered in a general legal research class.

This chapter describes how the book is organized and lists certain conventions I am using. Chapter 2 introduces various types of authority, and Chapter 3 describes factors affecting the research process. Chapter 4 takes you through a problem that involves many of the sources you will study later in this book. Chapter 4 also includes some unsolved problems you can use to test your tax research skills.

The next group of chapters introduces each type of primary authority. Chapter 5 begins with the Constitution. That document's first three articles describe powers (and limits on those powers) of the three branches of government we encounter in Chapters 6 through 11. Although those chapters focus on primary authority—legislation, treaties, administrative pronouncements, and judicial opinions—they also cover some secondary authority produced by government entities. Those chapters discuss what is available and how to find it, why it is important, how to interpret it, and what deference it may receive in court.

Chapter 12 covers a familiar topic, citators, including two that cover only tax materials. Chapters 13 through 16 cover another familiar topic, finding and using secondary sources. These sources include looseleaf services and treatises, indexes to periodical articles and the articles themselves, form books, and newsletters.

The last group of chapters covers collections of primary or secondary source materials. The first of these chapters discusses microform services. The other chapters cover electronic services, both CD/DVD and online. I refer to and illustrate electronic materials throughout the book, but the earlier discussions focus only on particular items. The later chapters provide a global look at what these services cover and include some information about how to use them.

The book concludes with five Appendixes:

- Appendix A   Commonly Used Abbreviations
- Appendix B   Alternate Citation Forms
- Appendix C   Potential Research Errors
- Appendix D   Bibliography
- Appendix E   Commonly Owned Publishers

SECTION C. USER NOTES

1. Describing Sources

As noted in Section B, I may describe a service in one or more chapters because it is relevant to the topics covered in those chapters. I may also cover a service in more detail later in the book; this is particularly true for electronic services, which include significant amounts of primary and secondary authority. In making decisions about where to describe services, I have tried to avoid unnecessary repetition. I have also included several cross-references to other chapters.

A caveat is in order. My descriptions and illustrations cannot substitute for a service's user's guide. This is particularly important for electronic services, which vary in their search command structures and continually change both coverage dates and sources included. Pathfinders and other library-prepared reference materials are also useful guides for accessing materials.

2. Problem Assignments

Most chapters include short problems. Locating the primary source materials you need for solving problems in Chapters 4 through 11 often requires using materials described in later chapters. You should consult those descriptions on an as-needed basis. Although you can easily solve many of the problems using electronic sources, you may need to use print or microform materials when you search for older items.

3. Illustrations and Tables

This book includes illustrations and tables. Illustrations show primary and secondary source material as it appears in the source from which it is excerpted.[1] Tables compile useful information about particular topics.

Because I refer to some illustrations and tables in more than one chapter, I numbered them by chapter to make them easier to locate. These references to illustrations and tables appear in brackets rather than in parentheses [e.g., Illustration 3-1; Table 5-3].

4. Bold Face and Arrows

To emphasize terms discussed in this book, I put them in **bold face** type. Arrows ($\rightarrow$) indicate discussion relating to an illustration or table.

5. Citation Format

Legal citation format is prescribed in a variety of sources, including TaxCite, The Bluebook, and the ALWD Citation Manual.[2] These sources differ in their treatment of various items, and their citation format often differs from that used by the material's original publisher.

---

[1] Because I obtained several Illustrations by scanning or using a screen capture function, the font or text size may differ slightly from a publisher's original version. The final product is close to the original and should not inconvenience or confuse researchers.

[2] TAXCITE: A FEDERAL TAX CITATION AND REFERENCE MANUAL (1995) (compiled by The Virginia Tax Review, Tax Law Review, and the ABA Section of Taxation; the ABA group received assistance from student editors of The Tax Lawyer); THE BLUEBOOK: A UNIFORM SYSTEM OF CITATION (18th ed. 2005) (compiled by the editors of the Columbia Law Review, Harvard Law Review, University of Pennsylvania Law Review, and The Yale Law Journal); ALWD CITATION MANUAL: A PROFESSIONAL SYSTEM OF CITATION app. 7 (3d ed. 2006) (compiled by the Association of Legal Writing Directors and Darby Dickerson). Websites for the latter two citation manuals include additional material.

Citation differences are particularly notable for IRS material. For example, TaxCite uses P.L.R. to cite private letter rulings (e.g., P.L.R. 2009-40-003). The Bluebook uses I.R.S. Priv. Ltr. Rul. (e.g., I.R.S. Priv. Ltr. Rul. 2009-40-003). The ALWD Manual uses either P.L.R. or Priv. Ltr. Rul. (e.g., P.L.R. 2009-40-003 or Priv. Ltr. Rul. 2009-40-003). Although all three hyphenate the ruling numbers, the IRS itself does not use hyphens and is likely to use PLR rather than the other identifiers. If you search for 200940003, you can easily find it online; if you search for 2009-40-003, you may be less successful. Thus, it is critical to determine which format(s) the service you use recognizes. Note that print services are likely to use a single format; some electronic services recognize more than one format.

Because citation manuals, law reviews, and courts use different citation formats, Appendix B includes several variations for selected primary sources. Before submitting your research, remember to format each citation in the style your recipient mandates.

Note that I do not italicize signals (such as "see" and "compare") or Latin terms (such as "i.e." and "e.g.") in text or footnotes. I also use italics and small capitals very sparingly in both footnotes and text. I generally limit italics and small capitals to footnote references to articles and reports. I made these formatting decisions primarily to enhance readability. They do not reflect a preference for a particular citation system.

6. Abbreviations

As the example in Subsection 5 illustrates, different services use different abbreviations for the same item. Even if every service uses the same abbreviation, you may not know what the letters mean. Appendix A provides an extensive list of abbreviations.

7. Cut-Off Dates

This edition went into production in late March 2010. Most illustrations and descriptions were completed between December 2009 and early March 2010. It is likely that some services, particularly those delivered electronically, will change their layout or coverage before a new edition appears. LexisNexis and Westlaw are currently updating their systems.

8. A Note on Free Sources

As this book illustrates, there are numerous subscription and free services available, and many items are available in multiple formats and from multiple publishers. If you are a student, you may never use some of the materials described here. For example, you may not need to read public comments on proposed regulations or determine if a proposed regulation has an impact on small business. Likewise, because you probably have free access to a variety of subscription services, you may have no need for free government websites or print materials. If you are a practitioner, or a student clerking for one, you may find that free sources provide the information you need in a cost-effective way. I have tried to accommodate both groups in discussing research materials.

9. Bibliography

This book's primary purpose is to familiarize you with various types of authority and how to find them. If you are interested in particular topics addressed in the book (for example, deference), the bibliography in Appendix D may be a useful starting point.

CHAPTER 2. TYPES OF AUTHORITY

SECTION A. INTRODUCTION

Because many factors influence the process, there is no "right" way to begin and end a tax research project. Your method of attack depends on the nature of the problem and your familiarity with the subject matter. While many research efforts begin with the relevant statutory provisions, others start with explanatory materials. The appropriate ending place depends on the type of problem and the number of sources you need to consult before resolving the issues raised.

At various points between the start and finish, most research efforts involve both primary and secondary authority. Primary authority carries more weight than does secondary authority. In addition, some primary authorities carry more weight than do others.

SECTION B. PRIMARY AND SECONDARY AUTHORITY

Primary authority emanates from a branch of government: legislative; executive (including administrative); or judicial. In addition to the Constitution, it includes statutes, treaties, Treasury regulations, Internal Revenue Service (IRS) documents, and judicial decisions. If a problem has international aspects, you may have to consult primary authorities from multiple countries or from international organizations. **Secondary authorities**—including treatises, looseleaf services, and articles—explain (and sometimes criticize) primary authorities.

Some publications (e.g., Code of Federal Regulations) contain one type of primary authority; others (e.g., Internal Revenue Bulletin) contain several types. Many services (e.g., United States Tax Reporter, LexisNexis, and Checkpoint) contain both primary and secondary authorities. In considering primary authority, remember two facts. First, some documents published by the government do not qualify as primary authority. These include the legislative histories discussed in Chapter 7, which have characteristics of both primary and secondary authority.[3] Second, an authority doesn't lose its status as primary when it is reproduced by a nongovernment publisher.

---

[3] This book describes legislative histories in the chapters on primary sources because (1) they emanate from a branch of government; (2) the IRS considers them authority for avoiding the substantial understatement penalty described later in this chapter; and (3) you would consult them immediately after reading statutory text in many research efforts. Nevertheless, many legislative history documents are considered secondary sources.

SECTION C. HIERARCHY OF AUTHORITY

Not all authorities are equal in value. Primary authorities carry more weight than do secondary authorities, and some primary authorities carry more weight than others. An authority's value varies depending upon the body reviewing it and the purpose for which it is being submitted. The subsections below, covering precedential, persuasive, and substantial authority, illustrate these distinctions.

1. Precedential and Persuasive Authority

The Treasury Department and IRS recognize a hierarchy of sources. Courts also value some authorities more than others. Certain holdings constitute **binding precedent**, which must be followed. Others are considered merely **persuasive** and receive little, if any, deference. Secondary sources fall into the latter category, but so do many primary sources. For example, the IRS will follow a Supreme Court decision in its dealings with other taxpayers. It may, however, choose to ignore an adverse lower court opinion and continue litigating a particular issue. The telephone tax litigation is one example of the IRS continuing to litigate an issue.[4]

An authority is not precedential merely because a court or administrative agency issued it. The type of document is also important. In some instances, for example, the IRS is not bound by its own pronouncements. Although it issues both officially published revenue rulings and privately published letter rulings, third parties with comparable facts may rely on the revenue rulings but not on the letter rulings. The relationship of one deciding body to another is also relevant. One trial court (e.g., the Tax Court) may refuse to treat as precedential an opinion issued by another trial court (e.g., the Court of Federal Claims). These limitations are discussed further in Chapters 9 through 11, which cover administrative and judicial sources.

2. Substantial Authority

An authority may have value even if the IRS rejects it. First, the Service might be incorrect. A court (perhaps even the Supreme Court) may rely on the particular authority in rendering its decision. Second, litigation involves more than the underlying substantive issue; penalties are

---

[4] See Notice 2006-50, 2006-25 I.R.B. 1141, in which the IRS announced it would stop litigating this issue, which it had lost in five appellate courts. The most recent round of telephone tax litigation concerns the IRS mechanism for claiming telephone tax refunds. See, e.g., Cohen v. United States, 578 F.3d 1 (D.C. Cir. 2009). IRS announcements concerning its litigation plans are discussed in Chapters 10 and 11.

also relevant. If the Service asserts the Code section 6662(b)(2) penalty for substantial understatement of income tax liability, the authority you found may shield the taxpayer from liability.

Section 6662(d)(2)(B)(i) waives this 20 percent penalty if the taxpayer has **substantial authority** for a position. This determination requires that the taxpayer's position be backed by recognized authority and that the authority be substantial.

A Treasury regulation lists the items below as authority for this purpose.[5] Note that several of them may be binding precedent, while others are at best persuasive authority.

• applicable provisions of the Internal Revenue Code and other statutory provisions;

• proposed, temporary and final regulations construing such statutes;

• revenue rulings and revenue procedures;

• tax treaties and regulations thereunder, and Treasury Department and other official explanations of such treaties;

• court cases;

• congressional intent as reflected in committee reports, joint explanatory statements of managers included in conference committee reports, and floor statements made prior to enactment by one of a bill's managers;

• General Explanations of tax legislation prepared by the Joint Committee on Taxation (the Blue Book);

• private letter rulings and technical advice memoranda issued after October 31, 1976;

• actions on decisions and general counsel memoranda issued after March 12, 1981 (as well as general counsel memoranda published in pre-1955 volumes of the Cumulative Bulletin);

• Internal Revenue Service information or press releases; and

• notices, announcements and other administrative pronouncements published by the Service in the Internal Revenue Bulletin.

---

[5] Treas. Reg. § 1.6662-4(d)(3)(iii). Taxpayers can also avoid this penalty by adequately disclosing the relevant facts if there is a reasonable basis for the tax treatment claimed. I.R.C. § 6662(d)(2)(B)(ii). The section 6662 regulations also constitute authority for avoiding the understatement penalty imposed on tax return preparers for taking an unreasonable position. See I.R.C. § 6694(a)(2); Treas. Reg. § 1.6694-2(b).

Conclusions reached in treatises or other legal periodicals and opinions rendered by tax professionals do not constitute authority for avoiding this penalty. In addition, the regulation provides rules by which overruled and reversed items lose their status as authority and older items receive less regard.[6]

3. Compiling a Table of Authorities

As part of your research effort, you could categorize authorities you locate in a table format. Table 2-1 illustrates one possible format. In the interest of brevity, it covers only five items of authority. If you do use this method, remember that an item's status as precedential is affected by the entity to which you are submitting it. Thus, a Fourth Circuit decision will be precedential in a District Court located in Virginia but would be only persuasive if you are litigating in Tennessee, which is located in the Sixth Circuit. A recent private letter ruling is more valuable as authority than one issued in 2000.

Table 2-1. Categorizing Authority

Item	Precedential Authority	Substantial Authority
Supreme Court decision	Yes	Yes
Fourth Circuit decision	Maybe	Yes
Private Letter Ruling	No	Maybe
Field Service Advice	No	No
Law Review Article	No	No

SECTION D. EXAMPLES

1. Precedential Authority

Examples of statements concerning precedent appear in Chapters 9 through 11, which cover administrative and judicial authority.

2. Substantial Authority

The judicial decisions and IRS rulings[7] below involved taxpayers who claimed they had substantial authority. Westlaw and LexisNexis cita-

---

[6] "An older private letter ruling, technical advice memorandum, general counsel memorandum or action on decision generally must be accorded less weight than a more recent one. Any document described in the preceding sentence that is more than 10 years old generally is accorded very little weight." Treas. Reg. § 1.6662-4(d)(3)(ii). This limitation does not apply to other IRS documents, such as revenue rulings. See Field Service Advisory (Nov. 17, 1994), 1994 WL 1725562, 1994 FSA LEXIS 464.

[7] Litigation remains an option for a taxpayer whose claim is denied by the IRS.

tions are provided so that you can determine what types of authority were involved. You can also find these items on Checkpoint and Intelli-Connect.

a. Successful Claims

• Technical Advice Memorandum 9022001, available at 1990 WL 699510, 1989 PLR LEXIS 4097

• TIFD III-E Inc. v. United States, 660 F. Supp. 2d 367, 396–99 (D. Conn. 2009)

b. Unsuccessful Claims

• Technical Advice Memorandum 200326034, available at 2003 WL 21483117, 2003 PLR LEXIS 345

• Ackerman v. Commissioner, 97 T.C.M. (CCH) 1392 (2009), T.C.M. (RIA) 2009-080, available at 2009 WL 1010861, 2009 Tax Ct. Memo LEX-IS 81

Citation format is not relevant to the discussion in this chapter. Nevertheless, you should note the differences in the LexisNexis and Westlaw citations for the IRS Technical Advice Memoranda and Field Service Advisory (also referred to as Field Service Advice) listed above. Always keep database differences in mind when you use multiple research services.

CHAPTER 3. RESEARCH PROCESS

SECTION A. INTRODUCTION

This chapter continues the overview discussion begun in Chapters 1 and 2. As noted there, your research will involve primary and secondary authorities and will consider the relative weight of each authority you find. This chapter focuses on process. What are your research goals? What methods will you use to find the materials you need? What factors favor using print or electronic sources? These questions reappear in later chapters as part of the discussion of various sources.

SECTION B. RESEARCH TASKS

As is true in other areas of the law, tax research begins with an assignment. To complete the assignment, you must (1) determine the relevant facts and issues; (2) find authorities that are on point (either directly or by analogy); (3) try to reconcile conflicting findings; (4) update your findings; and (5) communicate your conclusions. These are techniques you learned in a basic legal research course.

The type of assignment will influence the course your research takes and the product you produce. Are you structuring a new transaction? Are you litigating the effects of a transaction your clients already completed? Are you testifying before Congress or the Treasury Department to advocate a statutory or administrative change?

In the first situation, future legislation and regulations may be as important as existing law. Because retroactive effective dates are a fact of life, you must be able to locate pending legislation and proposed regulations. Because your client does not want unexpected tax consequences after the transaction closes, you may consider requesting a letter ruling to provide comfort that the IRS agrees with your tax analysis. Your ruling request will include authority that supports the ruling you are requesting.

When the IRS challenges a completed transaction, the statutes in effect when the transaction closed will be more important than future legislation.[8] You may also search for judicial opinions and information about cases currently being litigated. If your client's substantive position fails,

---

[8] But technical corrections bills may affect transactions that took place several years earlier.

you may need to locate sufficient authority to avoid the substantial understatement penalty described in Chapter 2.[9]

In testifying at congressional or Treasury Department hearings, you may want to include detailed history supporting your position. You can find previous legislative and regulatory changes and their effects by tracing rules back to their inception and reading cases and commentary about prior versions.

The above list is not exclusive. You may be researching sources for an article, bibliography, CLE presentation, or class assignment. Your assignment may be narrow in scope (e.g., go to the Tax Court website and find all opinions authored by Judge Vasquez in 2009), or it may require you to consult a variety of primary and secondary sources (e.g., research and write an article arguing for the reinstatement of income averaging). No matter what your goal is, successful research requires an ability to locate relevant sources.

SECTION C. RESEARCH METHODOLOGY

1. In General

As noted above, tax research has much in common with the research techniques covered in a basic research course. Using a set of facts presented, you determine the relevant issues and ascertain any additional facts that might be important. Because a project may be completed over a period of weeks or months, you must regularly update your research by looking for newer materials and using a citator. For the same reason, you must compile a list of sources you consulted and dates you used them.

2. Primary Sources

To resolve the issues you isolate, you must locate any governing statutory language. Legislative history or administrative pronouncements would be the next step if you desire guidance in interpreting the statute. You may then search for judicial decisions interpreting the statute or administrative provisions. In addition to interpreting statutes or regulations, judges may rule on their validity. Judicial decisions may cover constitutional challenges to statutes and regulations. In addition, courts may

---

[9] I.R.C. § 6662(b). In addition, you may need to avoid I.R.C. § 6694(a) preparer penalties. See also Treas. Dept. Circular 230, § 10.34 (31 C.F.R. § 10.34), Standards with respect to tax returns and documents, affidavits and other papers. On the other hand, if the client prevails, you may look for authority to justify charging part of your legal fees to the government. I.R.C. § 7430 provides for recovery of attorneys' fees if the government's position was not substantially justified and the taxpayer meets certain other requirements.

determine whether a regulation or ruling appropriately interprets a statute.[10] If your problem involves non-U.S. source income or citizens of other countries, your research expands to include applicable treaties and related materials.

3. Secondary Sources

If you are familiar with the subject matter involved, you might locate the relevant primary sources without using any secondary materials other than a citator. When you lack such familiarity, you might start your project by consulting secondary materials. Secondary sources have two advantages. First, they explain the topic you are researching. Second, they provide citations to the relevant Code sections and other primary sources. Looseleaf services, treatises, and periodical articles are particularly useful for this purpose. You may also resort to legal dictionaries or even annotated form books.

The "experienced start with primary sources, inexperienced start with secondary sources" rule does not always apply. Even an experienced researcher may begin the project by consulting a treatise or looseleaf service. In addition to covering potential issues, the author will cite to relevant primary sources. The discussion of potential issues is particularly important if the experienced researcher knows the tax rules but is less comfortable with nontax issues involved in the problem.[11]

How much time should you spend using secondary sources? Your level of knowledge may be the most important factor. Even if you have taken a basic tax course, you may have little or no knowledge about a particular specialty within tax law. You may not have encountered—or only brushed the surface of— employment taxes, exempt organizations, natural resources, and pensions. These areas involve complex Code sections and overlap with nontax rules (e.g., ERISA). Because tax law changes rapidly and there are so many sources to consult, even less complex topics may initially seem overwhelming.

How much secondary material is likely to be available? A clearly written statute should require less explanation than a complex one, and settled questions are written about less often than litigated issues. Timing is also important. For example, an older statute will have been explained

---

[10] Chapters 9 and 10 discuss the degree of deference courts give administrative determinations.

[11] If the research project involves a relatively recent statute or administrative pronouncement, articles in practitioner-oriented journals or newsletters are likely to be better starting points.

more thoroughly than a newer one.[12] You may need to be creative when researching recent changes. For example, if materials discussing a recent statutory amendment are limited, secondary materials criticizing the original provision may be useful guides to the change. If the change involves a completely new Code section, the Joint Committee reports and newsletter articles may be the best source of explanatory material.

4. Sample Problems

Chapter 4 illustrates solving a research problem. Because the problem includes both primary and secondary sources, it should assist you in approaching the variety of research tools and levels of authority involved in a tax problem.

This problem appears in a separate chapter to facilitate using it as both an introduction to the research process and a reference tool for subsequent material. Chapter 4 also includes, but does not solve, other problems that could involve more than one type of primary or secondary authority. Research problems in other chapters cover particular types of authority relevant to those chapters.

SECTION D. LOCATING MATERIALS

1. In General

As discussed above, tax research involves many of the techniques used in other types of research. Likewise, you can often use traditional legal research sources in solving tax research problems.[13] Even if you can use traditional materials, you will find that materials focusing on taxation make research easier.

Before starting your research in print materials, make sure you know where the tax materials are located.[14] Most library collections contain tax-oriented print materials but differ in how they shelve them. Many libraries shelve them together in a "tax alcove." Other libraries group some tax-oriented materials (e.g., treatises, looseleaf services, and legis-

---

[12] These factors also influence the availability of explanatory sources for administrative materials and judicial opinions.

[13] Because I assume users have some familiarity with traditional legal research tools, I devote relatively little space to such items. In some instances, particularly if a library lacks a tax-oriented tool, you may need to consult traditional materials.

[14] The librarians may have prepared a research guide or Pathfinder focusing on taxation. That document may even include the location for each print and microform service.

lative histories) together and shelve others (e.g., tax-oriented periodicals) in the general collection. Even if dispersed throughout the collection, tax research sources are no more difficult to locate or use than are traditional research tools.

Electronic research follows a similar pattern. You can select from general services (e.g., Westlaw and LexisNexis) that include tax libraries, or you can use services (e.g., IntelliConnect and Checkpoint) that focus on tax materials. In addition to subscription services, you can use general or tax-only government websites. Each service operates somewhat differently and varies in the material covered.

If your university has a business or public policy school, its library (or the general university library) may carry print or electronic services that aren't available in the law school library. You may be able to access those sources by virtue of your status as a law student.[15]

2. Subscription Services

Because there are so many available materials, a library or database may lack some materials discussed in this book or may contain materials omitted here. Fortunately, many alternative services cover primary and secondary sources. Because it focuses on the types of materials available, this book should help you conduct successful tax research in virtually any law library or electronic resource.

If you are still in school, you have free access to subscription services that may not be available to you in practice. Your firm may limit itself to LexisNexis or to Westlaw. It may carry only one of the tax-oriented electronic services; it may not carry any of them. Even if it carries a particular service, it may not subscribe to all of its available databases. It may carry some services in print and others electronically. You don't know today what subscription services you can access in practice, and clients won't want to pay for you to learn how to use them. Using all available services now can pay dividends in the future.

3. Government Websites

Don't overlook government websites, which include significant amounts of primary source material. They are not as easy to use as the commercial services, their coverage generally begins much later, and you may have to access multiple sites to obtain your information, but access is free.

---

[15] If you are a business school student, you may have similar privileges with respect to some or all of the law school's collection.

SECTION E. PRINT VERSUS ELECTRONIC RESEARCH

Given the large number of materials available in both print (bound and looseleaf), microform, and electronic (DVD, CD, and online) formats, how do you decide which format to select? Although that question has no single correct answer, factors discussed in the following paragraphs and in the chapters covering electronic research will influence your choice.[16]

1. Availability of Materials

What is available in your library? Although electronic services continue to add retrospective coverage, older materials are often available only in print or in microform. For example, if you don't have access to a source such as HeinOnline, you may be limited to print or microform versions of early legislative history materials. In other situations, the library may not carry print subscriptions to materials available in electronic format. Decisions not to carry might reflect shelf space and filing costs,[17] availability of similar services from another publisher, or relative lack of use by library patrons.

If you subscribe to an electronic service, to which of its files do you have access? Many subscription services have pricing options that allow access to different databases. The service may carry a particular item, but you can't access it unless your library subscription covers it.

Another aspect of availability relates to mobility. If you have Internet access, you can access electronic services from remote locations. The biggest inconvenience may involve remembering your passwords. Your access to print materials is likely to depend on having an accessible library.

2. Updating Frequency

How often is each source updated? Some print materials are updated weekly; others receive less-frequent supplementation. CD/DVD materials are not updated more frequently than monthly; some are updated even less frequently. Online databases should be updated at least as often as print sources and often are updated more frequently. Primary source materials posted by the government body that produces them may be avail-

---

[16] The discussion in this section largely ignores microforms. See Chapter 17 for a discussion of their advantages and disadvantages. In addition, as discussed in Chapter 18, DVD and CD services are likely to continue losing ground to online services.

[17] For example, IRS letter ruling services and the Daily Tax Report require extensive shelf space.

able immediately after being issued. This is particularly true for judicial opinions available at a court's website as well as IRS items.[18]

3. Type of Search

a. Indexes and Tables

Is the research best conducted based on indexes or by searching for words or concepts? Indexes are useful if you don't know all the relevant words or concepts. Tables of contents provide a structure for topics you are researching. Although both print and electronic services have indexes and tables of contents, the print versions are easier to browse than their electronic counterparts. In addition, it is harder to overlook them. A print volume (or set of volumes) has a table of contents at the beginning and an index at the end. It may also have tables indicating where the service covers specific cases, rulings, and other material. In an electronic environment, you may be tempted to go directly to the word search feature and skip the table of contents or index. That may not be the most effective way to research.

b. Words and Concepts

Judicially declared concepts such as "step-transaction doctrine" and "form over substance" are not specifically covered in citators because they are neither case names nor Code sections. You can find materials relevant to these concepts using a print source's index; you can often find them more quickly by doing an electronic search in the relevant database. The same is true for concepts that do appear in the Code (e.g., "effectively connected").

There are two risks associated with electronic searches for a particular word. First, if you (or the service itself) make a spelling error, you may not retrieve a document even though it exists. Words with variant spellings are particularly likely to cause problems. For example, "includible" and "excludible" might also be spelled "includable" and "excludable." If you know a word has variant spellings, you can use wildcards (discussed in Chapters 18 and 19) in your search. A second problem relates to specificity. For example, if you search for "car," you may miss sources that discuss automobile or motor vehicle. If an electronic service has a thesaurus option, using it reduces the risk of this type of error. Although specificity

---

[18] You can subscribe to a free email updating service the IRS provides for items that will later appear in the Internal Revenue Bulletin. These items often arrive several weeks before they appear in the I.R.B. The IRS website also has a page on which it lists advance releases. I.R.B. items are discussed further in Chapter 10.

may also be a problem when you use print services, "see also" references in a print service's index may point you in the right direction.

c. Code Cross-References

Electronic searches are more effective than print searches if you want to know which Code sections cite other sections. Their databases are updated more frequently than are print (or even electronic) Code cross-reference tables. In addition, because you can search directly by Code section, you do not have to worry about editorial errors in compiling the tables. Finally, because electronic databases include hyperlinks, you can jump directly from one Code section to another.

d. Names of Judges or Attorneys

Searches involving particular judges or attorneys are very difficult to accomplish using print materials. Finding every case in which Judge L. Paige Marvel authored an opinion after joining the Tax Court would require reading many volumes of opinions.[19] As illustrated below, that search can be easily accomplished electronically. Online searches can be restricted by judge name, attorney name, or date. If we wanted to know whether any of these cases involved a particular topic, such as compensation, we could add that as a search term.

Illustrations 3-1 through 3-4 illustrate Westlaw and LexisNexis searches for these decisions.[20] My search on December 22, 2009, yielded 182 decisions in Westlaw and 184 in LexisNexis.

Illustrations 3-5 and 3-6 cover a search in the Tax Court's website (www.ustaxcourt.gov). This search was not as successful. Because Judge Marvel did not join the court until 1998, the fact that the Tax Court's retrospective coverage begins in 1995 for Regular and Memorandum Opinions was not the problem; it could have been for a longer-serving judge. The problem related to the number of results generated. Although I requested all opinions, the results screen included the following message: "Over 50 Opinions matched search criteria, only first 50 displayed." And, because I used the Release Date sort option, the search did not return the most recent items. I could reduce or avoid that problem by limiting my search to particular years but that would increase the number of searches required.

---

[19] The search would be impossible to conduct using print sources if you needed to include Summary Opinions, which are not compiled in bound volumes.

[20] I used the Westlaw Tax tab and the LexisNexis Taxation tab. I did not use their specialized tax sites (LexisNexis Tax Center and Westlaw Tax). I cover those sites in Chapter 19.

This search project demonstrates the importance of memorializing when you conducted your search. Databases are constantly being updated to add new decisions. It also demonstrates decisions each provider makes about the order in which it presents results.

Illustration 3-1. Westlaw Search

Search

Selected Databases

Federal Taxation - Tax Court Cases (FTX-TCT) ⓘ

Terms and Connectors	Natural Language

Search: JU(Marvel)

Recent Searches & Locates   ▼

Dates: Unrestricted   ▼

Fields: Select an Option   ▼

Add Connectors or Expanders Help

Illustration 3-2. Westlaw Search: First Five Opinions Listed

Results: 182 Documents   Add Search to WestClip

SELECT TO PRINT, EMAIL, ETC.

☐   1. Palm Canyon X Investments, LLC v. C.I.R.,
T.C. Memo. 2009-288, 2009 WL 4824326, T.C.M. (RIA) 2009-288, 2009 RIA TC Memo 2009-288, U.S.Tax Ct., December 15, 2009 (NO. 5610-06)

☐ C 2. TG Missouri Corp. v. C.I.R.,
133 T.C. No. 13, 2009 WL 3790315, Tax Ct. Rep. (CCH) 57,991, U.S.Tax Ct., November 12, 2009 (NO. 8333-06)

☐ H 3. Wiener v. C.I.R.,
T.C. Memo. 2009-256, 2009 WL 3762970, 98 T.C.M. (CCH) 430, T.C.M. (RIA) 2009-256, 2009 RIA TC Memo 2009-256, U.S.Tax Ct., November 10, 2009 (NO. 17984-04)

☐ H 4. Vincentini v. C.I.R.,
T.C. Memo. 2009-255, 2009 WL 3739461, 98 T.C.M. (CCH) 427, T.C.M. (RIA) 2009-255, 2009 RIA TC Memo 2009-255, U.S.Tax Ct., November 09, 2009 (NO. 7166-03)

☐ C 5. Bucaro v. C.I.R.,
T.C. Memo. 2009-247, 2009 WL 3571348, 98 T.C.M. (CCH) 388, T.C.M. (RIA) 2009-247, 2009 RIA TC Memo 2009-247, U.S.Tax Ct., November 02, 2009 (NO. 17659-07)

→Westlaw listed cases in reverse chronological order and did not separate them by opinion type.

→I set the Result Options to Hide Terms in List because I didn't need a line or two highlighting the judge's name.

→Westlaw also offers a Judicial Reversal Reports summary option.

Illustration 3-3. LexisNexis Search

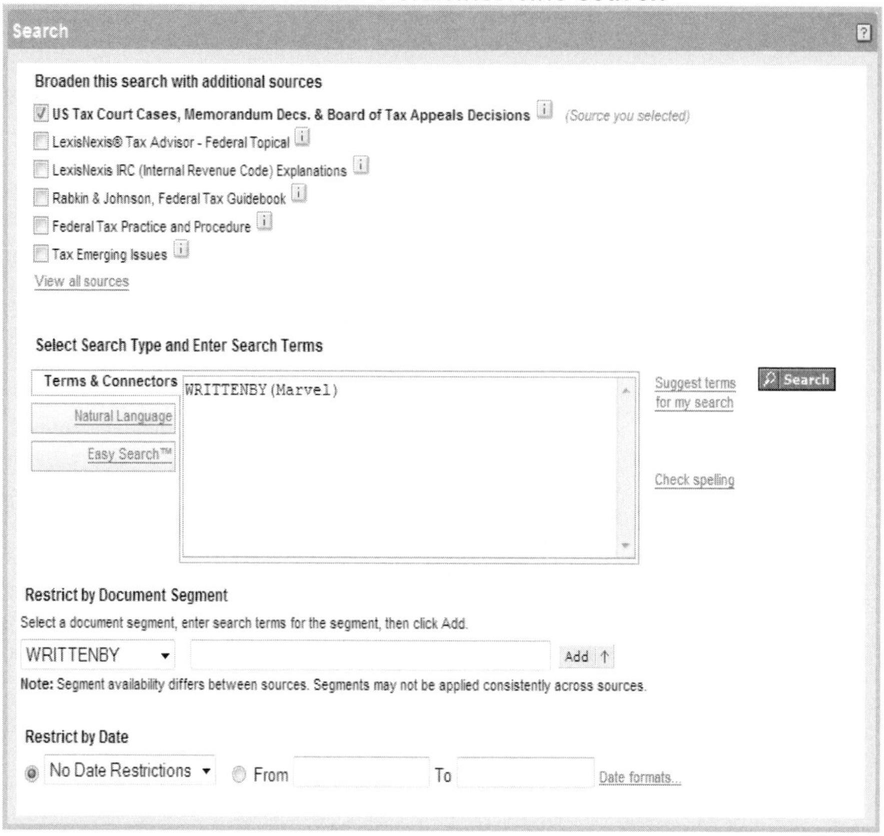

Illustration 3-4. LexisNexis Search: First Five Opinions Listed

→LexisNexis listed the cases by opinion type, with Regular (T.C.) Opinions first. Within each group, cases appear in reverse chronological order.

→I did not activate the Show Hits feature because I searched on a judge's name and not on a key word.

Illustration 3-5. Tax Court Website Search

Opinions Search

Go to » Today's Opinions

TC and Memorandum Opinions starting 09/25/95; Summary Opinions starting 01/01/01*

Date Search:		[By Day: MM/DD/YY] [By Month
Case Name Keyword:		(e.g., petitioner's last name)
Judge:	Marvel ▾	
Opinion Type:	All Types ▾	
Sort By:	Release Date ▾	
Text Search Opinion contains word(s):		Number of hits to display: 5 ▾ [Excluded Words List]

Search   Reset

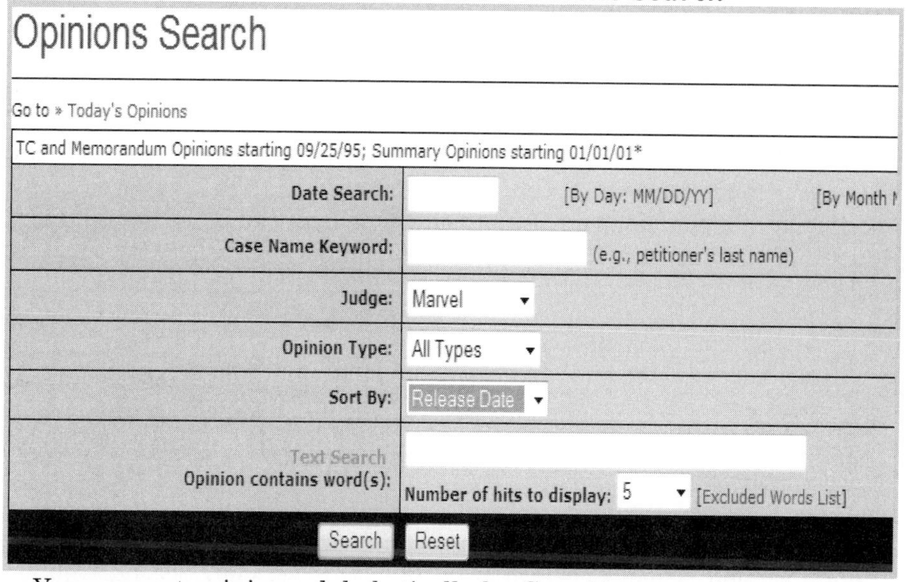

→ You can sort opinions alphabetically by Case Name or chronologically by Release Date.

Illustration 3-6. Tax Court Website Search: First Five Opinions Listed

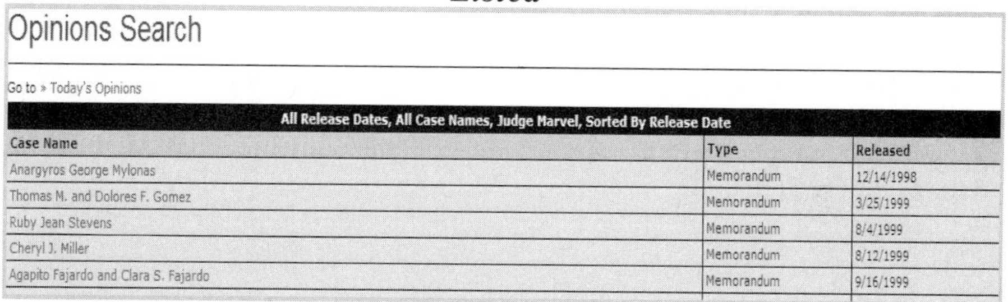

Opinions Search

Go to » Today's Opinions

All Release Dates, All Case Names, Judge Marvel, Sorted By Release Date		
Case Name	**Type**	**Released**
Anargyros George Mylonas	Memorandum	12/14/1998
Thomas M. and Dolores F. Gomez	Memorandum	3/25/1999
Ruby Jean Stevens	Memorandum	8/4/1999
Cheryl J. Miller	Memorandum	8/12/1999
Agapito Fajardo and Clara S. Fajardo	Memorandum	9/16/1999

→The results include the opinion type and date but not the issue.

e. Articles

Electronic searching is likely to be more efficient than print if you are searching for articles by author or topic. Print articles indexes are not cumulative. Each volume covers one or more years, necessitating a lengthy search. The process is further complicated because each index covers slightly different publications; at least one index imposes minimum page requirements for articles.

Although their electronic versions also have coverage limitations, you can search electronic databases far more quickly. More important, the electronic service may compile a list of "hits" that you can print out and return to as needed.

Two important limitations apply in selecting between print and electronic articles indexes. The first relates to availability; the second, to coverage dates. Neither Index to Federal Tax Articles, which has the most extensive retrospective coverage, nor Federal Tax Articles is currently available in any electronic format. Although both Index to Legal Periodicals and Current Law Index are available in electronic formats, the LexisNexis and Westlaw versions do not include pre-1980 materials.[21] A separate Wilson electronic publication, Index to Legal Periodicals Retrospective, covers articles written since 1908. It is available on WilsonWeb but not on LexisNexis or Westlaw. Articles indexes are discussed further in Chapter 14.

f. Citators

There are at least three advantages to using a citator online. First, the online version is more current than the print version. Second, you can accomplish the search more quickly because you won't have to consult several volumes of print materials. Third, online citators provide easy access to the citing material. You can print out a list of citations or jump to them directly using hyperlinks. Citators are discussed further in Chapter 12.

Electronic services can also quickly perform citator-like searches. Even if, for example, a CD/DVD case service lacks a citator, you can use the initial case name or citation as a search term and find all later cases or other material citing it.

4. Cost

Research tools are not free. Both your time and the cost of materials must be factored into a decision between competing sources. As noted in Subsection E.1, your library may have limited your choice by deciding which materials it carries. Cost may determine which materials you select from those available to you.

You do not pay separately to use print and CD/DVD materials; the subscription price is a fixed cost. You pay nothing to use free online materials, such as those available at government websites. Although law

---

[21] LexisNexis indicates that its coverage of Legal Resource Index (the electronic version of Current Law Index) begins in 1977 and its coverage of Index to Legal Periodicals begins in 1978. Westlaw coverage for those services begins in 1980 for Current Law Index and 1981 for Index to Legal Periodicals.

students have unlimited, free access to services such as LexisNexis and Westlaw, that may not be true for law firms.[22] Pricing for subscription services may be based on a fixed fee or may include time charges. You should consider both the time savings in speed (your "hourly rate" as a practitioner) and any incremental cost (fee for use) associated with subscription services.

If you are trying to familiarize yourself with a topic, print services may be preferable to electronic sources. The less you know about the topic, the more time you will spend reading explanatory material. Although you can reduce online time by downloading text, your lack of familiarity with the topic may result in your downloading too much or too little. If you have difficulty reading large amounts of text from a computer screen, you must factor in physical "costs" when deciding between print and electronic sources. The print version also forces you to keep reading. There are no hyperlinks to primary sources to distract you from the analytical material. This can be an important distinction if you are relatively unfamiliar with the topic.

5. Need for Original Page Citations

If you must cite to the original volume and page numbers, the original print source obviously provides that information. Many online services also include original pagination; CD/DVD services are less likely to do so. If you need to cite more than one publication (e.g., official and unofficial citations), online services are more likely to include parallel citations (and page numbers within each service) than are print materials.

When using electronic sources, you take a slight risk that citations or pagination will be incorrect. Many websites, particularly those of government entities, avoid this problem by providing documents in PDF format. Westlaw also does this for the West reporter services. This format doesn't merely add pagination at appropriate breaks; it actually reproduces the original document. In most cases, you will be able to perform word searches in these PDF documents.[23]

---

[22] See, e.g., Heidi W. Heller, _The Twenty-First Century Law Library: A Law Firm Librarian's Thoughts,_ 101 L. LIBR. J. 517, 518–19 (2009); Patrick Meyer, _Law Firm Legal Research Requirements for New Attorneys_, 101 L. LIBR. J. 297, 311–13, 329–30 (2009).

[23] If the service offers both text (with hyperlink) and PDF options, you can use the text version's hyperlinks to follow sources cited within the document while relying on the easy-to-read pagination of the PDF version.

SECTION F. EXTERNAL FACTORS AFFECTING RESEARCH

Three phenomena affect the research process: proliferation of sources; technological change; and publishing industry consolidation.

The number of primary and secondary authorities continually expands. Since this book's first edition, for example, the Internal Revenue Service has stopped issuing some types of guidance but has added different items. The Tax Court began public release of Summary Opinions in 2001, and additional law reviews focusing on tax have appeared.

Technology, particularly CD and DVD materials, web-based research sites, and even blogs, enhances the research process by covering many sources and allowing for easy database searching.[24] Although some online sites require subscriptions, many others offer free access to materials. The federal government has been quite active in providing free online access to primary source materials and in making its sites more user-friendly. Many libraries have reduced their print collections of materials that are available online. Recognizing the increasing importance of these sources, I have increased this book's focus on electronic materials.

Finally, the publishing industry continues to consolidate. Several once-independent companies are now commonly owned.[25] Many services have been renamed, eliminated, or limited to electronic format. Others now appear only on platforms (e.g., LexisNexis or Westlaw) owned by their common parent. No one knows when this process will end. Because I focus on general tax research principles, you should be able to adapt your research strategy to the appearance of new materials and the disappearance of old ones.

SECTION G. SUMMARY

Research generally involves using both primary and secondary sources. Various factors influence the order in which you consult them and the format in which you conduct your research. These factors include:

• how complicated the problem is in relation to your knowledge of the subject matter;

• the specific tools available in your library;

• the frequency with which services are updated;

---

[24] Your clients can access a wide array of free, but not necessarily authoritative, electronic sources. Don't be surprised if they ask you about tax results based on misleading information they've read online.

[25] Appendix E lists commonly owned publishers.

- where you are located when conducting your research;

- the usefulness of tables of contents, indexes, and other finding aids;

- the cost-effectiveness of each service for the particular task;

- your need for correct page citations; and

- personal preferences you develop as you gain research expertise.

Remember that your research is not complete until you use appropriate updating tools to check your authorities.

CHAPTER 4. ILLUSTRATIVE PROBLEMS

The problem in Section A illustrates sources you can consult in doing tax research. Section B includes additional problems you might use to test your research skills.

SECTION A. FACT PATTERN 1

Your clients recently refinanced their mortgage. When they purchased their home two years ago, interest rates were quite high and their credit rating wasn't particularly good. They made a down payment of $20,000 and borrowed $130,000 at 11.5 percent interest; their home was secured by a mortgage to Friendly Bank. The agreement with Friendly required them to refinance the loan or repay its full balance within four years. The original loan was qualified residence indebtedness and met the tests for acquisition indebtedness.

When interest rates dropped to five percent last month, your clients decided not to wait until the fourth year to refinance the $127,000 they still owed. Generous Bank loaned your clients $127,000 and charged two points ($2,540). They repaid the $127,000 owed to Friendly Bank. They paid the points charged by Generous Bank with funds in their checking account at Country Bank.

1. Goals for Research

Your clients wonder how much of this year's interest they can deduct and how to handle the points, which are prepaid interest.

Because they approached you after completing this transaction, your goals include assessing the tax consequences and advising on the appropriate tax return treatment. If they had approached you before refinancing, you might have advised them to pay a higher interest rate instead of paying the points. That advice would involve the interplay of tax consequences and their estimate of how long they plan to own the home.

Note that I excluded some potential issues from consideration. For example, because I stated that the original loan qualified as acquisition indebtedness, you do not have to determine whether your clients properly deducted interest on the original debt. Likewise, because I indicated that points are prepaid interest, you need not research the difference between deductible interest and nondeductible loan fees.[26] Finally, because the $2,540 was on deposit with a third bank and not added to the new loan, you can avoid researching when interest is treated as having been paid.

2. Research Strategy

Depending on how familiar you are with this topic, you may complete the steps below in a different order.

a. Determine the Issues

If you are reasonably familiar with the deductions for mortgage interest and points, you likely have isolated two issues for research:

• If the taxpayer refinances acquisition indebtedness, to what extent can the new loan qualify as acquisition indebtedness for purposes of the interest expense deduction?

• If the taxpayer pays points as part of the refinancing, are the points deductible in the year paid or must they be deducted pro rata over the life of the new loan?

In a real-world research effort, you may need to refine those issues or add new ones. As noted above, I stipulated away many of those issues for purposes of this exercise.

b. Locate the Relevant Statutes

Because federal tax rules are grounded in statutory provisions, locating relevant statutory text is critical. The method you use to locate that text is affected by your degree of familiarity with the subject matter. To carry out this part of the project, I will use looseleaf services that (1) either include statutory language or refer to the relevant statutes and (2) also include explanations.

(1) Code Section Index

If you were familiar with the Internal Revenue Code, you could go directly to Code section 163, which provides the rules for deducting interest, and section 461, which applies to prepayments. If you did not remember the section numbers, you could obtain that information from the

---

[26] Because section 461(g)(2) has not been amended since 1976, you don't have to research changes in statutory language. Many research projects do require that step.

subject index accompanying the Code. [See Illustrations 4-1 through 4-5, which are from Checkpoint.]

Illustration 4-1. Checkpoint Home Page: Index Option

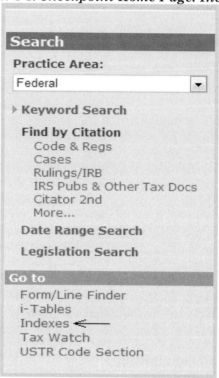

Illustration 4-2. Available Indexes

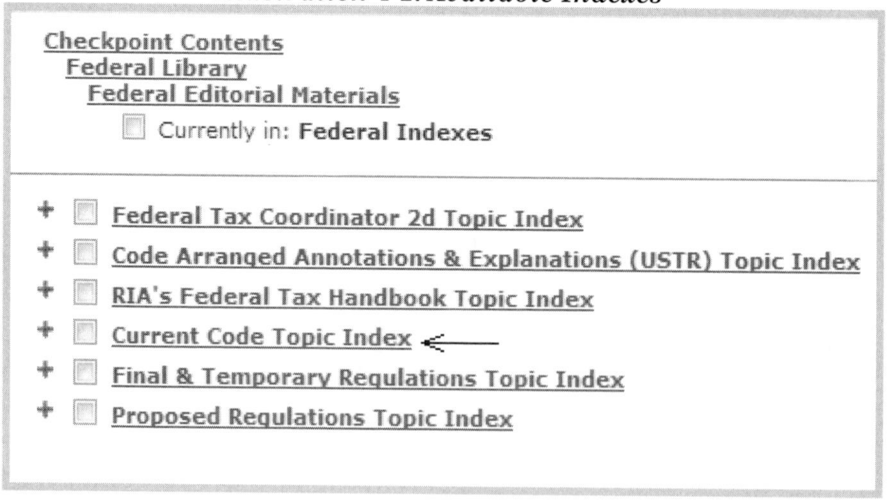

Checkpoint Contents
  Federal Library
    Federal Editorial Materials
        ☐ Currently in: **Federal Indexes**

+ ☐ **Federal Tax Coordinator 2d Topic Index**

+ ☐ **Code Arranged Annotations & Explanations (USTR) Topic Index**

+ ☐ **RIA's Federal Tax Handbook Topic Index**

+ ☐ **Current Code Topic Index** ⟵

+ ☐ **Final & Temporary Regulations Topic Index**

+ ☐ **Proposed Regulations Topic Index**

Illustration 4-3. Current Code Topic Index: Interest Options

> 📄 💼 <u>Intelligence community</u>
> 📄 💼 <u>Intercity rail facilities, high-speed</u>
> 📄 💼 <u>Interest</u>
> 📄 💼 <u>Interest expense</u>
> 📄 💼 <u>Interest-free loans</u>

→Of the two choices, Interest expense looked more relevant.

Illustration 4-4. Current Code Topic Index: Interest Expense

> Interest expense
> . .definition   265
> . .financial institution
> . . . allocation of to exempt interest 265

→Interest expense was the wrong choice.

Illustration 4-5. Current Code Topic Index: Interest

. .mortgages, residential property ⟵	25 ; 163
. .nonpayment of tax	6601 ; 6621
. .notice requirement	6631
. .obligations, tax-exempt	265
. .original issue discount	163
. . . current reporting	1272
. . . ratable daily portion	1272
. .overpayments, on	
. . . payment of estimated tax	6611
. . . rates, determination of	6621
. .paid	
. . . information returns	6049
. . . purchase or carry, to	
. . . .market discount bonds	1277
. . . .short-term obligations issued at discount	1282
. . . taxable year of deduction	461
. .penalties	6601
. .personal holding companies	543
. .personal interest	
. . . disallowance of deductions	163
. .points, deduction ⟵	461
. .prepaid, taxable year of deduction ⟵	461
. .rates, undiscounted losses	846

→Several index entries look helpful. For purposes of this problem, I will look at Code sections 163 and 461. If I were uncertain whether it also applied, I would add section 25 to my reading list.

(2) Secondary Source Topic Index

If you were less familiar with the issues, you might consult a treatise or looseleaf service, using its topical index to locate discussions of interest and points paid as an interest substitute. Those discussions would refer you to sections 163 and 461. Illustrations 4-6 through 4-10 cover topic indexes in Federal Tax Coordinator 2d and United States Tax Reporter on Checkpoint. These services are commonly owned, but their indexes are not identical.

Illustration 4-6. Federal Tax Coordinator 2d Topic Index

Intercompany transactions
Interest. See also "Interest expense"; "Interest income"
Interest allocation rules. See "Interest expense"
Interest charge DISCs
Interest charge Domestic International Sales Corporations. See "Interest charge DISC"
Interest coupons
Interest coverage test, interest deduction for obligations issued in corporate acquisitions
Interested parties, pension or profit sharing plans
Interest expense
Interest expenses
Interest-free or low-interest loans
Interest income
Interest on Lawyers Trust Accounts (IOLTA)
Interest on taxes
Interests

→Several of the entries above look promising.

Illustration 4-7. Federal Tax Coordinator 2d Topic Index:
Interest expense

. .personal interest	K-5510 et seq.
. . . defined	K-5511
. . . prohibition of deductions	K-5510 et seq.
. . . taxes, interest on underpaid or deferred taxes	K-5513
. . . trade or business debt interest as	K-5512
. .person entitled to deduction	K-5120 et seq.
. .points paid in connection with mortgage	K-5178 et seq. ⟵⎯⎯
. . . annual deduction for points deductible ratably over life of loan	K-5184
. . . borrower, payment by	K-5026
. . . capitalized points on refinancing, deductibility	K-5181
. . . purchase or improvement of residence, refinanced debt incurred for	⟵ K-5180 , K-5181

→Because the Topic Index links are to discussion, references are to paragraphs in Federal Tax Coordinator 2d, not to Code sections.

Illustration 4-8. Code-Arranged Annotations & Explanations (USTR) Topic Index

- Intercompany transactions and agreements
- Interest (See also Interest expense)
- Interest and principal allocation (See Allocation and apportionment)
- Interest charge DISC
- Interest equalization tax (See also Excise Taxes Volume Index)
- Interest expense
- Interest on interest
- Interest paid or accrued
- Interest rates (See Interest, subhead rates)
- Interest received or credited
- Interest reinvestment loans
- Interference with tax law administration

→The Topic Index entries for Interest, Interest expense, and Interest expenses all look promising.

Illustration 4-9. USTR Index: Interest

. .relative, interest paid by	1635.018 (15)
. .residence interest, qualified (See Residence interest, qualified)	←

Illustration 4-10. USTR Index: Residence Interest, Qualified

Residence interest, qualified			
. .accrued interest treatment, pre-1-1-1994	1634.052		
. .acquisition indebtedness	1634.052 ; 1635.052(5)		
. .allocation of indebtedness			
. . . portion of residence used for nonresidential purposes	1634.052		
. .alternative minimum tax	564.02		
. .cooperative housing corporations			
. . . debt secured by stock of tenant-stockholder	1634.052		
. .debt incurred on or before 10-13-1987	1634.052		
. .deductibility	1634 ;	1634.052 ; 1635.052	
. .definitions concerning	1634		
. .dollar cap on qualified debt	1634.052		
. .dual purpose debts	1634.052		
. .foreclosure	1635.052(10)		
. .grandfathered debt	1634.052		
. .home equity indebtedness	1634.052		
. .more than two residences	1634.052		
. .mortgage insurance premiums paid or accrued in 2007			
. . . treatment as interest	1634.052		
. .points as	1634.052		

→Note that the cross-references to paragraphs in the USTR service begin with the Code section number (163 in this case). USTR numbers its explanations and annotations based on the underlying Code sections.

c. Read the Code Sections

(1) Code Section 163(h)(3)(B)

Your research indicates that Code section 163 is an appropriate place to begin. Language relevant to your first issue appears in the flush language of subparagraph (h)(3)(B). Because debt resulting from refinancing acquisition indebtedness qualifies, the new loan is treated as acquisition indebtedness.

Illustration 4-11. Excerpt from I.R.C. § 163(h)(3)(B)

(B) Acquisition indebtedness.—
    (i) In general.—The term "acquisition indebtedness" means any indebtedness which—
    (I) is incurred in acquiring, constructing, or substantially improving any qualified residence of the taxpayer, and

....

Such term also includes any indebtedness secured by such residence resulting from the refinancing of indebtedness meeting the requirements of the preceding sentence (or this sentence) ....

→Language that is flush to a subdivision's margin modifies the entire subdivision. The flush language above applies to all of 163(h)(3)(B)(i), not merely to a smaller part of it (such as 163(h)(3)(B)(i))(I)).

(2) Code Section 461(g)

Because section 163 does not specifically address points, we must continue our research. The index shown in Illustration 4-5 indicates that Code section 461 applies to prepaid interest, so we might read that section next. Section 461(g) generally disallows a current deduction for prepaid interest. It allocates the interest to the period "with respect to which the interest represents a charge for the use or forbearance of money." In other words, your clients would prorate their deduction of the $2,540 over the life of the loan. However, they may qualify for a current deduction under section 461(g)(2), reproduced below.

Illustration 4-12. I.R.C. § 461(g)(2) (emphasis added)

This subsection shall not apply to points paid in respect of any indebtedness incurred _in connection with the purchase_ or improvement of, and secured by, the principal residence of the taxpayer to the extent that, under regulations prescribed by the Secretary, such payment of points is an established business practice in the area in which such indebtedness is incurred, and the amount of such payment does not exceed the amount generally charged in such area.

Section 461 uses the term "in connection with the purchase" rather than the term "to purchase." It provides no rules for determining if points are paid in connection with a purchase. Because your clients' loan had onerous terms, including a four-year window for refinancing or paying in full, you want to argue that they meet the "in connection with" test.

d. Locate Additional Authority

If you research the "in connection with" issue, your initial question involves statutory interpretation. Does indebtedness incurred "in connection with" a purchase or improvement differ from indebtedness incurred "to" purchase or improve?

Normally, your first step would be taken in the Code itself. Many sections include definition provisions designed to limit the meaning of a particular word or phrase. In other instances, definitions are provided elsewhere in the Code. For example, section 7701 includes an extensive list of definitions. Unfortunately, neither Code section 461 nor section 7701 defines "in connection with" in this context.

Because the Code contains no definition, you must focus your research on authorities interpreting the statutory language. For that step, you would consider what sources are available and which to consult first. You might start with congressional reports and progress to Treasury regulations, IRS rulings, and judicial opinions. You would consult treatises and other secondary sources as necessary throughout this process.

I locate IRS materials and judicial opinions using citators (Chapter 12) and reference materials that provide citations to particular Code sections, Treasury regulations, and IRS rulings. Looseleaf service supplement sections (Chapter 13) and newsletters (Chapter 16) are useful for locating recent changes.

Illustrations 4-13 through 4-29 present selected materials relevant to our issue. Most of these materials are available in both print and electronic formats.

(1) Legislative History

If I researched the legislative history of Code section 461(g), I would find that Congress enacted it in the Tax Reform Act of 1976.[27] The 1976 Act had three committee reports that I could search for references to the meaning of "in connection with."[28]

---

[27] Pub. L. No. 94-455, § 208(a). Chapter 7 discusses methods for tracing a Code section's history.

[28] H.R. REP. NO. 94-658 (House Ways and Means Committee); S. REP. NO. 94-938 (Senate Finance Committee); H.R. REP. NO. 94-1515 (Conference Committee).

I began with the Conference Report because this document indicates whether the provision was added by the House or the Senate and how differences, if any, were reconciled. It contains the following language:

Illustration 4-13. Excerpt from H.R. Rep. No 94-1515, at 416–17

205. Prepaid Interest

House bill.—Under present law, a taxpayer reporting his income on the accrual method of accounting can deduct prepaid interest only in the period or periods in which the interest represents the cost of using the funds during that period. However, generally, a cash method taxpayer can deduct expenses in the year he actually pays them. It is unsettled, however, whether a cash method taxpayer can deduct prepaid interest in full in the year paid. Recent court decisions have supported the Internal Revenue Service in requiring a cash method taxpayer to allocate his deductions for prepaid interest over the period of the loan.

The House bill requires a cash method taxpayer to deduct prepaid interest over the period of the loan to the extent the interest represents the cost of using the borrowed funds during each period. The House bill also requires points paid on a loan to be deducted ratably over the term of the loan, except in the case of a mortgage incurred in connection with the purchase or improvement of, and secured by, the taxpayer's principal residence. The House bill applies to prepayments made after September 16, 1975, except for prepayments made before January 1, 1976, pursuant to a binding contract or loan commitment in existence on September 16, 1975 (and at all times thereafter).

Senate amendment.—The Senate amendment is the same as the House bill, except that the rule permitting current deductibility of points on a home mortgage is amended to apply only if points are generally charged in the geographical area where the loan is made and to the extent of the number of points generally charged in that area for a home loan. The Senate amendment applies to prepayments of interest on and after January 1, 1976, except for interest paid before January 1, 1978, pursuant to a binding contract or written loan commitment in existence on September 16, 1975.

Conference agreement.—The conference agreement follows the Senate amendment; however, the exception for prepayments of interest pursuant to a binding contract or written loan commitments in existence on September 16, 1975, applies only to prepayments made before January 1, 1977.

A separate Ways and Means Report (H.R. REP. NO. 94-1380) discusses estate and gift tax changes that are not germane to our research.

The Conference Report simply states the rule that appears in section 461(g)(2). What about the House and Senate reports? Senate Report 94-938 (pt. I) includes the following language (emphasis added)[29]

Illustration 4-14. Excerpt from S. Rep. No. 94-938, at 105

> The committee amendment permits points paid by a cash method taxpayer on an indebtedness incurred in connection with the purchase or improvement of (and secured by) his principal residence to be treated as paid in the taxable year of actual payment. *A loan will not qualify under this exception, however, if the loan proceeds are used for purposes other than purchasing or improving the taxpayer's principal residence*, or if loan proceeds secured by property other than his principal residence are used to purchase or improve his residence. The exception applies only to points on a home mortgage, and not to other interest costs on such a mortgage. A further limitation is that in order to qualify under this exception, the charging of points must reflect an established business practice in the geographical area where the loan is made, and also the deduction allowed under this exception may not exceed the number of points generally charged in the area for this type of transaction.

We might interpret the italicized language as requiring that the points be paid as part of the original purchase, in which case our clients must deduct the points pro rata over the loan term instead of deducting them all in the year paid.

Because none of the reports indicates why the term "in connection with" was used, I might continue research by checking for hearings, comments recorded in Congressional Record, or other contemporary legislative history. Those sources are covered in Chapter 7. Because courts have given legislative history less deference in recent years, and the clients' potential tax savings are already outweighed by the cost of this research effort, I will move on regulations.

(2) Treasury Regulations

As explained in Chapter 9, Treasury regulations are easier to locate than other administrative materials because the regulations section number generally includes the Code section number. I will start my research in the regulations for Code section 461; these begin with section 1.461-1. Section 1.461-3 Prepaid Interest, would be on point; unfortunately, that section is listed as [Reserved]; no regulations have been issued.[30]

---

[29] The language that I italicized above also appears in the House Report, H.R. REP. NO. 94-658, at 101.

[30] This example skips two other steps with regard to this regulation: checking to see if there are proposed regulations and checking the Unified Agenda and

I then checked the section 163 regulations to see if they addressed this issue. I found a temporary regulation that was issued in 1987.[31]

Illustration 4-15. Temp. Treas. Reg. § 1.163-10T

Section 1.163-10T Qualified residence interest (temporary).

(a) *Table of contents.* This paragraph (a) lists the major paragraphs that appear in this § 1.163-10T.

....

(j) *Determination of interest paid or accrued during the taxable year—* (1) *In general.* For purposes of determining the amount of qualified residence interest with respect to a secured debt, the amount of interest paid or accrued during the taxable year includes only interest paid or accrued while the debt is secured by a qualified residence.

(2) *Special rules for cash-basis taxpayers—*(i) *Points deductible in year paid under section 461(g)(2).* If points described in section 461(g)(2) (certain points paid in respect of debt incurred in connection with the purchase or improvement of a principal residence) are paid with respect to a debt, the amount of such points is qualified residence interest.

→The above provision fails to define the term "in connection with."

→This regulation was issued for Code section 163, but it focuses on Code section 461(g)(2). Interestingly, Code section 163 does not mention section 461 or cross-reference to it.

(3) IRS Material

(a) Revenue Rulings

Perhaps the IRS has issued a ruling interpreting section 461(g)(2)'s "in connection with" language.[32] I can research IRS material in a variety of ways. One source is the Code–Rulings Table in Mertens, Law of Federal Income Taxation, a print-only source that covers revenue rulings but not private letter rulings.[33] Instead, I searched in an electronic database that focuses on IRS material [Illustration 4-16] and located Revenue Ruling 87-22 [Illustration 4-17].

Although the ruling does not support our clients' position, we may be able to distinguish it. First, the time period between the two loans described in the ruling is longer than that in our situation. Second, our

---

Priority Guidance Plan to see if regulations are likely to appear in the next year. These topics are discussed in Chapter 9.

[31] Temporary regulations are discussed in Chapter 9.

[32] Rulings and other IRS material are covered in Chapter 10.

[33] Mertens is discussed in Chapter 13.

clients' loan agreement required them to refinance within four years. The ruling does not indicate that refinancing was mandatory.

Illustration 4-16. Westlaw Search for Revenue Rulings

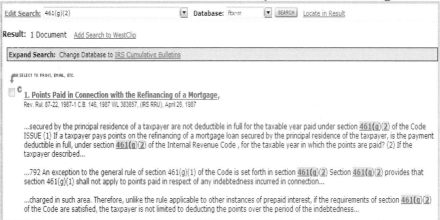

→I could not have found this ruling using the free IRS website; its retrospective coverage begins in 1996.

(b)Letter Rulings and Technical Advice Memoranda

At this point, I have choices. I could look for judicial opinions discussing section 461(g)(2) or Revenue Ruling 87-22, or I could look for non-precedential IRS rulings. Because electronic databases allow searching across categories, I could also take a short-cut and search for cases and rulings together.

I continued here with IRS materials simply to keep judicial decisions separate. I selected a database covering technical advice memoranda[34] and again used 461(g)(2) as my search term. Illustrations 4-18 and 4-19 illustrate this process.

---

[34] I chose the Technical Advice Memoranda database instead of the Private Letter Ruling database on the assumption that a taxpayer would be unlikely to ask for an advance ruling on this issue. IRS documents are discussed in detail in Chapter 10.

Illustration 4-17. Excerpt from Rev. Rul. 87-22, 1987-1 C.B. 146

ISSUE

(1) If a taxpayer pays points on the refinancing of a mortgage loan secured by the principal residence of the taxpayer, is the payment deductible in full, under section 461(g)(2) of the Internal Revenue Code, for the taxable year in which the points are paid?

....

FACTS

Situation 1. In 1981, *A* obtained a 16-percent mortgage loan (old mortgage loan) exclusively for the purchase of a principal residence. On August 20, 1986, *A* refinanced the old mortgage loan, which had an outstanding principal balance of $100,000, with a $100,000, 30-year, 10-percent mortgage loan (new mortgage loan) from *L*, a lending institution. The new loan was secured by a mortgage on *A*'s principal residence. Principal and interest payments were due monthly, with the first payment due October 1, 1986, and the last payment due September 1, 2016. In order to refinance, *A* paid 3.6 points ($3,600) to *L* at the loan closing.

....

LAW AND ANALYSIS

....

An exception to the general rule of section 461(g)(1) of the Code is set forth in section 461(g)(2). Section 461(g)(2) provides that section 461(g)(1) shall not apply to points paid in respect of any indebtedness incurred in connection with the purchase or improvement of, and secured by, the principal residence of the taxpayer to the extent that such payment of points is an established business practice in the area in which such indebtedness is incurred and the amount of such payment does not exceed the amount generally charged in such area. Therefore, unlike the rule applicable to other instances of prepaid interest, if the requirements of section 461(g)(2) of the Code are satisfied, the taxpayer is not limited to deducting the points over the period of the indebtedness. *Schubel v. Commissioner*, 77 T.C. at 703-04.

In *Situation 1*, the proceeds of the new mortgage loan were used solely to repay an existing indebtedness. The legislative history of section 461(g)(2) of the Code states that a loan does "not qualify under [the] exception [in section 461(g)(2)] . . . if the loan proceeds are used for purposes other than purchasing or improving the taxpayer's principal residence. . . ." H.R. Rep. No. 94-658, 94th Cong., 1st Sess. 101 (1975), 1976-3 (Vol. 2) C.B. 695, 793. Although the indebtedness secured by the new mortgage was incurred in connection with *A*'s continued ownership of *A*'s principal residence, the loan proceeds were used for purposes other than purchasing or improving the residence, and thus the indebtedness was not "incurred in connection with the purchase or improvement of" that residence, as that language is used in section 461(g)(2). Accordingly, the points paid by *A* with respect to *A*'s new mortgage loan do not meet the requirements of section 461(g)(2) of the Code.

Illustration 4-18. Westlaw Search for TAMS

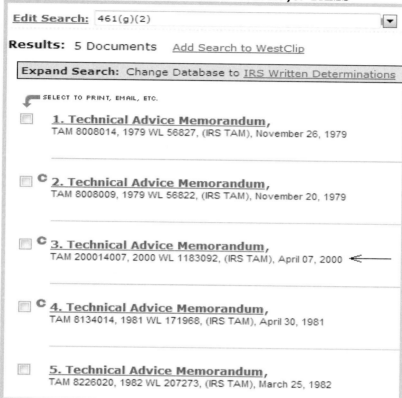

I chose TAM 200014007, the only item that came after Revenue Ruling 87-22. As the excerpt below indicates, it has nothing to do with prepaid interest. But it does refer to a judicial decision (*Huntsman*) construing the "in connection with" language in section 461(g)(2).

Illustration 4-19. Excerpt from TAM 200014007

> C
>
> **Technical Advice Memorandum**
> TAM 200014007
> April 07, 2000 (Approx. 4 pages)
>
> Cases that have construed the term "in connection with" as used in other tax statutes suggest that the term should be construed broadly. See Snow v. Commissioner, 416 U.S. 500 (1974) (holding experimental expenditures to be deductible under § 174 as incurred "in connection with" the taxpayer's trade or business even though, at the time incurred, the activities did not constitute a trade or business for purposes of § 162); Huntsman v. Commissioner, 905 F.2d 1182 (8th Cir. 1990) (holding that a debt incurred three years after the taxpayer purchased his residence was incurred "in connection with" the purchase of the residence as required by § 461(g)(2) when the debt replaced three-year balloon debt incurred at the time the residence was purchased); Alves v. Commissioner, 734 F.2d 478, 481-82 (9th Cir. 1984) (stock purchased by an employee was in connection with the performance of services under § 83 even though purchased at full market value and not considered compensation). When Congress used "in connection with" in § 108(c)(3)(A) it was aware of the Supreme Court's interpretation of this same language in Snow. Therefore, it is reasonable to assume that it intended the same broad interpretation be given to the language in § 108(c)(3)(A). See Miller v. Commissioner, 836 F.2d 1274, 1282 (10th Cir. 1988).

(4) Judicial Decisions

Should I search for judicial decisions using section 461(g)(2) as my search term? Or should I use Revenue Ruling 87-22? I decided to begin with the revenue ruling because I suspected it would yield fewer decisions that merely mention the search term in a different context. Although I found *Huntsman* by chance in the previous search, I decided to conduct this search as though I hadn't found it.

I had two other choices. I could have gone to a database for tax decisions and used 87-22 as my search term or I could have gone directly to a citator and searched for it there. I chose the citator route, but you might want to try searching in a tax decisions database instead.

The illustrations below show results from the electronic versions of four citators, CCH Citator, Shepard's, KeyCite, and RIA Citator 2nd, all of which are covered in greater detail in Chapter 12.

Illustration 4-20. CCH Citator Results

Federal Tax Citator, 2009FED, Main Citator Table, Rev. Rul. 87-22

Rev. Rul. 87-22, 1987-1 CB 146

ANNOTATED AT ... 2009FED¶9402.043, ¶9402.60

1987 CCH ¶6422

→CCH did not list any cases. It did link to discussion and annotations.

Illustration 4-21. Shepard's Results

View: KWIC | Full　　　　　　　　　　　　　　　　　◁ 1 - 33 of 33 Total Cites ▷
Display Options ▶　　　　Save As Shepard's Alert® | Unrestricted | All Neg | All Pos | FOCUS™- Restrict By
　　　　　　　　　　　　　　　Shepard's® ❶ Rev. Rul. 87-22, Rev. Rul. 87-22

CITING DECISIONS (6 citing decisions)

U.S. TAX COURT

✓ Select for Delivery
☐ 1. **Cited by:**
　　　Huntsman v. Commissioner, 91 T.C. 917, 1988 U.S. Tax Ct. LEXIS 141, 91 T.C. No. 57 (1988)

IRS AGENCY MATERIALS

☐ 2. **Cited by:**
　　　Field Serv. Adv. Mem., 1997 FSA LEXIS 479 (I.R.S. 1997)

☐ 3. **Cited by:**
　　　Action on Dec. CC-1991-02, AOD 1991-02, 1991 AOD LEXIS 4 (I.R.S. 1991)

→Shepard's retrieved both primary and secondary source material.

Illustration 4-22. KeyCite Results

C

Points Paid in Connection with the Refinancing of a Mortgage
Rev. Rul. 87-22
April 26, 1987

Citing References

(Showing 118 documents)

Positive Cases (U.S.A.)

SELECT TO PRINT, EMAIL, ETC.

★ ★ Cited

▶ 1 Huntsman v. C.I.R., 91 T.C. 917, 919+, 91 T.C. No. 57, 57+, 57 USLW 2329, 2329+, Tax Ct. Rep. (CCH) 45,174, 45174+, Tax Ct. Rep. Dec. (P-H) 91.57, 91.57+ (U.S.Tax Ct. Nov 17, 1988) (NO. 5883-87)

C 2 Brodsky v. Comptroller of Treasury, 1989 WL 109742, *1 (Md.Tax Sep 01, 1989) (NO. 2841)

Administrative Decisions (U.S.A.)

IRS Actions on Decisions

C 3 AOD- 1991-02, 1991 WL 537071, (IRS AOD Feb 11, 1991) ★ ★

IRS Field Service Advice

4 Field Service Advisory, 1997 WL 33314881, *33314881 (IRS FSA Jun 11, 1997) ★ ★

5 Field Service Advisory, 1997 WL 33314893, *33314893 (IRS FSA Jun 11, 1997) ★ ★

→Most of the 118 references are secondary sources discussing the ruling.

Illustration 4-23. RIA Citator 2nd Results

Filter this Document by Court: ALL   ▼

Rev Rul 87-22, 1987-1 CB 146, ,

Judicial History

Same case or ruling : IR- 87-34 , 1987 PH ¶54,743 , ,

Cited In

Cases reconciled : Huntsman, James Richard & Zenith Annette, <u>91 TC 919</u> , 91 PH TC 458 *(11/17/1988)*

Cited in dissent : Huntsman, James Richard & Zenith Annette, <u>91 TC 922</u> , 91 PH TC 459 *(11/17/1988)*

Cited favorably : Rev Proc 87-15 , 1987-1 CB 625 , ,

→I used the Checkpoint version for this search. The Westlaw version of this citator gave the same results.

→Page 919 (majority opinion) contains the citation to the ruling; it is not the first page of the opinion.

→The PH reference above is to Prentice-Hall. When Prentice-Hall owned this service, it was called P-H Federal Taxes.

Because I found references to *Huntsman v. Commissioner* in several sources, I decided to read it. Selected excerpts appear below.

Illustration 4-24. Excerpts from Huntsman v. Commissioner, 91 T.C. 917, 919–20 (1988)

We have not had occasion to interpret the meaning of 'in connection with the purchase or improvement' as used in section 461(g). We note, however, that in other cases dealing with the exception in section 461(g)(2), we have construed the terms used therein narrowly, requiring taxpayers to comply with all requirements for the exception therein to apply. See Schubel v. Commissioner, 77 T.C. 701 (1981).[4] We think that, in light of the legislative history of section 461(g), a limited reading of the term 'in connection with the purchase or improvement' is appropriate here and therefore sustain respondent's position.

....

[5]We do not herein decide that all types of refinancing of a principal residence fall outside the exception of sec. 461(g)(2). An example may be the building of a residence with a construction loan replaced upon completion with a permanent mortgage loan. Another example may be a 'bridge' loan, depending upon the circumstances. Since the record herein does not permit the conclusion that the instant case falls within either category, we do not reach the questions involved.

→Footnote 5 implies that more compelling facts could lead the Tax Court to a different outcome.

e. Checking Subsequent History

When I checked the Tax Court decision in a citator, I learned that the appellate court reversed the Tax Court and found for the taxpayer.

Illustration 4-25. KeyCite Results for Huntsman (Tax Court)

Direct History

SELECT TO PRINT, EMAIL, ETC.

➡1 KeyCited Citation:
Huntsman v. C.I.R., 91 T.C. No. 57, 91 T.C. 917, 57 USLW 2329, Tax Ct. Rep. (CCH) 45,174, Tax Ct. Rep. Dec. 91.57 (U.S.Tax Ct. Nov 17, 1988) (NO. 5883-87)

Judgment Reversed by

▷2 Huntsman v. C.I.R., 905 F.2d 1182, 58 USLW 2746, 66 A.F.T.R.2d 90-5020, 90-2 USTC P 50,340 (8th Cir. Jun 14, 1990) (NO. 89-1672)

Reading the appellate decision would be the next step.

Illustration 4-26. Excerpt from Huntsman v. Commissioner, 905 F.2d 1182, 1184 (8th Cir. 1990)

> **[2]** In determining the scope of section 461(g)(2), we first look to the language of the statute. *United States v. James*, 478 U.S. 597, 604, 106 S.Ct. 3116, 3120, 92 L.Ed.2d 483 (1986) (citing *Blue Chip Stamps v. Manor Drug Stores*, 421 U.S. 723, 756, 95 S.Ct. 1917, 1935, 44 L.Ed.2d 539 (1975) (Powell, J., concurring)). The statute merely requires a taxpayer's indebtedness to be "in connection with" the purchase or improvement of the taxpayer's residence. Thus, we find a fair reading of the statute requires that the indebtedness need only have an "association" or "relation" with the purchase of the taxpayer's residence.[5] The statute does not require all indebtedness to be *"directly related* to the actual acquisition of the principal residence." *Huntsman*, 91 T.C. at 921 (emphasis added).

→The illustrations for citations to Revenue Ruling 87-22 omit the appellate court decision because the Eighth Circuit did not cite this ruling.

Although the KeyCite listing for the Tax Court decision showed a flag, I read that decision before checking its validity. Because the Tax Court has national jurisdiction, appeal in your client's case might be to a different court. In addition, I wanted to see how the Tax Court interpreted section 461(g)(2).

Because the KeyCite listing for the Eighth Circuit opinion has a flag [Illustration 4-25], I must also check its validity.

Illustration 4-27. KeyCite Results for Huntsman (8th Circuit)

Direct History

SELECT TO PRINT, EMAIL, ETC.

▶1 Huntsman v. C.I.R., 91 T.C. No. 57, 91 T.C. 917, 57 USLW 2329, Tax Ct. Rep. (CCH) 45,174, Tax Ct. Rep. Dec. (P-H) 91.57 (U.S.Tax Ct. Nov 17, 1988) (NO. 5883-87)

    Judgment Reversed by

➡2 KeyCited Citation:
Huntsman v. C.I.R., 905 F.2d 1182, 58 USLW 2746, 66 A.F.T.R.2d 90-5020, 90-2 USTC P 50,340 (8th Cir. Jun 14, 1990) (NO. 89-1672)

Negative Citing References (U.S.A.)

Disagreed With by

C3 AOD- 1991-02, 1991 WL 537071 (IRS AOD Feb 11, 1991)

Distinguished by

C4 Chief Industries, Inc. v. C.I.R., T.C. Memo. 2004-45, 2004 WL 377058, 87 T.C.M. (CCH) 1002, T.C.M. (RIA) 2004-045, 2004 RIA TC Memo 2004-045 (U.S.Tax Ct. Mar 02, 2004) (NO. 2007-00)   **HN: 2,3 (F.2d)**

Illustration 4-27 lists an IRS action on decision (AOD) as a negative citing reference.[35] My next step is to read that document and learn what the Service's plans are with respect to litigating this issue. The excerpt in Illustration 4-28 indicates that the IRS has conceded this issue only in the Eighth Circuit.

Illustration 4-28. Excerpt from AOD 1991-02

The test that the Eighth Circuit has created requires examination of the facts of each case to determine if the refinancing is sufficiently connected with the purchase or improvement of the taxpayer's residence. The Service believes that Congress enacted section 461(g)(2) to eliminate the case-by-case approach to deductibility of points. Moreover, the legislative history indicates that Congress intended to limit the exception to points paid on indebtedness incurred to purchase or improve the taxpayer's principal residence. Accordingly, the Service maintains its position that points paid for a loan to refinance a mortgage on a taxpayer's principal residence are not deductible under I.R.C. § 461(g)(2). Thus it will not follow the court's holding with respect to this type of refinancing agreement outside of the Eighth Circuit. However, in the absence of an intercircuit conflict, the Service is of the opinion that the issue lacks sufficient demonstrable administrative importance to warrant a petition for certiorari.

RECOMMENDATION:

No certiorari

f. Starting with Secondary Sources

Illustrations 4-6 through 4-10 showed index references to discussion in looseleaf services. Instead of beginning with the primary sources discussed above, I might have begun with one of those discussions.

Illustration 4-29 demonstrates how a looseleaf service covers this issue. In addition to discussion, ¶K-5180 includes footnote references to legislative history, Revenue Ruling 87-22, both *Huntsman* decisions (and several other decisions that might have relevance[36]), and AOD 1991-02. If I

---

[35] I cover IRS litigation plans in Chapters 10 and 11.

[36] Dicta in the Ninth Circuit's unpublished opinion in *Cao v. Commissioner* [mentioned in Illustration 4-29] implies that the Ninth Circuit panel approved the Eighth Circuit's holding in *Huntsman*: "Nothing in the record indicates that the taxpayers refinanced the existing indebtedness on their residence in connection with the purchase of their house rather than for some other financial reason, such as lowering the interest rate on their original loan. See Huntsman v. Commissioner, 905 F.2d 1182, 1185 [66 AFTR 2d 90-5020] (9th Cir. 1990) (loan fees

had started my research here, I would have saved considerable time compiling an initial list of primary source materials to read.

Illustration 4-29. Discussion in Federal Tax Coordinator 2d

¶K-5180. Whether refinancing debt is considered to be incurred in connection with the purchase or improvement of a residence.

In order to qualify under the special rule allowing deduction of certain "points" in year they are paid, the points must be paid in respect of indebtedness incurred in connection with the purchase or improvement of residence, see ¶ K-5178 . Where the taxpayer does not establish that a refinancing of a loan is in connection with the purchase of their residence, rather than for some other reason, such as lowering the interest rate on the original loan, the loan fees are not deductible. [30]

    ✍ **sample client letter:** A sample client letter on home mortgage refinancing appears in Client Letters ¶ 1328 .

    ✍ **sample client letter:** A sample client letter on the deductibility of points with regard to the refinancing of a personal residence appears in Client Letters ¶ 1330 .

---

[30]

Cao, Phuoc v. Com., (1996, CA9) 77 AFTR 2d 96-1113 , 96-1 USTC ¶50167 (unpublished), affg (1994) TC Memo 1994-60 , RIA TC Memo ¶94060 , 67 CCH TCM 2171 .

IRS and the courts have considered the question of when, if ever, a debt that refinances a debt that was originally used for the purchase or improvement of a residence may itself be treated as incurred in connection with the purchase or improvement of a residence.

IRS has said that the points paid on a refinancing mortgage loan are not incurred in connection with the purchase or improvement of residence. [30.1] In so doing, it cited a Congressional Committee Report which said that a loan does not qualify for the exception described in ¶ K-5178 "if the loan proceeds are used for purposes other than purchasing or improving the taxpayer's principal residence." [31]

[30.1]

→Illustration 4-7 included a reference to Federal Tax Coordinator 2d ¶K-5180.

3. Drawing Conclusions

Your research did not uncover a definitive answer. Unless your clients live in the Eighth Circuit, the IRS will litigate this issue.[37] Even if your clients live in the Eighth Circuit, they cannot rely 100 percent on the decision in Huntsman. First, the Huntsmans had to refinance in three years; your clients were given four years. Second, your clients had mixed motives for refinancing in the second year instead of waiting until the end of year four.

---

related to acquiring a permanent mortgage and finalizing the purchase of a house were deductible under section 461(g)(2))." Note that your clients had a deadline for refinancing but they also wanted to take advantage of lower rates.

[37] Instructions for Form 1098 (2010), which the lender completes, include the following language on page 3: "Do not report as points on Form 1098 amounts paid:... ●For a refinancing ...." If your clients deduct amounts not shown on the Form 1098, their return might be selected for audit.

SECTION B. OTHER FACT PATTERNS

1. Financially Distressed Clients

The clients in Section A could afford their mortgage payments but had a loan that required refinancing in four years. Your new clients have financial problems and are having trouble making their monthly payments. Their lender agreed to lower the loan amount and the interest rate. Your clients anticipate being able to make the reduced payments.

Your clients currently have two assets: the home (cost $220,000; current value $250,000); vested pension rights that are exempt from levy under state law (current value $150,000). They owe $300,000 on the mortgage ($160,000 original loan and $140,000 home equity indebtedness, incurred to pay college tuition at a time when the home was worth considerably more than it is now). In addition, your clients guaranteed a $200,000 loan their son incurred when he started a business. Their son is making his monthly payments, but the business has not been doing well and there is a chance your clients will have to pay this debt.

If the lender reduces your clients' loan, must your clients report the entire reduction as gross income?

2. Entrepreneurial Client

Another client, who has a friend who breeds catfish, has decided to breed groupers. He will sell some of the offspring to restaurants and will retain others to increase the size of his breeding stock (and to replace those who die from old age or disease). Your client is worried about having an excess of male or female groupers. If he trades male groupers to another breeder and receives female groupers in exchange (or vice versa), what are his tax consequences? What other issues do you see?

3. Extended Family

Your next client has a complicated family situation. Her pregnant daughter moved into your client's apartment last December and was arrested this May. Your client is a widow. She has a low-paying job and few assets; she can't afford her daughter's bail. Her daughter will be in jail until her trial, which is scheduled for mid-November but might be delayed until next January. If the daughter is acquitted, she will return to your client's apartment. The baby is due in late July and will probably live with your client until the daughter's legal situation is resolved. Your client wants to know what her tax status will be this year and whether she will be entitled to any tax benefits with respect to her daughter and granddaughter. Her daughter earned no income this year.

CHAPTER 5. CONSTITUTION

SECTION A. INTRODUCTION

The United States Constitution serves several functions. First, in articles I, II, and III, it establishes the three branches of government: legislative, executive, and judicial. Second, it lists powers exercised by each branch and indicates situations in which a second branch is involved. For example, Congress (the legislative branch) has the power to impose taxes but legislative proposals generally do not become law without the President's signature. The President (executive branch) has the power to make treaties but only with the concurrence of the Senate. The judicial branch has the power to hear cases arising under the Constitution, statutes, and treaties, but the Constitution establishes only the Supreme Court and gives Congress has the power to establish any lower courts.

In addition to establishing the branches of government and allocating power between them, the Constitution imposes limits on the exercise of those powers. The first type of limitation is alluded to above; certain powers require the participation or acquiescence of a second branch of government. In addition, the constitution imposes limitations that do not involve a second branch of government. Many of these limitations, covered in the next section, relate to the imposition of taxes.

SECTION B. TAXING POWER AND LIMITATIONS

The Constitution gives Congress the power to impose taxes but provides several limitations on its ability to do so. Some limitations are substantive: direct taxes must be apportioned, and other taxes must be uniform throughout the United States. Other limitations are procedural: bills for raising revenue must originate in the House of Representatives. Table 5-1 includes provisions that specifically mention taxation.

Because the income tax is specifically authorized by the Constitution's sixteenth amendment, it avoids an earlier holding that it was a direct tax subject to apportionment based on population.[38] The estate and gift taxes, on the other hand, are indirect taxes; they are subject only to the requirement that they be uniform throughout the United States.

---

[38] Pollock v. Farmers' Loan & Trust Co., 158 U.S. 601 (1895); cf. Springer v. United States, 102 U.S. 586 (1881), concluding the Civil War income tax was indirect.

Table 5-1. Constitutional Provisions Regarding Federal Taxes

Art. I, § 2, cl. 3: Representatives and direct Taxes shall be apportioned among the several States which may be included within this Union, according to their respective Numbers .... (Before amendment)

Art. I, § 7, cl. 1: All Bills for raising Revenue shall originate in the House of Representatives; but the Senate may propose or concur with Amendments as on other Bills.

Art. I, § 8, cl. 1: The Congress shall have Power To lay and collect Taxes, Duties, Imposts and Excises, to pay the Debts and provide for the common Defence and general Welfare of the United States; but all Duties, Imposts and Excises shall be uniform throughout the United States;

Art. I, § 9, cl. 4: No Capitation, or other direct, Tax shall be laid, unless in Proportion to the Census or Enumeration herein before directed to be taken.

Art. I, § 9, cl. 5: No Tax or Duty shall be laid on Articles exported from any State.

Art. I, § 9, cl. 6: No Preference shall be given by any Regulation of Commerce or Revenue to the Ports of one State over those of another; nor shall Vessels bound to, or from, one State, be obliged to enter, clear, or pay Duties in another.

Amend. XVI: The Congress shall have power to lay and collect taxes on incomes, from whatever source derived, without apportionment among the several States, and without regard to any census or enumeration.

→Article I, § 10, includes limitations on the power of states to impose taxes and duties.

SECTION C. CONSTITUTIONAL LITIGATION

1. Items Challenged

Because several constitutional provisions explicitly mention taxation, courts may be asked to decide if a Code section violates the limitations shown in Table 5-1. Examples of such litigation appear in Table 5-2. Most cases discussing constitutional claims involve provisions that do not mention taxation, such as those listed in Table 5-3. Tax claims involving the Constitution do not generate a substantial body of important litigation in any year.

Table 5-2. *Litigation Involving Tax Provisions*

Mobley v. United States, 8 Cl. Ct. 767 (1985) (the apportionment clause–art. I, § 2, cl. 3)

Moore v. United States House of Representatives, 733 F.2d 946 (D.C. Cir. 1984) (the origination clause–art. I, § 7, cl. 1)

United States v. Ptasynski, 462 U.S. 74 (1983) (the uniformity clause–art. I, § 8, cl. 1)

United States v. International Business Machines Corp., 517 U.S. 843 (1996) (the export clause–art. I, § 9, cl. 5)

Murphy v. Internal Revenue Service, 460 F.3d 79 (D.C. Cir. 2006) (definition of income–amend. XVI)[39]

2. Supreme Court Litigation Versus Constitutional Litigation

Keep two facts in mind. First, lower courts dismiss many constitutional claims; most of these claims never reach the United States Supreme Court. Second, most substantive tax litigation involves interpreting statutes or other rules rather than resolving constitutional claims. If Congress disagrees with a Supreme Court decision regarding interpretation, it can "overrule" the Court by amending the statute.

SECTION D. IRS CONSIDERATION OF CONSTITUTIONAL CHALLENGES

Only a court can declare a statute or administrative interpretation unconstitutional. But the IRS can consider constitutional challenges in its dealings with taxpayers. If the Service decides a challenge is valid, it can concede the disputed tax before the matter reaches a court. Many of these challenges are so-called "frivolous" challenges—e.g., that the sixteenth amendment was not properly ratified. An annual IRS document, The Truth About Frivolous Tax Arguments, includes citations to cases and rulings covering constitutional and other challenges to federal taxes. It is available on the IRS website.

---

[39] The decision above was later vacated. In its later decision, the court upheld the tax as an excise tax that met the uniformity requirement. 493 F.3d 170 (D.C. Cir. 2007).

Table 5-3. Litigation Involving Nontax Provisions

Demko v. United States, 216 F.3d 1049 (Fed. Cir. 2000) (nondelegation doctrine–judicially derived from art. I, § 1)

NationsBank of Texas, N.A. v. United States, 269 F.3d 1332 (Fed. Cir. 2001) (separation of powers doctrine–art. I, § 7, cl. 2)

Clinton v. City of New York, 524 U.S. 417 (1998) (the presentment clause–art. I, § 7, cl. 2)

United States v. Rosengarten, 857 F.2d 76 (2d Cir. 1988) (ex post facto laws–art. I, § 9, cl. 3)

Freytag v. Commissioner, 501 U.S. 868 (1991) (the appointments clause–art. II, § 2, cl. 2)

United States v. Hatter, 532 U.S. 557 (2001) (the compensation clause–art. III, § 1)

Hernandez v. Commissioner, 490 U.S. 680 (1989) (establishment of religion and free exercise of religion–amend. I)

Regan v. Taxation with Representation, 461 U.S. 540 (1983) (freedom of speech and association–amend. I; equal protection–amend. V)

United States v. Carlton, 512 U.S. 26 (1994) (retroactivity as a denial of due process–amend. V)

Manufacturers Hanover Trust Co. v. United States, 775 F.2d 459 (2d Cir. 1985) (equal protection/sex discrimination–amend. V)

Ianniello v. Commissioner, 98 T.C. 165 (1992) (double jeopardy–amend. V; excessive fines and cruel and unusual punishments–amend. VIII)

South Carolina v. Baker, 485 U.S. 505 (1988) (infringement on powers reserved to states–amend. X)

Shapiro v. Baker, 646 F. Supp. 1127 (D.N.J. 1986) (judicial doctrine of intergovernmental tax immunity)

SECTION E. RESEARCH PROCESS

You can use citators to determine if a court or the IRS has considered a challenge based on constitutional grounds. KeyCite and the electronic version of Shepard's are the best citators for this purpose.[40] Instead of using a citator, you can search electronic services for specific constitutional provisions or common terms (e.g., due process).

The sources listed below discuss constitutional challenges. Each includes citations to authority.

• Standard Federal Tax Reporter volume 1, available in print and on IntelliConnect

• Mertens, Law of Federal Income Taxation chapter 4, available in print and on Westlaw

• The Truth About Frivolous Tax Arguments, available on the IRS website

• Bittker & Lokken, Federal Taxation of Income, Estates and Gifts chapter 1, available in print and on Westlaw

Because substantive tax research rarely involves the Constitution, you may decide to perform your research using nontax materials.[41]

SECTION F. PROBLEMS

1. Indicate which of the Constitution's tax provisions was involved in

    a. Prescott v. Commissioner, 561 F.2d 1287 (8th Cir. 1977)

    b. Burk-Waggoner Oil Association v. Hopkins, 269 U.S. 110 (1925)

    c. Kohl v. United States, 128 F. Supp. 902 (D. Wis. 1954)

    d. Peony Park, Inc. v. O'Malley, 121 F. Supp. 690 (D. Neb. 1954)

2. Indicate which of the Constitution's nontax provisions was involved in

    a. United States v. Lee, 455 U.S. 252 (1982)

    b. United States v. Miller, 307 U.S. 174 (1939)

    c. United States v. Josephberg, 459 F.3d 350 (2d Cir. 2006)

    d. Stelly v. Commissioner, 804 F.2d 868 (5th Cir. 1986)

---

[40] Many of the print Shepard's series did not cover IRS material or Tax Court Memorandum decisions; the CCH and RIA citators do not provide citations to statutes or regulations.

[41] The most useful materials are annotated Constitutions, such as those included in United States Code Annotated and United States Code Service, and digests.

3. Cite to the decision that involved the constitution and these facts and indicate its holding.

a. 2009 Sixth Circuit opinion involving an IRS violation of the Internal Revenue Manual

b 2001 Ninth Circuit opinion involving a challenge to the United States–France Income Tax Treaty based on the origination clause

c. 1983 Tax Court opinion involving a challenge to Code section 482 based on the nondelegation doctrine

d. 1966 Fifth Circuit opinion involving a challenge to the constitutionality of the Tax Court based on the separation of powers doctrine

e. 1951 District Court opinion involving a claim that different rates for the estate tax and gift tax violated the uniformity clause

4. Indicate which constitutional claim the IRS rejected in

a. Revenue Ruling 2007-19

b. Field Service Advisory 200242008

c. Technical Advice Memorandum 200045009

d. Technical Advice Memorandum 9842003

CHAPTER 6. STATUTES

SECTION A. INTRODUCTION

This chapter discusses statutes authorized by the United States Constitution and enacted by Congress. It covers terminology used to describe statutes, lists sources in which you can locate current, repealed, and pending statutes, and introduces rules of interpretation. The primary focus of this chapter is the Internal Revenue Code.

In interpreting statutes, judges and administrative agencies may look to legislative history, a topic covered in Chapter 7. If a taxpayer has ties to another country, treaties may also be relevant. Treaties and their relationship to statutes are discussed in Chapter 8.

Your goals for Chapters 6 and 7 include finding relevant documents, determining their relative importance, and updating your research to encompass pending items. In accomplishing these goals, you should become familiar with the process by which statutes are enacted and the terminology used to describe statutory and legislative history documents.

SECTION B. FUNCTIONS OF STATUTES

The Constitution gives Congress the power to levy taxes. As noted in Chapter 5, the Constitution provides limits on congressional power, but it does not provide rules for measuring income or value, allowing deductions, or determining rates. Congress accomplishes those tasks by enacting statutes covering taxation.

Statutes define the tax base and penalties for noncompliance, provide effective dates, authorize administrative agencies to interpret the laws, and direct those same agencies to make reports to Congress. Your research may require you to locate statutes serving these purposes.

SECTION C. TERMINOLOGY

This chapter's discussion of statutes uses terms related both to the statutes themselves and to the process by which they are enacted. The latter topic is discussed in more detail in Chapter 7.

1. Internal Revenue Code and United States Code

The **United States Code** is a subject-based codification of federal statutes. It is divided into titles, and each title is further subdivided into smaller units. A tax research project may involve several U.S.C. titles, but your primary focus is likely to be title 26, **Internal Revenue Code**. Most titles of U.S.C. are referred to by title number rather than by name. For example, you would generally say title 29 rather than the Labor title. Title 26, on the other hand, is generally referred to as the Internal Revenue Code.[42] Because other titles of U.S.C. include tax-related material, make sure you know whether you are looking for an answer in the I.R.C. or in another title of U.S.C.

The Internal Revenue Code contains the vast majority of statutes covering income, estate and gift, excise, and employment taxes. The 1986 Code replaced the 1954 Code, which had replaced the 1939 Code. I refer to the 1986 statutory materials as the Code or the I.R.C. throughout this book. When I refer to the two previous Codes (1939 and 1954), I will include the Code year.[43]

Although the current Code was enacted in 1986, it has been amended many times. You will frequently see references to the Internal Revenue Code of 1986, as amended. That usage is appropriate. A reference to the Internal Revenue Code of 2010 would be incorrect.

2. Bills and Acts

Before a provision can be added to the Internal Revenue Code (or to any other part of U.S.C.), it must first be enacted.[44] The starting point is the introduction of a **bill** in Congress. A bill contains the initial draft of proposed legislation. As discussed in Chapter 7, that language may be changed at various points before the bill is finally enacted.

Each bill is assigned a bill number. Each chamber numbers its bills separately in chronological order. A House bill is referred to as H.R. (e.g., H.R. 3838); a Senate bill is identified as S. Senators introduce bills involving taxation despite the constitutional requirement that bills for raising revenue originate in the House.[45]

---

[42] Title 26 is currently the only U.S.C. title that has the word Code in its name.

[43] Before 1939, tax statutes were reenacted in their entirety, or with necessary changes, on a regular basis. Because many current provisions can be traced back to the 1939 Code or even earlier—I.R.C. § 263, for example, contains language taken almost verbatim from § 117 of the 1864 Act—cross-references to these earlier materials are extremely useful. See Act of June 30, 1864, ch. 173, 13 Stat. 223, 281–82. Chapter 7 covers materials used to trace statutory language.

[44] Amendments to, or repeal of, statutory provisions, go through the same process.

[45] If the House objects, it "blue-slips" the bill and returns it to the Senate.

Even though a bill may die because it failed to pass both the House and Senate, don't be surprised to hear it referred to as an act.[46] Unfortunately, that term is not reserved for actual statutes. The bill's original name is likely to include the word "Act."

3. Public Laws, Slip Laws, and Statutes at Large

Each enacted bill is called a **Public Law** and receives a Public Law Number (Pub. L. No.). These numbers are chronological by Congress.[47] They bear no relation to the original bill number and provide no information about the session of that Congress.[48] Congress began using Public Law Numbers in 1957; bills enacted before then have chapter numbers instead of Public Law Numbers.

Public Laws are first published in pamphlet form as **slip laws**. They are later printed in **Statutes at Large** in Public Law Number order [Illustration 6-1]. Even though it is a separate pamphlet, each slip law includes the volume and page numbers it will have in Statutes at Large.

Statutes at Large prints Public Laws in chronological order by session of Congress. United States Code rearranges statutes, as amended by Public Laws. As noted in Subsection C.1, United States Code is arranged by subject matter.

As Illustration 6-2 shows, Public Laws can affect multiple I.R.C. sections. Because Internal Revenue Code provisions are often a minor part of a Public Law enacted for other purposes, the act generally affects many other titles of U.S.C. Language that appears together in Statutes at Large, because it is part of a single act section, may be dispersed into several titles of U.S.C.

If statutory language will be added to U.S.C., the Public Law generally refers to the relevant U.S.C. title. In addition to language that will be added to U.S.C., the Public Law includes enactment dates, effective

---

[46] Unless a bill is enacted by the time a particular Congress ends, it dies. Its supporters must reintroduce it in a subsequent Congress and start the legislative process over. This rule does not apply to treaties (Chapter 8), which remain alive for action by a subsequent Congress.

[47] Statutes enacted before 1957 have chapter numbers instead of Public Law numbers.

[48] For example, the Tax Increase Prevention and Reconciliation Act of 2005 is Pub. L. No. 109-222. The Public Law number indicates that it was passed in the 109th Congress; it does not indicate in which of the two sessions. TIPRA was introduced in the 109th Congress as H.R. 4297.

dates, instructions to administrative agencies, and provisions that will not be codified in U.S.C.

Illustration 6-1. First Page of Pub. L. No. 110-245

122 STAT. 1624   PUBLIC LAW 110–245—JUNE 17, 2008

Public Law 110–245
110th Congress

An Act

June 17, 2008

[H.R. 6081]

To amend the Internal Revenue Code of 1986 to provide benefits for military personnel, and for other purposes.

Be it enacted by the Senate and House of Representatives of the United States of America in Congress assembled,

Heroes Earnings Assistance and Relief Tax Act of 2008.
26 USC 1 note.

SECTION 1. SHORT TITLE, ETC.

(a) SHORT TITLE.—This Act may be cited as the "Heroes Earnings Assistance and Relief Tax Act of 2008".

26 USC 1 et seq.

(b) REFERENCE.—Except as otherwise expressly provided, whenever in this Act an amendment or repeal is expressed in terms of an amendment to, or repeal of, a section or other provision, the reference shall be considered to be made to a section or other provision of the Internal Revenue Code of 1986.

(c) TABLE OF CONTENTS.—The table of contents for this Act is as follows:

→In addition to the Public Law Number, the first page includes the enactment date, and the original bill number.

→The first page also includes the title (To amend the Internal Revenue Code, etc.) and the short title (Heroes Earnings Assistance and Relief Tax Act of 2008).

→If an act has additional short titles, those will appear in the relevant parts of the act.

Illustration 6-2. Page of Pub. L. No. 110-245

TITLE I—BENEFITS FOR MILITARY

SEC. 101. RECOVERY REBATE PROVIDED TO MILITARY FAMILIES.

(a) IN GENERAL.—Subsection (h) of section 6428 (relating to identification number requirement) is amended by adding at the end the following new paragraph: 26 USC 6428.

"(3) SPECIAL RULE FOR MEMBERS OF THE ARMED FORCES.— Paragraph (1) shall not apply to a joint return where at least 1 spouse was a member of the Armed Forces of the United States at any time during the taxable year.".

(b) EFFECTIVE DATE.—The amendments made by this section shall take effect as if included in the amendments made by section 101 of the Economic Stimulus Act of 2008.   26 USC 6428 note.

SEC. 102. ELECTION TO INCLUDE COMBAT PAY AS EARNED INCOME FOR PURPOSES OF EARNED INCOME TAX CREDIT.

(a) IN GENERAL.—Clause (vi) of section 32(c)(2)(B) (defining earned income) is amended to read as follows:

"(vi) a taxpayer may elect to treat amounts excluded from gross income by reason of section 112 as earned income.".

(b) CONFORMING AMENDMENT.—Paragraph (4) of section 6428(e) is amended by striking "except that—" and all that follows through "(B) such term shall" and inserting "except that such term shall".

(c) SUNSET NOT APPLICABLE.—Section 105 of the Working Families Tax Relief Act of 2004 (relating to application of EGTRRA sunset to this title) shall not apply to section 104(b) of such Act.   26 USC 32 note.

(d) EFFECTIVE DATE.—The amendments made by this section shall apply to taxable years ending after December 31, 2007.   26 USC 32 note.

→The marginal notes to sections 101 and 102 of the act indicate the Code sections being amended.

→The "note" language indicates provisions that are not codified but are related notes following a particular Code section.

There are three important differences between Statutes at Large and United States Code. The first, discussed above, is arrangement: Statutes at Large is chronological; U.S.C. is subject-based. The second relates to uncodified items. U.S.C. deletes Statutes at Large language that won't be added to any of its titles or includes this language only in notes.

The third difference relates to how each Code section appears. Statutes at Large prints only the language in the Public Law. If a Public Law amends an existing Code section, it includes only the amending language.

As a result, Statutes at Large does not show how the pre- or post-amendment Code section reads. [See Illustration 6-3.] If you need to see current Code language, the I.R.C. is more useful than Statutes at Large.

Illustration 6-3. Original, Amending, and Amended Language of I.R.C. Code § 24(a)

I.R.C. § 24(a) Before Amendment	Pub. L. No. 110-351, § 501(c)(1), amending I.R.C. § 24(a)	I.R.C. § 24(a) After Amendment
a) Allowance of credit.–There shall be allowed as a credit against the tax imposed by this chapter for the taxable year with respect to each qualifying child of the taxpayer an amount equal to $1,000.	(c) Restrict Qualifying Child Tax Benefits to Child's Parent. (1) Child tax credit.–Section 24(a) of such Code is amended by inserting ``for which the taxpayer is allowed a deduction under section 151" after ``of the taxpayer".	(a) Allowance of credit.–There shall be allowed as a credit against the tax imposed by this chapter for the taxable year with respect to each qualifying child of the taxpayer for which the taxpayer is allowed a deduction under section 151 an amount equal to $1,000.

→The Public Law section number (501(c)(1)) has nothing to do with the Code section number (24(a)). Because there is a Code section 501(c)(1), you will not find what you need if you search for Code section 501(c)(1).

4. Codified and Uncodified Provisions

Most provisions, with the exception of the dates described below, are **codified** in the I.R.C. or in another title of U.S.C. Three types of provisions are not likely to be codified. These are effective and enactment dates (discussed below); directions to another branch of government (usually an administrative agency); and statutory provisions that Congress has chosen not to codify.

5. Enactment Date, Effective Date, and Sunset Date

These terms are critical aspects of tax research. Because pending legislation may add new legislation or amend or repeal existing law, it can totally change the outcome of a planned transaction.

a. Enactment Date and Effective Date

Most acts have two relevant dates. The **enactment date** is the date the President signs the act (or allows it to become law without a signature) or Congress overrides a presidential veto. The **effective date**, on which the act's provisions apply to particular transactions, may coincide with, follow, or even precede the enactment date.[49]

Tax legislation often involves separate effective dates for individual sections of an act. It is risky to assume that the enactment date is the effective date or that the effective date of one section applies to all parts of a new act. Remember that effective dates rarely become part of the Code, but they do appear in the act itself.[50] Sources that include statutory text are discussed in Section G.

When working with effective dates, be careful to look for **transition rules**. In appropriate circumstances, Congress will provide exemptions from a particular effective date. This is particularly likely to occur for transactions that occur after the new effective date but which were subject to a binding contract on a specified earlier date.[51] An example appears in Table 6-1.

Illustration 6-4 illustrates separate effective dates in one act. Illustration 6-5 and Table 6-1 show the importance of effective dates.

Illustration 6-4. Effective Date Provisions in Housing and Economic Recovery Act of 2008, § 3022

(d) EFFECTIVE DATE.—
    (1) HOUSING BONDS.—The amendments made by subsection (a) shall apply to bonds issued after the date of the enactment of this Act.
    (2) LOW INCOME HOUSING CREDIT.—The amendments made by subsection (b) shall apply to credits determined under section 42 of the Internal Revenue Code of 1986 to the extent attributable to buildings placed in service after December 31, 2007.
    (3) REHABILITATION CREDIT.—The amendments made by subsection (c) shall apply to credits determined under section 47 of the Internal Revenue Code of 1986 to the extent attributable to qualified rehabilitation expenditures properly taken into account for periods after December 31, 2007.

→The enactment date was July 30, 2008.

---

[49] If the effective date precedes the enactment date, aggrieved taxpayers may challenge the retroactivity. Constitutional challenges are discussed in Chapter 5.

[50] Effective dates do appear in the Code for provisions that phase in over time or which apply in a different manner in different years. For example, the depreciation dollar limits in the 2009 version of I.R.C. § 179(b)(1) varied based on the year the property is placed in service.

[51] Some acts include transition rules that benefit specific taxpayers. See, e.g., Pub. L. No. 99-514, § 204, 100 Stat. 2085, 2146 (1986).

Illustration 6-5. Excerpt from Polone v. Commissioner[52]

> Here, the Tax Court held that pre-amendment § 104 applied to Polone's May 1996 payment from UTA, but that post-amendment § 104 applied to the November 1996, May 1997, and November 1998 payments because Polone received those payments after the amendment's effective date. _Polone,_ T.C. Memo 2003–339 at 66.

Table 6-1. Timeline in Polone v. Commissioner

Action	Date
Employer fires Polone	April 21, 1996
Polone sues for defamation	April 24, 1996
Settlement of $4 million; Polone receives first $1 million	May 3, 1996
Bill (H.R. 3448) introduced in Congress	May 14,1996
I.R.C. § 104(a)(2) amended to include "physical" requirement	August 20, 1996 (effective date unless binding agreement, decree, or award in effect or issued before September 13, 1995)
Polone receives second installment	November 11, 1996
Polone receives third and fourth installments	May 5, 1997 & November 11, 1998

The exact language Congress uses is critical for determining an effective date. Table 6-2 indicates effective date formats with quite different meanings.

Table 6-2. Effective Date Formats

Effective for transactions occurring in taxable years beginning after December 31, 2010
Effective for transactions occurring after December 31, 2010
Effective for transactions occurring in taxable years ending after December 31, 2010

→If a taxpayer has a calendar year, the three effective dates above might yield the same results. If a taxpayer instead has a fiscal year that ends January 31, a transaction that occurs January 15, 2011, will be covered by the second and third effective dates but not by the first.

---

[52] 505 F.3d 966, 970 (9th Cir. 2007), cert. denied, 552 U.S. 1280 (2008).

b. Sunset Date

As a general rule, Code provisions remain in effect until amended, repealed, or declared unconstitutional. Congress may provide a specific **sunset date** for an individual Code provision. Unlike effective dates, sunset dates generally do appear in the Code.

Acts subject to sunset dates may be referred to as **expiring provisions**. Unless extended by Congress in subsequent legislation, the Code section dies (expires). The term **extenders** is commonly used for tax bill provisions postponing sunset dates. Unless Congress extends it, section 45O [Illustration 6-6] will sunset at the end of 2012. Section 30D [Illustration 6-7] will sunset over several years.

Illustration 6-6. Sunset Date for I.R.C. § 45O

(i) TERMINATION.–This section shall not apply to any amount paid or incurred after December 31, 2012.

Illustration 6-7. Sunset Dates for I.R.C. § 30D

(e) TERMINATION.–This section shall not apply to any property purchased after–
(1) in the case of a new qualified fuel cell motor vehicle (as described in subsection (b)), December 31, 2014,
(2) in the case of a new advanced lean burn technology motor vehicle (as described in subsection (c)) or a new qualified hybrid motor vehicle (as described in subsection (d)(2)(A)), December 31, 2010,
(3) in the case of a new qualified hybrid motor vehicle (as described in subsection (d)(2)(B)), December 31, 2009, and
(4) in the case of a new qualified alternative fuel vehicle (as described in subsection (e)), December 31, 2010.

Although sunset dates are generally calendar dates, specific events may also cause a provision to sunset. For example, the section 30B credit for alternative motor vehicles includes a phase-out based on the number of hybrid vehicles sold.[53]

6. Act Names

a. Short Titles and Popular Names[54]

Acts are often referred to by a so-called **popular name**. The name may be an acronym (e.g., the Economic Recovery Tax Act of 1981 is generally

---

[53] I.R.C. § 30B(f).

[54] Some examples of short titles appear in Table 6-8.

referred to as ERTA). It may be a descriptive phrase (e.g., Inmate Tax Fraud Prevention Act of 2008). It may be something as simple as Revenue Act of 1924. Congress often "names" legislation by including one or more **short titles** in the Public Law. A short title appears in an act section, usually the first one, and reads: "This Act may be cited as ...." Congress may also provide separate short titles for some (or all) of an act's major subdivisions. In that case, the beginning of the subdivision would read: "This [division, title, subtitle] may be cited as ...."

Short titles and popular names can be confusing. If an act has multiple short titles, you may not realize that you've been given the name of a subdivision. In addition, practitioners aren't bound by the language Congress uses. As noted above, ERTA is a popular name, but it is not the act's short title. Finally, many short titles are similar; in the case of Revenue Acts, the year may be the only differentiating part of the names.

Although short titles and popular names may differ, if an act has only one short title, it and the popular name generally will be the same. This book generally uses the terms interchangeably.

b. Revenue Acts and Other Act Names

Acts that have "Revenue" or "Tax" in their names clearly announce their relevance to taxation. Other acts that are likely to include substantive tax law include those with "Deficit Reduction," "Income," "Trade," or "Investment" in their titles.

The name of an act may contain no hint that it includes tax provisions. Other acts that include tax provisions may lack popular names altogether. For example, the Ricky Ray Hemophilia Relief Fund Act of 1998 treats certain payments as damages for purposes of Code section 104(a)(2).[55] Public Law Number 107-22, which changed the name of Education IRAs to Coverdell Education Savings Accounts, has no popular name.[56]

SECTION D. INTERNAL REVENUE CODE

This section covers how the Code is organized. It introduces topics that are covered in greater detail in Section E.

---

[55] Pub. L. No. 105-369, § 103(h), 112 Stat. 3368, 3371 (1998).

[56] 115 Stat. 196 (2001). Pub. L. No. 107-22 began as a Senate bill. S. 1190, 107th Cong., 1st. Sess. (2001). It had no revenue implications and thus did not violate the origination clause. U.S. CONST. art. I, § 7, cl. 1.

1. Code Subdivisions

Because the Internal Revenue Code is a title of U.S.C., its first subdivisions are subtitles. The Code currently has 11 subtitles.

Table 6-3. *Internal Revenue Code Subtitles*

Subtitle	Subject
A	Income Taxes
B	Estate and Gift Taxes
C	Employment Taxes
D	Miscellaneous Excise Taxes
E	Alcohol, Tobacco, and Certain Other Excise Taxes
F	Procedure and Administration
G	The Joint Committee on Taxation
H	Financing of Presidential Election Campaigns
I	Trust Fund Code
J	Coal Industry Health Benefits
K	Group Health Plan Requirements

Each subtitle is further subdivided into smaller units. Table 6-4 illustrates these smaller units: chapter; subchapter; part; subpart; section; subsection; paragraph; subparagraph; clause; and subclause. On occasion, you will encounter references to sentences within a larger subdivision.

Table 6-4. *Code Subdivisions: I.R.C. § 45F(c)(1)(A)(i)(I)*

Subdivision	Heading or Text
Title 26	Internal Revenue
Subtitle A	Income Taxes
Chapter 1	Normal Taxes and Surtaxes
Subchapter A	Determination of Tax Liability
Part IV	Credits Against Tax
Subpart D	Business Related Credits
Section 45F	Employer-provided child care credit
Subsection (c)	Definitions. For purposes of this section—
Paragraph (1)	Qualified child care expenditure
Subparagraph (A)	In general. The term "qualified child care expenditure" means any amount paid or incurred—
Clause (i)	to acquire, construct, rehabilitate, or expand property—
Subclause (I)	which is to be used as part of a qualified child care facility of the taxpayer,

→Subdivisions may include only headings, only text, or both text and headings.

The section is the basic unit used in finding the law. The Code contains only one section 1, not one for each part, chapter, or other unit. Although sections are numbered sequentially, breaks in the sequence provide room for Congress to insert new sections as needed.

2. Code Subdivision Numbering System

Titles, chapters, parts, and sections are identified by number. Sub-titles, subchapters, and subparts are identified by letter. Most subsections are identified by letter (e.g., subsection 163(d)), but a few are designated by number (e.g., subsection 212(1)). Successive subdivisions bear letters or numbers, as appropriate. The Code uses both upper and lower case letters and both Roman and Arabic numerals.

Code section 45F [Table 6-4] is not unique. Many Code sections have so many subdivisions that it is easy to lose track of where you are. Checkpoint includes a tool that lets you know exactly what Code section subdivision you are reading. IntelliConnect labels each subdivision.

Illustration 6-8. Checkpoint Compass Feature

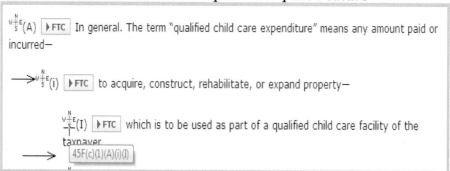

→Let your mouse hover over a compass sign. The box gives you the full citation.

Illustration 6-9. IntelliConnect Code Labels

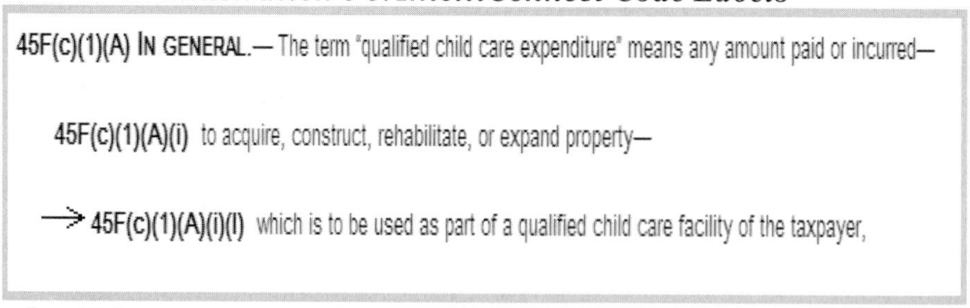

45F(c)(1)(A) IN GENERAL.— The term "qualified child care expenditure" means any amount paid or incurred—

  45F(c)(1)(A)(i) to acquire, construct, rehabilitate, or expand property—

  ➤ **45F(c)(1)(A)(i)(I)** which is to be used as part of a qualified child care facility of the taxpayer,

→IntelliConnect always shows the full Code section and relevant subdivisions.

3. Unique and Repeated Code Subdivisions

Title, subtitle, chapter, and section numbers and letters are used only once. Other subdivision classifications are used multiple times. For example, there are several Subchapter As, but there is only one Chapter 1 (which appears in Subtitle A). The first chapter in Subtitle B is Chapter 11.

Although subchapter, part, and subpart classifications are used multiple times, subchapters are the most likely to cause a problem if you aren't careful. Practitioners frequently refer to four groups of sections in Subtitle A by their subchapter designation—Subchapter C, Subchapter J, Subchapter K, and Subchapter S.[57] If you receive an assignment to research a particular subchapter, be sure to ascertain the correct one before you begin.

4. Similar Section Numbers

In using the Code's numbering system, be careful to note whether a letter is part of the section number or the subsection number. Code sections that include capital letters are most likely to cause problems. For example, section 2056(a) is not the same as section 2056A. Also be careful when working with sections that share a common number followed by different capital letters. These include sections 45A through 45N and sections 280A through 280H. Perhaps the most confusing numbering system is that used in the sections dealing with Recovery Zone Bonds; those sections are numbered 1400U-1 through 1400U-3. That format has characteristics of the system used for numbering regulations (Chapter 9).

5. I.R.C. and Other Section Numbers

The Code, the Public Laws amending it or otherwise affecting taxation, and the bills that may become Public Laws all divide their provisions into sections. These section numbering systems bear no relationship to each other. It is critical that you match the section number to the particular bill version, act, or Code you are researching.[58]

---

[57] These subchapters cover, respectively, corporations, trusts and estates, partnerships, and "small business" corporations. Although Subtitle A has several Subpart Fs, international practitioners often refer to Subpart F as a shorthand designation for the controlled foreign corporation Code sections in Chapter 1, Subchapter N, Part III.

[58] As noted in Subsection G.1, the 1939 Code section numbers bear no relationship to the 1954 and 1986 Code section numbers.

Take for example, Code section 1202(a)(1), which reads as follows:

> In general.—In the case of a taxpayer other than a corporation, gross income shall not include 50 percent of any gain from the sale or exchange of qualified small business stock held for more than 5 years.

Congress added the original version of that section to the Code in 1993, including it as section 13113(a) of the Revenue Reconciliation Act of 1993. The provision began as section 14113(a) of H.R. 2264, the Omnibus Budget Reconciliation Act of 1993, a subtitle of which was the Revenue Reconciliation Act of 1993.

SECTION E. WORKING WITH THE INTERNAL REVENUE CODE

As noted in Sections B and D, taxes are imposed by statutes, and most statutes relevant to tax research are in the Internal Revenue Code. These facts lead us to three tasks: finding the relevant Code provisions; reading them; and interpreting them. The problem in Chapter 4 introduced these tasks. The discussion in this section and Sections F and G includes additional information about the process.

Your research may involve two more tasks. The first is using a citator to determine if a court has ruled on the statute's validity; Section H introduces citators, which are discussed in more detail in Chapter 12. The second is checking for pending legislation that could change the result. This is particularly important if you are researching a proposed transaction.

1. Finding Code Sections

Your research project will probably involve more than one Code section. You might locate those sections in secondary sources, which discuss the issues raised in your project. Alternatively, you might use a Code section index to locate relevant Code sections. Think about the Code's structure and look for cross-references as you look for relevant Code sections.

a. Working with the Code's Structure

The Code has a structure that you should keep in mind in conducting your research. First, the subtitles [Table 6-3] give a starting point for research. For example, income tax provisions begin in Subtitle A; estate tax provisions begin in Subtitle B. Subtitle F includes various procedural rules.

Second, chapters and subchapters [Table 6-5] within each subtitle guide you to sections that may be relevant. This is particularly true for the income tax. In addition to issues related to credits, exclusions, deductions, timing, and character, your project may involve allocating income and deductions between individuals and entities or between United States and foreign sources. The problem in Chapter 4 involved sections from two subchapters of Subtitle A, Chapter 1: section 163 is in Subchapter B, Computation of Taxable Income; section 461 is in Subchapter E, Accounting Periods and Methods of Accounting. If our clients also planned to sell their home, you would read sections in Subchapters O and P (Gain or Loss on Disposition of Property; Capital Gains and Losses).

Table 6-5. Subchapters in Subtitle A, Chapter 1

Subch.	Heading	I.R.C. §§
A	Determination of Tax Liability	1–59B
B	Computation of Taxable Income	61–291
C	Corporate Distributions and Adjustments	301–385
D	Deferred Compensation	401–436
E	Accounting Periods and Methods of Accounting	441–483
F	Exempt Organizations	501–530
G	Corporations Used to Avoid Income Tax on Shareholders	531–565
H	Banking Institutions	581–597
I	Natural Resources	611–638
J	Estates, Trusts, Beneficiaries, and Decedents	641–692
K	Partners and Partnerships	701–777
L	Insurance Companies	801–848
M	Regulated Investment Companies and Real Estate Investment Trusts	851–860L
N	Tax Based on Income from Within or Without the United States	861–999
O	Gain or Loss on Disposition of Property	1001–1111
P	Capital Gains and Losses	1201–1298
Q	Readjustment of Tax Between Years and Special Limitations	1301–1351
R	Election to Determine Corporate Tax on Certain International Shipping Activities Using Per Ton Rate	1352–1359
S	Tax Treatment of S Corporations and Their Shareholders	1361–1379
T	Cooperatives and Their Patrons	1381–1388
U	Designation and Treatment of Empowerment Zones, Enterprise Communities, and Rural Investment Development Areas	1391–1397E
V	Title 11 Cases	1398–1399
W	District of Columbia Enterprise Zone	1400–1400C
X	Renewal Communities	1400E–1400J
Y	Short-Term Regional Benefits	1400L–1400U-3

Table 6-5 illustrates some important facts. First, Code sections for several entities have their own subchapters; these include exempt organizations, partnerships, and insurance companies). If your problem involves one of these taxpayers, start with the relevant subchapter. Second, an income tax project may include subchapters that are scattered throughout Subtitle A, Chapter 1. For example, gains and losses are relevant to the computation of taxable income, but those Code sections are in a separate subchapter.

Table 6-5 suggests a third fact to remember. Although some subchapters involve only a few Code sections, others—such as Subchapter B—include many sections. If you want to use subdivision headings as a research guide, you should look to parts [Table 6-6] and subparts.

Table 6-6. Parts in Subtitle A, Chapter 1, Subchapter B

Part	Heading	I.R.C. §§
I	Definition of Gross Income, Adjusted Gross Income, Taxable Income, etc.	61–68
II	Items Specifically Included in Gross Income	71–90
III	Items Specifically Excluded from Gross Income	101–140
IV	Tax Exemption Requirements for State and Local Bonds	141–150
V	Deductions for Personal Exemptions	151–153
VI	Itemized Deductions for Individuals and Corporations	161–199
VII	Additional Itemized Deductions for Individuals	211–224
VIII	Special Deductions for Corporations	241–249
IX	Items Not Deductible	261–280H
X	Terminal Railroad Corporations and Their Shareholders	281
XI	Special Rules Relating to Corporate Preference Items	291

b. Cross-References[59]

Subchapter B in Table 6-6 includes several parts that list deductions, but it also includes Part IX, Items Not Deductible. Presumably the sections in Part IX modify those earlier sections. In other words, the Code provides for deductions in some Code sections but might take them away in other sections. Ideally, the Code would include cross-references between sections in each group.

---

[59] This chapter covers using statutory language, including cross-references within the Code. Chapter 7 covers using cross-reference tables to trace how a Code section has evolved over time.

If two sections interact, each section may refer to the other. For example, section 267(e)(6) states: "For additional rules relating to partnerships, see section 707(b)." Section 707(b)(1) includes several references to section 267. This is the ideal situation because you find the relationship no matter which section you read first.

Alternatively one section may refer to another section, but the second section may not mention the first. Section 104(a) refers to section 213, but section 213 does not mention section 104. Assume, for example, you are researching what looks like a simple question: did a particular outlay your client made qualify for the section 213 medical expense deduction. If you did not know that she had previously been awarded damages to cover future medical expenses, you might ask whether her outlays were covered by Blue Cross but not ask about damages from a prior lawsuit.[60]

In the worst-case scenario, neither section refers to the other. For example, section 280B contains no cross-references. It could be relevant to sections 162, 212, 165, and 1016. None of those sections mentions section 280B.[61]

(1) Locating Cross-References

There are two methods you can use to determine if a particular Code section is mentioned by another section: cross-reference tools and electronic searches. Cross-reference tools, which are illustrated below, collect the information for you but are subject to editorial errors. Electronic searches for all Code sections that mention the section in which you are interested are less likely to include editor errors. But, unless you search widely enough, you still may miss a relevant statute. For example, if you search only in the I.R.C., you may miss relevant provisions in other U.S.C. titles or in a statute's uncodified provisions.

Cross-reference tables listing Code sections citing to a particular section appear in Standard Federal Tax Reporter (Chapter 13). Although electronic services lack tables, they may have other finding aids you can use to find cross-references. The OneDisc, for example, provides cross-references in the Background Notes for most Code sections.

As Illustrations 6-10 through 6-12 indicate, different sources may yield different results. There is no substitute for reading the Code sections to be sure the cross-reference is valid and relevant to your project.

---

[60] Careful reading of section 213(a) would avoid this result; the language covers expenses "not compensated for by insurance *or otherwise*." (emphasis added)

[61] Section 280B is mentioned in sections 179B, 198, and 198A.

Illustration 6-10. Cross-References for I.R.C. § 1 in United States Code Service on LexisNexis

> This section is referred to in 7 USCS § 940d; 26 USCS §§ 2, 3, 15, 23, 24, 25A, 32, 41, 42, 55, 57, 59, 63, 68, 132, 135, 137, 146, 151, 162, 163, 179, 213, 219, 220, 221, 301, 306, 453A, 460, 468B, 511, 512, 513, 531, 541, 584, 641, 646, 685, 691, 702, 774, 854, 857, 871, 876, 877, 891, 904, 911, 936, 962, 1022, 1260, 1291, 1301, 1398, 1446, 2032A, 2503, 2631, 3402, 3406, 4001, 4261, 4985, 6014, 6015, 6039F, 6242, 6323, 6334, 6428, 6601, 6655, 6662A, 6867, 7430, 7518, 7519, 7701; 46 USCS Appx § 1177.

→The Related Statutes & Rules segment for each section includes references in other titles of United States Code Service.

Illustration 6-11. Cross-References for I.R.C. § 1 in OneDisc

> **Section Referred to in Other Sections**
>
> This section is referred to in sections 2, 3, 15, 32, 41, 42, 59, 63, 68, 132, 135, 402, 453A, 460, 468B, 511, 513, 641, 691, 871, 876, 877, 891, 904, 962, 1291, 1398, 1446, 4001, 6014, 6103, 6652, 6655, 6867, 7518, 7519 of this title; title 7 section 940d; title 42 section 629; title 46 App. section 1177.

→The Background Notes includes references in other titles of U.S.C.

Illustration 6-12. Cross-References for I.R.C. § 1 in Standard Federal Tax Reporter Code Volume I Cross-Reference Table III

Internal Revenue Code (Standard Federal version), Cross-Reference Table III

CROSS-REFERENCES WITHIN THE INTERNAL REVENUE CODE OF 1986

(As of January 19, 2004)

Section	Referred to in
1	Sections 2, 3, 15, 23, 24, 25A, 32, 41, 42, 55, 59, 63, 68, 132, 135, 137, 146, 162, 163, 179, 213, 219, 220, 221, 223, 301, 306, 453A, 460, 468B, 511, 512, 513, 584, 641, 646, 685, 691, 702, 774, 854, 857, 871, 876, 877, 891, 904, 911, 936, 962, 1022, 1260, 1291, 1301, 1398, 1446, 2032A, 2503, 2631, 3402, 3406, 4001, 4261, 6014, 6015, 6039F, 6103, 6242, 6323, 6334, 6428, 6601, 6652, 6655, 6867, 7430, 7518, 7519.

→This table does not include cross-references in other titles of U.S.C. It has not been updated since 2004.

(2) Limitations of Relying on Cross-Reference Tools

As noted above, cross-reference tools are worthless if Code sections interact but don't explicitly refer to each other. Even if sections do refer to each other, an infrequently updated cross-reference tool may not reflect the most recent statutory changes. Using a term search in an online service presents much less risk that your source will not be current.

Cross-reference tools and electronic searches may induce a dangerous sense of security. After all, neither method can produce a cross-reference that doesn't exist. If you are an experienced practitioner, you know which types of provisions affect others. In approaching a deductibility problem, for example, you would consider sections allowing the deduction as well as potential disallowance sections and timing provisions. You can locate these in the Code's table of contents, in a subject matter Code section index, or in a subject-oriented looseleaf service or treatise (Chapter 13). Less-experienced researchers should probably start with a looseleaf service. Illustrations 4-1 through 4-10 and 4-29 illustrate these options.

(3) Limitations on Cross-References as Interpretive Aids

While cross-references are useful in locating relevant statutory material, they may lack independent interpretive significance. Code section 7806(a) provides that "[t]he cross references in this title to other portions of the title, or other provisions of law, where the word 'see' is used, are made only for convenience, and shall be given no legal effect." If you are using cross-references only to help you find relevant material, that limitation is not a problem.

2. Reading Code Sections

Illustrations 6-10 through 6-12 demonstrate that you can't rely on an editor's decision about cross-references. The same is true for explanations. If you rely on someone else's description of what the Code says, you risk missing an exception or election that applies to your client but was omitted in a general discussion.

Read each Code section carefully. First, determine what general rules it provides. Then look for exceptions, both within that section and in other sections that might apply. Finally, make sure that the applicable rules apply in the relevant time period. Focus on the effective date and the sunset date, if any. Remember that an effective date may include transition rules. These concepts are discussed in Subsection C.5.

Subscription-based versions of the Code are generally more helpful than the official U.S.C. version. First, the U.S.C. is revised only every six years, with annual supplements. Second, subscription-based services are more likely to alert you to incorrectly numbered sections, sunset dates that do not appear in the Code section, and pending legislation that might amend the section.

3. Interpreting Code Language

a. Definitions

As you read each Code section, you are likely to encounter terms that need to be defined. For example, the problem in Chapter 4 turned on the meaning of the phrase "in connection with." When searching for definitions, be cognizant of where they are likely to appear, but don't expect that every term will be defined.

The first place to look for a definition is in the Code section that uses the term. Unfortunately, the Code does not consistently use a "Definitions" label in each section. Definitions may appear in subsections (or smaller subdivisions) entitled Definitions, Special Rules, or [Term] Defined; often the heading for the definition is simply the term being defined. Examples appear in Table 6-7.

Table 6-7. Examples of Definition Placement

I.R.C. §	Heading
108(d)	Meaning of terms; special rules relating to certain provisions
108(i)(5)	Other definitions and rules
213(d)	Definitions
217(b)	Definition of moving expenses
217(f)	Self-employed individual
453(b)	Installment sale defined

→A Code section may include definitions in more than one subdivision.

Another place to look is in a group of provisions that apply to more than one Code section. Chapter 79 of the Code includes several definition provisions, most of which apply to the entire Code. If you cannot locate a definition in an individual section, be sure to check the definitions in Subtitle F, Chapter 79 (Code sections 7701–7704).

Many terms appear in the Code without definition. "Gross income" is one example. Other terms are defined in a section solely for purposes of that section. For example, section 1202(c) defines "qualified small business stock" for purposes of section 1202. Still other definitions apply only to a portion of a Code section. If you can't locate a Code definition that applies to your project, you should look in regulations, rulings, and judicial decisions. Researching in those sources is covered in Chapters 9 through 11.

If you find a definition, be careful to use it correctly. A Code section definition may apply to only a portion of that Code section, or it may contain a term that also needs defining. Many Code sections refer to definitions in other statutes. Illustration 6-13 demonstrates these limitations.

Illustration 6-13. Definitions in I.R.C. § 44

(a) General rule.–For purposes of section 38, in the case of an eligible small business, the amount of the disabled access credit determined under this section for any taxable year shall be an amount equal to 50 percent of so much of the eligible access expenditures for the taxable year as exceed $250 but do not exceed $10,250.

(b) Eligible small business.–**For purposes of this section**, the term "eligible small business" means any person if–

(1) either–

(A) the gross receipts of such person for the preceding taxable year did not exceed $1,000,000, or

(B) in the case of a person to which subparagraph (A) does not apply, such person employed not more than 30 full-time employees during the preceding taxable year, and

(2) such person elects the application of this section for the taxable year.

For purposes of paragraph (1)(B), an employee shall be considered full-time if such employee is employed at least 30 hours per week for 20 or more calendar weeks in the taxable year.

....

 (d) Definition of disability; special rules.–**For purposes of this section**–

(1) Disability.–The term "disability" has the same meaning as when used in the Americans With Disabilities Act of 1990 (as in effect on the date of the enactment of this section).

→The first highlighted definition applies for purposes of section 44. The second applies to a term used in section 44(b)(1)(B); its definition of full-time applies only to that provision.

→The final highlighted definition sends you to another statute and sets the date on which the other statute's language applies. Not only must you find the ADA, but you must find its language on the date Code section 44 was enacted.

b. Scope Limitations

Definitions and scope limitations share a common trait: both indicate whether their rule applies to the entire Code (e.g., "this title") or to a smaller subdivision (e.g., "this subtitle" or "this paragraph"). Definitions define words or phrases. Scope limitations indicate when a particular rule applies. As is true for definitions, if you misread a scope limitation, you risk drawing erroneous conclusions. Illustration 6-14 demonstrates a scope limitation.

Illustration 6-14. Scope Limitation in I.R.C. § 1041(b)

> (b) Transfer treated as gift; transferee has transferor's basis.–In the case of any transfer of property described in subsection (a)–
> (1) for purposes of this subtitle, the property shall be treated as acquired by the transferee by gift, and
> (2) the basis of the transferee in the property shall be the adjusted basis of the transferor.

→The transfer is treated as a gift only for purposes of the income tax ("this subtitle"). It is not treated as a gift for purposes of other subtitles, including Subtitle B, which includes the gift tax.

c. Provisions Affecting Multiple Subtitles

Some Code provisions affecting more than one type of tax (separate subtitles) appear in neither subtitle. Instead, they are found in Subtitle F, Chapter 80, Subchapter C (Code sections 7871–7874). Two of these provisions, section 7872 (loans with below-market interest rates) and section 7874 (expatriated entities) have potentially broad application; the other two will be relevant to taxpayers representing Indian tribal governments or taxpayers dealing with them.

d. Judicial Construction

When litigation involves what a statute means or whether it applies to a particular set of facts, someone must interpret it. Although Congress has delegated the authority to issue interpretive rules to the Treasury Department (Chapter 9),[62] regulations rarely follow on the heels of a law's enactment.

In addition to administrative interpretations, or in their absence when none are available, courts may turn to legislative history documents (Chapter 7) as expressions of congressional intent. Legislative history materials take on particular significance if administrative rules are alleged to be unreasonable and the statute's "plain meaning" is in doubt.[63]

Judges cite various rules of statutory construction in the course of interpreting statutes. The decisions listed below state or repeat several of

---

[62] I.R.C. § 7805.

[63] Supreme Court rulings on deference paid administrative interpretations are discussed in Chapters 9 and 10.

these rules.[64] To appreciate their effect, you should read the opinions cited for each proposition. The weight given legislative history is discussed in Chapter 7; that given administrative interpretations is discussed in Chapters 9 and 10.

• The fundamental principle of statutory construction, expressio unius est exclusio alterius, applies. There is a firm presumption that everything in the I.R.C. was intentionally included for a reason and everything not in the code was likewise excluded for a reason—the expression of one thing is the exclusion of another. Speers v. United States, 38 Fed. Cl. 197, 202 (1997).

• "Under the principle of ejusdem generis, when a general term follows a specific one, the general term should be understood as a reference to subjects akin to the one with specific enumeration." .... In the usual instance, the doctrine of ejusdem generis applies where a "catch-all" term precedes, or more often follows, an enumeration of specific terms in order to expand the list without identifying every situation covered by the statute. Host Marriott Corp. v. United States, 113 F. Supp.2d 790, 793 (D. Md. 2000).

• [T]he presumption is against interpreting a statute in a way which renders it ineffective or futile. Matut v. Commissioner, 86 T.C. 686, 690 (1986).

• [T]he courts have some leeway in interpreting a statute if the adoption of a literal or usual meaning of its words "would lead to absurd results *** or would thwart the obvious purpose of the statute." .... Or, to put it another way, we should not adopt a construction which would reflect a conclusion that Congress had "legislate[d] eccentrically." Edna Louise Dunn Trust v. Commissioner, 86 T.C. 745, 755 (1986).

• We should avoid an interpretation of a statute that renders any part of it superfluous and does not give effect to all of the words used by Congress. Beisler v. Commissioner, 814 F.2d 1304, 1307 (9th Cir. 1987).

• [T]he whole of [the section's] various subparts should be harmonized if possible. Water Quality Association Employees' Benefit Corp. v. United States, 795 F.2d 1303, 1307 (7th Cir. 1986).

---

[64] The Code also includes rules of construction: "No inference, implication, or presumption of legislative construction shall be drawn or made by reason of the location or grouping of any particular section or provision or portion of this title, nor shall any table of contents, table of cross references, or similar outline, analysis, or descriptive matter relating to the contents of this title be given any legal effect." I.R.C. § 7806(b).

• In terms of statutory construction, the context from which the meaning of a word is drawn must of necessity be the words of the statute itself. Strogoff v. United States, 10 Cl. Ct. 584, 588 (1986).

• [H]eadings and titles are not meant to take the place of the detailed provisions of the text. Nor are they necessarily designed to be a reference guide or a synopsis. Where the text is complicated and prolific, headings and titles can do no more than indicate the provisions in a most general manner;.... Factors of this type have led to the wise rule that the title of a statute and the heading of a section cannot limit the plain meaning of the text. Stanley Works v. Commissioner, 87 T.C. 389, 419 (1986).

• When a statute does not define a term, we generally interpret that term by employing the ordinary, contemporary, and common meaning of the words that Congress used. Merkel v. Commissioner, 192 F.3d 844, 848 (9th Cir. 1999).

• As a matter of statutory construction, identical words used in different parts of the Internal Revenue Code are normally given the same meaning. Disabled American Veterans v. Commissioner, 94 T.C. 60, 71 (1990).

• Stated another way, Congress must make a clear statement that a double benefit is intended before we will construe a provision to allow this result. Transco Exploration Co. v. Commissioner, 949 F.2d 837, 841 (5th Cir. 1992).

SECTION F. WORKING WITH OTHER STATUTES

Several tax-related provisions appear outside the Internal Revenue Code. These include provisions codified in other titles of United States Code and provisions that are not part of U.S.C. And, although it may ultimately be codified, pending legislation is at best a pre-statute.

1. Other United States Code Titles

Although most substantive tax provisions are included in the Internal Revenue Code, other titles of United States Code may include provisions relevant to your research. A provision may appear in another title of U.S.C. because an agency other than the Treasury Department has primary responsibility for the area of law involved. For example, many rules affecting retirement benefits appear in 29 U.S.C., the title that covers Labor.[65] In addition, as demonstrated in Illustration 6-13, a Code section may refer to a nontax statute that appears in another title of U.S.C. or is uncodified.

---

[65] See also 37 U.S.C. § 558, providing tax deferments for military personnel while they are missing in action.

You can locate provisions in other titles using a subject matter index to U.S.C. The Related Statutes materials in Standard Federal Tax Reporter Code volume II include texts of many of these statutes. You can also perform an electronic search through U.S.C. to locate relevant material in other titles. Finally, you can use popular name tables if, as shown in Illustration 6-13, the Code includes the name of an act and doesn't give a cross-reference to U.S.C.

2. Uncodified Provisions

As noted in Section C, many tax-related provisions are never added to U.S.C. Most uncodified provisions involve effective dates for particular Code sections. Others may direct an agency (usually the Treasury Department or IRS) to take a particular action.[66] [See Illustration 6-15.] A third group involves substantive law provisions. [See Illustration 6-16.]

Illustration 6-15. Material Omitted from Code

SEC. 11144. TREASURY STUDY OF HIGHWAY FUELS USED BY TRUCKS FOR NON-TRANSPORTATION PURPOSES.
(a) STUDY.—The Secretary of the Treasury shall conduct a study regarding the use of highway motor fuel by trucks that is not used for the propulsion of the vehicle. As part of such study—
(1) in the case of vehicles carrying equipment that is unrelated to the transportation function of the vehicle—
(A) the Secretary of the Treasury, in consultation with the Secretary of Transportation, and with public notice and comment, shall determine the average annual amount of tax-paid fuel consumed per vehicle, by type of vehicle, used by the propulsion engine to provide the power to operate the equipment attached to the highway vehicle, and

→This excerpt is from is Pub. L. No. 109-59, § 11144, 119 Stat. 1144, 1965 (2005). Studies such as this may lead to future legislation.[67]

Because we expect statutes to have effective dates, it is second nature to look for them in the act itself or in a Code publication that includes effective date notations. The other types of information are less common, however, and may well escape notice by someone who has not followed the progress of the particular legislation.

---

[66] Congress may ask for a report, impose a moratorium on Treasury regulations, or issue some other mandate to Treasury and IRS.

[67] In § 1(a), Congress provided two alternate short titles for this act: Safe, Accountable, Flexible, Efficient Transportation Equity Act: A Legacy for Users; and SAFETEA-LU. Several titles and subtitles have their own popular names. Act Title XI, which contains numerous amendments to the Code, does not have a separate short title.

Uncodified substantive provisions are traps for the unwary. A very troublesome example involves so-called section 530 relief. Although you might assume that was its Code section number, you would be mistaken. Code section 530 involves Coverdell Education Savings Accounts. Section 530 relief has nothing to do with tax benefits for education. Instead, it is an act section involving guidance in the employee–independent contractor area.[68] It is not codified anywhere.

Illustration 6-16. Material Omitted from Code

SEC. 803. NO FEDERAL INCOME TAX ON RESTITUTION RECEIVED BY VICTIMS OF THE NAZI REGIME OR THEIR HEIRS OR ESTATES.

(a) IN GENERAL.—For purposes of the Internal Revenue Code of 1986, any excludable restitution payments received by an eligible individual (or the individual's heirs or estate) and any excludable interest—

(1) shall not be included in gross income; and

(2) shall not be taken into account for purposes of applying any provision of such Code which takes into account excludable income in computing adjusted gross income, including section 86 of such Code (relating to taxation of Social Security benefits).

For purposes of such Code, the basis of any property received by an eligible individual (or the individual's heirs or estate) as part of an excludable restitution payment shall be the fair market value of such property as of the time of the receipt.

→This excerpt is from the Economic Growth and Tax Relief Reconciliation Act of 2001, Pub. L. No. 107-16, § 803, 115 Stat. 38, 149 (2001). Although these provisions affect tax consequences, they are not codified.

3. Pending Legislation

As illustrated earlier in this chapter, legislation occasionally has retroactive effect. Pending legislation is also relevant if you are researching for a transaction that has not yet closed; the law could change before you finalize the transaction.

When you look for pending legislation, don't limit yourself to the first bill that you find. Several members of Congress may introduce bills covering the same Code section. Fortunately, because each Congress lasts only two years, searches for pending legislation generally involve current

---

[68] Revenue Act of 1978, Pub. L. No. 95-600, § 530, 92 Stat. 2763, 2885, extended indefinitely by the Tax Equity and Fiscal Responsibility Act of 1982, Pub. L. No. 97-248, § 269(c), 96 Stat. 324, 552, and amended by various subsequent acts. U.S.C. provides references to section 530 and its amendments in notes following Code section 3401.

material and can be conducted electronically in THOMAS or in a bill-tracking service. These searches are discussed in Section G.

4. Potential Legislation

Long before a bill is introduced, taxpayers may receive hints that legislation is likely. In presidential election years, for example, party platforms include potential legislative agendas. Presidential budget messages may also serve this function. Items of this nature appear in newsletters and in general interest newspapers. You can also find presidential documents at the President's website, www.whitehouse.gov. Political parties have their own sites.

Prior congressional action is another source of potential legislation. Treasury Department studies mandated in one act [Illustration 6-15] may lead to provisions enacted in a later year.[69] In addition, acts that die in one Congress are often reintroduced in a later Congress. Legislators frequently issue press releases announcing they are working on bills.

Although Treasury regulations usually follow (and interpret) statutes, there are occasional role reversals. Legislation may be enacted to codify positions taken in regulations.[70] Unpopular administrative positions or court decisions may also trigger legislative activity.[71]

SECTION G. FINDING STATUTES

The method you use to find statutes, and what service you read them in, depends on several, interrelated factors. First, do you need Code section text or Public Law text? Second, are you looking for current law, repealed law, or pending law? Third, do you want to read one version of a Code or do you want to compare versions over time? Fourth, do you have a full citation to the material you want, only a short title or popular name, or neither? The paragraphs below discuss these interrelated concepts.

---

[69] These and other government studies are discussed in Chapter 7. Reports issued by nongovernmental groups are discussed in Chapter 14.

[70] This occurred in 1996 for life insurance benefits paid before death during a terminal illness (I.R.C. § 101(g)), in 1984 for certain fringe benefits (I.R.C. § 132), and in 1971 for asset depreciation range (ADR) depreciation (1954 I.R.C. § 167(m)).

[71] See, e.g., I.R.C. § 108(d)(7)(A), a response to Gitlitz v. Commissioner, 531 U.S. 206 (2001). See also Pub. L. No. 111-5, § 1261, 123 Stat. 115, 342 (2009), prospectively repealing Notice 2008-83, 2008-42 I.R.B. 905.

1. Using Citations

a. Code Section Citations

(1) Current Law

If you have a citation to the most recent Code, you can read the relevant section(s) in any commercial Code service. Unless the section was enacted before 2006, and not amended since then, the government-published United States Code is not a good choice. The official U.S.C. is completely revised every six years; it is supplemented annually in the interim.[72] Unofficial services are better choices. The four versions below are regularly updated during the year.

- United States Code Service (print and LexisNexis)

- United States Code Annotated (print and Westlaw)

- United States Tax Reporter Code (print and Checkpoint)

- Standard Federal Tax Reporter Code (print and IntelliConnect)

You can use any of these for I.R.C. sections. Use U.S.C.A. and U.S.C.S. for provisions that are codified in other titles of U.S.C.

(2) Prior Law: Since 1939

(a) In General

If you have a citation to the Code as it read in a previous year, use a source that covers the Code by year. Pay attention to dates when you use these sources. If you need to know how your section read on March 15, a Code that is current as of January 1 won't be accurate if the law changed on February 1. And, because it is possible that your section was revised again in November, a Code that is current as of January 1 of the following year could also cause problems. You need the version that includes the February change but not the November change.

Services that provide earlier versions of the Code include:

- Checkpoint (annual since 1990)

- IntelliConnect (annual since 1978; pre-1954 version of 1939 Code and pre-1986 version of 1954 Code)

---

[72] HeinOnline carries each version of U.S.C. since 1925–26. The government's GPO Access website begins with the 1994 edition. U.S.C. is likely to be added to FDsys by the time this book appears.

• Internal Revenue Code of 1939 (Statutes at Large; doesn't reflect amendments)

• Internal Revenue Code of 1954 (Statutes at Large; doesn't reflect amendments)

• LexisNexis Tax Center USCS Archive (end of each legislative session since 1992)

• U.S. Code Congressional & Administrative News—Internal Revenue Code (print; annual update; 1954 on)

• Westlaw Tax Historical Codes (annual USCA since 1990; original versions of 1939 and 1954 Codes)

• Westlaw Tax Code (Table of Contents allows searching by "effective date" since 1996)[73]

If you don't have access to a source that provides statutory text on the date you want, you can recreate the prior text by starting with a Code version as close in time to your date as you can get. Then use the historical notes accompanying that Code to find amending language. You can use that language to recreate the Code as it read on the date you need.

Illustrations 6-17 and 6-18 illustrate reconstructing language using Checkpoint's Archive Materials section. Checkpoint includes December 31 language beginning in 1990 and has a separate database for history.

Illustration 6-17. Excerpt from I.R.C. § 104 as of December 31, 1990

RIA   §104 (as of 12/31/1990) Compensation for injuries or sickness.
Internal Revenue Code (as of 12/31/1990) (RIA)

☑ Show Permalinks

§ 104 Compensation for injuries or sickness.

(a) In general.
Except in the case of amounts attributable to (and not in excess of) deductions allowed under section 213 (relating to medical, etc., expenses) for any prior taxable year, gross income does not include—

(1) amounts received under workmen's compensation acts as compensation for personal injuries or sickness;

(2) the amount of any damages received (whether by suit or agreement and whether as lump sums or as periodic payments) on account of personal injuries or sickness;

→Illustration 6-18 describes the 1983 change to § 104(a)(2).

---

[73] Differences between Westlaw and Westlaw Tax (and between LexisNexis and LexisNexis Tax Center) are discussed in more detail in Chapter 19. Each of the specialized interfaces can be launched from the main service's tax tab.

Illustration 6-18. Excerpt from I.R.C. § 104 History as of December 31, 1990

RIA

§104 (as of 12/31/1990) Compensation for injuries or sickness.
Internal Revenue Code History (as of 12/31/1990) (RIA)

⤢ Show Permalin

History for Code Section 104

In **1989**, P.L. 101-239, Sec. 7641(a), added the last sentence to subsec. (a), effective for amounts received after 7/10/89, in tax. yrs. end. after 7/10/89, except as provided in Sec. 7641(b)(2) of this Act which reads:

"(2) Exception.—The amendment made by subsection (a) shall not apply to any amount received—

"(A) under any written binding agreement, court decree, or mediation award in effect on (or issued on or before) July 10, 1989, or

"(B) pursuant to any suit filed on or before July 10, 1989."

In **1983**, P.L. 97-473, Sec. 101(a), substituted "whether by suit or agreement and whether as lump sums or as periodic payments" for "whether by suit or agreement" in para. (a)(2), effective for tax. yrs. end. after 12/31/82.

You can use the services below for tracing statutory language. All but Mertens are discussed in Chapter 7.

• Barton's Federal Tax Laws Correlated (1913–1952)[74]

• Legislative History of the Internal Revenue Code (1954–65)

• Mertens, Law of Federal Income Taxation—Code (1954–85) (Chapter 13)

• RIA Cumulative Changes (separate services for 1939, 1954, and 1986 Codes)

• Seidman's Legislative History of Federal Income and Excess Profits Tax Laws (1861–1953)[75]

• Tax Management Primary Sources (1969–2003)

• The Internal Revenue Acts of the United States: 1909–1950; 1950–1972; 1973–

Each is available in print; all but Mertens, Cumulative Changes, and Primary Sources are also available in HeinOnline. Keep in mind that if a

---

[74] Barton's covers through 1969 but prints statutory text only through 1952.

[75] If Seidman's is unavailable, you can use Eldridge, The United States Internal Revenue System. It provides annotated text for revenue acts prior to 1894 but does not give as much information as does Seidman's.

provision predates the 1954 Code, it has a different section number. You can locate the section numbers from earlier Codes by using the cross-reference tables discussed in Chapter 7.

(b)Revised Code Section Numbers

Congress occasionally changed Code section numbers in the 1954 or 1986 Codes, but this was not a regular occurrence. And, when Congress replaced the 1954 Code with the 1986 Code, it generally retained the 1954 Code section numbers. Notes following Code sections generally indicate if a section number has been changed.

When Congress replaced the 1939 Code with the 1954 Code, it changed the section numbers and rearranged much of the Code. If your research project includes the 1939 Code, you can use tools that cross-reference from one Code to another to locate the relevant Code section number. These tools are described in Chapter 7.

(3)Prior Law: Before 1939

There was no Internal Revenue Code before 1939. Instead each Congress reenacted revenue laws with whatever amendments were necessary. If you have a citation, the best full-text sources for pre-1939 statutes are Statutes at Large and The Internal Revenue Acts of the United States: 1909–1950. The Barton's and Seidman's materials listed above may also be useful, particularly if you need quick access to multiple statutory changes. All are available in print and in HeinOnline.

b.Public Law Citations

If you are researching current law, you are most likely to need the Internal Revenue Code or some other title of U.S.C. If you want to read instructions to the Treasury Department or other uncodified provisions, you might instead select a source that includes the text of the relevant Public Law.

As was the case with the Code itself, your choice of service will be affected by how long ago the law was enacted. If you are using the print Statutes at Large (or the online version available on HeinOnline), you are not constrained by date. On the other hand, several of the services described below have limited retrospective coverage.

(1)Free Services

If you have the Public Law Citation, you can find the act in the print version of Statutes at Large. Government websites include either Statutes at Large or individual Public Laws. The government's FDsys website currently covers 2003 to 2006 for Statutes at Large; the FDsys Public and Private Laws collection begins in 1995. The latter section includes Statutes at Large pagination but does not include its tables.

The THOMAS website also has a Public Law search function. Coverage begins in 1989, with the 101st Congress.[76] Beginning with the 104th Congress, THOMAS links to the same material available in the FDsys website. THOMAS provides more information about the Public Law's legislative history (covered in Chapter 7), so you may prefer it to FDsys.

Illustration 6-19. Advanced Search Option in FDsys

ADVANCED SEARCH

Publication Date:
If publication date is not available, search is performed on date of submission into FDsys.

All Dates ▼

Collections:

Full-Text of Publications and Metadata	Selected Collections
Associated Bill Citation	Statutes at Large
Branch	
Category	Add >>
Citation	
Congress Number	<< Remove
Congress Session	
Congressional Bills Citation	
Congressional Report Citation	
Government Author	
Is Appropriation	
Legislation Type	
Popular Name	
President	
Public or Private Law Citation	
Statutes at Large Citation	
Subject	
Sudoc Class Number	
Title	
Volume Number	

Full-Text of Publications and Metadata ▼ for _____

Full-Text of Publications and Metadata ▼ for _____

→You can search Statutes at Large by all of the categories listed above.

→Not every category in the left-hand box is available for each database. The categories available for a Public Law search do not currently include

---

[76] THOMAS provides information, but not text, for laws enacted since 1973. THOMAS often gives PDF, printer-friendly, and hyperlink reading options.

popular name, but a word search using the Title option will often yield the same results.

(2) Subscription Services

You can also find Public Laws by citation on subscription services. Westlaw has a Statutes at Large database covering 1789–1972; its United States Public Laws database lets you find legislation from the current Congress by Public Law Number; its Federal Taxation Public Laws database lets you find legislation by Public Law Number since 1973. The LexisNexis USCS – Public Laws database begins in 1988.

Checkpoint provides hyperlinks to enacted legislation in Pub. L. No. order in its enacted legislation file. Coverage begins with the 104th Congress. The IntelliConnect citation feature lets you find a Public Law by its citation. For older legislation, it links to the version printed in the Cumulative Bulletin, which may be limited to the act's tax provisions. IntelliConnect currently divides older materials into two Historical Legislative Documents files: 1954–2002 and 2003–2008.

When researching in an individual act, remember that the act section is not the same as the Code section. Act sections generally add, amend, or repeal Code sections. Illustration 6-18 shows how section 101(a) of a Public Law enacted in 1983 amended Code section 104(a)(2).

c. Short Title and Popular Name Citations

If you lack the Code section number and the Statutes at Large citation, but you have the act's short title or popular name, you can use that information to find the relevant Public Law. Once you find the Public Law, you can determine which Code sections have been affected.

When you search for popular names, keep four facts in mind. First, the "short title" that Congress assigns an act is often what practitioners use as its popular name, but that is not always true. Practitioners often refer to an act by the initials of its popular name rather than by the full name. For example, the Tax Increase Prevention and Reconciliation Act of 2005 is usually referred to as TIPRA.[77] Second, Congress may assign one short title name to an act and separate short titles to different subdivisions of the same act, or it may simply assign short titles to the individual subdivisions and not to the act as a whole. [See Table 6-8.] Third, some names are very similar to each other (e.g., Revenue Act of 1924, Revenue Act of 1926); be very careful with those names. Finally, Congress does not assign a short title to every act.

---

[77] Pub. L. No. 109-222, 120 Stat. 345 (2006).

If the act's short title includes a year, it is usually easy to locate the act's text in Statutes at Large. In some situations, the year in the act's name is the year before the year of enactment. That is the case with the Tax Increase Prevention and Reconciliation Act of 2005, which is mentioned in the preceding paragraph. If the year is not part of the name, use Shepard's Acts and Cases by Popular Names to obtain a Statutes at Large citation. You can also obtain citations from popular names tables in the print or electronic versions of U.S.C.,[78] U.S.C.A., or U.S.C.S. These tables list short titles and popular names; they may also list acronyms by which an act is known.

Table 6-8. Short Title Information: Selected 2008 Legislation

Pub. L. No.	Short Title: Act	Short Title: Revenue Subdivisions
110-458	Worker, Retiree, and Employer Recovery Act of 2008	No separate short title
110-343	Emergency Economic Stabilization Act of 2008 (technically only the short title for Subdivision A; also includes tax provisions)	Energy Improvement and Extension Act of 2008 (Subdivision B); Tax Extenders and Alternative Minimum Tax Relief Act of 2008 (Subdivision C)
110-289	Housing and Economic Recovery Act of 2008	Housing Assistance Tax Act of 2008
110-246	Food, Conservation, and Energy Act of 2008	Heartland, Habitat, Harvest, and Horticulture Act of 2008
110-245	Heroes Earnings Assistance Relief Tax Act of 2008	No separate short title
110-185	Economic Stimulus Act of 2008	No separate short title
110-141	No short title	Not applicable

→Acronyms can be formed from the initials of the words in short titles for Pub. L. Nos. 110-245 and 110-246.

You can also search in government websites using the act's short title. Both THOMAS and FDsys allow this type of search. THOMAS gives you multiple versions of the act (e.g., bill as introduced, bill as passed in each chamber, bill sent to President) with hyperlinks to each of them. Be sure to select the correct version.[79]

---

[78] The electronic U.S.C. Popular Name Tool is not as up-to-date as the tables prepared by commercial services, but its scroll function makes it almost as easy to read as a print table. It is available on the Office of the Law Revision Counsel website at http://uscode.house.gov/popularnames/popularnames.htm.

[79] Chapter 7 discusses the various bill versions.

Free services such as Statutes at Large are also available in online subscription services. You can also search subscription services by Public Law name and retrieve the full text of the act.[80] Those services are covered in the discussion of finding statutes using Public Law citations.

d. Pending Legislation

(1) Citations[81]

Pending legislation does not appear in either Statutes at Large or U.S.C. If you have a citation to the bill number, you can find the bill's text in THOMAS or in the FDsys Congressional Bills section. Westlaw, LexisNexis, and other commercial services have databases that provide the text of pending bills. Because the House and Senate both begin numbering at 1, include H.R. or S.[82] in your database search.

Illustrations 6-20 through 6-22 illustrate finding H.R. 2989, 111th Congress, 1st Session, in two services.

Illustration 6-20. Searching by Bill Number in THOMAS

---

[80] You can also find acts in three print services, the Cumulative Bulletin, Internal Revenue Acts—Text and Legislative History, and Mertens, Law of Federal Income Taxation—Code volumes. The Mertens service included the text of new acts for the 1954 Code. It remains useful for 1954 Code historical research. The Cumulative Bulletin stopped printing new legislation after 2003.

[81] The CCH Congressional Index bill-tracking service provides citations but not text.

[82] The database may accept HR or S in addition to (or instead of) H.R. or S. See Illustration 6-20.

Illustration 6-21. Results of Bill Number Search in THOMAS

H.R.2989

Title: To amend the Employee Retirement Income Security Act of 1974 to provide special reporting and disclosure rules for individual account plans and to provide a minimum investment option requirement for such plans, to amend such Act to provide for independent investment advice for participants and beneficiaries under individual account plans, and to amend such Act and the Internal Revenue Code of 1986 to provide transitional relief under certain pension funding rules added by the Pension Protection Act of 2006.

Sponsor: Rep Miller, George [CA-7] (introduced 6/23/2009)   Cosponsors (2)

Related Bills: H.R.1984, H.R.1988, S.401

Latest Major Action: 12/11/2009 House Committee on Ways and Means Granted an extension for further consideration ending not later than Jan. 19, 2010.

House Reports: 111-244 Part 1

All Information (except text)	Text of Legislation	CRS Summary	Major Congressional Actions
Titles	Cosponsors (2)	Committees	All Congressional Actions
Related Bills	Amendments	Related Committee Documents	All Congressional Actions with Amendments With links to *Congressional Record* pages, votes,reports
CBO Cost Estimates	Subjects		

→On the day I searched, I learned that the bill was still in the House Committee on Ways and Means, a committee had issued a report, and several related bills had been introduced.

→Using hyperlinks, I can read the text of H.R. 2989, the committee report, and the related bills.

Illustration 6-22. Finding H.R. 2989 in Westlaw Federal Taxation Congressional Bills Database

Edit Search: ti(hr 2989) & da(aft 12/31/2008)   ▼   **Database:** ftx-billtxt   ▼   SEARCH   Locate in Result

Results: 41 Documents   Add Search to WestClip

☐   **24.** 2009 CONG US HR 2989 111th CONGRESS, 1st Session HR 2989 Introduced in House June 23, 2009 H. R. 2989

...United States Library of Congress HR 2989 Introduced in House June 23, 2009 H. R. **2989** To amend the Employee Retirement Income Security Act of 1974 to provide special reporting and disclosure rules for individual ...

(2) Code Section Number

Many commercial services alert you that pending legislation may affect an existing Code section. Westlaw flags Code sections to indicate pending legislation and provides links to the pending material. The Shepardize function in LexisNexis includes a link to pending legislation.

You can also search by Code section number in THOMAS to see if a pending bill would modify an existing Code section. When conducting this type of search, you might want to include both the section number and a word or phrase that is likely to appear (or include the term Internal Revenue Code).

Searching by section number always involves risk: a pending bill may not amend an existing section directly. It may instead amend it indirectly with a second section that affects, but doesn't include a cross-reference to, the original section. Commercial services that track legislation, including the Daily Tax Report and Tax Notes Today newsletters, are likely to point out these indirect effects. Bill-tracking services are discussed further in Chapter 7.

e. Unenacted Legislation

Because a bill that was not enacted during an earlier Congress may be introduced again, you may want to read the earlier bill. If you know the H.R. or S. number for the earlier bill, and the Congress in which it was introduced, you can find it in THOMAS. Full-text coverage in THOMAS begins in 1989. GPO Access and FDsys let you search for legislation introduced since 1993. You can search by bill number or by words and phrases. Several commercial services also have unenacted legislation files.

2. No Citations

What if you need information about actual or proposed legislation, but you have no citations to the Code, Public Law, bill number, or other identifier? For example, you have been asked to find current Code sections covering employee achievement awards. Alternatively, you are preparing a survey article and need to know which Code sections were amended in a particular year. Or perhaps you need to find a statute indicating whether "Cash for Clunkers" rebates are taxable. Finally, what if you need to know which Code sections are subject to sunset and when that will occur?

The particular assignment determines how you proceed. The first problem is relatively simple. You should be able to find sections 74 and 274 by using the Code's table of contents or index. You could also use a looseleaf service to find the relevant materials. These searches would be similar to those illustrated in Chapter 4.

The second type of problem initially looks more time-consuming. You know that I.R.C. sections are amended by Public Laws that focus on taxation as well as by Public Laws that primarily deal with other areas of the law. [See Table 6-8.] Certainly, you don't want to read every Public Law enacted in a given year. Even searching THOMAS or another site for the terms Internal Revenue Code or Title 26 will be a time-consuming effort. This research assignment is probably best accomplished using a table of Code sections affected during that year. The ideal format for such a table would be a list of changes in Code section order by year (or at least by Congress). Less useful, but still better than no listing, is a table of changes by Public Law. Illustrations 6-23 through 6-25 demonstrate Checkpoint and USCCAN table formats.

If you cannot locate a table, you may have to find each act. The Joint Committee on Taxation Bluebook (discussed in Chapter 7) lists Tax Legislation passed in a particular Congress. However, it won't appear until after the two-year session ends.

Illustration 6-23. Checkpoint Listing: 109th Congress

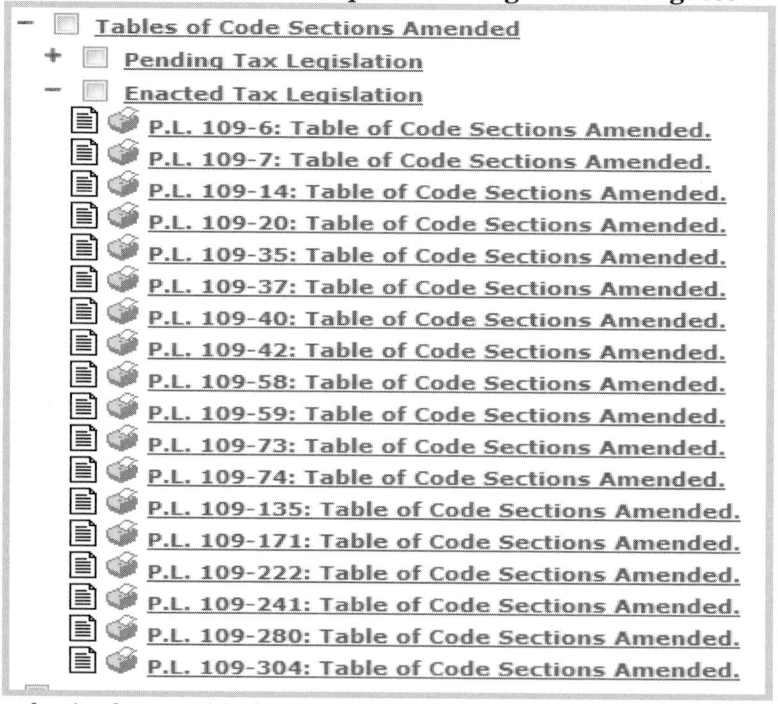
– Tables of Code Sections Amended
+ Pending Tax Legislation
– Enacted Tax Legislation
P.L. 109-6: Table of Code Sections Amended.
P.L. 109-7: Table of Code Sections Amended.
P.L. 109-14: Table of Code Sections Amended.
P.L. 109-20: Table of Code Sections Amended.
P.L. 109-35: Table of Code Sections Amended.
P.L. 109-37: Table of Code Sections Amended.
P.L. 109-40: Table of Code Sections Amended.
P.L. 109-42: Table of Code Sections Amended.
P.L. 109-58: Table of Code Sections Amended.
P.L. 109-59: Table of Code Sections Amended.
P.L. 109-73: Table of Code Sections Amended.
P.L. 109-74: Table of Code Sections Amended.
P.L. 109-135: Table of Code Sections Amended.
P.L. 109-171: Table of Code Sections Amended.
P.L. 109-222: Table of Code Sections Amended.
P.L. 109-241: Table of Code Sections Amended.
P.L. 109-280: Table of Code Sections Amended.
P.L. 109-304: Table of Code Sections Amended.

→Checkpoint has a table for each Public Law, grouped by Congress.[83]

→To reach these tables, use the Table of Contents function and search in the Pending and Enacted Legislation option under Federal Source Materials in the Federal Library.

---

[83] The Cumulative Bulletin's legislation volume had a 1986 Code Sections Affected by Public Laws listing; it was by act rather than by Code section and has not been published since 2003.

Illustration 6-24. Checkpoint Table: Pub. L. No. 109-73

RIA

P.L. 109-73: Table of Code Sections Amended.
109th Congress - Tables of Internal Revenue Code Sections Amended (RIA)

Code Sec. 72(t)	Bill Sec. 101(a)
Code Sec. 170(e)(3)	Bill Sec. 305(a)
Code Sec. 170(e)(3)	Bill Sec. 306(a)
Code Sec. 7508(a)(1)	Bill Sec. 403(a)

→The Checkpoint table is in Code section order, but you have to search each act individually.

→Checkpoint does not include Statutes at Large page numbers but does provide hyperlinks.

Illustration 6-25. USCCAN Table: 110th Congress, 2d Session

TABLE 3—AMENDMENTS AND REPEALS

U.S.Code and U.S.C.A.		2008–110th Cong.		122 Stat. at Large and 2008 Cong. News
Title	Sec.	P.L.	Sec.	Page
26	6103 nt	428	2(d)	4840
	6109	234	4002(b)(1)(B)	1096
		246	4(a)	1664
			4002(b)(1)(B)	1857
			4002(b)(2)(O)	1858
	6211(b)(4)(A)	185	101(b)(1)	615
		289	3011(b)(2)	2891
	6213(g)(2)(L)	185	101(b)(2)	616
	6401	246	4(a)	1664
	6401(b)(1)	234	15316(c)(3)	1511
		246	15316(c)(3)	2273

→USCCAN has a table in Code section order for each session of Congress.

→USCCAN tables include Pub. L. No., act section number, and page in Statutes at Large.

With respect to the third search, you should check a popular names table to see if the term "Cash for Clunkers" appears. A search using Google or another search engine is also likely to succeed. Once you obtain the citation, you can read the act in Statutes at Large.

Illustration 6-26. USCA Popular Name Table on Westlaw

USCA POPULAR NAME INDEX

Case-Zablocki Act

Cash Discount Act

Cash for Clunkers (Consumer Assistance to Recycle and Save Act of 2009)

Cash Management Improvement Act of 1990 (CMIA)

Cash Management Improvement Act Amendments of 1992

→Click on the popular name to get a citation and other information.

→LexisNexis carries the USCS popular names table; as of mid-January 2010, it listed the act by its short title but not by "Cash for Clunkers."

The final search, involving tax provisions that will sunset, is best conducted in two steps. First, use the Joint Committee on Taxation pamphlet, available on the JCT website. The version available in January 2010 (JCX-3-10) covered provisions expiring between 2009 and 2020. Second, read any provisions in one of the Code services discussed in this chapter. The JCT pamphlet is arranged in expiration date order; it does not have a separate Code section order division.

SECTION H. CITATORS FOR STATUTES

After Congress passes an act, litigation may ensue over the constitutionality or interpretation of individual Code sections. Constitutional litigation is discussed in Chapter 5, which includes examples of such claims. Litigation is more likely to involve disputes between the IRS and taxpayers over conflicting interpretations of statutory provisions.

Citators are an excellent tool for determining if a federal court has ruled on a statute's constitutionality. Because they are updated much more frequently, online citators are more useful search tools than are print citators. Online services also allow different types of searching. For example, if you use an electronic service, you may not even need its citator features. Instead, you can find constitutional challenges using a word search that includes the Code section and a variant of constitutional.

Not only do print citators lack the frequency and word search advantages, they may also have coverage issues. The Shepard's print citators did not cover Tax Court decisions as extensively as electronic citators do. These limitations even applied to the earliest volumes of Shepard's Federal Tax Citations. The CCH and RIA print citators did not cover statutes at all. Citators are discussed in greater detail in Chapter 12.

SECTION I. PROBLEMS

1. Indicate the subtitle, chapter, subchapter, part, and subpart for the Code section listed below.

   a. 302

   b. 731

   c. 4081

   d. 5601

2. Give the bill number for the Pub. L. No. listed below.

   a. 89-719

   b. 95-427

   c. 100-647

   d. 104-117

3. Indicate the popular name for the act listed below.

   a. Pub. L. No. 85-866

   b. Pub. L. No. 95-618

   c. Pub. L. No. 101-380

   d. Pub. L. No. 111-13

4. Indicate the full Statutes at Large citation, including Public Law or chapter number, for the act listed below.

   a. Revenue Act of 1935

   b. Individual Income Tax Act of 1944

   c. Tax Treatment Extension Act of 1977

   d. Technical and Miscellaneous Revenue Act of 1988

5. Indicate the Code section covered by the act section listed below.

   a. Support for East European Democracy (SEED) Act of 1989, Pub. L. No. 101-179, § 307

   b. United States National Tourism Organization Act of 1996, Pub. L. No. 104-288, § 3(c)

   c. Museum and Library Services Act of 2003, Pub. L. No. 108-81, § 503

d. Coast Guard and Maritime Transportation Act of 2006, Pub. L. No. 109-241, § 902(i)

6. Indicate the study mandated in the act below.

a. Gramm-Leach-Bliley Act, § 721

b. Ticket to Work and Work Incentives Improvement Act of 1999, § 303(a)

c. Higher Education Opportunity Act, § 1117

d. Energy Improvement and Extension Act of 2008, § 117

7. Indicate the Code section added by the act section listed below.

a. Pub. L. No. 94-455, § 1201(a)

b. Pub. L. No. 97-248, § 351(a)

c. Pub. L. No. 105-34, § 101(a)

d. Pub. L. No. 107-16, § 431(a)

8. Indicate the enactment date for the act listed below and the effective date for the act section indicated.

a. Revenue Act of 1942, § 127

b. Revenue Act of 1971, § 302(a)

c. Taxpayer Bill of Rights 2, § 1301(a)

d. Michelle's Law, § 2(c)(1)

9. Give the sunset date for the Code section as it read on December 31, 2009. If it has changed since then, indicate the new sunset date.

a. 139B

b. 164(b)(5)

c. 108(a)(1)(E)

d. 25D(g)

10. Indicate the scope limitations (e.g., subtitle, section, clause) for Code section

a. 66(a)

b. 84(a)

c. 269B(a)(1)

d. 645(a)

11. Indicate which Code section defines

  a. Federal irrigation water

  b. purpose built passenger vehicle

  c. unprocessed timber

  d. qualified housing interest

12. Congress occasionally defines Code section terms by citing to other federal statutes. Find a Code section that takes its definition from

  a. District of Columbia Retirement Protection Act of 1997

  b. Foreign Service Act of 1980

  c. Comprehensive Environmental Response, Compensation, and Liability Act of 1980

  d. Federal Deposit Insurance Act

13. List all Code sections that refer to the Code section listed. If possible, use more than one service in finding this information and list any differences between the services.

  a. 512

  b. 721

  c. 1245

  d. 2603

14. Do an electronic search to find a more recent judicial decision citing a principle of interpretation listed in Section E. Your instructor may assign a particular principle for you to research.

15. Print out (or provide a URL for) the tax planks from the Democratic and Republican platforms from the most recent presidential campaign.

16. Print out (or provide a URL for) any tax proposals from the President's most recent State of the Union Address and Budget Message.

CHAPTER 7. LEGISLATIVE HISTORIES

SECTION A. INTRODUCTION

This chapter continues the discussion of statutes begun in Chapter 6 by describing legislative history materials and indicating where they can be found. In addition to hearings, reports by tax-writing committees, and congressional floor debate, it includes reports by other committees and by entities such as the Government Accountability Office. This chapter also explains the process for tracing current statutes back to earlier versions. Legislative history documents for treaties are covered in Chapter 8.

Your goals for this chapter include familiarizing yourself with the documents comprising a statute's legislative history, learning where to find them, and understanding how judges view them when interpreting statutes. Refer to discussion in Chapter 6 as needed.

SECTION B. GROUPS INVOLVED IN LEGISLATION[84]

1. Congressional Committees

The **House Committee on Ways and Means** and the **Senate Committee on Finance** have primary jurisdiction over revenue bills. Other relevant committees include each chamber's **Budget Committee** and committees with jurisdiction over other areas with tax implications.[85] Each of these committees has subcommittees that may act with respect to pending legislation. If the House and Senate pass different versions of a bill, a **Conference Committee** meets to resolve these differences.

Five members each from Ways and Means and Finance sit on the **Joint Committee on Taxation** (JCT).[86] JCT Committee members are assisted by a staff of accountants, attorneys, and economists. The JCT may issue proposals and reports, but it is not charged with drafting legislation. As a result, courts treat its reports as having less interpretive significance than those issued by the tax-writing committees.

---

[84] Table 7-1 provides website information for entities described in this section.

[85] E.g., the Subcommittee on Finance and Tax of the House Committee on Small Business. Subcommittee names may change over time; this subcommittee was previously named the Subcommittee on Tax, Finance, and Exports.

[86] I.R.C. §§ 8001–8023. The JCT is charged with investigating the operation and effects of the tax system, its administration, and means of simplifying it. Id. § 8022. It also reviews tax refunds exceeding $2,000,000. Id. § 6405. This committee was the Joint Committee on Internal Revenue Taxation between 1926 and 1975.

The JCT website lists reports for each year, beginning with 1981. Those issued beginning in 1992 are available in PDF format from the JCT website. The JCT's **General Explanation** of legislation enacted by Congress (which has been referred to as the **Bluebook** or the **Blue Book**) can be used as authority if a taxpayer is disputing the substantial underpayment penalty discussed in Chapter 2.

The **Joint Economic Committee**, which is also comprised of members of each chamber, reviews the economy and recommends improvements in economic policy. It occasionally issues reports and other documents related to taxation.[87]

2. Congressional Support Entities

Three entities are organized as nonpartisan support services. Each issues reports on various tax administration and policy issues. Two of them [Illustrations 7-7 and 7-8] make their reports available online.

The **Government Accountability Office** is the investigative arm of Congress. The GAO audits the operation of federal agencies, reports on how well government programs meet their objectives, investigates allegations of illegal and improper activities, performs policy analyses, and issues legal decisions and opinions.[88] The GAO issues numerous reports on tax administration and on substantive tax topics. It is headed by the Comptroller General of the United States.

The **Congressional Budget Office** provides analyses to aid in economic and budget decisions. Although it may prepare reports for all committees, it gives priority to the Committees on Budget, Appropriations, Ways and Means, and Finance.[89]

The **Congressional Research Service** (known as the Legislative Reference Service between 1914 and 1970) provides policy and legal analysis to members of Congress. Its work is confidential, and the CRS website does not provide access to its reports.[90]

---

[87] See, e.g., Free E-Filing Makes Sense for Both Taxpayers and the IRS (Economic Fact Sheet, Apr. 14, 2008).

[88] GAO website, About GAO page (Jan. 16, 2010). The GAO was called the General Accounting Office until July 7, 2004.

[89] CBO website, About GPO page, "Preparing and Distributing Estimates and Analyses" section (Jan. 16, 2010).

[90] "[T]he CRS Website is accessible only to House and Senate offices and other legislative branch agencies." Congressional Research Service, Annual Report Fiscal Year 2008, at 43, at http://www.loc.gov/crsinfo/. No more recent Annual Report appeared as of mid-January 2010.

Although the CRS does not publish its reports, many of them are available from other sources, several of which are listed in Section D.

3. The Executive Branch

a. Executive Office of the President

The **President** may propose legislation, which a member of Congress will introduce, in messages to Congress (e.g., the State of the Union Address) or in other speeches. The **Office of Management and Budget** (OMB) assists the President in formulating a budget and works with administrative agencies to ensure that their reports and testimony are consistent with the President's goals. The **Council of Economic Advisers** (CEA) provides analysis and advice on developing and implementing economic policy.

The OMB and CEA are part of the **Executive Office of the President**. Other entities in the Executive Office include the National Economic Council, the Office of the United States Trade Representative, and the President's Economic Recovery Advisory Board. You can reach all of these entities (and reports they issue) from the White House website.

b. Other Executive Branch Agencies

Several other executive branch entities issue reports with respect to taxation. As discussed in Chapter 6, Congress often asks the **Treasury Department** or other agencies to study and report on issues. The **IRS National Taxpayer Advocate** issues two reports to Congress each year. The first outlines objectives planned for the next year. The second discusses serious issues facing taxpayers and recommendations for solving them.[91] The National Taxpayer Advocate may also issue recommendations for legislation. These groups are discussed in Chapters 9 and 10.

c. URL Listings for Relevant Government Entities

Table 7-1 lists current URLs for government entities involved in the legislative process. The table includes both legislative bodies and entities that provide analysis or suggestions before or after legislation is enacted. If you need a URL for another entity, you can access government sites in the Government Agencies section of the USA.gov website (www.usa.gov). GPO Access (www.gpoaccess.gov) links to an agency listing maintained by Louisiana State University Libraries (www.lib.lsu.edu/gov/index.htm).

---

[91] See Tax Notes Today, 2002 TNT 41-1 (Mar. 1, 2002) for a report on possible legislative initiatives in response to the Advocate's December 2001 report.

Table 7-1. Entities That Enact, Suggest, or Analyze Legislation

Entity	URL
Congressional Budget Office (CBO)	cbo.gov
Congressional Research Service (CRS)	loc.gov/crsinfo/aboutcrs.html
Council of Economic Advisers (CEA)	www.whitehouse.gov/administration/eop/cea/
Government Accountability Office (GAO)	gao.gov
House of Representatives	house.gov
Budget Committee	budget.house.gov
Ways and Means Committee	waysandmeans.house.gov
Internal Revenue Service (IRS)	www.irs.gov
IRS National Taxpayer Advocate	www.irs.gov/advocate
Joint Economic Committee (JEC) [92]	jec.senate.gov/
Joint Committee on Taxation (JCT)	jct.gov
National Economic Council (NEC)	www.whitehouse.gov/administration/eop/nec
Office of Management and Budget (OMB)	www.whitehouse.gov/omb
Office of the United States Trade Representative (USTR)	www.ustr.gov/
President	www.whitehouse.gov
President's Economic Recovery Advisory Board (PERAB)	www.whitehouse.gov/administration/eop/perab
Senate	senate.gov
Budget Committee	budget.senate.gov
Finance Committee	finance.senate.gov
Treasury Department	treas.gov
Inspector General for Tax Administration (TIGTA)	treas.gov/tigta
Office of the Benefits Tax Counsel (BTC)	treas.gov/offices/tax-policy/offices/btc.shtml
Office of the International Tax Counsel (ITC)	treas.gov/offices/tax-policy/offices/itc.shtml
Office of Tax Analysis (OTA)	treas.gov/offices/tax-policy/offices/ota.shtml
Office of the Tax Legislative Counsel (TLC)	treas.gov/offices/tax-policy/offices/tlc.shtml
Office of Tax Policy (OTP)	treas.gov/offices/tax-policy/

→If www appears in Table 7-1, the website would not open without it or it displayed www despite opening without it.

---

[92] The JEC's website includes links to the minority party's websites.

4. Other Groups

Members of Congress regularly receive written input from constituents, professional societies, trade associations, and lobbyists. These groups also testify at hearings on proposed legislation. Several of these groups are listed in Chapter 14.

SECTION C. LEGISLATIVE PROCESS

The process for enacting tax legislation is almost identical to that used for other federal laws. The major difference relates to the constitutional limitation discussed in Chapter 5: revenue-raising bills must originate in the House of Representatives.[93] This section discusses the legislative process; Section D covers finding the documents discussed in this section.

1. Introduction of Bill

The sponsoring legislator may present remarks for inclusion in the **Congressional Record** at the bill's introduction. If the administration is proposing an item, a presidential message may accompany the proposal transmitted to Congress.

The bill receives a number when it is introduced. Similar bills may be introduced in the same chamber; each receives its own number. [See Illustration 7-1.] The same is true for bills introduced in both the House and Senate; they receive separate numbers in each chamber.

Illustration 7-1. Example of Related Bills Introduced in 2009

H.R.3508
Title: To amend the Internal Revenue Code of 1986 to provide for improved treatment of HSA account provisions, and for other purposes.
Sponsor: Rep Paulsen, Erik [MN-3] (introduced 7/31/2009)   Cosponsors (36)
Related Bills: H.R.3610 ←——
Latest Major Action: 7/31/2009 Referred to House committee. Status: Referred to the House Committee on Ways and Means.

→The Related Bills listed in THOMAS are not necessarily identical. If they relate to a topic you are tracking, make sure you read each of them.

Bill numbers are sequential for each term of Congress (e.g., H.R. 1; S. 1); there is not a separate numbering system for each session within the two-year term. Occasionally, a bill number will be reserved for major legislation; that bill may be introduced after a bill with a higher number.

---

[93] See James V. Saturno, Blue-Slipping: The Origination Clause in the House of Representatives (Congressional Research Service Report, 2002), available on LexisNexis at 2002 TNT 114-16.

2. Referral to Committee and Committee Action

After its introduction, the bill is referred to the appropriate committee, generally the House Ways and Means Committee or the Senate Finance Committee. The committee (or a subcommittee thereof) may hold hearings, which will be published. It usually issues a committee report to accompany the bill that is reported out of committee. These reports are numbered by Congress (e.g., H.R. Rep. No. 109-13, 109th Cong., 1st Sess. (2005)).

The version of the bill that the committee chair initially issues is referred to as the **chairman's mark**.[94] After committee deliberation, which may include input from committee, IRS, and Treasury staffs and from other groups described in Section B, the marked-up bill may differ significantly from its initial version.

The bill, or a similar version, may have been simultaneously considered in the other chamber or considered after being passed in the first chamber. The process in the second chamber, generally the Senate, is comparable to that described above.

3. House and Senate Floor Debate

A bill sent to the floor by committee can die in one chamber, pass intact, or pass with amendments. Each chamber separately deliberates on the bill before voting. Although Senate rules permit more extensive debate and floor amendments than do House procedures, each chamber can change the bill. A bill passed by one chamber and sent to the other is called an **engrossed** bill.

Questions and answers and other statements made during floor debate can illuminate the meaning of legislation.[95] Be aware, however, that statements can be made to an empty chamber or added as text but not spoken.

If both chambers pass the bill with identical terms, it can be sent to the President. If the versions differ, a Conference Committee is appointed.

---

[94] As of January 2010, all tax-writing committee chairs have been male.

[95] In Ashburn v. United States, 740 F.2d 843 (11th Cir. 1984), the court referred to committee reports and congressional debates as evidence of the meaning of a phrase in the Equal Access to Justice Act. See also Commissioner v. Engle, 464 U.S. 206 (1984), in which the Court's opinion on the meaning of I.R.C. § 613A cited to testimony at hearings, floor debate, and committee reports. Be aware that the Supreme Court has become less receptive to using legislative history materials in construing statutes.

4. Conference Committee Action

The Conference Committee meets to resolve House and Senate differences. It generates a third report, the **Conference Report**. That document is usually numbered as a House report. The Conference Report explains the resolution of House–Senate differences. [See Illustration 7-2.]

Illustration 7-2. Excerpt from H.R. Rep. No. 107-84, 107th Cong., 1st Sess. (2001), at 158

a skill required in a trade or business currently engaged in by the taxpayer, or (2) meets the express requirements of the taxpayer's employer, applicable law or regulations imposed as a condition of continued employment. However, education expenses are generally not deductible if they relate to certain minimum educational requirements or to education or training that enables a taxpayer to begin working in a new trade or business.[31]

HOUSE BILL

No provision.

SENATE AMENDMENT

The provision extends the exclusion for employer-provided educational assistance to graduate education and makes the exclusion (as applied to both undergraduate and graduate education) permanent.

Effective date.—The provision is effective with respect to courses beginning after December 31, 2001.

CONFERENCE AGREEMENT

The conference agreement follows the Senate Amendment.

5. Floor Action on Conference Report

Unlike the pre-conference bills, a bill that emerges from the Conference Committee cannot be further amended during floor debate. Each chamber must pass it or reject it as written. That "final" version (the **enrolled** bill) is then prepared for submission to the President.

6. Correcting Drafting Errors

Unlike treaties, bills die when a Congress's second session ends.[96] Members work under extreme time pressure to pass pending legislation by that date. As a result, a Conference Report's version may contain errors, which Congress passes along with the rest of the bill. If both cham-

---

[96] Chapter 8 discusses other differences between statutes and treaties.

bers agree, Congress can adopt a **concurrent resolution** making necessary changes before the act is enrolled for submission to the President. If they do not agree, or find the errors too late, a **technical corrections** bill is inevitable.[97]

7. Presidential Action

The President has four options. The bill becomes law if the President signs it within ten days of its presentment. It also becomes law if the President does nothing so long as Congress remains in session during that period. Alternatively, the President can veto the bill; Congress can override a veto only by a two-thirds vote in each chamber.[98] If the President does nothing and the congressional session ends during the ten-day period, the bill is "pocket-vetoed." The President may issue a statement when signing or vetoing a bill.

In 1996, Congress gave the President a different option, a so-called line-item veto over certain direct spending items and "limited tax benefits." The Supreme Court held that the line-item veto violated the Constitution's presentment clause.[99]

SECTION D. LOCATING LEGISLATIVE HISTORY DOCUMENTS: CITATIONS AND TEXT

The process used for locating legislative history documents varies depending on whether you are using print materials or electronic services. If you are using print materials, your research may involve two steps. First you must obtain citations for the documents you need.[100] Then you

---

[97] See, e.g., H.R. Con. Res. 328, 98th Cong., 2d Sess. (1984), 98 Stat. 3454 (1984), making technical changes to the Tax Reform Act of 1984. Compare H.R. Con. Res. 395, 99th Cong., 2d Sess. (1986), which failed to pass, leaving flaws in the 1986 Act. When using the THOMAS website, search for resolutions as H Res and concurrent resolutions as H Con Res rather than HR Res or HR Con Res. The site will retrieve the document whether or not you use periods in H.R. Use S Res and S Con Res (with or without periods) for Senate resolutions.

[98] Congress overrode President Franklin Roosevelt's veto of the Revenue Act of 1943, ch. 63, 58 Stat. 21 (1944). More recently, it overrode President George W. Bush's veto of the Food, Conservation, and Energy Act of 2008, Pub. L. No. 110-246, 122 Stat. 1651 (2008). See Table 6-8 for the short title of that act's tax title.

[99] Clinton v. City of New York, 524 U.S. 417 (1998). House and Senate Rules currently include procedures for reporting on "limited tax benefits" in pending bills. See House Rule XXI and Senate Rule XLIV.

[100] Beginning in 1975, Statutes at Large includes citations to committee reports, Congressional Record items, and presidential messages immediately following the text of each act.

must locate those documents. When researching electronically, you may be able to skip the first step and find your documents using word and Code section searches or by searching directly for the act or its history.

Many of the illustrations in this section cover government websites, which have excellent coverage of legislative history materials from the past 15 or so years (and in some cases even earlier). Illustrations of commercial materials are provided for older legislative history materials.

1. Versions of the Bill

A bill that is enacted into law is often amended during the enactment process. Versions include the bill as introduced, as reported by a committee, as passed by one chamber of Congress (engrossed bill), as reported by a committee of the other chamber of Congress, as passed by the other chamber of Congress, and as reported by the Conference Committee, passed by both chambers, and sent to the President (enrolled bill).[101]

THOMAS includes versions of each bill introduced since 1989 (the 101st Congress). You can search THOMAS by phrase [Illustrations 7-3 and 7-4] or bill number [Illustration 7-5]. If you need bills from earlier sessions of Congress, check to see if your library has the microfiche set entitled United States Congress Public Bills and Resolutions; it covers bills introduced in the 96th through 106th Congresses.

The Internal Revenue Acts of the United States: 1909–1950, and subsequent legislative history sets published by William S. Hein & Company include different versions of enacted legislation. These legislative histories are available in print. They are also included in the HeinOnline Taxation & Economic Reform in America library.

Fee-based services include the text of more recent bills in addition to older proposed legislation. When using these services, check the relevant database for coverage dates. Retrospective coverage in some databases does not begin earlier than the coverage in the THOMAS site. For example, the LexisNexis Federal Bill Text Combined Archive database contains the full text of each version, but its coverage begins in 1989. Its Federal Tax Legislation, Congressional Reports, & Bills file begins in 1954 but provides only "selective" coverage. Checkpoint and IntelliConnect also provide full-text coverage.

---

[101] You can use a subscription bill-tracking service to follow legislation through Congress. These include CCH Congressional Index, a looseleaf service that provides brief digests of pending legislation; LexisNexis Bill-Tracking Report – Current Congress; and Westlaw US-BILLTRK. IntelliConnect includes status information in its Bills Worth Watching section.

Illustration 7-3. THOMAS Search for Bills by Phrase

Search Bill Text for the 110th Congress (2007-2008)

🖨 Print   📶 Subscribe   ☑ Share/Save

Search Bill Text | **Search Bill Summary, Status** | **Search Multiple Congresses**

Select Congress:
111 | 110 | **109** | **108** | **107** | **106** | **105** | **104** | **103** | **102** | **101**

❂ Help

⊘ **Browse by Bill Number**

Enter Search
| Word/Phrase ▾ | internal revenue |
⦿ Exact Match Only   ⊙ Include Variants (plurals, etc.)

Which Bills?
☒ All Bills
⊙ Bills with Floor Action   What is a floor action?
⊙ Enrolled Bills   What is an enrolled bill?

From Where?
⊙ Both House and Senate
⦿ House Bills Only
⊙ Senate Bills only

→This search for House bills in the 110th Congress used the phrase "internal revenue." I could have searched for a specific bill (or Public Law) if I had the bill or act number.

Illustration 7-4. Results of THOMAS Search for Bills by Phrase

1000 Bills from the 110th Congress ranked by relevance on *"internal+revenue "*.
   1000 bills containing your phrase **exactly as entered.**
   0 bills containing all your search words **near each other in any order.**
   0 bills containing all your search words **but not near each other.**
   0 bills containing **one or more of your search words.**

Listing of **1000** bills containing your phrase **exactly as entered.**

1. Enhanced Protection of the Internal Revenue Service and Its Employees Act of 2007 (Introduced in House)[H.R.2527.IH][PDF]
2. Providing for consideration of the bill (H.R. 3056) to amend the Internal Revenue Code of 1986 to repeal the authority of the Internal Revenue Service to use private debt collection... (Reported in House)[H.RES.719.RH][PDF]
3. To amend the Internal Revenue Code of 1986 to extend certain expiring energy conservation provisions and to provide a tax credit for certain individuals using home heating oil. (Introduced in House)[H.R.4297.IH][PDF]
4. Providing for consideration of the bill (H.R. 7201) to amend the Internal Revenue Code of 1986 to provide incentives for energy production and conservation, and for other purposes and... (Reported in House)[H.RES.1516.RH][PDF]
5. To amend the Internal Revenue Code of 1986 to repeal the reduction in the deductible portion of expenses for business meals and entertainment. (Introduced in House)[H.R.2648.IH][PDF]

→This search found 1000 items. The same search using only enrolled bills yielded a more manageable 48 items.

→The parentheticals (e.g., Introduced in House) explain the abbreviations (e.g., IH)

Illustration 7-5. Bill Versions for H.R. 3996 in THOMAS

There are 6 versions of Bill Number H.R.3996 for the 110th Congress

1. Temporary Tax Relief Act of 2007 (Introduced in House)[H.R.3996.IH][PDF]
2. Temporary Tax Relief Act of 2007 (Reported in House)[H.R.3996.RH][PDF]
3. Temporary Tax Relief Act of 2007 (Engrossed as Agreed to or Passed by House)[H.R.3996.EH][PDF]
4. Temporary Tax Relief Act of 2007 (Placed on Calendar in Senate)[H.R.3996.PCS][PDF]
5. Tax Increase Prevention Act of 2007 (Engrossed Amendment as Agreed to by Senate)[H.R.3996.EAS][PDF]
6. Tax Increase Prevention Act of 2007 (Enrolled as Agreed to or Passed by Both House and Senate)[H.R.3996.ENR][PDF]

→Click on the hyperlinked bill number or the PDF to read the bill in your preferred format.

→Another screen, Bill Summary & Status, provides links to the Public Law included in Statutes at Large.

2. Statements on the Floor of Congress

The Congressional Record prints introduced bills and statements made at their introduction. It also prints statements, questions, and answers made during floor debate. Make sure you check whether your citation is to the bound or daily version. Page numbers indicate H for House and S for Senate.

Congressional Record can be accessed through its indexes, but it is easier to search online. The service you use for this purpose will depend on the year involved.

The THOMAS website provides two methods of accessing the Congressional Record back to 1989. First, you can use its Congressional Record page to search by key word, date, or speaker. In addition to statements relating to bills, this method will also recover statements made without respect to particular pending legislation. This search screen is shown in Illustration 7-6. Second, if you know the bill or Public Law Number, you can search its history as shown in Illustration 7-8.

The government also makes Congressional Record available online through GPO Access, beginning with 1994.[102] Beginning in 1995, the GPO Access version is available in PDF, making it easier to read than the THOMAS version. THOMAS often offers a link to the GPO PDF.

Remember that GPO Access is migrating to FDsys. The latter already carries the bound version of the Congressional Record (1999–2001) and

---

[102] See www.gpoaccess.gov/crecord/index.html.

the daily version (since 1994). FDsys includes the Congressional Record Index since 1983.

Illustration 7-6. Congressional Record Search in THOMAS

Search the Congressional Record for the 110th Congress (2007-2008)

The Congressional Record is the official record of the proceedings and debates of the U.S. Congress. ⊚ More about the Congressional Record

🖶 Print 📶 Subscribe 🌐 Share/Sav

Search the Congressional Record | Latest Daily Digest | Browse Daily Issues

Browse the Keyword Index

Select Congress:
111 | 110 | 109 | 108 | 107 | 106 | 105 | 104 | 103 | 102 | 101

❷ Help

Enter Search

AMT

⦿ Exact Match Only   ◌ Include Variants (plurals, etc.)

→THOMAS also lets you search by name of the legislator, by section of Congressional Record, and by session of the particular Congress.

Illustration 7-7. Partial Results of Congressional Record Search in THOMAS

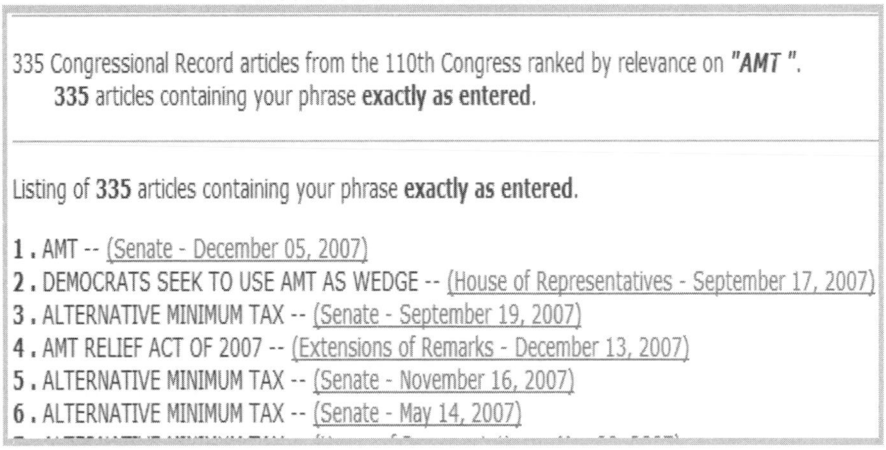

335 Congressional Record articles from the 110th Congress ranked by relevance on *"AMT"*.
   335 articles containing your phrase **exactly as entered**.

Listing of **335** articles containing your phrase **exactly as entered**.

1. AMT -- (Senate - December 05, 2007)
2. DEMOCRATS SEEK TO USE AMT AS WEDGE -- (House of Representatives - September 17, 2007)
3. ALTERNATIVE MINIMUM TAX -- (Senate - September 19, 2007)
4. AMT RELIEF ACT OF 2007 -- (Extensions of Remarks - December 13, 2007)
5. ALTERNATIVE MINIMUM TAX -- (Senate - November 16, 2007)
6. ALTERNATIVE MINIMUM TAX -- (Senate - May 14, 2007)

Illustration 7-8. Congressional Record Search Results
for H.R. 6081 (2008)

138 Congressional Record articles from the 110th Congress ranked by relevance on **"hr+6081 "**.
    1 article containing your phrase **exactly as entered.**
    0 articles containing all your search words **near each other in any order.**
    0 articles containing all your search words **but not near each other.**
    137 articles containing **one or more of your search words.**

Listing of **1** article containing your phrase **exactly as entered.**

1 . HEROES EARNINGS ASSISTANCE AND RELIEF TAX ACT OF 2008 -- (House of Representatives - May 20, 2008)

Listing of **137** articles containing **one or more of your search words.**

2 . HEROES EARNINGS ASSISTANCE AND RELIEF TAX ACT OF 2008 -- (Extensions of Remarks - May 23, 2008)
3 . PERSONAL EXPLANATION -- (Extensions of Remarks - May 22, 2008)
4 . BILL PRESENTED TO THE PRESIDENT -- (House of Representatives - June 09, 2008)
5 . PERSONAL EXPLANATION -- (Extensions of Remarks - May 20, 2008)

→H.R. 6081 became Public Law Number 110-245 [Illustration 6-1].

Illustration 7-9. Congressional Record Search in FDsys

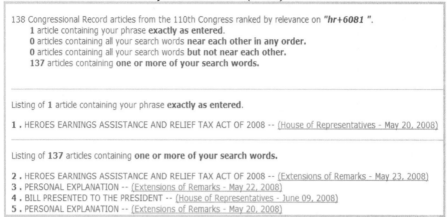

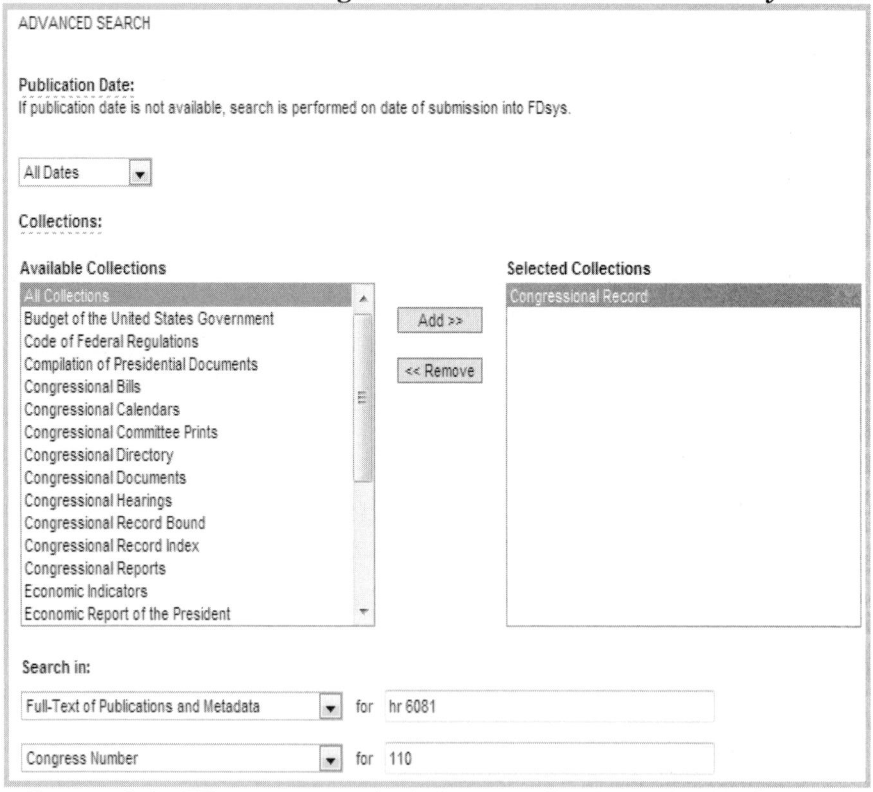

→To search in FDsys, you can include up to five items in the Search in: function.

→This search yielded 18 items; THOMAS had 138 hits.

You can search Congressional Record online through Westlaw and LexisNexis. Both begin in 1985. It is possible your library will offer access to LexisNexis Congressional that is separate from any subscription to the general LexisNexis service. HeinOnline currently carries the bound Congressional Record (1873–2004) and the daily Congressional Record since 1994.[103] If you don't have access to HeinOnline, you may be able to locate older volumes of Congressional Record in the library's microform collection.

Three services print excerpts from Congressional Record: Tax Management Primary Sources (1969–2003); Internal Revenue Acts—Texts and Legislative History (since 1954); and Seidman's Legislative History of Federal Income and Excess Profits Tax Laws (1863–1953). Barton's Federal Tax Laws Correlated, provides page citations for the period from 1953 through 1969.[104]

Illustration 7-10. Excerpt from Congressional Debate in Seidman's

| 1028 | 1864 ACT | [See inside back cover |

Congressional Discussion

Discussion—Senate (Cong. Globe, 38th Cong., 1st Sess.).—THE PRESIDING OFFICER. The question now is on inserting the following words at the end of section one hundred and fifteen²:

And provided further, That net profits realized by sales of property upon investments made within the year, for which income is estimated, shall be chargeable as income; and losses on sales of property purchased within the year, for which income is estimated, shall be deducted from the income of such year.

accumulates from year to year.

MR. JOHNSON. Has it been so construed under the old law?

MR. FESSENDEN. That was the construction the Commissioner put upon it in writing. Our difficulty was to fix any ratio of income. If anything could be considered as income in such case, it is the increase of value for the year. If, for instance, you buy property one year and hold it, and by last year's accumulation

→Seidman's prints excerpts from an act's legislative history.

3. Committee Hearings

Transcripts of hearings can be located in the library's government documents section or in its microform collection. Online versions are available through services as Westlaw, LexisNexis, and LexisNexis Congressional; coverage dates vary.

---

[103] HeinOnline also includes predecessor documents, e.g., the Congressional Globe.

[104] Seidman's and Barton's are also available in HeinOnline.

Beginning with the 104th Congress, you can find transcripts of hearings (including written submissions) using the GPO's FDsys website. Congressional websites also include some transcripts. The House Ways and Means Committee website links to hearings beginning with 2003.

Illustration 7-11. *Hearings Listing on House Ways and Means Site*

HEARINGS

Congress: 110 ▼ **Subcommittee:** Select Revenue Measures ▼
(To filter content, choose your options above and submit) Submit Options

Hearing on Individual Retirement Accounts (IRAs) and their role in our retirement system
Thursday, June 26, 2008

Hearing on Education Tax Incentives
Thursday, May 01, 2008

Hearing on Tax Treatment of Derivatives
Wednesday, March 05, 2008

4. Committee Reports

You can find committee reports in the library's government documents or microform collections if you have the appropriate citation. Reports are numbered sequentially by Congress, not by committee. The numbering does not restart when a term of Congress goes into its second session.

Citations include initials to indicate which chamber issued them, but they do not indicate which committee. Although I omitted these from Table 7-2, citations do indicate the number and session of Congress.

As the entry for Pub. L. No. 109-222 indicates, legislation may be enacted without all three reports. Some legislation is enacted without any committee reports.

Table 7-2. *Illustrative Committee Report Citations*

	Taxpayer Relief Act of 1997, Pub. L. No. 105-34, 111 Stat. 788 (1997)	Tax Increase Prevention and Reconciliation Act of 2005, Pub. L. No. 109-222, 120 Stat. 345 (2006)
House	H.R. Rep. No. 105-148	H.R. Rep. No. 109-304
Senate	S. Rep. No. 105-33	None
Conference	H.R. Rep. No. 105-220	H.R. Rep. No. 109-455

→ The House report for Pub. L. No. 105-34 came from the Budget Committee, rather than from Ways and Means.

a. Citations

Online sources provide immediate access to reports even if you lack citations. Unfortunately, they rarely cover pre-1954 Code material. If you need a citation to a report, several services provide that information.[105]

• Bulletin Index–Digest System (1954–1994)

• Barton's Federal Tax Laws Correlated (through 1969) (print and HeinOnline) [Illustration 7-12]

• Standard Federal Tax Reporter—Citator (Cumulative Bulletin rather than report number citations for amendments to 1954 and 1986 Codes; listed in Code section order)

• TaxCite (citations to reports printed in the Cumulative Bulletin for commonly cited statutes enacted between 1913 and 1993)

• Legislative History of the Internal Revenue Code of 1954 (1954 through 1969)

If you know the act number, title, or subject matter, you may also be able to obtain citations from a source such as LexisNexis Congressional, which covers a government legislative history compilation known as the Serial Set. Your library microform collection may also have this set.

Illustration 7-12. Legislative History Citations in Barton's

TABLE E						Amendments – Legislative History				
Public Law						House of Representatives				
Number	Date	Cong.	Stats. at Large	Cum. Bull.	USCCAN	H. Rept.	Cong./Date	Cum. Bull.	USCCAN	Floor debate
86-594	7-6-60	86/2	74:333	60-2/685	86-2/389	1054	86-1/8-26-59			105 CR 18829
86-624	7-12-60	86/2	74:411	60-2/686	86-2/477	1564	86-2/5-2-60			106 CR 10353, 15009
86-667	7-14-60	86/2	74:534	60-2/687	86-2/610	1145	86-1/9-3-59			105 CR 18826, 106 CR 15248

→The HeinOnline version has two pages for each act. The second page for each act covers the Senate and Conference Committees.

---

[105] The government occasionally publishes legislative history information. See, e.g., Joint Committee on Taxation, Listing of Selected Federal Tax Legislation Reprinted in the IRS Cumulative Bulletin, 1913–1990 (JCS-19-91) (Dec. 19, 1991). This study appeared as a supplement to Daily Tax Report. It is also available on LexisNexis and IntelliConnect.

b. Text in Print

Once you have a citation, you can find full or partial text of committee reports in several publications. Print sources include the following:

• Standard Federal Tax Reporter (limited coverage)

• United States Tax Reporter (limited coverage)

• Rabkin & Johnson, Federal Income, Gift and Estate Taxation (1954 Code only)

• Cumulative Bulletin (1913–2003)[106]

• Internal Revenue Acts—Text and Legislative History (since 1954)

• Tax Management Primary Sources (1969–2003)

• Seidman's Legislative History of Federal Income and Excess Profits Tax Laws (1863–1953) (print and HeinOnline)

• The Internal Revenue Acts of the United States: 1909–1950; 1950–1972; 1973– (print and HeinOnline)

Each service has limitations. These include providing only partial texts, printing only one committee report rather than all reports for an act, or omitting original pagination. Seidman's omits estate and gift taxes altogether.

The Internal Revenue Acts of the United States: 1909–1950 (and later series) provides full text with original pagination for all materials. Because it omits pre-1909 material, you should consult Seidman's, which includes partial texts, for earlier reports.

c. Text in Electronic Format

If you need reports published in the last ten to fifteen years, online services provide the most comprehensive coverage and are the easiest to search. The government makes committee reports for the 104th and later Congresses available online through both the THOMAS and FDsys websites. Those published in PDF format retain original pagination.

The Westlaw Federal Tax Legislative History database (FTX-LH) begins in 1948 with selective coverage and provides full coverage since 1990. LexisNexis includes reports since 1954 in its Federal Tax Legisla-

---

[106] Committee reports for 1913 through 1938 appear in 1939-1 (pt. 2) C.B. With the exception of the 1954 Code, for which none are included, reports for most acts appeared in the Cumulative Bulletin, often in a separate volume. The government stopped including reports in the C.B. after 2003.

tion, Reports, & Bills file. Checkpoint includes committee reports since the 104th Congress (1995) [Illustration 7-13]. IntelliConnect has several files that include reports. One file covers major legislation beginning with the Tax Reform Act of 1986 through the prior Congress (a separate file covers the current Congress). The Historical Legislative Documents (1954–2002) file includes earlier reports. Finally, HeinOnline includes committee reports in its Taxation & Economic Reform in America library. Its retrospective coverage begins in 1909.

Illustration 7-13. Conference Committee Report in Checkpoint

Committee Report for conf109-455, pl109-222 , Conference

TAX INCREASE PREVENTION AND RECONCILIATION ACT OF 2005

Click here for a PDF of Conference Report 109-455 *Click here for a PDF of the Estimated Revenue Effects of Conference Report 109-455*

Contents

I. EXTENSION AND MODIFICATION OF CERTAIN PROVISIONS

A. Allowance of Nonrefundable Personal Credits Against Regular and Alternative Minimum Tax Liability (sec. 101 of the House bill, sec. 107 of the Senate amendment, and sec. 26 of the Code)

→Checkpoint offers both PDF and hyperlink reading options for many of these reports.

5. Other Congressional Reports

a. Joint Committee on Taxation

One of the most important reports issued by the Joint Committee on Taxation's staff is the General Explanation ("Bluebook") of tax legislation.[107] That document can be used as authority if a taxpayer is disputing the substantial underpayment penalty discussed in Chapter 2.

---

[107] The relevant nomenclature can be confusing. First, although the JCT website currently uses the term Bluebook, these documents have also been referred to as the Blue Book, as is done in Treas. Reg. § 1.6662-4. Second, the General Explanation issued by the JCT staff is not the only "Blue Book." Until 2009, the Treasury Department's General Explanations of the Administration's Fiscal [Year] Revenue Proposals were referred to as the Blue Book). The Treasury document for fiscal 2010, released in May 2009, is the "Green Book." Although the fiscal 2003 through 2010 documents include "Revenue Proposals" in their titles, the fiscal 2002 document instead uses the term "Tax Relief Proposals." Treasury General Explanations issued since 2001 are in the Tax Policy Documents section (Miscellaneous Tax Policy Documents) of the Office of Tax Policy website.

Because the Joint Committee is not an official tax-writing committee, the General Explanation is not an official committee report. Services that cover committee reports may include these reports with other committee reports, cover them in a separate database, or not cover them at all. The same is true for other Joint Committee staff reports and for reports of legislative subcommittees.

The JCT website includes both Bluebooks and other reports. Be careful when using the JCT website. In January 2010, the Publications By Year tab listed documents beginning in 1981. The by-year lists for 1981 through 1991 indicate that these publications (including Bluebooks) are not available electronically. The Publications Bluebooks tab, on the other hand, includes PDF versions of Bluebooks beginning with the Tax Reform Act of 1969 (issued in 1970).

Several subscription services carry JCT reports: Westlaw (Bluebooks since 1976 and other documents since 1992), LexisNexis (Bluebooks since 1970 and other documents since 1981), Checkpoint (since 1996), and IntelliConnect (Bluebooks since 1976 and limited coverage of other documents at least since 1985).

Illustration 7-14. Document Categories on JCT Website

Home	Publications	About Us	Careers	Resources	Contact Us	
By Year	Estimating Methodology	Macroeconomics	Tax Expenditures	Bluebooks	Presidents' Budget	Expiring Provisions

b. Joint Economic Committee

The JEC website categorizes documents into reports, charts, and issues. It may be easier to find documents by browsing than by using a search feature.

c. Congressional Support Entities

You may also want access to reports issued to Congress by congressional support entities, including the Congressional Budget Office, Congressional Research Service, and Government Accountability Office.

You can find these items online, in microform collections, and in library government documents collections. Government websites are particularly likely to include documents generated after 1993.[108] An important advantage of locating these documents online, whether through gov-

---

[108] See Government Printing Office Electronic Information Access Enhancement Act of 1993, Pub. L. No. 103-40, 107 Stat. 112, codified at 44 U.S.C. § 4101.

ernment websites or subscription services, is your ability to search for them based on concept rather than by document number. Illustrations 7-15 and 7-16 cover show the search features available on the CBO and GAO websites.

As noted earlier, the CRS does not post its reports to its website. They are available online from the following sources:

• IntelliConnect CRS Reports and Other Studies (since 2003)

• Westlaw FTX-CRS database (reports released since 1989)

• Tax Analysts (Tax Notes Today, also available on LexisNexis)

• opencrs (http://opencrs.com)

• University of North Texas UNT Digital Library (http://digital.library.unt.edu/explore/collections/CRSR/)

Illustration 7-15. Search Interfaces on CBO Website

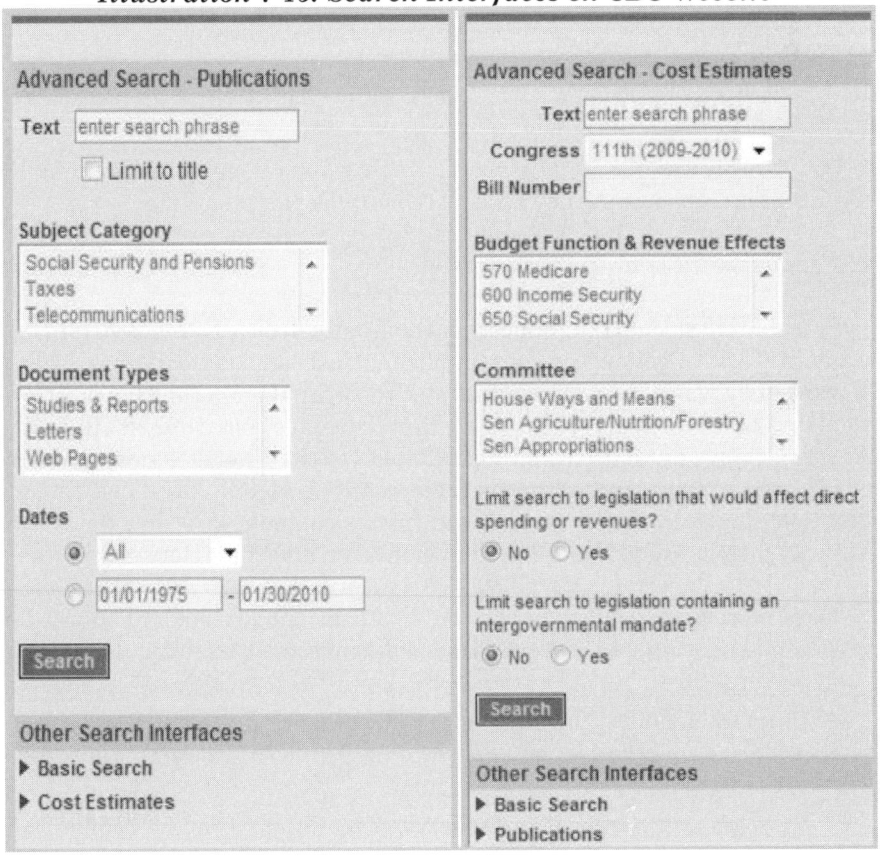

Illustration 7-16. Search Results on GAO Website

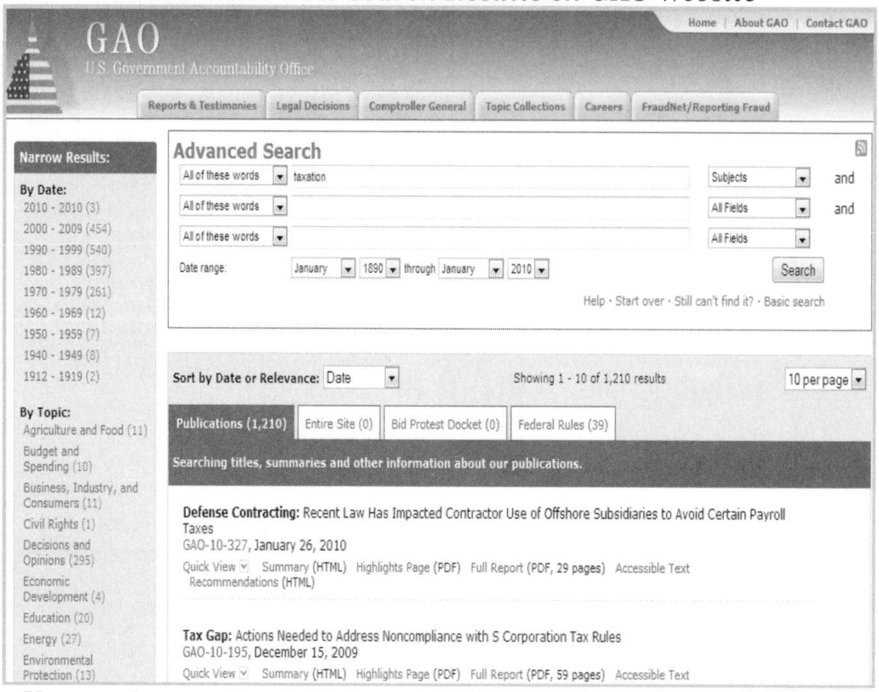

→You can browse the GAO Reports & Testimonies page by Topic or by Agency. The relevant agency is the Treasury Department.

6. Executive Branch Documents[109]

Presidential documents appear in the Compilation of Presidential Documents. This collection has been published daily since late January 2009; it previously was a weekly publication. It is available on the GPO's FDsys website; coverage begins in 1992 (but coverage for 1992 is limited). Another FDsys database, the Public Papers of the Presidents of the United States, includes messages to Congress.[110] Use the Advanced Search function shown in Illustration 7-9 to find documents in either database. You can also locate presidential documents at the White House website.

The American Presidency Project[111] is a free, nongovernment source for presidential documents since George Washington. It includes documents

---

[109] Chapters 9 and 10 also include executive branch documents, particularly those related to interpreting or implementing legislation. Chapter 8 discusses documents related to treaties.

[110] Messages transmitting proposed legislation also appear in the Congressional Record.

[111] www.presidency.ucsb.edu/index.php.

in the Compilation and Public Papers series. It also includes political party platforms, presidential candidate debates, and other documents. Presidential materials are also available in subscription services.[112]

Documents issued by the Office of Management and Budget, the Council of Economic Advisors, and other executive branch offices listed in Subsection B.3 can be found at their websites [Table 7-1].

SECTION E. UNENACTED BILLS

Subscription and free services don't limit their coverage to enacted legislation. You can locate "legislative history" documents such as those described above even for bills that do not become law. For most unenacted legislation, the introduced bill may constitute the entire history: the bill may never reemerge from the committee to which it is referred.

The following services provide legislative history documents for unenacted legislation:

• THOMAS [Illustration 7-17]

• FDsys History of Bills file (easier to use if you have a citation)

• Checkpoint Pending and Enacted Legislation file

• IntelliConnect Federal Tax Legislation files (various sub-files)

• LexisNexis and Westlaw bill-tracking files

Illustration 7-17. Unenacted Bill–History in THOMAS

H.R.194
Title: To amend the **Internal Revenue Code** of 1986 with respect to the purchase of prescription drugs by individuals who have attained retirement age, and to amend the Federal Food, Drug, and Cosmetic Act with respect to the importation of prescription drugs and the sale of such drugs through Internet sites.
Sponsor: Rep. Paul, Ron [TX-14] (introduced 1/4/2007)   Cosponsors (None)
Latest Major Action: 2/2/2007 Referred to House subcommittee. Status: Referred to the Subcommittee on Health.

ALL ACTIONS:

1/4/2007:
    Referred to the Committee on Energy and Commerce, and in addition to the Committee on Ways and Means, for a period to be subsequently determined by the Speaker, in each case for consideration of such provisions as fall within the jurisdiction of the committee concerned.
1/4/2007:
    Referred to House Energy and Commerce
    2/2/2007:
        Referred to the Subcommittee on Health.
1/4/2007:
    Referred to House Ways and Means
    1/18/2007:
        Referred to the Subcommittee on Health.
1/5/2007:
    Sponsor introductory remarks on measure. (CR E9)

---

[112] For example, the HeinOnline U.S. Presidential Library includes both the Weekly Compilation (1965–2009) and the Public Papers (1931–2004). Several Westlaw databases cover presidential documents. LexisNexis has a Public Papers of the Presidents file.

SECTION F. USING LEGISLATIVE HISTORY
IN STATUTORY INTERPRETATION

After a bill becomes law, the interpretive process begins. Whether you are researching to determine the best way to structure a transaction, or because litigation is already in process, you must locate authoritative interpretations of the law. In addition to locating legislative history materials issued for a current act, you may need to trace a Code section back to its original version.

1. In Lieu of Administrative Interpretations

Because Congress authorizes the Treasury Department to issue rules and regulations, you might start searching for interpretations in Treasury regulations (Chapter 9) or IRS documents (Chapter 10). These agencies cannot issue guidance as quickly as Congress enacts major legislation, and they invariably have a backlog of regulations and rulings projects.[113]

If no regulations are available, you can consult legislative history materials to ascertain congressional intent. Even after regulations appear, you can use legislative history to challenge their validity.[114] As discussed in Section H, courts vary in the degree of weight they grant legislative history.[115] Do not overlook this fact in doing your research.

2. Tracing Changes in Statutory Language

Legislative history necessarily includes the process by which a section evolved from its original version. Most 1986 Code provisions were continued from the 1954 Code using the same section numbering scheme. Although the 1939 Code's number system is quite different, you can easily trace current provisions to that Code or to earlier revenue acts.

---

[113] In a worst-case scenario, regulations lag several years behind statutes. For example, Congress enacted I.R.C. § 385 in 1969; regulations adopted in 1980, and subsequently amended, were ultimately withdrawn. Regulations interpreting I.R.C. § 501(c)(9) were issued in 1980; Congress enacted that section's predecessor in 1928. Even if regulations do exist, they may not reflect amended Code language.

[114] See, e.g., United States v. Nesline, 590 F. Supp. 884 (D. Md. 1984), holding invalid a regulation that varied from the plain language of the statute and had no support in the committee reports; cf. Tutor-Saliba Corp. v. Commissioner, 115 T.C. 1 (2000), holding that a regulation comported with congressional intent.

[115] The Treasury Department and IRS cite to legislative history in administrative documents. See, e.g., T.D. 8810, 64 Fed. Reg. 3398 (1999) (conference report); Rev. Rul. 88-64, 1988-2 C.B. 10 (statement during floor debate).

Chapter 6 lists sources publishing the texts of prior laws. The materials below aid you in determining which sections of those laws are relevant.

a. 1986–1954–1939 Code Cross-Reference Tables

Code cross-reference tables provide cross-references between the 1939 and 1954 Codes. Although cross-references directly from the 1986 Code would also be helpful, the 1954 Code tables will suffice so long as the 1954 and 1986 section numbering systems remain substantially identical.

Certain limitations affect your use of cross-reference tables. First, Congress changed section numbers (adding new items and deleting or moving old ones) after enacting the 1954 Code and again in the 1986 Code. Cross-reference tables may not reflect these changes.[116] You must determine when each provision received its current section number. If the table has not been amended since then, use the previous section number in your tracing effort.

A second limitation is also worth noting. These tables reflect their compilers' opinions as to the appropriate cross-references. Different publishers' tables may yield different results. Illustrations 7-18 and 7-19 reflect this phenomenon for 1939 Code section 47.

These services provide tables cross-referencing the 1954 and 1939 Codes:

• United States Statutes at Large (Appendix in volume 68A following text of 1954 Code) (print and HeinOnline)

• Standard Federal Tax Reporter (Code volume I) (print and IntelliConnect)

• Rabkin & Johnson, Federal Income, Gift and Estate Taxation (volume 7B) (print)

• Mertens, Law of Federal Income Taxation—Code (1954–58 Code volume) (1954 to 1939 only) (print)

• Cumulative Changes (1954 Code volume I) (print)

---

[116] For example, Code cross-reference tables list 1939 Code § 23(aa)(1) as the predecessor of 1954 Code § 141. However, 1986 Code § 141 deals with an entirely different topic. 1954 Code § 141 corresponds to 1986 Code § 63(c). The Westlaw FTX-IRC54 file contains the 1954 Code as it read immediately before the adoption of the 1986 Code. Westlaw has a comparable file, FTX-IRC39, for the 1939 Code. IntelliConnect also has 1939 and 1954 Code files.

• Barton's Federal Tax Laws Correlated (looseleaf volume) (print and HeinOnline)

• Seidman's Legislative History of Federal Income and Excess Profits Tax Laws (1953–1939 volume II) (print and HeinOnline)

• Legislative History of the Internal Revenue Code of 1954 (print and HeinOnline)

• Joint Committee on Taxation, Derivations of Code Sections of the Internal Revenue Codes of 1939 and 1954 (JCS-1-92) (Jan. 21, 1992) (JCT website)[117]

Illustration 7-18. Excerpt from Seidman's Code References Table I

1954 CODE REFERENCES

[1953 Code section index precedes subject index]

TABLE I

1953 CODE SEC.	1954 CODE SEC.	1953 CODE SEC.	1954 CODE SEC.	1953 CODE SEC.	1954 CODE SEC.
13(a)	—	23(n)	167	44	453, 7101
15(a)	11	23(o)(1)-(5)	170	45	482
15(c)	1551	23(p)	404	46	442
21	63	23(q)(1)-(3)	170	47(b)-(c)	443, 6011(a)
22(a)	61	23(r)(1)	591	48	441, 7701

→Seidman's ceased publication when the 1954 Code was adopted. Its 1953–1954 table reflects the initial version of the 1954 Code. It does not reflect any section renumbered in a later year. This table is page 3005 of 1953–1939 volume II.

Illustration 7-19. Excerpt from CCH Cross Reference Table I

46	442
47(a)	443, 6011(a)
47(c)	443
47(e)	443
47(g)	443
48(a)	441, 7701(a)(23)

---

[117] The JCT tables are derived from tables in Statutes at Large, volumes 53 and 68A.

b. Tracing Pre-1939 Statutes

You can use these tools to trace provisions that predate the 1939 Code:

• United States Statutes at Large (Appendix in volume 53 (pt. 1) following text of 1939 Code) (separate tables trace sections predating the Revised Statutes of 1875 back to their origin) (print and HeinOnline) [Illustration 7-20]

• Barton's Federal Tax Laws Correlated (print and HeinOnline)

• Seidman's Legislative History of Federal Income and Excess Profits Tax Laws (print and HeinOnline)

• Joint Committee on Taxation, Derivations of Code Sections of the Internal Revenue Codes of 1939 and 1954 (JCS-1-92) (Jan. 21, 1992) (JCT website)

Illustration 7-20. Derivation of 1939 Code in 53 Statutes at Large

Part I—Reference Tables

TABLE A.—*Derivation of Internal Revenue Code*

[* = Amending statute.   † = Reenacting statute.   ‡ = Adding statute.]

I. R. C. section	Date	Volume	Page	Chapter	Section
1, page 4	1938, May 28	52	452	289	1.
2 do	do	52	452	289	2.
3 do	do	52	452	289	3.
4 do	do	52	452	289	4.
11	do	52	452	289	11.
12	do	52	453	289	12.
13	do	52	455	289	13.
14	do	52	456	289	14.
15	do	52	457	289	15.
21	do	52	457	289	21.
22 (a)–(i)	do	52	457	289	22.
22 (j)					
23	1938, May 28	52	460	289	23.
24	do	52	464	289	24.
25	do	52	466	289	25.
26	do	52	467	289	26.
27	do	52	468	289	27.
28	do	52	470	289	28.
31	do	52	472	289	31.
32	do	52	472	289	32.
33	do	52	473	289	33.
41	do	52	473	289	41.
42	do	52	473	289	42.
43	do	52	473	289	43.
44	do	52	473	289	44.
45	do	52	474	289	45.
46	do	52	474	289	46.
47	do	52	475	289	47.
48	do	52	475	289	48.
51	do	52	476	289	51.
52 (a)	do	52	476	289	52.
52 (b)					
53	1938, May 28	52	477	289	53.
54	do	52	477	289	54.
55 (a) (1)	1926, Feb. 26	44	51	27	257 (a).
	1938, May 28	52	478	289	55 (a).
55 (a) (2)	1936, June 22	49	1671	690	55 (a).
	1938, May 28	52	478	289	55 (a).
55 (a) (3)	1926, Feb. 26	44	51	27	257 (a).
55 (b) (1)	do	44	51	27	257 (c).

→This table is on the Page v that follows Page 504, not on the first Page v.

SECTION G. LEGISLATIVE HISTORY COLLECTIONS

This section provides additional information about several legislative history services discussed at various points in this chapter. Each began as a bound or looseleaf print service. These collections are invaluable for researching material that predates the government's move to electronic access. Unfortunately, most are out of print or infrequently updated.[118]

1. Barton's Federal Tax Laws Correlated

Five hardbound volumes trace income, estate, and gift tax provisions from the Revenue Act of 1913[119] through the Tax Reform Act of 1969. Barton's is no longer being published, but it is available in HeinOnline.

a. 1909 through 1952

Barton's reproduces in Code or act section order the text of the various tax acts. Because the acts are lined up in several columns on each page, you can read across a page and see every version of a particular section for the period that volume covers.[120] Barton's often uses different typefaces to highlight changes.

Illustration 7-21. Tracing Statutory Changes in Barton's

INDIVIDUAL CREDITS AGAINST NET INCOME. 65		
Act of 1932.	**Act of 1928.**	**Act of 1926.**
Sec. 25. Credits of individual against net income.	Sec. 25. Credits of Individual Against Net Income.	CREDITS ALLOWED INDIVIDUALS.
There shall be allowed for the purpose of the normal tax, but not for the surtax, the following credits against the net income:	There shall be allowed for the purpose of the normal tax, but not for the surtax, the following credits against the net income:	Sec. 216. For the purpose of the normal tax only there shall be allowed the following credits:
Sec. 25. (a) Dividends. — The amount received as dividends—	Sec. 25. (a) Dividends. — The amount received as dividends—	Sec. 216. (a) The amount received as dividends (1) from a domestic corporation other than a cor-
Sec. 25. (a) (1) from a domestic corporation which is subject to taxation under this title, or	Sec. 25. (a) (1) from a domestic corporation, or	poration entitled to the benefits of section 262 [100], and other than a

→Congress changed the statutory language in both 1928 and 1932.

---

[118] HeinOnline includes some, but not all, of the discontinued services.

[119] The original second edition (vol. 1) also contained the text of the income tax laws from 1861 through 1909. The reproduced second edition omits this material.

[120] Volume 1 covers 1913–24; volume 2 covers 1926–38; volume 3 covers 1939–43; volume 4 covers 1944–49; volume 5 covers 1950–52.

The first two volumes provide a citation to Statutes at Large for each act. Volume 1 includes case annotations, and each volume has a subject matter index. The volumes covering the 1939 Code include tables indicating amending acts and effective dates for 1939 Code sections. Volume 5 has a retrospective table cross-referencing sections to pages in the four previous volumes.

b. 1953–1969

The looseleaf sixth volume does not print the text of Code sections. Its Tables instead provide citations to primary sources that print the desired material. Tables A–D are in Code section order; Table E is in Public Law number order.

Table A provides the history of the 1954 Act. It indicates Statutes at Large page; House, Senate, and Conference report page (official and U.S. Code Congressional & Administrative News); 1939 Code counterpart; Revenue Act where the provision originated; and relevant pages in volumes 1–5. Table C is similar to Table A, but it covers the 1939 Code. It gives the 1954 Code section; the origin of the 1939 Code provision; and cross-references to volumes 1 through 5.

Table B covers amendments to the 1954 Code. For each section it provides Public Law number, section, and enactment date; Statutes at Large citation; House, Senate, and Conference report numbers and location in the Cumulative Bulletin; comment (e.g., revision, amendment); and effective date information. Table D is the same as Table B, but it covers post-1953 changes to the 1939 Code.

Table E [Illustration 7-12] provides citations to legislative history for all acts from 1953 through 1969. It also provides the following information for each act: Public Law number; date of enactment; congressional session; Statutes at Large, Cumulative Bulletin, and USCCAN citations for the act; congressional sessions, dates, and Cumulative Bulletin and USCCAN citations for House, Senate, and Conference report numbers; and Congressional Record citations for floor debate. Acts are not cited by popular name.

2. Seidman's Legislative History of Federal Income and Excess Profits Tax Laws

Seidman's stops in 1953, but it remains useful for determining the legislative history of provisions that originated in the 1939 Code or even earlier.[121] The two volumes covering 1939 through 1953 include both taxes.

---

[121] I.R.C. § 263, for example, contains language taken almost verbatim from § 117 of the 1864 Act. See Act of June 30, 1864, ch. 173, 13 Stat. 223, 281–82.

Separate volumes for the income tax and the excess profits tax were used for the earlier materials, covering 1861 through 1938 and 1917 through 1946, respectively. Seidman's is no longer in print, but it is available in HeinOnline.

Seidman's follows each act, beginning with the most recent, presenting the text of Code sections, followed by relevant committee reports and citations to hearings and the Congressional Record. In some cases, Seidman's excerpts these documents. [See Illustrations 7-10 and 7-22.] Seidman's uses different typefaces to show where in Congress a provision originated or was deleted.

Seidman's prints proposed sections that were not enacted along with relevant history explaining their omission. This information can aid you in interpreting provisions Congress did enact.

Although its coverage has great breadth, Seidman's does not print every Code section. It omits provisions with no legislative history, items lacking substantial interpretive significance, and provisions the editor considered long outmoded. Seidman's does not cover gift, estate, or excise taxes.

Seidman's has three indexes. The Code section index lists each section by act and assigns it a key number. The same key number is assigned to corresponding sections in subsequent acts. The key number index indicates every act, by section number and page in the text, where the item involved appears. A subject index lists key numbers by topic. A table in Volume II of the 1953–1939 set cross-references 1953 and 1954 Code sections covered in Seidman's. [See Illustration 7-18.]

Illustration 7-22. *Statutory Language and History in Seidman's*

388   1934 ACT   [See inside back cover

Report—Senate Finance Committee (73d Cong., 2d Sess., S. Rept. 558).—   Same, except for clerical changes, as Ways and Means Committee Report. (p.42)

Sec. 204(c)(8)

[SEC. 204. INSURANCE COMPANIES OTHER THAN LIFE OR MUTUAL.]

[(c) Deductions Allowed.—* * *]

(8) The amount of interest earned during the taxable year which under section 22(b) (4) is (107) exempt to a corporation from the taxes imposed by this title *excluded from gross income*;

Committee Reports

Report—Ways and Means Committee (73d Cong., 2d Sess., H. Rept. 704).—The additional language "to a corporation" in subsection (c) (8) is merely a clarifying change. The lan-   Amendments nos. 98, 99, 101, 102, 104, 105, 107, and 108: These amendments carry out in the case of insurance companies the same policy as do amendments nos.¹ 15 and 25 in the case of other cor-

→Note how Seidman's indicates changes in statutory language.

3. The Internal Revenue Acts of the United States: 1909–1950; 1950–1972; 1973–

a. Original Series

This set, edited by Bernard D. Reams, Jr., provides comprehensive legislative histories of all the services discussed in this chapter. In addition to each congressional version of revenue bills, the 144 original volumes (1909–1950) contain the full texts of hearings, committee reports, Treasury studies, and regulations. Official pagination is retained for relevant documents. In addition to income and excise taxes, this set includes estate and gift, social security, railroad retirement, and unemployment taxes. This set is available in print, microfiche, and HeinOnline.

An Index volume contains several indexes for locating relevant materials. A chronological index lists each act and every item comprising its legislative history. That index indicates the volume, but not the page, where each item is located.[122] Other indexes cover miscellaneous subjects, such as hearings on items that did not result in legislation; Treasury studies; Joint Committee reports; regulations; congressional reports; congressional documents; bill numbers; and hearings. Unfortunately, there is neither a Code section nor a subject matter index.

Full-text materials appear by type of document rather than by the act involved. All hearings are printed together, as are all bills, laws, studies, and regulations. If you use the print version, you will need to use several volumes to assemble all materials for a particular law or provision. This is by no means a substantial drawback to using this set; assembling the same materials from elsewhere in the collection (assuming they are all available) would be far more difficult.

b. Subsequent Series[123]

Professor Reams subsequently compiled materials to extend this set's coverage to later years. The later volumes are similar in coverage and format to the 1909–50 materials, but hearings receive less attention.

The 1954 volumes include committee reports, hearings, debates, and the final act. Revenue bills and Treasury studies do not appear. Because

---

[122] These volumes are not consecutively paginated, so neither a detailed table of contents nor an index will lead you to the correct page. Although you will have to page through the particular volume to reach the material you seek, that is a minor inconvenience.

[123] Check the library catalog to determine which sets your library has and where it shelves each set.

the IRS Cumulative Bulletins do not cover the 1954 Act, these materials are particularly valuable. A two-volume update published in 1993 includes fifty House and Senate bills missing from the original volumes. The 11 volumes of the original 1954 series are also available in HeinOnline.

Additional sets cover 1950–51, 1953–72, 1969, 1971, 1975, 1976, 1978, 1980, 1984, 1985 (Balanced Budget), 1986, 1987 (Balanced Budget), 1988, 1990, and 1993. Two other sets, covering the Taxpayer Relief Act of 1997 and the Economic Growth and Tax Relief Reconciliation Act of 2001, were edited by William Manz. These sets and others, some of which are compiled by government agencies, are available on HeinOnline as part of its Taxation & Economic Reform in America library. These electronic versions are easier to navigate than their print counterparts.

Illustration 17-23. Excerpt from The Internal Revenue Acts of the United States Index Volume

```
                        REVENUE ACT OF 1916


                                                        Volume

BILL IN ITS VARIOUS FORMS
     Passed Senate, 64th Cong., 1st session,
     H.R. 16763.   In the House of Representatives.
     September 6, 1916.   Ordered to be printed
     with the amendments of the Senate numbered  ..........  61

SLIP LAW
     Public No. 271, 64th Cong., (H.R. 16763),
     an act to increase the revenue, and for
     other purposes.   Approved September 8, 1916,
     39 Stat. 756 .........................................  93

REPORTS
     To increase the revenue, and for other
     purposes, report, H.Rpt. 64-922, July 5, 1916 ........  93

     To increase the revenue, report, S. Rpt.,
     64-793, pt. 1, August 16, 1916 ......................  93

     To increase the revenue.   Views of the
     minority.   S.Rpt. 64-793, pt. 2,
     August 16, 1916 ......................................  93

     The revenue bill, conference report,
     H.Rpt. 64-1200, September 7, 1916 ...................  93

HEARINGS
     To increase the revenue.   Hearings before
     the subcommittee of the Committee on Finance
     U.S. Senate, 64th Cong., 1st session on
     H.R. 16763.   Sections relating to wines and
     liqueurs, dyestuffs, drugs and coal tar
     products, and munitions manufacturers' tax,
     July 17, 1916 ........................................  58
```

4. Eldridge, The United States Internal Revenue System

This reprint of early legislative materials is a useful complement to The Internal Revenue Acts of the United States, discussed above. It includes texts of revenue acts passed through 1894. There is extensive textual material as well as annotations for the various acts. It also contains a descriptive history of the various acts. This text is available online in The Making of Modern Law: Legal Treatises 1800–1926. Hein published a reprint in 1994.

5. Legislative History of the Internal Revenue Code of 1954

Prepared for the Joint Committee on Internal Revenue Taxation in 1967, this volume tracks all changes to the 1954 Code through October 23, 1965. It is arranged in Code section order and provides full text of the original 1954 language and all changes. It also includes ancillary provisions (both in other parts of U.S.C. and not in U.S.C.) and citations to Statutes at Large. There are four tables: 1939 Code sources of each 1954 provision; corresponding sections of the two Codes; post 1954 amendments to the 1939 Code; and amendatory statutes. The last table includes the Public Law number; date enacted; bill number; congressional report numbers; Act name; and Statutes at Large citation. This volume is available in HeinOnline.

6. Cumulative Changes

This multivolume looseleaf service tracks changes in the Code and Treasury regulations. There are series for the 1939, 1954, and 1986 Codes and regulations; many libraries lack the 1939 Code series. Cumulative Changes covers employment taxes and provides limited coverage of excise taxes.

The Code and regulations materials appear separately, arranged in Code section order.[124] The 1954 service includes parallel citation tables for the 1939 and 1954 Codes.

A chart for each Code section indicates its original effective date. The chart includes the Public Law number, section, and enactment and effective dates of each amendment and the act section prescribing the effective date. The chart covers Code section subdivisions (subsections, paragraphs, and even smaller subdivisions). It does not include Statutes at Large citations.

---

[124] Using Cumulative Changes to trace regulations is discussed in Chapter 9.

The format of Cumulative Changes changed slightly in the mid-1990s. The later format gives citations for dates rather than the dates themselves. Illustration 7-24 includes both formats for Code section 51.

The pages following each chart reproduce each version (except the current one) since the provision's original introduction in the relevant Code. The current version can be found in any service that includes the current Code. RIA no longer advertises this service, and it is not updated frequently to reflect recent congressional action.

Illustration 7-24. Excerpt from Cumulative Changes

[See definitions preceding chart on page 1 of this section.]

SEC. 51 '86 I.R.C.	SUBSECTIONS					
	(f)—(h)	(i)(1)	(i)(2)	(i)(3)	(j)	(k)
Pub. Law 99-514, 10-22-86				Added by 1701(c) 1701(e)* Note 1		Redesig. 1878(f)(1) 1881* Note 1
AMENDING ACTS						
Pub. Law 103-66 8-10-93		13302(d) 13303* 8-10-93				

Public Law	Law Sec.	IRC Sec.	Eff. Date
P.L. 104-188	1201(a)	51(a)	1201(g)*
	1201(e)(1)	51(a)	1201(g)*
	1201(f)	51(c)(1)	1201(g)*
	1201(d)	51(c)(4)	1201(g)*
	1201(b)	51(d)	1201(g)*
	1201(e)(1)	51(g)	1201(g)*
	1201(c)	51(i)(3)	1201(g)*
	1201(e)(5)	51(j) Heading	1201(g)*
P.L. 105-34	603(b)(2)	51(d)(2)(A)	
	603(c)(2)	51(d)(9)-(11) Redes (10)-(12)	
	603(d)(2)	51(i)(3)	
P.L. 105-277	1002(a)	51(c)(4)(B)	1002(b)
	4006(c)(1)	51(d)(6)(B)(i)	

7. Primary Sources

Primary Sources presents legislative history information for 1954 and 1986 Code sections and the Employee Retirement Income Security Act (ERISA). Unfortunately, its usefulness is limited to the period from 1969 to 2003. Materials presented for each Code section include presidential messages, committee reports, Treasury Department testimony at hearings, and discussion printed in Congressional Record.

The legislative histories are published in several series, each of which covers several years.[125] Within each series, material appears in Code section order. Each series contains a Master Table of Contents in Code section order; these tables cover the current series and all prior series

Illustration 7-25. Excerpt from Primary Sources, Series IV

IV-26   § 168 [1981] pg. (i)

SEC. 168 – ACCELERATED COST RECOVERY SYSTEM

Table of Contents

                                                      Page

STATUTE — [As Added by the Economic Recovery Tax Act of 1981
     (P.L. 97-34)] .... § 168 [1981] pg. 1

LEGISLATIVE HISTORY

     Background
         97th Congress, 1st Sess. (H.R. 3849)
             Treasury Dept. Tech. Explanation of H.R. 3849 .... § 168 [1981] pg. 28

     House of Representatives
         Ways and Means Committee
             Committee Hearings
                 Statement of Donald Regan, Sec'y of Treasury   § 168 [1981] pg. 34
             Committee Report .... § 168 [1981] pg. 35

     Senate
         Finance Committee
             Committee Hearings
                 Statement of Donald Regan, Sec'y of Treasury   § 168 [1981] pg. 43
             Committee Press Releases
                 No. 81-19 (June 24, 1981) .... § 168 [1981] pg. 44
                 No. 81-21 (June 26, 1981) .... § 168 [1981] pg. 45
             Committee Report .... § 168 [1981] pg. 46
         Senate Discussion
             Vol. 127 Cong. Rec. (July 20, 1981) .... § 168 [1981] pg. 55
             Vol. 127 Cong. Rec. (July 23, 1981) .... § 168 [1981] pg. 58

---

[125] Series I begins with sections affected by the Tax Reform Act of 1969; Series II begins with the 1976 Tax Reform Act; Series III begins with the Revenue Act of 1978; Series IV begins with the Economic Recovery Tax Act of 1981; Series V begins with the Tax Reform Act of 1986. Series I includes the 1939 Code version for many Code sections.

SECTION H. JUDICIAL DEFERENCE

Although judicial opinions cite legislative history documents in deciding between conflicting statutory interpretations, many judges prefer to resolve cases based on the so-called "plain meaning" of the statute. Those judges may give more deference to Treasury regulations than to legislative history if the statute is deemed ambiguous.[126]

The following items illustrate judicial statements regarding the deference courts give legislative history. Several of these statements reiterate statements made in earlier cases.

• Delving into the legislative history is unnecessary because the statutes' language is unambiguous. United States v. Farley, 202 F.3d 198, 210 (3d Cir. 2000).

• While the court makes its holding under the plain meaning rule of statutory construction, the court's conclusion is supported by the predecessor to § 402(a) which was § 165(b) of the IRC of 1939 which had its beginnings in § 219(f) of the Internal Revenue Act of 1921. Shimota v. United States, 21 Cl. Ct. 510, 518 (1990).

• The language of the statute leaves us with uncertainty .... The Secretary has not issued any regulations under section 613(e)(3), that might have provided guidance. We look to the legislative history behind the statute for assistance. Newborn v. Commissioner, 94 T.C. 610, 627 (1990).

• Indications of congressional intent contained in a conference committee report deserve great deference by courts because "the conference report represents the final statement of terms agreed to by both houses, [and] next to the statute itself it is the most persuasive evidence of congressional intent." RJR Nabisco, Inc. v. United States, 955 F.2d 1457, 1462 (11th Cir. 1992).

• [The Bluebook] is not part of the legislative history although it is entitled to respect.... Where there is no corroboration in the actual legislative history, we shall not hesitate to disregard the General Explanation as far as congressional intent is concerned. Redlark v. Commissioner, 106 T.C. 31, 45 (1996).

• [The Blue Book] of course does not rise to the level of legislative history, because it was authored by Congressional staff and not by Congress.

---

[126] Deference to administrative interpretations is discussed in Chapters 9 and 10. Even if not accorded deference for purposes of resolving an issue, committee reports, managers' statements in the conference report, pre-enactment floor statements by one of a bill's managers, and the Bluebook all constitute authority for purposes of avoiding the substantial understatement penalty discussed in Chapter 2.

Nevertheless, such explanations are highly indicative of what Congress did, in fact, intend. Estate of Hutchinson v. Commissioner, 765 F.2d 665, 669–70 (7th Cir. 1985)

• Congress conveys its directions in the Statutes at Large, not in excerpts from the Congressional Record, much less in excerpts from the Congressional Record that do not clarify the text of any pending legislative proposal. Begier v. Internal Revenue Service, 496 U.S. 53, 68 (1990) (Scalia, J., concurring).

• While Congress's later view as to the meaning of pre-existing law does not seal the outcome when addressing a question of statutory interpretation, it should not be discounted when relevant. Sorrell v. Commissioner, 882 F.2d 484, 489 (11th Cir. 1989).

• While headings are not compelling evidence of meaning in themselves, the corresponding section of the Senate report clarifies and reinforces this analysis. That section is headed "Production, acquisition, and carrying costs" (emphasis added) and expresses the intent that "a single, comprehensive set of rules should govern the capitalization of costs of producing, acquiring, and holding property" (emphasis added). Reichel v. Commissioner, 112 T.C. 14, 18 (1999).

• Surrounding sentences are context for interpreting a sentence, but so is the history behind the sentence—where the sentence came from, what problem it was written to solve, who drafted it, who opposed its inclusion in the statute. Sundstrand Corp. v. Commissioner, 17 F.3d 965, 967 (7th Cir. 1994).

• We also find the Government's reading more faithful to the history of the statutory provision as well as the basic tax-related purpose that the history reveals. O'Gilvie v. United States, 519 U.S. 79, 84 (1996).

• Legislative history that is inconclusive, however, should not be relied upon to supply a provision not enacted by Congress. St. Laurent v. Commissioner, 71 T.C.M. (CCH) 2566, 2570 (1996).

SECTION I. PROBLEMS

1. Who introduced the following bill? What Code section would it add or amend?

    a. S. 1168, 103d Cong.

    b. H.R. 3602, 106th Cong.

    c. H.R. 5602, 106th Cong.

    d. S. 2421, 110th Cong.

2. Indicate the proposed popular name and all action for the bill described below.

   a. H.R. 5638, 102d Cong.

   b. H.R. 622, 107th Cong.

   c. H.R. 1779, 108th Cong.

   d. H.R. 6908, 110th Cong.

3. Who is the first person named on the witness list for the hearing described below?

   a. Hearing on Corporate Tax Reform, held by the House Ways and Means Subcommittee on Select Revenue Measures, May 9, 2006

   b. Hearing on Earned Income Tax Credit Outreach, held by the House Ways and Means Subcommittee on Oversight, Feb. 13, 2007

   c. Hearing on the New Markets Tax Credit Program, held by the House Ways and Means Subcommittee on Select Revenue Measures, June 18, 2009

4. Provide House, Senate (and Conference, if one exists) report numbers for the act listed.

   a. Revenue Act of 1950

   b. Crude Oil Windfall Profit Tax Act of 1980

   c. Tariff Suspension and Trade Act of 2000

5. Print the first page of the report requested.

   a. Conference Committee report for the Excess Profits Tax Act–1950

   b. Senate Finance Committee report for the Miscellaneous Trade and Technical Corrections Act of 1999

   c. House Ways and Means Committee report for the Job Creation and Worker Assistance Act of 2002

6. With respect to the document listed, provide the information requested by your instructor (author, month of issue, portion of text, etc.).

   a. a 2009 CRS report: Tax Havens: International Tax Avoidance and Evasion

   b. a 2009 TIGTA report: Combat Zone Indicators on Taxpayer Accounts Are Frequently Inaccurate

c. a 2009 Treasury Department report: Report on the Taxation of Social Security and Railroad Retirement Benefits in Calendar Years 1997 through 2004

d. a 2009 CBO report: Tax Preferences for Collegiate Sports

e. a 2009 GAO report: Actions Needed to Address Noncompliance with S Corporation Tax Rules

f. a 2007 JCT report: Modeling The Federal Revenue Effects Of Proposed Changes In Cigarette Excise Taxes

7. Provide a Congressional Record citation for the statement below.

a. Statement by Representative Poe in February 2008: "Mr. Speaker, if you tax something, you get less of it. If you subsidize it, you get more of it. So in this day of homegrown energy depletion, Congress made the absurd choice of putting more taxes on American oil companies and, instead, chose to subsidize the special interest groups of unproven, undeveloped, and even nonexistent sources of energy."

b. Statement by Representative Stearns in August 2001: "My colleagues, the message is clear, Republicans giveth and Democrats taketh away. Americans are just now receiving their tax refund checks, and Democrats are already trying to yank it back so they can spend more here on wasteful programs in Washington, D.C."

c. Statement by Representative Armey in April 1993: "If you think you're safe, he'll tax your VAT. If you scream too loud, he'll tax your cat. If you drink a bit, he'll tax your beer. If you think too much, he'll tax your fear. If you take tobacco, he'll tax your smoke. If you think it's funny, he'll tax your joke. If you want to drive, he'll tax your gas. If you want to cry, he'll tax your past."

8. Which 1954 Code section corresponds to the 1939 Code section listed?

a. 1939 I.R.C. § 252

b. 1939 I.R.C. § 813(b)

c. 1939 I.R.C. § 1400

9. If the 1939 Code section listed in item 8 originated before 1939, indicate the original act and section number.

CHAPTER 8. TREATIES AND OTHER INTERNATIONAL MATERIAL

SECTION A. INTRODUCTION

This chapter discusses treaties and other documents you can consult when researching the treatment of taxpayers with ties to both the United States and another country.

Treaties are agreements between two (bilateral) or more (multilateral) countries. If the United States has a tax treaty with another country, that document probably applies to your international research project, but it is not the only relevant document. You may also need to locate statutes; congressional, State Department, and presidential documents; regulations; rulings; and judicial opinions. In addition to sources of relevant United States law, your research is likely to involve the treaty partner's internal law. In appropriate situations, you may also have to consult documents issued by international organizations, including the United Nations and World Trade Organization.

Your goals include locating all relevant documents, determining their relative hierarchy and validity, and updating your research to encompass pending items. In accomplishing these goals, you should become familiar with the process by which treaties enter into force and the terminology used to describe treaty documents. You must also take into account changes in sovereignty. Newly independent or merged countries are not always covered by a treaty between the United States and the country with which they were formerly (or are currently) affiliated.

SECTION B. FUNCTIONS OF TREATIES

Although United States citizens residing abroad pay United States income tax on both domestic and foreign-source income, they may also be taxed in the foreign country of residence. Similar problems may arise with regard to property and transfer taxes. Several statutory mechanisms exist to reduce the burden of taxation by more than one country. These include credits or deductions for certain foreign taxes and exclusions for certain foreign source income.[127] Treaties between the United States and others countries may also limit harsh tax consequences.

Treaties serve other tax-related purposes. These include promoting trade by reducing tariffs and reducing tax evasion through exchanges of information with other countries. Although the United States may have

---

[127] I.R.C. §§ 27, 164(a), 911, 912 & 2014.

separate income, estate, gift, and other tax treaties with a given country, in many instances the only tax treaty will be that covering income.

SECTION C. RELATIONSHIP OF TREATIES AND STATUTES

1. Authority for Treaties

Treaties are authorized by the Constitution. Article II, section 2, clause 2, provides that the President "shall have Power, by and with the Advice and Consent of the Senate, to make Treaties, provided two thirds of the Senators present concur ...." Article VI, clause 2, includes both statutes and treaties as the "supreme Law of the Land."

2. Conflict Between Treaties and Statutes

In determining which governs a transaction, neither a treaty nor a statute automatically receives preferential treatment by virtue of its status. As noted, the Constitution includes both treaties and statutes as the "supreme Law of the Land." While normally the "last in time" rule applies to reconcile conflicts between a treaty and a statute, that rule does not always apply.

In enacting Code sections, Congress can decide that treaty provisions will override statutory rules governing income earned (or property transferred) abroad by a United States citizen or resident or transactions undertaken in this country by a foreign national.[128] Congress can also provide that statutory rules will apply instead of treaty language.

In addition, treaties can be overruled by a later statute, by a later treaty, or by treaty termination. Statutory repeal is an extraordinary step, taken in the 1986 Act for cases of treaty shopping.[129] Section J includes several judicial decisions discussing the interplay between statutes and treaties.[130]

---

[128] See I.R.C. §§ 894(a) & 7852(d). Disclosure requirements apply to taxpayers who claim that a tax treaty overrules or modifies an internal revenue law. I.R.C. § 6114; Treas. Reg. § 301.6114-1; IRS Form 8833. See also I.R.C. § 7701(b); Treas. Reg. § 301.7701(b)-7.

[129] Pub. L. No. 99-514, § 1241(a), 100 Stat. 2085, 2576 (1986), modified for income tax treaties in 1988 by Pub. Law. No. 100-647, § 1012(q)(2)(A), 102 Stat. 3342, 3523. I.R.C. § 884(e)(1) currently reads: "No treaty between the United States and a foreign country shall exempt any foreign corporation from the tax imposed by subsection (a) . . . unless— (A) such treaty is an income tax treaty, and (B) such foreign corporation is a qualified resident of such foreign country."

[130] See S. REP. NO. 100-445, 100th Cong., 2d Sess. 316 (1988), for a discussion of the relationship of statutes and treaties and the amendment of I.R.C. § 7852 by Pub. L. No. 100-647, § 1012(aa), 102 Stat. 3342, 3531 (1988).

SECTION D. TREATY TERMINOLOGY

Treaties are often referred to as **conventions**. They are generally amended by documents called **protocols**. Because there may be a long delay before a signed treaty is actually ratified, a pending treaty may be amended several times before it goes into force. A treaty may also be amended after it **enters into force**. Congress may consider protocols along with the original treaty or at a later date.

The Senate can consent to the treaty as signed by the parties or it can express **reservations**. If the countries involved accept these reservations, the treaty process goes forward. If they do not, the treaty may be renegotiated or it may effectively die. A **ratified treaty** enters into force only after the governments exchange instruments of ratification. A treaty that has been signed but which has not undergone whatever actions are necessary to bring it into force is often referred to as **unperfected**.

Each treaty partner designates a **competent authority** to resolve disputes that may arise over which country has jurisdiction to tax an item. The competent authorities may enter into a **memorandum of understanding**. This document is not part of the treaty ratification process.

As was true for statutes, you must take note of **effective dates**. A treaty can become effective on the date it enters into force, at a later date, or even at an earlier date. Different treaty provisions may become effective at different dates. If a treaty is later amended by a protocol, the protocol is subject to the ratification process that applied to the original treaty and may have its own set of date limitations.

SECTION E. TREATY NUMBERING SYSTEMS

Treaties are numbered in a variety of ways, depending on which source is involved. Relevant numbering systems are those used by the State Department, the Senate, and the United Nations.

The State Department assigns treaties a Treaties and Other International Acts Series (T.I.A.S.) number.[131] T.I.A.S. began in 1945. The government previously published treaties in Treaty Series (T.S.) (1–994) and in Executive Agreement Series (E.A.S.) (1–506). T.I.A.S. numbering begins at 1501 to reflect that it continues the other series.

---

[131] Treaties in Force uses the letters NP (not printed in Treaties and Other International Act Series) to indicate treaties that will not be covered by T.I.A.S. If a treaty is part of T.I.A.S. but does not yet have a number, Treaties in Force prints "TIAS" with no further explanation.

A treaty also receives a Senate Executive Document number or a Senate Treaty Document number. The Senate Executive Document system assigned each treaty a letter and a number based on the Congress that received the treaty for ratification. The Senate Treaty Document nomenclature began in the 97th Congress; this system gives each treaty a number and also indicates in which Congress the Senate Foreign Relations Committee published its recommendation to the full Senate.

The United Nations numbering system applies to treaties registered with that body (United Nations Treaty Series; UNTS). The United States is party to some, but not all, of these treaties.

You will rarely need to know treaty numbers if your goal is limited to finding a treaty. The sources noted in Section G let you locate treaties by country. The T.I.A.S. number is important if you are using Shepard's Federal Statute Citations to find decisions interpreting treaties through 1995. The print Shepard's stopped covering treaties at that point.

Table 8-1. Treaty Numbers for the 1975 Income and Capital Tax Convention Between the United States and Iceland

Numbering System	Number
State Department	T.I.A.S. 8151
Senate	S. Exec. E, 94-1
United Nations	Reg. No. 14972, 1020 UNTS 211

Table 8-2. Treaty Numbers for the 1989 Income and Capital Tax Convention Between the United States and Germany

Numbering System	Number
State Department	T.I.A.S. not yet assigned
Senate	S. Treaty Doc. 101-10
United Nations	Reg. No. 29534, 1708 UNTS 3

→Treaties in Force (2009) lists no T.I.A.S. number for this treaty, which entered into force in 1991, or its protocol, which entered into force in 2008.

SECTION F. TREATY HISTORY DOCUMENTS

The treaty history discussed in this section is illustrated by excerpts from documents for the income tax treaty between the United States and Denmark. These documents were obtained from the Treasury Department, IRS, GPO FDsys, and THOMAS websites. Section G lists other sources for treaty documents.

Treaties, in common with statutes, involve both legislative and executive branches of government. However, the order in which each group acts is reversed. Treaties begin with the executive branch and are negotiated by representatives of each government. Unlike acts, pending treaties do not expire at the end of a Congress.

Although State Department representatives are consulted, the Treasury Office of Tax Policy has primary responsibility for negotiating a tax treaty.[132] The treaty signing process has two steps. Changes can be made after a treaty is **initialed** but not after it has been **signed**. The Treasury Department issues a press release after a tax treaty has been signed.

The State Department submits the treaty to the President, asking that the treaty be transmitted to the Senate.[133] The letter from the State Department to the President is a **letter of submittal**; the letter from the President to the Senate is a **letter of transmittal**. The Senate Foreign Relations Committee receives the treaty and both letters. It issues a **Senate Treaty Document**, which contains all three documents.

The Treasury Department prepares a **Technical Explanation** for use by the Senate Foreign Relations Committee. The Joint Committee on Taxation also issues reports. The Foreign Relations Committee holds hearings. The Committee issues a **Senate Executive Report** transmitting the treaty to the full Senate for ratification. Debate by the full Senate appears in the Congressional Record.

After the treaty is ratified by the appropriate government entities in each country, the countries exchange **instruments of ratification** and announce that the treaty has **entered into force**. The Treasury Department issues a press release announcing this information.

Some treaties involve more documents than others. For example, some treaties do not have protocols. Others may not involve diplomatic notes or memoranda of understanding. As Table 8-3 indicates, individual government websites often cover only a few of the relevant documents. As a result, a treaty service is a better source for determining which documents exist and often for accessing those documents. Unfortunately, as is true for government sources, many subscription treaty services limit the type of documents they carry. Government websites and other services carrying treaties and treaty history documents are covered in Section G.

---

[132] The treaty will be signed by a State Department official, not a Treasury official.

[133] The House of Representatives plays no role in the treaty ratification process. Some bilateral agreements, such as those regarding Social Security, are transmitted to both the House and Senate but do not require ratification. [See Illustration 8-17.]

Illustration 8-1. Press Release Announcing Treaty Signing

FROM THE OFFICE OF PUBLIC AFFAIRS

August 19, 1999
LS-64

UNITED STATES AND DENMARK SIGN NEW INCOME TAX TREATY

The Treasury Department announced Thursday that Assistant Secretary for Tax Policy Donald C. Lubick and Danish Chargé daffaires Lars Møller signed a new income tax Treaty between the United States and Denmark at the State Department in Washington. This tax Treaty, if ratified, will replace the current Treaty that entered into force on December 1, 1948, and will represent an important step toward achieving Treasurys goal of updating the United States existing tax treaty network.

→The release number (LS-64) reflects the initials of Lawrence Summers, the Secretary of the Treasury at the time.

Illustration 8-2. Letter of Submittal

LETTER OF SUBMITTAL

DEPARTMENT OF STATE,
Washington, September 7, 1999.

The PRESIDENT,
The White House.

THE PRESIDENT: I have the honor to submit to you, with a view to its transmission to the Senate for advice and consent to ratification, the Convention Between the Government of the United States of America and the Government of the Kingdom of Denmark for the Avoidance of Double Taxation and the Prevention of Fiscal Evasion with Respect to Taxes on Income, signed at Washington on August 19, 1999 ("the Convention"), together with a Protocol.

This Convention replaces the current convention between the United States of America and the Government of the Kingdom of Denmark signed at Washington on May 6, 1948. This proposed Convention generally follows the pattern of the U.S. Model Tax Treaty while incorporating some features of the OECD Model Tax Treaty and recent U.S. tax treaties 'with developed countries. The proposed Convention provides for maximum rates of tax to be applied to various types of income, protection from double taxation of income and exchange of information. It also contains rules making its benefits unavailable to persons that are engaged in treaty shopping. Like other U.S. tax conventions, this Convention provides rules specifying when income that arises in one of the countries and is attributable to residents of the other country may be taxed by the country in which the income arises (the "source" country).

→Note the references to two model treaties, the U.S. Model Tax Treaty and the OECD Model Tax Treaty.

→The United Nations Model Double Taxation Convention Between Developed and Developing Countries would not be relevant to this treaty.

Illustration 8-3. President's Letter of Transmittal

LETTER OF TRANSMITTAL

THE WHITE HOUSE, *September 21, 1999.*

To the Senate of the United States:

I transmit herewith for Senate advice and consent to ratification the Convention Between the Government of the United States of America and the Government of the Kingdom of Denmark for the Avoidance of Double Taxation and the Prevention of Fiscal Evasion with Respect to Taxes of Income, signed at Washington on August 19, 1999, together with a Protocol. Also transmitted for the information of the Senate is the report of the Department of State concerning the Convention.

It is my desire that the Convention and Protocol transmitted herewith be considered in place of the Convention for the Avoidance of Double Taxation, signed at Washington on June 17, 1980, and the Protocol Amending the Convention, signed at Washington on August 23, 1983, which were transmitted to the Senate with messages dated September 4, 1980 (S. Ex. Q, 96th Cong., 2d Sess.) and November 16, 1983 (T. Doc. No. 98-12, 98th Cong., 1st Sess.), and which are pending in the Committee on Foreign Relations. I desire, therefore, to withdraw from the Senate the Convention and Protocol signed in 1980 and 1983.

→Note how long the prior proposed treaty was pending.

Illustration 8-4. Treasury Technical Explanation

DEPARTMENT OF THE TREASURY TECHNICAL EXPLANATION OF THE CONVENTION BETWEEN THE GOVERNMENT OF THE UNITED STATES OF AMERICA AND THE GOVERNMENT OF THE KINGDOM OF DENMARK FOR THE AVOIDANCE OF DOUBLE TAXATION AND THE PREVENTION OF FISCAL EVASION WITH RESPECT TO TAXES ON INCOME SIGNED AT WASHINGTON, AUGUST 19, 1999

GENERAL EFFECTIVE DATE UNDER ARTICLE 29: 1 JANUARY 2001

INTRODUCTION

This is a Technical Explanation of the Convention and Protocol between the United States and Denmark signed at Washington on August 19, 1999 (the "Convention" and "Protocol"). References are made to the Convention between the United States and Denmark for the Avoidance of Double Taxation and the Prevention of Fiscal Evasion with Respect to Taxes on Income signed at Washington, D.C., on May 6, 1948 (the "prior Convention"). The Convention replaces the prior Convention.

Negotiations took into account the U.S. Treasury Department's current tax treaty policy, as reflected in the U.S. Treasury Department's Model Income Tax Convention of September 20, 1996 (the "U.S. Model") and its recently negotiated tax treaties, the Model Income Tax Convention on Income and on Capital, published by the OECD in 1992 and amended in 1994, 1995 and 1997 (the "OECD Model"), and recent tax treaties concluded by Denmark.

The Technical Explanation is an official guide to the Convention and Protocol. It reflects the policies behind particular Convention provisions, as well as understandings reached with respect to the application and interpretation of the Convention and Protocol. In the discussions of each Article in this explanation, the relevant portions of the Protocol are discussed. This Technical Explanation has been provided to Denmark. References in the Technical Explanation to "he" or "his" should be read to mean "he or she" and "his or her."

Illustration 8-5. JCT Explanation (JCS-8-99)

INTRODUCTION

This pamphlet,[1] prepared by the staff of the Joint Committee on Taxation, describes the proposed income tax treaty, as supplemented by the proposed protocol, between the United States of America and the Kingdom of Denmark ("Denmark"). The proposed treaty and proposed protocol were both signed on August 19, 1999.[2] The Senate Committee on Foreign Relations has scheduled a public hearing on the proposed treaty and proposed protocol on October 13, 1999.

Part I of the pamphlet provides a summary with respect to the proposed treaty and proposed protocol. Part II provides a brief overview of U.S. tax laws relating to international trade and investment and of U.S. income tax treaties in general. Part III contains an article-by-article explanation of the proposed treaty and proposed protocol. Part IV contains a discussion of issues with respect to the proposed treaty and proposed protocol.

Illustration 8-6. Hearings, S. HRG. 106-356

BILATERAL TAX TREATIES AND PROTOCOL: ESTONIA—TREATY DOC. 105–55; LATVIA—TREATY DOC. 105–57; VENEZUELA—TREATY DOC. 106–3; DENMARK—TREATY DOC. 106–12; LITHUANIA—TREATY DOC. 105–56; SLOVENIA—TREATY DOC. 106–9; ITALY—TREATY DOC. 106–11; GERMANY—TREATY DOC. 106–13

WEDNESDAY, OCTOBER 27, 1999

U.S. SENATE,
COMMITTEE ON FOREIGN RELATIONS,
Washington, DC.

The committee met, pursuant to notice, at 3:05 p.m. in room SD–419, Dirksen Senate Office Building, Hon. Chuck Hagel presiding.

Present: Senators Hagel and Sarbanes.

Senator HAGEL. Good afternoon.

The committee meets today to consider bilateral income tax treaties between the United States and Estonia, Latvia, Lithuania, Venezuela, Denmark, Italy, and Slovenia as well as an estate tax protocol with Germany.[1]

The United States has tax treaties with 59 countries. This global network of treaties is designed to protect U.S. taxpayers from double taxation and to provide the IRS with information and data to prevent tax evasion and avoidance.

The treaties prevent international double taxation by setting down rules to determine what country will have the primary right to tax income and at what rates. These bilateral international tax treaties are important for America's economic growth.

As we move into the next millennium, today's global economy will be even more interconnected and more interdependent on international tax treaties. The treaties pending before this committee represent new treaty relationships between the United States and Estonia, Latvia, Lithuania, Venezuela and Slovenia.

The treaties with Denmark and Italy would modernize existing treaty relationships. These treaties generally track with the U.S. tax treaty model, although some deviate to various degrees from the U.S. model.

Illustration 8-7. Senate Foreign Relations Committee Executive Report

106TH CONGRESS *1st Session*	SENATE	EXEC. RPT. 106–9

TAX CONVENTION WITH DENMARK

NOVEMBER 3, 1999.—Ordered to be printed

Mr. HELMS, from the Committee on Foreign Relations,
submitted the following

REPORT

[To accompany Treaty Doc. 106–12]

The Committee on Foreign Relations, to which was referred the Convention between the Government of the United States of America and the Government of the Kingdom of Denmark for the Avoidance of Double Taxation and the Prevention of Fiscal Evasion with Respect to Taxes on Income, signed at Washington on August 19, 1999, together with a Protocol, having considered the same, reports favorably thereon, with one declaration and one proviso, and recommends that the Senate give its advice and consent to ratification thereof, as set forth in this report and the accompanying resolution of ratification.

Illustration 8-8. Senate Executive Report 106-9, at 5

The Congressional tax-writing committees and this Committee have made it clear in the past that treaties are not the appropriate vehicle for granting credits for taxes that might not otherwise be creditable under the Code or Treasury regulations. The Committee believes that it would be more appropriate for the United States to address unilaterally problems of the sort raised by special oil and gas taxes imposed by foreign countries. The Committee believes that treaties should not be used in the future to handle foreign tax credit issues which are more appropriately addressed either legislatively or administratively. Nevertheless, the Committee believes that given the circumstances surrounding the Danish hydrocarbon tax, it is justifiable to provide a credit for such tax in this case.

→Note the discussion of using treaties to grant tax credits.

Illustration 8-9. 145 Cong. Rec. (Bound) 28857–58 (1999)

TAX CONVENTION WITH DENMARK

The resolution of ratification is as follows:

Resolved, (two-thirds of the Senators present concurring therein), That the Senate advise and consent to the ratification of the Convention between the Government of the United States of America and the Government of the Kingdom of Denmark for the Avoidance of Double Taxation and the Prevention of Fiscal Evasion with Respect to Taxes on Income, signed at Washington on August 19, 1999, together with a Protocol (Treaty Doc. 106–12), subject to the declaration of subsection (a) and the proviso of subsection (b).

(a) DECLARATION.—The Senate's advice and consent is subject to the following declaration, which shall be binding on the President:

(1) TREATY INTERPRETATION.—The Senate affirms the applicability to all treaties of the constitutionally based principles of treaty interpretation set forth in Condition (1) of the resolution of ratification of the INF Treaty, approved by the Senate on May 27,

28858   (

1988, and Condition (8) of the resolution of ratification of the Document Agreed Among the States Parties to the Treaty on Conventional Armed Forces in Europe, approved by the Senate on May 14, 1997.

(b) PROVISO.—The resolution of ratification is subject to the following proviso, which shall be binding on the President:

(1) SUPREMACY OF CONSTITUTION.—Nothing in the Convention requires or authorizes legislation or other action by the United States of America that is prohibited by the Constitution of the United States as interpreted by the United States.

→Note the limitations on the President in the Declaration and Proviso.

Illustration 8-10. Treaty as Transmitted to Senate

The Government of the United States of America and the Government of the Kingdom of Denmark, desiring to conclude a Convention for the avoidance of double taxation and the prevention of fiscal evasion with respect to taxes on income, have agreed as follows:

ARTICLE 1
General Scope

1. Except as otherwise provided in this Convention, this Convention shall apply to persons who are residents of one or both of the Contracting States.

2. This Convention shall not restrict in any manner any benefit now or hereafter accorded:
      a) by the laws of either Contracting State; or
      b) by any other agreement between the Contracting States.

3. Notwithstanding the provisions of subparagraph 2b):
      a) the provisions of Article 25 (Mutual Agreement Procedure) of this Convention exclusively shall apply to any dispute concerning whether a measure is within the scope of this Convention, and the procedures under this Convention exclusively shall apply to that dispute; and
      b) unless the competent authorities determine that a taxation measure is not within the scope of this Convention, the non-discrimination obligations of this Convention exclusively shall apply with respect to that measure, except for such national treatment or most-favored-nation obligations as may apply to trade in goods under the General Agreement on Tariffs and Trade. No national treatment or most-favored-nation obligation under any other agreement shall apply with respect to that measure.

Illustration 8-11. Press Release That Treaty Entered Into Force

FROM THE OFFICE OF PUBLIC AFFAIRS

April 3, 2000
LS-521

TREASURY ANNOUNCES EFFECTIVE DATES OF NEW TAX AGREEMENT WITH
DENMARK

The Treasury Department on Monday announced that a new income tax treaty with Denmark entered into force on March 31, 2000. The treaty, to which the U.S. Senate gave advice and consent to ratification in November, 1999, replaces the existing tax treaty between the United States and Denmark, which was signed in 1948.

On March 31, Denmark notified the United States that Denmark had complied with the constitutional requirements for entry into force of the bilateral income tax treaty between the two countries. The United States had previously provided reciprocal notification to the Denmark, and accordingly, the treaties entered into force on March 31. The treaties apply, with respect to taxes withheld at source, in respect of amounts paid or credited on or after May 1, 2000 and, with regard to other taxes, in respect of taxable years beginning on or after January 1, 2001.

→Note the different effective dates.

Illustration 8-12. Press Release for Protocol to Treaty

May 3, 2006
JS-4231

United States and Denmark Sign Protocol to
Income Tax Treaty

Washington – Today the Treasury Department announced that U.S. Ambassador James P. Cain and Danish Tax Minister Kristian Jensen signed a new Protocol to amend the existing bilateral income tax treaty, concluded in 1999, between the two countries. The Protocol was signed Tuesday.

The agreement significantly reduces tax-related barriers to trade and investment flows between the United States and Denmark. It also modernizes the treaty to take account of changes in the laws and policies of both countries since the current treaty was signed. The Protocol brings the tax treaty relationship with Denmark into closer conformity with U.S. treaty policy.

The most important aspect of the Protocol deals with the taxation of cross-border dividend payments. The Protocol is one of a few recent U.S. tax agreements to provide for the elimination of the source-country withholding tax on dividends arising from certain direct investments and on dividends paid to pension funds. The Protocol also strengthens the treaty's provisions preventing so-called treaty shopping, which is the inappropriate use of a tax treaty by third-country residents.

→John Snow (JS) was Secretary of the Treasury in May 2006.

Illustration 8-13. Exchange of Notes in Connection with Protocol

Copenhagen, May 2, 2006

Excellency:

I have the honor to refer to the Protocol signed today between the Government of the United States of America and the Government of the Kingdom of Denmark Amending the Convention for the Avoidance of Double Taxation and the Prevention of Fiscal Evasion with Respect to Taxes on Income, and to confirm, on behalf of the Government of the United States of America, the following understandings reached between our two Governments.

In reference to clause a) (iv) of paragraph 3 of Article 10 (Dividends) of the Convention, as amended by the Protocol, it is understood that the U.S. competent authority generally will exercise its discretion to grant benefits under such paragraph to a company that is a resident of Denmark if:

→The reference to Article 10 (Dividends) refers to the article numbering system in the original treaty.

→Note the reference to how the competent authority will act with respect to dividends.

Illustration 8-14. Protocol to Treaty

ARTICLE II

1.   Article 10 (Dividends) of the Convention shall be omitted and the

following shall be substituted:

"ARTICLE 10

Dividends

1.   Dividends paid by a resident of a Contracting State to a resident of the

other Contracting State may be taxed in that other State.

→Article II of the protocol amends Article 10 of the original treaty.

SECTION G. LOCATING TREATIES AND THEIR HISTORIES

When a treaty goes into force, it is added to the State Department's Treaties and Other International Acts Series (T.I.A.S.). T.I.A.S. is the treaty equivalent of Statutes at Large; the treaty document equivalent of United States Code is United States Treaties and Other International Agreements (U.S.T.). Because official treaty publications are not updated nearly as quickly as their statutory counterparts, you should use other sources to obtain the text of recent treaties.

Tax treaties and their revising protocols are published in various places, several of which are limited to tax treaties. Many sources also provide access to at least some treaty history documents. Unfortunately, few sources provide access to all relevant information.

The sources below illustrate the formats in which you can locate treaties and other documents. Your library may also carry them in microform.

1. United States Government Sources

The Internal Revenue Service website includes PDF versions of treaty texts other than the most recently ratified treaties. The site also includes Treasury Technical Explanations for many of the treaties, some diplomatic notes, and Publication 901. Publication 901 lists current treaties and provides information about how each treaty affects specific categories of taxpayers. This site does not include congressional action, Joint Committee explanations, or press releases.

The Treasury Department Office of Tax Policy website provides access to proposed treaties, diplomatic notes, press releases, Treasury testimony at hearings, and Treasury Technical Explanations. It has links to JCT explanations. It does not include all these items for every treaty, and it does not include congressional action. In addition, it does not cover documents issued before October 1996. Many of its documents are available in PDF formats.

GPO FDsys offers access to hearings, congressional debate, and committee reports for treaties. It also includes the letters of submittal and transmittal and treaty language. JCT explanations are available on the JCT site. The THOMAS site has a section giving a treaty's congressional history.

The weekly Internal Revenue Bulletin contains the most recent material, which is reprinted in the Cumulative Bulletin at six month intervals. Because of their arrangement, these publications are more useful for finding IRS material relating to treaties than for finding the treaties themselves. In addition to treaty texts, these services include the Senate Executive Reports and the Treasury Technical Explanations. The I.R.B. is available in print, online at the IRS website, and through subscription online services.[134]

Table 8-3. Government Sites Providing Treaty Documents

Document	Website
Congressional Record	FDsys
Diplomatic Notes	IRS, Treasury
Hearings	Treasury,[135] FDsys
JCT Explanations	JCT
Letters of Submittal and Transmittal	FDsys[136]
Press Releases	Treasury
Senate Executive Report	FDsys
Treasury Technical Explanation	IRS, Treasury
Treaty and Protocol texts	IRS, Treasury, FDsys
Treaty History Listing	THOMAS

2. Subscription Services

Subscription services that cover treaty materials are available in a variety of formats. In addition to online and CD/DVD coverage of treaty documents, many services also provide a print or microform version of these documents. Other services are limited to a single format. The discussion below indicates available formats.

a. CCH Tax Treaties

The CCH Tax Treaties looseleaf service is available in print and on IntelliConnect. It reproduces texts of United States income and estate tax treaties, exchange of information agreements, shipping and air transport treaties, and social security treaties. It reproduces selected treaty documents, including letters of submittal and transmittal, diplomatic notes,

---

[134] See Joint Committee on Taxation, Listing of Selected International Tax Conventions and Other Agreements Reprinted in the IRS Cumulative Bulletin, 1913–1990 (JCS-20-91), Dec. 31, 1991, for citations to older treaty documents and administrative guidance. This document is available on LexisNexis at 92 TNT 2-8. It is also available on IntelliConnect.

[135] The Treasury website includes only Treasury Department testimony.

[136] You can also find letters of transmittal on the White House website; these will be separate items rather than combined with the letter of submittal and the treaty text. The GPO's Compilation of Presidential Documents also includes letters of transmittal. The Compilations are discussed in Chapter 7.

and Treasury and congressional reports. CCH includes editorial comments and annotations, and it reproduces IRS publications providing withholding rate tables and Cumulative Bulletin citations for each treaty and protocol. It also includes texts of model treaties. Supplementation is monthly.

The IntelliConnect version includes full-text treaty history documents. It also provides links to texts of administrative documents (such as revenue procedures and letter rulings) and judicial decisions interpreting each treaty.

Illustration 8-15. IntelliConnect Documents: U.S.-Denmark Income Tax Treaty

☐ Income Tax Treaties

   ⊟ ☐ Treaty in Force

      ☐ TREATY, INCOME TAX TREATY BETWEEN DENMARK AND THE UNITED STATES

      ☐ PROTOCOL, Protocol Amending the Convention Between the Government of the |

      ☐ PROTOCOL, Protocol

      ☐ DIPLOMATIC NOTE, Exchange of Notes.—

      ☐ DIPLOMATIC NOTE, Letter of Transmittal.—

     ⊞ ☐ Report of the Senate Foreign Relations Committee on the Income Tax Protocol Bet

     ⊞ ☐ Joint Committee on Taxation Explanation of Proposed Income Tax Treaty and Prop

     ⊞ ☐ [¶2500G] Department of the Treasury Technical Explanation of the Convention Be

     ⊞ ☐ Joint Committee on Taxation, Explanation of Proposed Protocol to the Income Tax

     ⊞ ☐ [¶2500I] Testimony of The Staff of the Joint Committee on Taxation Before the Se

      ☐ TECHNICAL EXPLANATION, Department of the Treasury Technical Explanation of

     ⊞ ☐ [¶2500N] Denmark Income Tax Treaty

b. Federal Tax Coordinator 2d

The RIA Federal Tax Coordinator 2d looseleaf service is available in print and on Checkpoint. Volumes 20 and 20A, Chapter O, cover United States income and estate and gift tax treaties.

The textual discussion in the Checkpoint version is linked to the treaty text in the Checkpoint U.S. Tax Treaties in Force library. U.S. Tax Treaties in Force includes the text of treaties, protocols, and diplomatic notes, but it does not include legislative history documents.

Illustration 8-16. Federal Tax Coordinator 2d Discussion: U.S.–Denmark Income Tax Treaty

---

¶O-20442. U.S. and Denmark defined under Denmark tax treaty.

Under the U.S.-Denmark treaty, the term "U.S." means the U.S., and includes the states thereof and the District of Columbia. It also includes the territorial sea and the sea bed and subsoil of the submarine areas adjacent to the territorial sea over which the U.S. exercises sovereign rights under international law. However, Puerto Rico, the Virgin Islands, Guam, and other U.S. possessions or territories are excluded. [14] The extension to the territorial sea area applies only if the person, property or activity to which the treaty is being applied is connected with natural resource exploration or exploitation. Thus, it would not include any activity involving the sea floor of an area over which the U.S. exercised sovereignty for natural resource purposes if that activity was unrelated to the exploration and exploitation of natural resources. [15]

---

[14]

Denmark Treaty, Art. 3(1)(f) .

---

[15]

Treas. Tech Expl. p. 9.

---

c. BNA Publications

The Tax Management Portfolios—Foreign Income service is available in print and electronically.[137] This service covers individual countries in separate Portfolios (Business Operations Abroad series), but it does not yet publish a Portfolio for each treaty country. The Detailed Analysis sections contain explanations, significant cases, and other annotations. The Worksheets include treaty texts. Other Portfolios in this series cover general topics, such as the foreign tax credit and transfer pricing.

Other BNA products include an online Tax Treaties Analysis service (updated for new material), International Journal (monthly), International Tax Monitor (daily), and Transfer Pricing Report (biweekly).

d. Tax Analysts Publications

Tax Analysts covers treaty documents in its OneDisc Premium DVD and in an online Worldwide Tax Treaties service. LexisNexis also carries Tax Analysts publications.

---

[137] In addition to its own electronic service, BNA makes its Portfolios available on Westlaw. The Portfolios are not an available Westlaw option for every academic library subscription.

Treaty documents include full texts of treaties and all documents comprising each treaty's legislative history. The Integrated Treaty Texts option shows treaties as amended by subsequent protocols. Tax Analysts covers income, transfer tax, shipping and air transport, information exchange, and social security treaties. It also includes model treaties, administrative documents (such as revenue rulings and Chief Counsel advice), and judicial interpretations.

Tax Analysts also covers international news in Tax Notes International (weekly) and Worldwide Tax daily.

Illustration 8-17. OneDisc: Treaty History Options

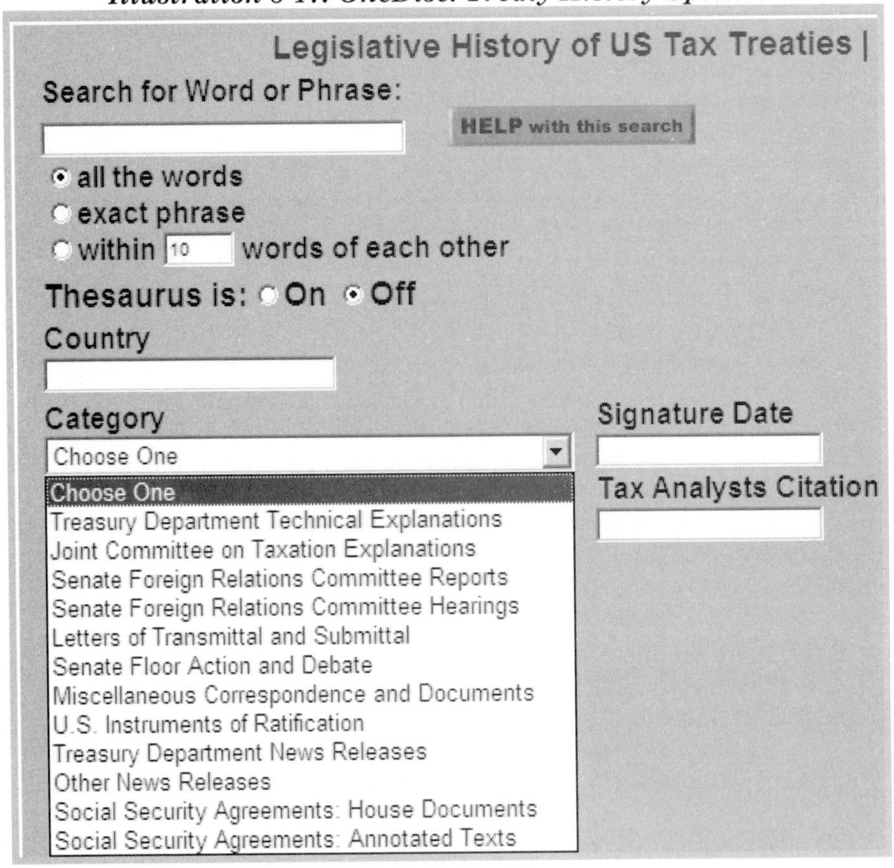

e. **Legislative History of United States Tax Conventions (Roberts & Holland Collection)**

This looseleaf service, introduced in 1986, updated and expanded a four-volume 1962 version prepared by the Joint Committee on Taxation staff. The twenty-one volumes contain the full text of treaties and legislative history documents, including presidential messages, Senate Executive Reports, floor debate, Joint Committee staff explanations, and hearings. Official pagination is retained.

This service focused on the history of the treaty rather than on subsequent judicial and administrative interpretations. Although the most recent supplement is from 2006, this service remains a valuable source of compiled treaty history documents. An electronic version is available in HeinOnline.

Illustration 8-18. Roberts & Holland Collection: Documents for U.S.–Denmark Income Tax Treaty

SECOND BASIC CONVENTION (signed Aug. 19, 1999).
  Treasury News, LS-64, Aug. 19, 1999 385
  Presidential Message of Transmittal to Senate,
    Senate Treaty Doc. 106-12, 106th Cong., 1st Sess.,
    Sept. 21, 1999 386
  Staff of Joint Comm. on Taxation, Explanation,
    JCS 8-99, Oct. 8, 1999 437
  Testimony, Lindy Paull, Chief of Staff of the
    Joint Committee on Taxation, JCX-76-99. 497
  Testimony, Philip R. West, Treasury International
    Tax Counsel, Treas. News, LS-177, Oct. 27, 1999. 501
  Treasury Dept., Technical Explanation 526
  Senate Executive Report, 106-9, 106th Cong.,
    1st Sess., Nov. 3, 1999 627
  Treasury News, LS-521, April 2, 2000 680
  Senate Resolution Ratifying Treaty 681
  TIAS   , entered into force March 31, 2000.
    (Not Available)

→Documents for the 2006 protocol are not covered.

f. Rhoades & Langer, U.S. International Taxation and Tax Treaties

This treatise covers the treaty and non-treaty aspects of both inbound and outbound transactions. Following the topical discussion in the main text sections, Appendix A prints the text of current, proposed, and prior income tax treaties. It also prints estate and gift tax treaties, information exchange agreements, transportation agreements, social security totalization agreements, and other relevant agreements. Appendix B includes model treaties: OECD; United States; and United Nations. In addition to the print version, this treatise is available on LexisNexis.

In addition to its T.I.A.S. citation, a brief legislative history accompanies each treaty. If a treaty no longer applies, the service still covers that country and indicates when the treaty went out of force. Cross-references to any pertinent regulations, revenue rulings and letter rulings follow each treaty article.

g. Other Sources

LexisNexis carries Tax Analysts materials and Rhodes & Langer, both of which are described above. It also includes general and country-specific information in its International Tax Planning and its Primary Law by Country or Region libraries. Westlaw carries RIA Tax Treaties and Explanations, RIA International Taxes Weekly, and Journal of International Taxation. Westlaw also includes Warren Gorham & Lamont international tax treatises. Oceana publishes Treaties and International Agreements Online.

SECTION H. PENDING TREATIES

The government regularly announces the status of treaty negotiations. This information is carried in newsletters, looseleaf services, and on government websites.

If you want to determine if a tax treaty has been signed and is pending before the Senate, you can locate this information in the CCH Congressional Index, Senate volume (Treaties–Nominations tab). Looseleaf services such as those discussed in Section G are a good source of information about pending treaties and treaties that are being negotiated.

SECTION I. CITATORS FOR TREATIES

Two sources that formerly provided citations to judicial and administrative decisions regarding treaties are of limited use. Shepard's Federal Statute Citations provides citations to court decisions involving treaties through 1995; you need the U.S.T. and T.I.A.S. citations to use this volume. Citations to IRS pronouncements (1954–1993/94) can be found in the Service's Bulletin Index-Digest System, discussed in Chapter 10.

In the absence of a formal citator, you can locate judicial and administrative rulings in looseleaf, CD/DVD, and online services that focus on treaties or that have extensive treaty coverage.

SECTION J. INTERPRETING TREATIES

1. Administrative Interpretations

In many instances, the executive branch must issue regulations and other rulings to implement or interpret treaty provisions. For example,

Title 26, Chapter I, Subchapter G of the Code of Federal Regulations provides regulations regarding tax treaties. These regulations do not follow the regulations numbering system described in Chapter 9, and they do not cover all treaty countries.[138] The Treasury Department's 2009–2010 Priority Guidance Plan includes Guidance under treaties as one of its items; regulations have not been ruled out in this context.[139]

The Internal Revenue Service issues revenue rulings and other guidance interpreting treaty provisions. You can locate these documents by using the treaty country as a search term instead of using a Code section. Chapter 10 discusses locating IRS documents.

2. Judicial Interpretations

Because treaties and statutes are both approved by Congress, many of the rules of interpretation applied to statutes apply to treaties. The list below illustrates interpretation rules applied to treaties and to situations involving a conflict between a treaty and a statute.

• [W]hen a treaty and an act of Congress conflict "the last expression of the sovereign will must control". Lindsey v. Commissioner, 98 T.C. 672, 676 (1992).

• Unless the treaty terms are unclear on their face, or unclear as applied to the situation that has arisen, it should rarely be necessary to rely on extrinsic evidence in order to construe a treaty, for it is rarely possible to reconstruct all of the considerations and compromises that led the signatories to the final document. However, extrinsic material is often helpful in understanding the treaty and its purposes, thus providing an enlightened framework for reviewing its terms. Xerox Corp. v. United States, 41 F.3d 647, 652 (Fed. Cir. 1994).

• The Government correctly notes that "[a]lthough not conclusive, the meaning attributed to treaty provisions by the Government agencies charged with their negotiation and enforcement is entitled to great

---

[138] See, e.g., Treas. Reg. § 513.2: "The fact that the payee of the dividend is not required to pay Irish tax on such dividend because of the application of reliefs or exemptions under Irish revenue laws does not prevent the application of the reduction in rate of United States tax with respect to such dividend."

[139] See Kristen A. Parillo, *Treasury Considering Supplemental Treaty Guidance, Official Says*, TAX NOTES TODAY, Dec. 9, 2008, 2008 TNT 238-3: "[Treasury deputy international tax counsel Gretchen] Sierra responded that Treasury has been considering providing some type of supplemental treaty guidance, such as treaty regs. She noted, however, that doing so would be a resource-intensive project. She said issuing regs would have advantages in that the government would be able to get reporting from taxpayers that take positions contrary to the regs."

weight." .... Courts nevertheless "interpret treaties for themselves.".... Moreover, because we are to interpret treaties so as to give effect to the intent of both signatories, ..., an agency's position merits less deference "where an agency and another country disagree on the meaning of a treaty," .... Finally, this court, when considering different provisions of the 1975 Treaty, has declined to defer to Treasury's contemporaneous interpretation where it conflicted with the contemporaneous intent of the Senate.... Westminster Bank, PLC v. United States, 512 F.3d 1347, 1358 (Fed. Cir. 2008) (citations omitted).

• Even where a provision of a treaty fairly admits of two constructions, one restricting, the other enlarging, rights which may be claimed under it, the more liberal interpretation is to be preferred. North West Life Assurance Co. of Canada v. Commissioner, 107 T.C. 363, 378 (1996).

• We construe a treaty like a contract. Amaral v. Commissioner, 90 T.C. 802, 813 (1988).

• It does appear, however, that in the case of treaties, courts have sometimes been more willing to resort to extra-textual, preparatory material to determine meaning, and also to allow for more liberal interpretation of the words of a treaty. In such instances the decision of the courts to resort to sources beyond the treaty language and/or to a more liberal interpretation of the written word often has occurred because the treaty language is not completely clear and requires further explanation. Snap-On Tools, Inc. v. United States, 26 Cl. Ct. 1045, 1065 (1992).

• Thus, to the extent that a treaty can reasonably be interpreted to avoid conflict with a subsequent enactment, such an interpretation is to be preferred. Norstar Bank of Upstate New York v. United States, 644 F. Supp. 1112, 1116 (N.D.N.Y. 1986).

SECTION K. UNITED NATIONS, OECD, AND WTO

The United States belongs to several international organizations whose activities may affect U.S. tax legislation and administration. Relevant organizations include the United Nations, OECD, and WTO.

1. United Nations

As noted in Section E, the United Nations numbers treaties that are registered with it. Its website includes a searchable treaty database.[140] The United Nations model tax treaty, Model Double Taxation Convention between Developed and Developing Countries, is also available on its website; the most recent version is from 2001. United States treaty histo-

---

[140] http://treaties.un.org/Pages/Home.aspx?lang=en.

ry documents indicate if the parties considered the United Nations model treaty.[141]

2. OECD

The Organisation for Economic Co-operation and Development was formed in December 1960 as a continuation of the Organisation for European Economic Co-operation. "Discussions at OECD committee-level sometimes evolve into negotiations where OECD countries agree on rules of the game for international co-operation. They can culminate in formal agreements by countries, for example on combating bribery, on arrangements for export credits, or on the treatment of capital movements. They may produce standards and models, for example in the application of bilateral treaties on taxation, or recommendations, for example on cross-border co-operation in enforcing laws against spam."[142]

The United States is a signatory to the OECD Mutual Administrative Assistance in Tax Matters Convention, which entered into force in 1995. The OECD has published several model treaties, such as the OECD Model Tax Convention on Income and on Capital, which the United States takes into account in negotiating tax treaties.[143] Treaty explanations indicate variances from the OECD Model Treaty. The Centre for Tax Policy and Administration page of the OECD website covers a wide array of tax-related projects.[144] The website also has hyperlinks to a variety of reports and news releases related to taxation.

---

[141] See, e.g., Staff of the Joint Committee on Taxation, Explanation of the Proposed Income Tax Treaty Between the United States and the People's Republic of Bangladesh, JCX-04-06 (2006): "The United States and the People's Republic of Bangladesh do not have an income tax treaty currently in force. The proposed treaty is similar to other recent U.S. income tax treaties, the 1996 U.S. model income tax treaty ("U.S. model"), the 1992 model income tax treaty of the Organization for Economic Cooperation and Development, as updated ("OECD model"), and the 1980 United Nations Model Double Taxation Convention Between Developed and Developing Countries, as amended in 2001 ("U.N. model"). However, the proposed treaty contains certain substantive deviations from these treaties and models."

[142] OECD website (http://www.oecd.org), "What We Do and How" section. This site includes OECD Model Treaty information.

[143] The most recent OECD Model Treaty was issued in mid-2008; a draft revised Article 7 (Business Profits) is pending. The most recent U.S. Model Treaty was issued in November 2006.

[144] The OECD regularly reports on countries that have not made a commitment to transparency and effective exchange of information. The OECD site also discusses so-called Harmful Tax Practices and issues progress reports on that topic.

3. WTO

The World Trade Organization was formed in 1995 to deal with the global rules of trade between nations. It succeeded the General Agreement on Tariffs and Trade (GATT). Trade disputes resolved by WTO panels extend beyond such traditional measures as tariffs. Its 2002 holding, that U.S. tax provisions favoring foreign sales corporations were invalid export subsidies, led to several changes in the Internal Revenue Code.[145]

The WTO website can be searched by country [Illustration 8-19], subject, year, and document type.

Illustration 8-19. WTO Disputes Involving the United States

Ecuador	1 cases:
	DS335
European Communities	31 cases:
	DS38, DS39, DS63, DS85,
	DS88, DS100, DS1⟋
	DS118, DS136, DS13
	DS151, DS152, DS160 Tax Treatment for "Foreign
	DS165, DS166, DS176 Sales Corporations"
	DS186, DS200, DS212,
	DS213, DS214, DS217,
	DS225, DS248, DS262,
	DS294, DS317, DS319,
	DS320, DS350, DS353

→Slide the mouse over a dispute number to see what it concerns.

SECTION L. OTHER INTERNATIONAL MATERIAL

1. General Information

If a transaction will take place in another country, you may need information about that country's tax laws and general business climate. Pamphlets published by major accounting firms and other organizations provide useful background information. Individual country websites are

---

[145] World Trade Organization Appellate Body ruling (WT/DS108/AB/RW) (Jan. 14, 2002) on appeal from Panel Report, United States – Tax Treatment for "Foreign Sales Corporations" – Recourse to Article 21.5. of the DSU by the European Communities (the "Panel Report"). The WTO Dispute Settlement Body adopted the Appellate Body ruling on January 29, 2002 (WT/DS/108/25). These and subsequent documents related to this dispute are available at the WTO website, http://www.wto.org. The WTO website can be searched by country and by type of dispute.

easy to access.[146] Background material appears in sources such as the Tax Management Portfolios (Chapter 13).

Although background materials provide an introduction, they cannot substitute for primary source materials. Many United States law libraries have collections of materials from other countries, particularly countries that use English as their primary language. Subscription databases, such as Westlaw and LexisNexis, also carry relevant information.

2. Material in Other Languages

Although not limited to international taxation, a practitioner may need access to materials in a language other than English. Treaties to which the United States is a signatory are published in both English and the official language of the other country. About 20 United States tax forms are available in Spanish on the IRS website. The website also includes several publications in Chinese, Korean, Russian, Spanish, and Vietnamese. The IRS Publication 850 series provides English–other language glossaries of words and phrases covering those languages.

3. Treaties with Native American Tribes

Treaties the United States entered into with Native Americans are beyond the scope of this book. You should be aware that tax rules applied to Native Americans may involve claims of treaty-based exemptions.[147]

SECTION M. PROBLEMS

1. Which tax treaties are in force between the U.S. and the country listed? Include income, estate, gift, exchange of information, and social security. Exclude air transport and shipping income, customs, and tariffs and trade agreements.

   a. Japan

   b. Sweden

   c. Venezuela

2. When were the following U.S.–(Country Listed) treaties signed?

   a. Italy–Income Tax

---

[146] See, e.g., http://www.hmrc.gov.uk/home.htm (United Kingdom Revenue & Customs); Being a business owner in Denmark link, Business Lounge page, at http://www.denmark.dk.

[147] See, e.g., Cook v. United States, 86 F.3d 1095 (Fed. Cir. 1996).

    b. Poland–Income Tax

    c. France–Estate and Gift Tax

3. What is the T.I.A.S. number for the following U.S.–(Country Listed) treaties, and when did they enter into force?

    a. Hungary–Income Tax

    b. Mexico–Exchange of Information

    c. Pakistan–Income

4. Locate and provide citations for as many of the treaty and treaty history items illustrated as you can for the treaty selected by your instructor.

5. Using Chapter 10 discussion as necessary, provide a citation for and holding of the IRS document described below.

    a. 2009 letter ruling concerning whether the taxpayer satisfied the 12-month stock ownership requirement of the U.S.–United Kingdom income tax treaty

    b. 2004 letter ruling concerning a lump sum distribution from a non-qualified retirement plan and the U.S.–Australia income tax treaty

    c. 2001 technical assistance memorandum concerning whether residents of East Timor are covered by the U.S.–Indonesia income tax treaty

    d. 1999 technical assistance memorandum concerning the classification of U.S. source endorsement income of nonresident alien athletes under U.S. income tax treaties

6. Using Chapter 11 discussion as necessary, locate and give the holding and any appeals action for the decision described below.

    a. a D.C. Circuit decision involving the alternative minimum tax limitation on foreign tax credits and the U.S.–Canada Income Tax Treaty, including the effect of two protocols that amended the treaty after the relevant Code section was enacted.

    b. a District Court decision as to whether an alien holding a "green card" was covered by the U.S.–China income tax treaty

    c. a Court of Federal Claims decision as to whether income from rental housing was covered by the U.S.–Australia income tax treaty as incidental to operation of aircraft

    d. a Tax Court decision as to whether lottery payments were annuities for purposes of the U.S.–Israel income tax treaty

7. Print out tax information from a country-specific website.

CHAPTER 9. TREASURY REGULATIONS

Section A. Introduction

This chapter discusses regulations, which Congress authorizes in the Internal Revenue Code and in other statutes. It explains the different types of regulations—proposed, temporary, and final—and the difference between legislative and interpretive regulations. It also covers other terms used to describe regulations, judicial deference to administrative positions, and sources in which you can find relevant documents. This chapter's coverage of regulations is similar to the coverage in Chapters 6 and 7 for statutes and their legislative history.

Your goals for this chapter include locating all relevant documents, determining their relative importance, and updating your research to include projects that may result in proposed regulations.

Section B. Functions of Administrative Guidance

As discussed in Chapters 6 and 7, Congress enacted the Internal Revenue Code and other statutes governing income, transfer, and excise taxes. Taxpayers interpret those statutes in determining their liability for these taxes. Courts become involved when there is a controversy between the government and a taxpayer. In interpreting statutes, both taxpayers and courts must consider administrative interpretations.[148]

The **Treasury Department** and **Internal Revenue Service** (IRS) interpret and enforce internal revenue laws. In some areas, such as employee benefits, they share their authority with other administrative agencies. This chapter focuses on one form of administrative guidance, regulations, primarily those issued as Treasury regulations. Chapter 10 focuses on IRS pronouncements.

Section C. Terminology

1. Proposed, Temporary, and Final Regulations

You should expect to encounter regulations in three different stages. The citation format indicates whether the item is a Proposed Regulation (e.g., Prop. Treas. Reg. § 1.801-4(g)); a Temporary Regulation (e.g., Temp. Treas. Reg. § 1.71-1T); or a Final Regulation (e.g., Treas. Reg. § 1.106-1). Assuming the citation is correct, a regulation that does not include either

---

[148] Administrative interpretations are also relevant for treaties ratified by the Senate. Treaties are discussed in Chapter 8.

a "Prop." or a "T" is a final regulation. Each type can be cited as authority for avoiding the substantial understatement penalty discussed in Chapter 2.

a. Proposed Regulations

Proposed regulations offer guidance for taxpayers seeking to comply with statutory rules. Taxpayers generally receive an opportunity to submit written comments or testify at hearings before proposed regulations become final.

b. Temporary Regulations

The IRS can simultaneously issue a proposed regulation as a **temporary regulation**. Unlike a proposed regulation, a temporary regulation is effective when it is published in the Federal Register. It provides immediate, binding guidance, and receives more deference than a proposed regulation. It becomes operative without the benefit of public comment.

Code section 7805(e) mandates that temporary regulations issued after November 20, 1988, also be issued as proposed regulations; this ensures that there will be a notice and comment procedure before regulations are finalized.[149] Section 7805(e) also requires that temporary regulations expire no more than three years after they are issued. This limitation does not apply to temporary regulations issued on or before that date, and several older temporary regulations are still in effect.

c. Final Regulations

Regulations issued after any necessary notice and comment period are referred to as final regulations. The **final regulations** may differ from the proposed or temporary regulations they replace for various reasons, including government response to taxpayer comments or judicial decisions. In addition to regulatory analysis information, described in Section E, the Preamble accompanying the Treasury Decision will indicate comments received and any changes made in response to comments.

2. Interpretive and Legislative Regulations

Most regulations are issued pursuant to the Code section 7805(a) general mandate. You may see these referred to as **general authority**, **interpretive**, or **interpretative regulations**. These contrast to regulations, issued for Code sections in which Congress included a specific grant of authority. The specific grant of authority allows IRS experts to

---

[149] Proposed regulations need not be issued as temporary regulations.

write rules for technical areas. You may encounter references to these regulations using the terms **specific authority** or **legislative regulations**.

The information accompanying each regulation indicates Treasury's authority for issuing the regulation, either a specific Code section (specific authority or legislative), Code section 7805(a) (general authority or interpretive), or both. If the regulation is a final or temporary regulation, the authority information is added to the appropriate part of the Code of Federal Regulations. As noted in Section K, courts give legislative regulations more deference than they accord interpretive regulations.

Understanding terminology is important. Interpretive and legislative relate to the authority for a particular regulation; proposed, temporary, and final relate to steps in the process for issuing regulations. For example, a regulation can be both final and interpretive.

3. Federal Register and Code of Federal Regulations

The **Federal Register** contains the text of proposed, temporary, and final regulations, including their Preambles and other information about the regulation. Items appear in the order in which they are filed; they are not arranged by subject matter or by issuing agency. The Federal Register is the regulatory equivalent of Statutes at Large, which is discussed in Chapter 6. The Federal Register is published each weekday.

The **Code of Federal Regulations** (C.F.R.) is the regulatory equivalent of United States Code. Final and temporary regulations are classified by topic into the appropriate C.F.R. title. Title 26 covers most tax provisions. Each C.F.R. title is updated only once a year in the official C.F.R. publication; title 26 is updated as of each April 1. A separate government website, e-CFR, is updated daily, but is not an "official legal edition" of the C.F.R.[150]

4. Treasury and Other Agency Regulations

a. Treasury Regulations

Title 26 of the Code of Federal Regulations (C.F.R.) is the Internal Revenue title of C.F.R. As such, it contains most of the regulations you will need for resolving tax problems. Instead of citing these regulations as 26 C.F.R. sections, you can cite them as **Treasury Regulations** (Treas. Reg.).

---

[150] The e-CFR site has not yet migrated to FDsys; see ecfr.gpoaccess.gov.

Some Treasury-issued regulations appear elsewhere in C.F.R. Regulations in 31 C.F.R. (Money and Finance: Treasury) cover other Treasury Department functions, including Practice Before the Internal Revenue Service.[151]

b. Other Agency Regulations

The Treasury Department is one of several Cabinet Departments, each of which may issue regulations. Regulations may also be issued by groups categorized as Other Executive Agencies or as Independent Regulatory Agencies. If another agency has authority for provisions affecting tax law, its regulations are also relevant. For example, the Department of Labor issues regulations in the employee benefits area. Those regulations appear in 29 C.F.R. One of the Other Executive Agencies whose regulations may be relevant is the Pension Benefit Guaranty Corporation (29 C.F.R.).

5. Numbering Systems

As was true for statutes, several numbering systems are relevant to regulations. In addition to the actual regulation number, these include the project number, Treasury Decision number, Regulation Identifier Number, Sequence Number, and OMB Control Number. You can use these numbers to find regulations, or information about their status, in various government documents and websites. You can also use some of them to find information about compliance with government mandates discussed in Section E. Because most of the numbering systems are different, the only ones likely to cause confusion are the RIN and OMB numbers.

a. Regulation Number

The **regulation number** is the number used to cite a regulation. If it is a Treasury regulation, its number reflects the underlying Code section and whether it is a proposed, temporary, or final regulation. Examples of regulations numbers appear in Section F.

b. Project Number

When the IRS opens a regulations project, it assigns it a **project number**.[152] It uses those project numbers for its proposed regulations. Although the project numbering system has changed several times, certain parts have remained constant.

---

[151] This group of sections begins at 31 C.F.R. § 10.0.

[152] A single project number (or T.D.) can cover multiple regulations sections.

Before an IRS reorganization in 1988, most projects were drafted in the IRS Legislation and Regulations Division and began with the letters LR. Employee benefits and exempt organization projects were designated EE; international projects, INTL. Projects begun under this system received new letter designations but not new numbers after 1988.

Between 1988 and August 1996, project numbers indicated the IRS division with responsibility for the project. [See Table 9-1.] The current numbering system began in August 1996. All project numbers now begin with REG, followed by a series of numbers, followed by the project's year. There is no indication of which IRS division has authority for the regulations project. A recent example of this numbering system is REG-127270-06, covering proposed regulations for Code section 104. The document appeared in the Federal Register in 2009. The -06 following the hyphen indicates it was a 2006 project.[153]

Although the numbering system no longer indicates which division produced the regulation,[154] that information does appear in the Drafting Information section included in the regulation's Preamble.

Table 9-1. IRS Project Designations, 1988–1996

Designation	Division
CO	Corporate
EE	Employee Benefits and Exempt Organizations
FI	Financial Institutions and Products
GL	General Litigation
IA	Income Tax and Accounting
INTL	International
PS	Passthroughs and Special Industries

c. Treasury Decision Number

Final and proposed regulations are issued as **Treasury Decisions** (T.D.). Treasury Decisions are numbered sequentially; the current numbering system began in 1900. It does not indicate the year of issue or the Code section involved. After the regulation text is added to the C.F.R.,

---

[153] 74 Fed. Reg. 47152 (2009).

[154] The IRS operating divisions that followed the Internal Revenue Service Restructuring and Reform Act of 1998, Pub. L. No. 105-206, 112 Stat. 685, don't replace the Chief Counsel units. The operating divisions (Wage and Investment; Small Business/Self-Employed; Large and Mid-Size Business (LMSB); and Tax Exempt and Government Entities) are not part of the Chief Counsel's office. The Chief Counsel division for exempt organizations is now called Tax Exempt and Government Entities; General Litigation has become part of Procedure and Administration.

the most important information in the T.D. is the Preamble. [See Illustration 9-1.]

d. Regulation Identifier Number

The Regulatory Information Service Center (RISC) assigns **Regulation Identifier Numbers** to agency rulemaking projects. Each RIN begins with a four-digit agency code, followed by a four-character alphanumeric code. The alphanumeric part of the number is assigned in the order in which the project is entered in the government database tracking rulemaking projects.

The RIN does not change as the item advances from prerule to final rule. The RIN appears in the Unified Agenda and in the headings of proposed and final regulations published in the Federal Register.

e. Sequence Number

The **sequence number** is likely the least important number you will encounter. Regulatory Agendas printed in the Federal Register include sequence numbers for each document. The sequence numbers indicate where the document appears in that Agenda; they change from Agenda to Agenda. Since fall 2007, the online Agendas omit the sequence numbers; the printed versions included in the Federal Register retain them.

f. OMB Control Number

If a regulation involves collection of information and is therefore subject to the Paperwork Reduction Act, the OMB assigns an **OMB Control Number**. These numbers appear in Treas. Reg. § 602.101. Each OMB Control number begins with a four-digit agency code, followed by another four-digit numerical code.

6. Additional Rulemaking Terminology

Regulations rarely appear immediately after a Code section is enacted or amended. Relevant stages include opening a regulations project, announcing a proposed rule (or making an advance announcement), and issuing proposed, temporary, or final regulations. Rules issued by agencies other than the IRS may use different names for their rulemaking projects even though the processes are much the same.

a. Advance Notice of Proposed Rulemaking

The Service may publish an **Advance Notice of Proposed Rulemaking** (ANPRM). Advance notices indicate rules the Service expects to propose. In the advance notice, the Service may request public comment, which could influence the resulting NPRM. The ANPRM includes the project number and the RIN. ANPRMs are issued in what the Unified Agenda refers to as the prerule stage. The Service does not issue an ANPRPM for every project in this stage.

b. Notice of Proposed Rulemaking

The IRS publishes the text of a proposed regulation and its accompanying Preamble as a **Notice of Proposed Rulemaking** (NPRM). Notices include the project number and the Regulation Identifier Number (RIN). Neither number reflects the underlying Code section number or the year the proposal is filed with the Federal Register. The NPRM is issued at the end of rulemaking stage of the process.

7. Dates

a. Filing and Publication Dates

Because they are not statutes, regulations are not enacted. Instead they are issued to the public by being filed with the Federal Register. The **filing date** generally precedes the **publication date** by a day or two. The T.D. information following each temporary and final regulation includes the Federal Register date. That date is also listed before Preambles to proposed, temporary, and final regulations. The date is important because of the rules concerning retroactivity discussed in Subsection E.2.

b. Effective Date

The Preamble to the T.D. or NPRM includes the regulation's **effective date**, which can vary from its filing and publication dates. The effective date for a proposed regulation is likely to read as follows: "These regulations are applicable to taxable years ending after the date final regulations are published in the Federal Register."

c. Sunset Date and "Stale" Regulations

Final regulations generally continue in effect indefinitely. Temporary regulations issued after November 20, 1988, **sunset** no later than three years after they are issued.

Although a final regulation continues in effect until it is withdrawn, its validity may be seriously compromised if the Code section it interprets is amended or if a judicial opinion rejects its reasoning. Use the T.D. date to determine when a regulation was promulgated or amended. If a regulation contradicts its Code section, it probably has not been amended to reflect the most recent statutory change.[155] If it varies from a judicial holding, the IRS may have decided to continue litigating its position rather than withdraw the regulation. Chapter 10 discusses administrative announcements regarding continuing litigation.

8. Preambles and Texts of Regulations

Preambles to T.D.s and NPRMs discuss the regulation and provide other useful information, much of which is discussed elsewhere in this chapter. Preambles appear in the Federal Register but not in the C.F.R.

Table 9-2. Preamble Segments

Paperwork Reduction Act
Background
Explanation of Provisions
Effective Date
Special Analyses
Comments and Public Hearing
Drafting Information
List of Subjects

Two items follow the Preamble. The first is the amendment to the affected C.F.R. subdivision. This amendment indicates the Code section authorizing each regulation, a concept discussed in Subsection C.2. The second item is the regulation's text. That language is added to the C.F.R. if it is a temporary or final regulation. If it is a proposed regulation, the text appears in the Federal Register but not the C.F.R. Preambles are illustrated in Illustrations 9-1 and 9-5.

9. Agendas and Guidance Plans

Agencies announce their regulatory plans twice a year in the Unified Agenda of Regulatory and Deregulatory Actions.[156] The **Unified Agenda** appears in the Federal Register and as a searchable database on the RegInfo.gov and Regulations.gov websites. The fall issue of the Agenda includes the **Regulatory Plan**. The Plan provides information about the most significant actions each agency plans for the coming year.

In addition, the Treasury and IRS issue an annual **Priority Guidance Plan**, which lists guidance they hope to issue during the next twelve months. The Priority Guidance Plan covers both regulations and

---

[155] Looseleaf services that print regulations often indicate that a regulation does not reflect a statutory change.

[156] This document is often referred to as the Semiannual Agenda.

other types of guidance. These documents are discussed further in Section I.

Illustration 9-1. Preamble to T.D. 9454

This section of the FEDERAL REGISTER contains regulatory documents having general applicability and legal effect, most of which are keyed to and codified in the Code of Federal Regulations, which is published under 50 titles pursuant to 44 U.S.C. 1510.

The Code of Federal Regulations is sold by the Superintendent of Documents. Prices of new books are listed in the first FEDERAL REGISTER issue of each week.

DEPARTMENT OF THE TREASURY

Internal Revenue Service

26 CFR Part 1

[TD 9454]

RIN 1545-BG37

Notification Requirement for Tax-Exempt Entities Not Currently Required To File

AGENCY: Internal Revenue Service (IRS), Treasury.

ACTION: Final regulations and removal of temporary regulations.

SUMMARY: This document contains final regulations as required by section 6033(i)(1) describing the time and manner in which certain tax-exempt organizations not currently required to file an annual information return under section 6033(a)(1) are required to submit an annual electronic notice including certain information required by section 6033(i)(1)(A) through (F). These regulations affect tax-exempt organizations whose annual gross receipts are not normally in excess of $25,000.

DATES: *Effective Date:* These regulations are effective on July 23, 2009.

Applicability Date: These regulations are applicable to annual periods beginning after 2006.

FOR FURTHER INFORMATION CONTACT: Monice Rosenbaum at (202) 622-6070 (not a toll-free number).

SUPPLEMENTARY INFORMATION:

Background

This document contains amendments to the Income Tax Regulations (26 CFR part 1) under section 6033(i)(1) relating to the notification requirement for entities not currently required to file an annual information return under section 6033(a)(1). Section 6033(i)(1) was added by section 1223(a) of the Pension

Protection Act of 2006, Public Law 109-280, 120 Stat. 1090 (2006) (PPA 2006), effective for annual periods beginning after 2006. Section 6033(i)(1) requires the Treasury Secretary to promulgate regulations that describe the time and manner in which certain tax-exempt organizations not currently required to file an annual information return are to submit an annual electronic notification including information set forth in section 6033(i)(1)(A) through (F).

On November 15, 2007, temporary regulations (TD 9366, 2007-52 IRB 1232) were published in the Federal Register (72 FR 64147) satisfying the requirement that the Treasury Secretary promulgate regulations as described in the preceding paragraph. Those temporary regulations were corrected on November 23, 2007 (72 FR 65667) and December 14, 2007 (72 FR 71060). A notice of proposed rulemaking (REG-104942-07, 2007-52 IRB 1264) cross-referencing the temporary regulations was published in the Federal Register (72 FR 64174) on November 15, 2007.

The IRS and the Treasury Department received four written comments from the public in response to the proposed and temporary regulations. No hearing was requested or held. After consideration of the comments received, it was determined that the proposed regulations would be finalized without change. Accordingly, the proposed regulations are adopted as amended by this Treasury decision and the corresponding temporary regulations are removed. The final regulations retain the provisions of the proposed and temporary regulations and make minor typographical changes.

Explanation of Revisions and Summary of Comments

One comment pointed out that there is no de minimis rule regarding the amount of income an organization receives during the year which would exempt it from having to submit an electronic notification. Section 6033(i) does not provide a *de minimis* rule, nor does it provide discretionary authority for the IRS and the Treasury Department to establish a *de minimis* exception for reporting under section 6033(i)(1).

Another comment objected to the requirement that the notification be submitted electronically. The IRS and the Treasury Department note that the statute requires that information be submitted electronically, and makes no

provision for paper notification. However, as stated in the preamble to the temporary regulations, if an organization that is required to submit an annual electronic notification files a complete Form 990, "Return of Organization Exempt from Income Tax," or Form 990-EZ, "Short Form Return of Organization Exempt from Income Tax," the annual notification required under section 6033(i) shall be deemed satisfied. The annual notification requirement is not satisfied if the Form 990 or Form 990-EZ contains only those items of information that would have been required by submitting the notification in electronic form.

One comment asked about the intent of the regulations and the application of the requirement to submit electronic notification to organizations that are local chapters or clubs of larger organizations. The intent of the regulations, which were required by statute, is to provide the public with the most accurate information about tax-exempt organizations. With respect to organizations that are local chapters or clubs of larger organizations, if the organization is a subordinate of a parent organization and the subordinate is included on the parent's group return, the subordinate need not submit the electronic notification. However, if an organization is not part of a group return and is a separate legal entity that meets the criteria for submitting the electronic notification, it must submit Form 990-N, "Electronic Notice (e-Postcard) for Tax-Exempt Organizations Not Required To File Form 990 or 990-EZ."

Finally, another comment asked about the applicability of the electronic notification requirement to Qualified State and Local Political Organizations (QSLPOs). QSLPOs are not organizations described in section 501(c) that are required to file a return under section 6033(a); therefore, the provisions of these final regulations do not apply to them. However, QSLPOs may have other reporting requirements under section 6033(g).

Special Analyses

It has been determined that this Treasury decision is not a significant regulatory action as defined in Executive Order 12866. Therefore, a regulatory assessment is not required. It also has been determined that section 553(b) of the Administrative Procedure

→Note the discussion of comments received.

→The Subjects covered by this T.D. are Income taxes and Reporting and recordkeeping requirements.

SECTION D. REGULATORY PROCESS

1. IRS and Treasury

Regulations begin as projects assigned to drafters in the relevant division of the IRS Chief Counsel's office. The Unified Agenda or Priority Guidance Plan will generally list these items. The Unified Agenda lists the Code section and Project Number and indicates a target date by which action, such as publishing the proposed regulations, will occur. The Priority Guidance Plan lists topics (e.g., Exempt Organizations, Financial Issues and Products) alphabetically. Within each topic, it lists both regulations and other guidance the Treasury Department and IRS hope to issue; Code sections are included for most items. For example, the initial version of the 2009–2010 Plan includes as an item within the Tax Administration group "Proposed regulations under §6015 updating the existing regulations regarding relief from joint and several liability."

Because the IRS may issue advance notices regarding its proposals,[157] researchers interested in future regulations must also check IRS documents discussed in Chapter 10.

After a **notice and comment period**, the IRS has several options. These include finalizing the proposed regulation without modifications, finalizing it with modifications, modifying it and asking for additional comments, or withdrawing it and starting the drafting process over again. Because proposed regulations, unlike temporary regulations, do not sunset after three years, the IRS can also retain the proposal in its original form without further action.

2. Congress

In March 1996, Congress added a congressional review procedure for agency rules. This procedure allows Congress to disapprove a "major" rule by a **joint resolution of disapproval**. A disapproved rule does not become effective unless the President vetoes the disapproval and Congress fails to override the veto. Major rules are suspended for up to 60 days for the congressional review and for additional time if needed for the override process.[158]

---

[157] See, e.g., Notice 2006-60, 2006-29 I.R.B. 82.

[158] 5 U.S.C. §§ 801–808. A major rule is "any rule that the Administrator of the Office of Information and Regulatory Affairs of the Office of Management and Budget finds has resulted in or is likely to result in–(A) an annual effect on the economy of $100,000,000 or more; (B) a major increase in costs or prices for consumers, individual industries, Federal, State, or local government agencies, or geographic regions; or (C) significant adverse effects on competition, employment,

Congress may intervene by imposing a moratorium on regulations in a particular area, as it did for "nonstatutory" fringe benefits before the enactment of Code section 132. Congress could also reject a regulation by changing the statute to produce a different outcome. A current area of practitioner frustration relates to Code sections with no regulations despite statutory language saying the Secretary "shall" issue regulations.

SECTION E. REGULATORY AUTHORITY

1. Entities Involved

The two most important entities involved in promulgating regulations are the Internal Revenue Service and the Treasury Department. Regulations are drafted by the Internal Revenue Service, but they are issued under the authority of the Secretary of the Treasury. Sections C and D describe various steps involved in issuing a regulation.

Code section 7805(a) authorizes the Secretary to "prescribe all needful rules and regulations for the enforcement" of the tax statutes. Other Code sections that refer to regulations also use the term "the Secretary." Code section 7701(a)(11)(B) defines that term to mean "the Secretary of the Treasury or his delegate." If the statute instead says "the Secretary of the Treasury," section 7701(a)(11)(A) prohibits delegation.

The Secretary has delegated the regulations drafting function to the Commissioner of Internal Revenue.[159] For that reason, this book generally refers to the IRS role in the regulations process. Nevertheless, you must refer to them as Treasury regulations, not IRS regulations.

2. Code Limitations on Authority

Section 7805(a) authorizes issuing regulations, but it is not an absolute grant of authority. Several limitations apply to the IRS's authority to issue regulations. These relate to retroactivity and taxpayer burden. The government describes its compliance with these rules in the Preambles that accompany regulations. [See Illustration 9-3.]

a. Retroactivity

Code section 7805(b) imposes limits on issuing regulations with retroactive effect. Beginning with statutes enacted on July 30, 1996, a pro-

---

investment, productivity, innovation, or on the ability of United States-based enterprises to compete with foreign-based enterprises in domestic and export markets." Id. § 804(2).

[159] Treas. Reg. § 301.7805-1(a).

posed, temporary, or final regulation cannot apply to any taxable period before the earliest of its filing with the Federal Register[160] or the date on which a notice substantially describing its expected contents is issued to the public. This rule does not apply to regulations filed or issued within 18 months of the statute's enactment, necessary to prevent abuse, or is-sued to correct procedural defects in previously issued regulations.[161]

b. Small Business

Code section 7805(f) requires the Treasury Department to submit pro-posed and temporary regulations to the Small Business Administration's Chief Counsel for Advocacy. The Chief Counsel for Advocacy is required to comment on the regulation's impact on small business. The Preamble accompanying the final regulations must discuss these comments.[162]

3. Other Limitations on Authority

a. Administrative Procedure Act

Agencies must publish notices of proposed rulemaking in the Federal Register.[163] These notices include information about the time and place for a public rulemaking procedure, indicate the agency's legal authority for promulgating the regulation, and indicate the terms or substance of the proposed rule. Publication generally must precede the effective date by at least 30 days. Although they are exempt from these requirements, interpretive tax regulations generally follow the act's requirements.[164]

b. Executive Order 12866

In 1993, President Clinton issued an order setting forth a statement of regulatory philosophy and principles and providing a regulatory planning and review process for proposed and existing regulations. The Office of Management and Budget is charged with ensuring that regulations fol-low the stated philosophy and principles. The order also requires that

---

[160] A final regulation can be retroactive to the date its proposed version was filed. It might even relate back to an IRS notice, described in Chapter 10.

[161] Congress can legislatively waive section 7805(b). In addition, the IRS can authorize taxpayers to elect retroactive application. I.R.C. § 7805(b)(6)&(7).

[162] Comparable requirements apply to final regulations that are not based on proposed regulations; those submissions must occur before the regulation is filed.

[163] 5 U.S.C. § 553.

[164] The legislative–interpretive distinction is also important when a court is de-ciding how much deference the rule merits. Deference is discussed in Section K.

agencies submit their regulatory plans for the year for OMB review.[165] You can search for agency submissions governed by Executive Order 12866 on the RegInfo.gov website.[166] [See Illustration 9-2.] You can also search directly in an online version of the Federal Register or in a service covering Preambles to regulations.

In January 2009, President Obama asked the Director of the Office of Management and Budget (OMB) to produce recommendations for a new Executive Order on regulatory review. Links to the OMB request for public comments, extension of the comments deadline, and public comments deadline all appear on the RegInfo.gov site. This process may lead to a replacement for, or revision of, Executive Order 12866.

Illustration 9-2. EO 12866 Regulatory Review Search Page

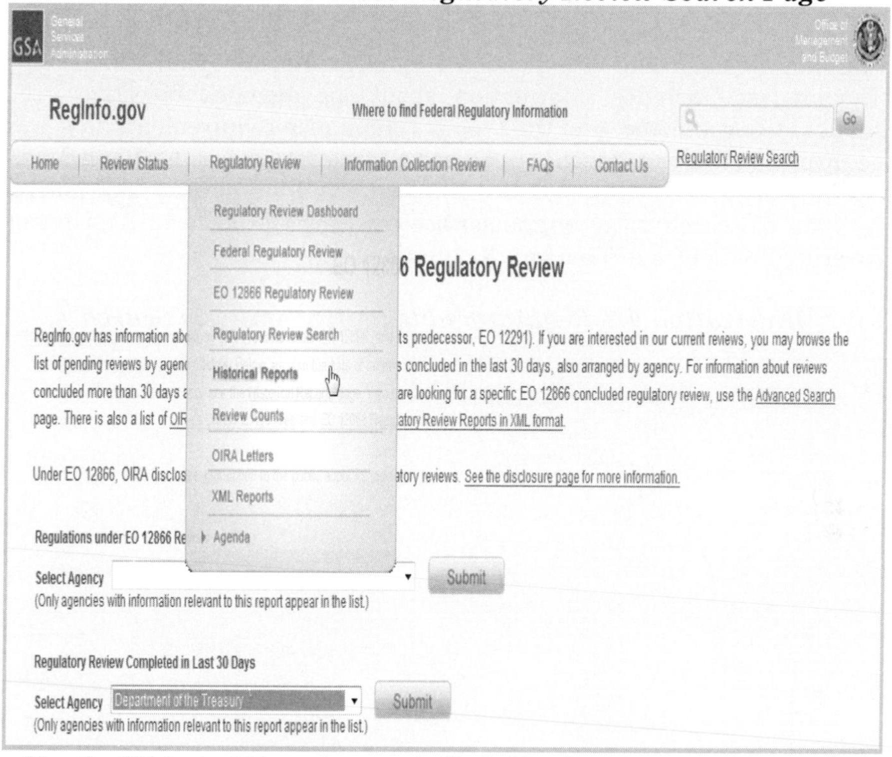

→Use the Historical Reports page to find older items.

---

[165] In Executive Order 13258, President Bush made changes to Executive Order 12866 to reflect personnel changes. 67 Fed. Reg. 9385 (2002). President Obama revoked Executive Order 13258 on January 30, 2009. Executive Order 13497, 74 Fed. Reg. 6113 (2009). Executive Order 12866 appears at 58 Fed. Reg. 51735 (1993).

[166] This site is produced by the Office of Management and Budget (OMB) and the General Services Administration (GSA).

c. Paperwork Reduction Act of 1995[167]

One of this act's goals is reducing duplication and burden on the public. The OMB performs this function by reviewing information requests. An agency that wants to require information submissions from the private sector must obtain OMB approval. The RegInfo.gov website lets you search for agency submissions involving information collection. A significant number of the results are tax return forms.

d. Regulatory Flexibility Act

Federal agencies that are required to publish notices of proposed rule-making must prepare and publish for comment an initial regulatory flexibility analysis. This requirement also applies to notices of proposed rulemaking for interpretive rules involving the internal revenue laws that impose information collection requirements on small business.[168] The analysis includes information about the agency's objectives, the small entities affected, and the type of compliance requirements that will be involved. You can use the Advanced Search feature of the RegInfo.gov site to search for such items. [See Illustrations 9-3 and 9-4.] Alternatively, you can search in an online service covering the Federal Register or covering Preambles to Treasury Regulations.

Illustration 9-3. Regulatory Flexibility Analysis Search

---

[167] The Paperwork Reduction Act begins at 44 U.S.C. § 3501,

[168] See 5 U.S.C. § 603. A final regulatory flexibility analysis, including a description of public comments and the agency's response, accompanies the final regulation. Id. § 604.

Illustration 9-4. Items Requiring Regulatory Flexibility Analysis

Executive Order Review Search Results

EO Review Search Criteria: Subagency=Internal Revenue Service.

Number Of Records Found: 4   New Search

Received Date	RIN	Agency	Rule Title	Status	Concluded Date	Conclusion Action
03/25/1991	1545-AP18	1545- TREAS/ IRS	Limitations on Corporate Net Operating Loss Carry Forwards	Concluded	04/25/1991	Consistent without Change
11/30/1990	1545-AN98	1545- TREAS/ IRS	Family Support Act Regulations -- Employee Business Expenses, Reporting and Withholding on Employee Business Expense Reimbursements and Allowances	Concluded	12/10/1990	Consistent without Change
09/05/1990	1545-AO56	1545- TREAS/ IRS	Nondiscrimination Requirements for Qualified Plans, Application of Average Benefit Percentage Test to ESOPs (Amends Proposed Rule Published 05/18/89 and 05/14/90)	Published	09/11/1990	Consistent without Change
01/04/1990	1545-AO08	1545- TREAS/ IRS	Excise Tax on Sale of Chemicals Which Deplete the Ozone Layer and of Products Containing Such Chemicals	Published	04/02/1990	Consistent with Change

Illustration 9-5. Preamble Discussion of Regulatory Constraints

published as final regulations in the **Federal Register**.

Special Analyses

It has been determined that this notice of proposed rulemaking is not a significant regulatory action as defined in Executive Order 12866. Therefore, a regulatory assessment is not required. It also has been determined that section 553(b) of the Administrative Procedure Act (5 U.S.C. chapter 5) does not apply to this regulation.

Pursuant to the Regulatory Flexibility Act (5 U.S.C. chapter 6), it is hereby certified that this regulation will not have a significant economic impact on a substantial number of small entities, because any effect on small entities by the rules proposed in this document flows directly from section 403 of the Energy Improvement and Extension Act of 2008, Division B of Public Law 110–343 (122 Stat. 3765, 3854 (2008)).

Section 403(a) of the Act modifies section 6045 to require that brokers report the adjusted basis of the securities and whether any gain or loss with respect to the securities is long-term or short-term when reporting the sale of a covered security. It is anticipated that this statutory requirement will fall only on financial

Section 403(d) of the Act adds new section 6045B, which requires issuer reporting by all issuers of specified securities regardless of size and even when the securities are not publicly traded. In implementing this statutory requirement, the regulation proposes to limit reporting to those items necessary to meet the Act's requirements. Additionally, the regulation proposes to mitigate the burden imposed by the Act by providing rules to permit issuers to report each action publicly as permitted by the Act instead of filing a return and furnishing each nominee or holder a statement about the action. The regulation therefore does not add to the statutory impact on small entities but instead eases this impact to the extent the statute permits.

Therefore, because this regulation will not have a significant economic impact on a substantial number of small entities, a regulatory flexibility analysis is not required. The Treasury Department and IRS request comments on the accuracy of this statement. Pursuant to section 7805(f) of the Code, this regulation has been submitted to the Chief Counsel for Advocacy of the Small Business Administration for comment on its impact on small business.

→This excerpt is from T.D. 8976, at 74 Fed. Reg. 67024 (Dec. 17, 2009). Discussion of the Paperwork Reduction Act appears at 74 Fed. Reg. 67010.

SECTION F. WORKING WITH REGULATIONS

1. Title 26, C.F.R.

a. Format

Title 26 of the C.F.R. has no subtitles and only one chapter (Chapter I – Internal Revenue Service, Department of the Treasury). Chapter I is divided into seven subchapters and numerous parts.

Table 9-3. List of Subchapters and Partial List of Parts

Subchapter A	Income Tax
Part 1	Income taxes
Part 2	Maritime construction reserve fund
Part 3	Capital construction fund
Part 4	Temporary income tax regulations under section 954 of the Internal Revenue Code
Part 5	Temporary income tax regulations under the Revenue Act of 1978
Subchapter B	Estate and Gift Taxes
Subchapter C	Employment Taxes and Collection of Income Tax at Source
Subchapter D	Miscellaneous Excise Taxes
Subchapter F	Procedure and Administration
Subchapter G	Regulations Under Tax Conventions
Subchapter H	Internal Revenue Practice
Part 601	Statement of procedural rules
Part 602	OMB control numbers under the Paperwork Reduction Act

→Subchapter E is currently Reserved.

There are subdivisions within each part, but they are not separately numbered and often lack formal titles (e.g., subpart). For example, one subdivision of Subchapter A, Part 1, is Normal Taxes and Surtaxes. Two of its subdivisions are Determination of Tax Liability and Computation of Taxable Income. Those units are themselves further subdivided.

b. Tables of Contents

Title 26 of C.F.R. has an overall table of contents, which lists parts, at the beginning of the title. In addition, it has a regulations section table of contents at the beginning of each part. A third type of table of contents exists for certain series of regulations within title 26. Regulations that merely list the contents have a 0 after the hyphen discussed in Subsection F.2.[169]

Illustration 9-6. Table of Contents for I.R.C. § 179 Regulations

Section 1.179-0 - Table of contents for section 179 expensing rules.	PDF | XML | More
Section 1.179-1 - Election to expense certain depreciable assets.	PDF | XML | More
Section 1.179-2 - Limitations on amount subject to section 179 election.	PDF | XML | More
Section 1.179-3 - Carryover of disallowed deduction.	PDF | XML | More
Section 1.179-4 - Definitions.	PDF | XML | More
Section 1.179-5 - Time and manner of making election.	PDF | XML | More
Section 1.179-6 - Effective dates.	PDF | XML | More

→FDsys offers several options for reading regulations.

c. Authority for Regulations

When a proposed, temporary, or final regulation is published in the Federal Register, the authority (Code section 7805 or another section) appears along with the regulation text. When a temporary or final regulation is published in C.F.R., the authority information is not part of the regulation's text but it is available elsewhere in C.F.R.

Authority information in C.F.R. appears immediately after a listing of sections in a particular part.

Illustration 9-7. Partial Authority Listing for Part 26

Internal Revenue Service, Treasury   **§ 26.2600-1**

§ 25.7701-1   Tax return preparer.

(a) *In general.* For the definition of a tax return preparer, see §301.7701-15 of this chapter.

(b) *Effective/applicability date.* This section is applicable to returns and claims for refund filed, and advice provided, after December 31, 2008.

[T.D. 9436, 73 FR 78452, Dec. 22, 2008]

PART 26—GENERATION-SKIPPING TRANSFER TAX REGULATIONS UNDER THE TAX REFORM ACT OF 1986

Sec.
26.2600-1   Table of contents.
26.2601-1   Effective dates.
26.2611-1   Generation-skipping transfer defined.
26.2612-1   Definitions.
26.2613-1   Skip person.
26.2632-1   Allocation of GST exemption.
26.2641-1   Applicable rate of tax.
26.2642-1   Inclusion ratio.

26.6694-2   Penalties for understatement due to an unreasonable position.
26.6694-3   Penalty for understatement due to willful, reckless, or intentional conduct.
26.6694-4   Extension of period of collection when preparer pays 15 percent of a penalty for understatement of taxpayer's liability and certain other procedural matters.
26.6695-1   Other assessable penalties with respect to the preparation of tax returns for other persons.
26.6696-1   Claims for credit or refund by tax return preparers.
26.7701-1   Tax return preparer.

AUTHORITY: 26 U.S.C. 7805 and 26 U.S.C. 2663.

Section 26.2632-1 also issued under 26 U.S.C. 2632 and 2663.
Section 26.2642-4 also issued under 26 U.S.C. 2632 and 2663.
Section 26.2642-6 also issued under 26 U.S.C. 2642.
Section 26.2662-1 also issued under 26 U.S.C. 2662.
Section 26.2663-2 also issued under 26 U.S.C. 2632 and 2663.
Section 26.6060-1 also issued under 26 U.S.C. 6060(a).

---

[169] Occasionally, a regulation ending in -0 provides effective dates instead of a table of contents. See, e.g., Treas. Reg. § 1.170-0.

2. Regulations Numbering Scheme

a. Subdivisions

Most regulations section numbers have two segments, which are separated by a decimal point, and a third segment, which follows a hyphen. The first segment, often called the **prefix**, indicates where the regulation appears; prefixes use the part numbers illustrated in Table 9-3.

The segment that follows the decimal point generally indicates the Code section being interpreted. Thus, Treas. Reg. § 1.106-1 interprets Code section 106. The third segment, which follows the hyphen, is similar to the subdivisions used for Code subsections and is discussed in Subsection F.4.

Each regulations section is further subdivided into

- paragraphs (e.g., Treas. Reg. § 1.23-2(a));

- subparagraphs (e.g., Treas. Reg. § 1.23-2(e)(2)); and

- subdivisions (e.g., Treas. Reg. § 1.23-2(d)(4)(iv)).

The regulations do not uniformly follow the nomenclature above. For example, Treas. Reg. § 1.61-2(d)(1) contains the following language: "Except as provided in paragraph (d)(6)(i) of this section ...."

Smaller units exist but do not receive formal names. For example, Treas. Reg. § 1.274-2(b)(1)(iii)(a) says: "Except as otherwise provided in (b) or (c) of this subdivision ...." The subdivision referred to is (iii); (a), (b), and (c) are smaller units of (iii).

b. Examples

Regulations frequently contain examples illustrating how the regulation applies to particular facts. These may appear in a separate Examples subdivision (e.g., Treas. Reg. § 1.119-1(f)) or as part of a subdivision to which the example applies (e.g., Treas. Reg. § 1.162-5(b)(3)(ii)). In some cases, a regulations section will be titled Examples (e.g., Prop. Treas. Reg. § 1.1058-2).

3. Significance of Regulations Prefixes

The prefix is critical for finding the correct regulation. First, regulations in different parts may interpret the same Code section. For example, Treas. Reg. §§ 1.7520-1, 20.7520-1, and 25.7520-1 all interpret Code section 7520. Differences in their texts reflect their application to different taxes.

Second, regulations in some parts don't interpret a Code section but the number following the prefix is a Code section number. For example, Treas. Reg. § 1.1-1 is an income tax regulation for Code section 1. Treas. Reg. § 2.1-1 is a definition section dealing with the maritime construction reserve fund; it has nothing to do with Code section 1.[170] Although its prefix (2) indicated it related to the maritime construction reserve fund [Table 9-3], that information alone would not have told you that the regulation had nothing to do with Code section 1.

4. Relationship of Code and Regulations Subdivisions

The portion of the regulation that follows the hyphen does not indicate the Code subsection involved. In fact, there may be significantly more regulations sections than Code subsections. Table 9-4 illustrates the relationship of Code and regulations sections for Code section 61(a).[171]

Table 9-4. _Relationship of Code and Regulations Subdivisions_

Code Subsection	Regulations Section
61(a)	1.61-1, 1.61-14, 1.61-22
61(a)(1)	1.61-2, 1.61-15, 1.61-21
61(a)(2)	1.61-3, 1.61-4, 1.61-5
61(a)(3)	1.61-6
61(a)(4)	1.61-7
61(a)(5)	1.61-8
61(a)(6)	1.61-8
61(a)(7)	1.61-9
61(a)(8)	1.61-10
61(a)(9)	1.61-10
61(a)(10)	1.61-10
61(a)(11)	1.61-11
61(a)(12)	1.61-12
61(a)(13)	1.61-13
61(a)(14)	1.61-13
61(a)(15)	1.61-13

→Some Code subdivisions have more than one regulations section; others share a regulations section.

---

[170] Regulations in Part 601 follow this pattern. Treas. Reg. § 601.101, for example, has nothing to do with I.R.C. § 101.

[171] The relationship between Treas. Reg. § 1.61-22, issued in 2003, and paragraphs in I.R.C. § 61(a) varies based on how the particular split-dollar life insurance arrangement is analyzed.

5. Letters Preceding Hyphen in Section Number

a. Formats

Most section numbers follow this format: Treas. Reg. § 1.61-1. Two other formats include a capital or lower case letter before the hyphen.

Capital letters must be used if the underlying Code section includes a capital letter. For example, Treas. Reg. § 1.263A-1 is a regulation for Code section 263A. Capital letters may also appear even though the Code section does not include a capital letter. Treas. Reg. § 1.170A-1 is an example of this situation. Section 170 regulations that lack the A (e.g., Treas. Reg. § 1.170-1) interpret the statute before its 1969 amendment.

Some regulations include lower case letters before the hyphen. Treas. Reg. § 1.672(a)-1 illustrates that format. The letter in parentheses may indicate the relevant Code subsection but does not necessarily do so.

b. Location in C.F.R.

If a section number includes a letter before the hyphen, it follows the regulations for the Code section that don't include a letter. If more than one letter is used, those regulations appear in alphabetical order. Temporary regulations always include a capital T, but it appears after the hyphen. Temporary regulations appear in the normal number order in C.F.R.

Illustration 9-8. Order of Section 25 Regulations in e-CFR

§1.25-1t	Credit for interest paid on certain home mortgages (Temporary).
§1.25-2t	Amount of credit (Temporary).
§1.25-3	Qualified mortgage credit certificate.
§1.25-3t	Qualified mortgage credit certificate (Temporary).
§1.25-4t	Qualified mortgage credit certificate program (Temporary).

→Although e-CFR uses a lower case t, the correct usage for a temporary regulation is an upper case T.

Illustrations 9-9 through 9-11 show the regulations order for Code section 142 in LexisNexis, the 2010 Standard Federal Tax Reporter (SFTR), and e-CFR. Each uses a different order.

Illustration 9-9. Order of Section 142 Regulations in LexisNexis

§ 1.142-0 Table of Contents.

§ 1.142-1 Exempt facility bonds.

§ 1.142(f)(4)-1 Manner of making election to terminate tax-exempt bond financing.

§ 1.142-2 Remedial actions.

§ 1.142-3 Refunding issues. [Reserved]

§ 1.142-4 Use of proceeds to provide a facility.

§ 1.142(a)(5)-1 Exempt facility bonds: Sewage facilities.

Illustration 9-10. Order of Section 142 Regulations in SFTR

§1.142-0. Table of contents

§1.142-1. Exempt facility bonds

§1.142-2. Remedial actions

§1.142-3. Refunding issues

§1.142-4. Use of proceeds to provide a facility

§1.103-7. Industrial development bonds

§1.103-8. Interest on bonds to finance certain exempt facilities

§1.103-8. Interest on bonds to finance certain exempt facilities, LR-190-78, 8/22/84.

§1.103-8. Interest on bonds to finance certain exempt facilities, LR-269-84, 11/7/85.

§1.103-8. Interest on bonds to finance certain exempt facilities, REG-140492-02, 9/16/2009.

§17.1. Industrial development bonds used to provide solid waste disposal facilities; temporary rules (Temporary)

§17.1. Industrial development bonds used to provide solid waste disposal facilities; temporary rules, REG-140492-02, 9/16/2009.

§1.103-9. Interest on bonds to finance industrial parks

§1.103-11. Bonds held by substantial users

§5c.103-1. Leases and capital expenditures (Temporary)

§5c.103-2. Leases and industrial development bonds (Temporary)

§5f.103-2. Public approval of industrial development bonds (Temporary)

§1.142(a)(5)-1. Exempt facility bonds: Sewage facilities

§1.142(a)(6)-1. Exempt facility bonds: solid waste disposal facilities, REG-140492-02, 9/16/2009.

§1.142(f)(4)-1. Manner of making election to terminate tax-exempt bond financing

→Standard Federal Tax Reporter includes final and temporary regulations, which are in C.F.R., and proposed regulations (REG), which are not. It also includes regulations that are not strictly tied to section 142.

Illustration 9-11. Order of Section 142 Regulations in e-CFR

§1.142-0	Table of contents.
§1.142-1	Exempt facility bonds.
§1.142-2	Remedial actions.
§1.142-3	Refunding Issues.--[Reserved]
§1.142-4	Use of proceeds to provide a facility.
§1.142(a)(5)-1	Exempt facility bonds: Sewage facilities.
§1.142(f)(4)-1	Manner of making election to terminate tax-exempt bond financing.

6. Regulations Issued for Prior Internal Revenue Codes

Regulations issued for 1954 Code sections also apply to the 1986 Code to the extent Code sections (or their numbers) remained unchanged. Regulations interpreting the 1939 Code followed a different numbering system. Unless I indicate otherwise, you can assume that references in this book cover regulations interpreting the 1986 Code.

7. Regulations for Other C.F.R. Titles

Each C.F.R. title has its own numbering system. The most common difference between Treasury regulations in 26 C.F.R. and other regulations relates to material following the decimal point. Table 9-5 illustrates tax-related section numbers from three other C.F.R. titles.

Table 9-5. Regulation Numbers in Other C.F.R. Titles

Citation	Caption
27 C.F.R. § 53.61	Imposition and Rates of Tax
29 C.F.R. § 2510.3-2	Employee Pension Benefit Plan
31 C.F.R. § 10.1	Director of the Office of Professional Responsibility

SECTION G. DEFINITIONS IN REGULATIONS

As was true for the Code itself, the regulations frequently define terms within individual sections, and a definition in one section may apply in interpreting another section. Some groups of regulations include a definitions section [Illustration 9-6]. In addition, several regulations sections enlarge upon definitions found in Internal Revenue Code Subtitle F, Chapter 79.[172] Finally, because several Code sections defer to other sta-

---

[172] See, e.g., Treas. Reg. § 301.7701-1.

tutes or agency interpretations, you may have to look for definitions in Statutes at Large, United States Code, or other titles of C.F.R.[173]

SECTION H. RULES AFFECTING MULTIPLE REGULATIONS SECTIONS

As is the case for the Code, rules appearing in a regulation section may apply only to that section, or a subdivision thereof, or they may apply to several sections. See, for example, Treas. Reg. § 1.414(r)-3(c)(5)(iii)(A):

> Solely for purposes of the separateness rules of this section and the assignment rules of section 1.414(r)-7, if an employee changes status as described in paragraph (c)(5)(iii)(B) of this section, an employer may, for up to three consecutive testing years after the base year (within the meaning of paragraph (c)(5)(iii)(B)(1) or (2) of this section), treat the employee as providing the same level of service to its lines of business as the employee provided in the base year.

SECTION I. LOCATING REGULATIONS DOCUMENTS

The first step in locating administrative documents is determining which items you need. The following paragraphs divide documents by type rather than by where you can find them.

Many of the items covered in this section can be located on government websites. Some items are included in more than one such site. These sites do not have identical coverage dates or search functions. Several items, particularly those of historical interest, are likely to be available only in print or microform or from subscription-based websites.

1. Unified Agenda and Priority Guidance Plan

The Unified Agenda of the Federal Regulatory and Deregulatory Actions and the Priority Guidance Plan relate to planned regulatory action. Unless you are tracking agency plans over time, you probably need only the most recent versions of each. Documents for the current year (and several prior years) are available on government websites.[174]

---

[173] See, e.g., I.R.C. § 4064(b)(1)(B): "The term 'automobile' does not include any vehicle which is treated as a nonpassenger automobile under the rules which were prescribed by the Secretary of Transportation ...."

[174] The RegInfo.gov site currently includes Agendas issued since fall 1995 and will eventually cover Agendas since spring 1983. You can also find Agendas issued since fall 2007 on the Regulations.gov website. The IRS website's Electronic Reading Room page includes Priority Guidance Plans since 1999.

a. Unified Agenda

The Unified Agenda is issued twice a year and published in the Federal Register. It is often referred to as the Semiannual Agenda or the Semiannual Regulatory Agenda.

The Treasury Department and agencies within its umbrella are grouped together in the Agenda. Agencies in addition to the IRS include the Alcohol and Tobacco Tax and Trade Bureau, the Comptroller of the Currency, and the Office of Thrift Supervision. In some instances, such as projects involving employee benefits, you may also need to consult the Agendas produced by other government agencies.

Although the Agenda is issued semiannually, a Regulatory Plan is required in the fall Agenda. That plan indicates the most important items that should be issued within the fiscal year.

The Treasury Department currently includes most of its regulatory projects only in the searchable RegInfo.gov database. Since fall 2007, it has limited its Federal Register listings to the Regulatory Plan and to rules that are subject to the Regulatory Flexibility Act.

The RegInfo.gov site groups projects by agency within the Treasury Department. Within each agency grouping, it subdivides them into five categories: Prerule Stage; Proposed Rule Stage; Final Rule Stage; Long-Term Actions; and Completed Actions. The items in each category appear in RIN order.[175] That number does not indicate the regulation section number, project number, or underlying Code section number.

If you know a project's RIN but not the actual project number, you can easily find it online in the Agenda. You can also search by project number or Code section using the site's Advanced Search function. If you are unsure whether a project exists, you can search for projects by agency.

The government currently includes Agendas since fall 2007 on the Regulations.gov website. Despite their similar names, the RegInfo.gov and Regulations.gov sites differ in their primary focus. RegInfo.gov lets you search for regulations projects based on a variety of criteria [Illustration 9-12]. Regulations.gov lets you search for pending regulations projects, comment on them, and read comments submitted by others. It is discussed in Subsection I.5.

---

[175] Projects appeared in sequence number order when the Treasury Department included its full Agenda in the Federal Register.

Subscription-based services, such as LexisNexis and Westlaw, that have Federal Register databases provide access to the Agenda. The Tax Analysts OneDisc also includes the Agenda. Its version is arranged in Code section order [Illustration 9-15] and can also be searched by word or phrase, including Code section number.

Illustration 9-12. Advanced Search in RegInfo.gov

RIN

Major
☐ Yes   ☐ No   ☐ Undetermined

Included in the Regulatory Plan
☐ Yes   ☐ No

RFA Section 610 Review
☐ Section 610 Review
☐ Completion of a Section 610 Review
☐ Rulemaking Resulting From a Section 610 Review

Government Levels Affected
☐ Federal   ☐ Local
☐ State   ☐ Tribal
☐ None   ☐ Undetermined

RIN Status
☐ First Time Published in The Unified Agenda
☐ Previously Published in The Unified Agenda

Agenda Stage of Rulemaking
☐ Prerule Stage
☐ Proposed Rule Stage   ☐ Final Rule Stage
☐ Long-Term Actions   ☐ Completed Actions

Federalism Implications
☐ Yes   ☐ No   ☐ Undetermined

Agency reported Affected Sectors using NAICS codes
☐ Yes   ☐ No

Small Entities Affected
☐ Business
☐ Governmental Jurisdictions
☐ Organizations   ☐ No   ☐ Undetermined

Unfunded Mandates
☐ State, Local, or Tribal Governments
☐ Private Sector
☐ No   ☐ Undetermined

Priority
☐ Economically Significant
☐ Other Significant
☐ Substantive, Nonsignificant
☐ Routine and Frequent   ☐ Info./Admin./Other

Regulatory Flexibility Analysis Required
☐ Business
☐ Governmental Jurisdictions
☐ Organizations
☐ No   ☐ Undetermined

Agency Has Prepared or Plans to Prepare Statement of Energy Effects   ☐ Yes   ☐ No   ☐ Undetermined

Agency has reported Compliance Cost Information
☐ Yes   ☐ No

International Impacts
☐ Yes   ☐ No   ☐ Not Collected

Legal Deadline - Action
☐ NPRM   ☐ Final   ☐ Other

Legal Deadline - Source
☐ Statutory   ☐ Judicial

Timetable - FR Citation

Timetable - Action(s) *
ANPRM
ANPRM Comment Period End
Begin Review

Terms **
"1012"

In Following Field(s) *
All
Abstract
Additional Information

→I reached this search screen after first entering Department of Treasury and Internal Revenue Service in the Agenda Advanced Search screen.

→I searched for 1012 to find any projects concerning I.R.C. § 1012.

Illustration 9-13. Agenda Search Results

View Rule

Printer-Friendly Version   Download RIN Data in XML

| TREAS/IRS | RIN: 1545-BI66 | Publication ID: Fall 2009 |

Title: oBasis Reporting by Securities Brokers

Abstract: This action proposes new and amended regulations under 26 CFR part 1 to provide guidance regarding the requirement that brokers begin reporting the basis of securities sold by customers on Form 1099-B. The requirement for basis reporting was added by section 403 of the Energy Improvement and Extension Act of 2008 enacted on October 3, 2008. The Act also amended section 1012 to provide new rules for determining the basis of certain securities subject to the new reporting requirements. The new reporting requirements and basis rules generally begin to take effect on January 1, 2011.

Agency: Department of the Treasury(TREAS)	**Priority:** Substantive, Nonsignificant
RIN Status: First time published in the Unified Agenda	**Agenda Stage of Rulemaking:** Proposed Rule Stage
Major: Undetermined	**Unfunded Mandates:** Undetermined

CFR Citation: 26 CFR 1 (To search for a specific CFR, visit the Code of Federal Regulations.)

Legal Authority: 26 USC 1012; 26 USC 6045; 26 USC 6045A; 26 USC 6045B; 26 USC 7805; ...

Legal Deadline: None

Timetable:

Action	Date	FR Cite
NPRM	12/00/2009	

Additional Information: REG-101896-09 Drafting attorney: Stephen J. Schaeffer (202) 622-4910 Reviewing attorney: James C. Gibbons (202) 622-4910 CC: PA: Branch 1

Regulatory Flexibility Analysis Required: No	**Government Levels Affected:** None

Federalism: No

Included in the Regulatory Plan: No

RIN Data Printed in the FR: No

Agency Contact:
Stephen J. Schaeffer

→The RIN for most tax-related items begins with 1545. Many ERISA projects begin with 1210.

Illustration 9-14. Example of Final Rule Stage Entry

View Rule

Printer-Friendly Version   Download RIN Data in XML

| TREAS/IRS | RIN: 1545-BH83 | Publication ID: Fall 2009 |

Title: Guidance on the Residential Mortgage Insurance Deduction

Abstract: These proposed regulations with cross-reference to temporary regulations provide guidance concerning how to allocate prepaid mortgage insurance premiums to determine the proper deduction in a particular taxable year for individual taxpayer. These proposed regulations also provide guidance to report entities receiving prepaid mortgage insurance premiums in issuing the Form 1098.

Agency: Department of the Treasury(TREAS)	**Priority:** Substantive, Nonsignificant
RIN Status: Previously published in the Unified Agenda	**Agenda Stage of Rulemaking:** Final Rule Stage
Major: No	**Unfunded Mandates:** No

CFR Citation: 26 CFR 1.163-11

Legal Authority: 26 USC 163(h); 26 USC 7805

Legal Deadline: None

Timetable:

Action	Date	FR Cite
NPRM	05/07/2009	74 FR 21295
NPRM Comment Period End	08/05/2009	
Final Action	06/00/2010	

Additional Information: REG-107271-08 Drafting attorney: Christopher F. Kane (202) 622-4950 Reviewing attorney: Christopher F. Kane (202) 622-4950 Treasury attorney: Jeanne F. Ross (202) 622-4950 CC: ITA

Regulatory Flexibility Analysis Required: No	**Government Levels Affected:** None
Small Entities Affected: No	**Federalism:** No

Included in the Regulatory Plan: No

RIN Data Printed in the FR: No

Related RINs: Related to 1545-BD82, Related to 1545-BH84

Agency Contact:
Christopher F. Kane

→Note the link to the NPRM in the Federal Register.

Illustration 9-15. Regulatory Agenda Search in OneDisc

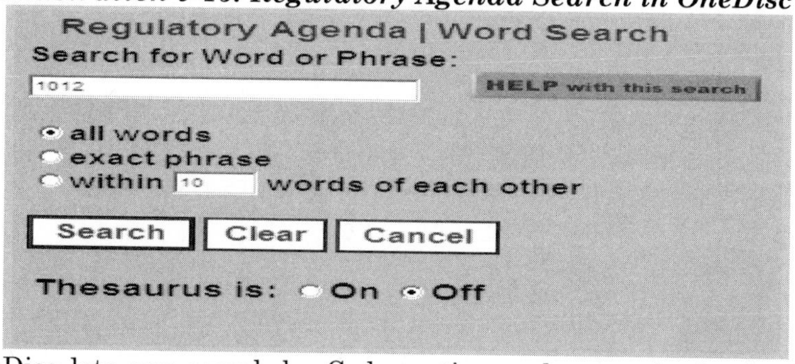

→OneDisc lets you search by Code section or key words. It also has a Code section table for projects. I again looked for 1012.

Illustration 9-16. Results of OneDisc Search

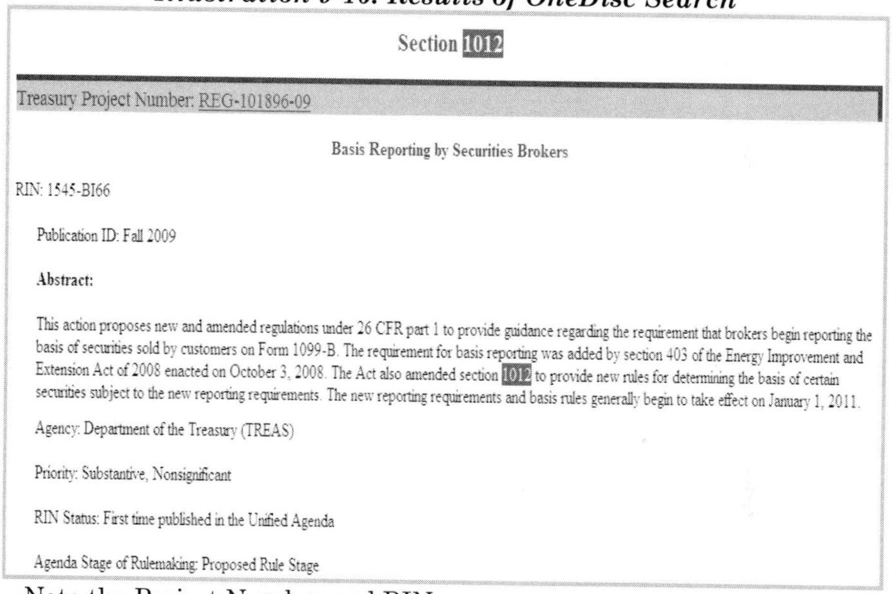

→Note the Project Number and RIN.

b. Priority Guidance Plan

The Priority Guidance Plan, which has also been referred to as the Business Plan and the Guidance Priority Plan, includes both regulations and other forms of guidance that Treasury and IRS plan to issue during the year. Until 2002, the Plan covered a calendar year. Beginning with the plan issued in 2002, it covers a fiscal year ending June 30. It is covered by newsletters such as Daily Tax Report and Tax Notes. Although you can find Plans for several years on the Treasury website, it is easier to locate all the Plans on the IRS site.

Illustration 9-17. 2009–2010 Priority Guidance Plan

INSURANCE COMPANIES AND PRODUCTS

1. Final regulations on the exchange of property for an annuity contract. Proposed regulations were published on October 18, 2006.

2. Guidance on the tax treatment of a partial exchange or partial annuitization of an annuity contract.

3. Guidance on the classification of certain cell captive insurance arrangements. Previous guidance was published in Not. 2008-19.

4. Guidance on tax issues arising under §807 as a result of the adoption by the National Association of Insurance Commissioners (NAIC) of an Actuarial Guideline setting forth the Commissioners' Annuity Reserve Valuation Methodology for variable annuities (AG 43).

5. Revenue ruling regarding the tax-free exchange of life insurance contracts subject to §264(f).

→The Guidance Plan covers regulations, rulings, and other guidance.

2. Proposed, Temporary, and Final Regulations

a. Federal Register

The Federal Register includes the text, including Preambles, of proposed, temporary, and final regulations. It also includes corrections that are filed after the initial publication. Because it includes the Preambles, you may prefer reading a new regulation in the Federal Register even if it also appears in C.F.R. If the IRS is simply amending an existing regulation, the Federal Register version includes only the amendment and not the full text. Illustration 6-3 illustrates an analogous situation for amendments to the I.R.C.

The government's FDsys site carries the Federal Register beginning with the 1994 volume. You can search the Federal Register by project number, Federal Register date, RIN, or underlying Code section.

If you need a volume of the Federal Register issued before 1994, your library may have it in print or microform. It is also available in subscription services, including HeinOnline (since 1936), LexisNexis (since 1980), and Westlaw (since 1936).

b. Code of Federal Regulations

The C.F.R. includes the text of temporary and final regulations. It also includes all T.D. numbers, dates, and Federal Register citations for each regulation.[176] The beginning of each C.F.R. part lists the authority (I.R.C. § 7805 or another Code section) for regulations in that part. The C.F.R. does not include proposed regulations, and it does not include Preambles.

Because the C.F.R. section numbers generally correspond to Code section numbers, it is easier to find temporary and final regulations in the C.F.R. than in the Federal Register.[177] As noted above, you might choose to use the Federal Register because it includes Preambles.

Although many libraries carry the print softbound C.F.R. volumes, they are best used for historical purposes. The government does not update C.F.R. volumes every time an agency promulgates a new regulation. Instead it republishes C.F.R. titles on an annual basis; several titles are replaced each calendar quarter. The annual reissue of Title 26 includes regulations issued as of April 1. Searching C.F.R. print updates for later material is a tedious process.[178]

The government's FDsys site carries the C.F.R. beginning with the 2007 volume.[179] If you know the regulations section number, you can go to it directly because C.F.R. is arranged in regulations section order. If you know the Code section number only, you can browse the regulations for that Code section until you find the relevant regulation. Alternatively, you can search the C.F.R. on FDsys by citation, T.D. number, date, or phrase.

The government does not update the online C.F.R. any more often than it updates the print version. To avoid missing temporary and final regulations issued since the last C.F.R. update, use e-CFR instead of C.F.R. You can also use a subscription service, such as LexisNexis or Westlaw, which updates its C.F.R. database as new regulations are issued.

---

[176] If a 1954 Code regulation was originally published before 1960, the IRS may have republished it that year in T.D. 6498, 6500, or 6516. The C.F.R. begins the regulation's history at that point.

[177] The method for issuing regulations in the Federal Register makes that publication analogous to Statutes at Large for revenue acts. Each T.D. is listed separately by publication date rather than by Code section. The Code of Federal Regulations, which is in section number order, is analogous to United States Code for statutes.

[178] There is also an electronic version of the C.F.R.'s List of Sections Affected (LSA). Basic legal research texts discuss using LSA. Because it is easier to use e-CFR, this book ignores the LSA search process.

[179] The GPO Access site, which FDsys is replacing, begins its C.F.R. coverage in 1996.

If you need a volume of C.F.R. that precedes the date on which the government began publishing it electronically, you may be able to find it in the library's print or microform collection. It is also available in subscription services, including HeinOnline (since 1938), LexisNexis (since 1981), and Westlaw (since 1984).

Illustration 9-18. Search in C.F.R. for Disregarded Entity

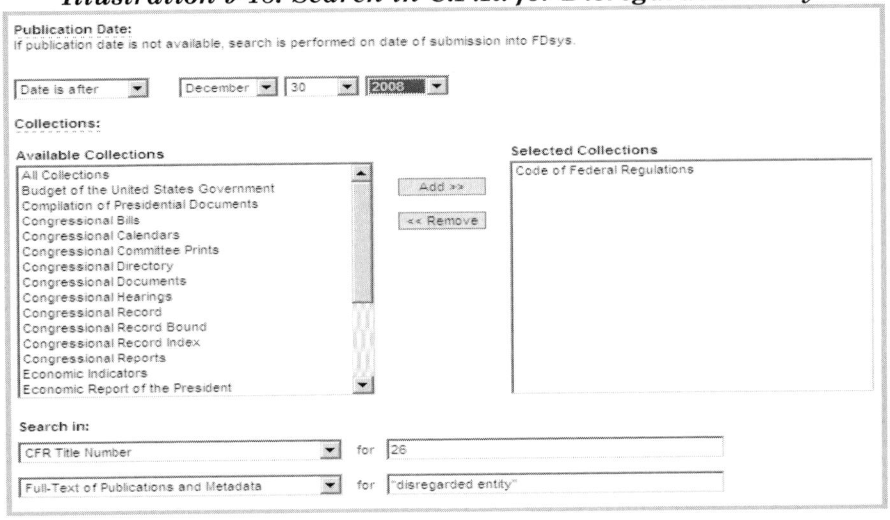

Illustration 9-19. Disregarded Entity Regulations

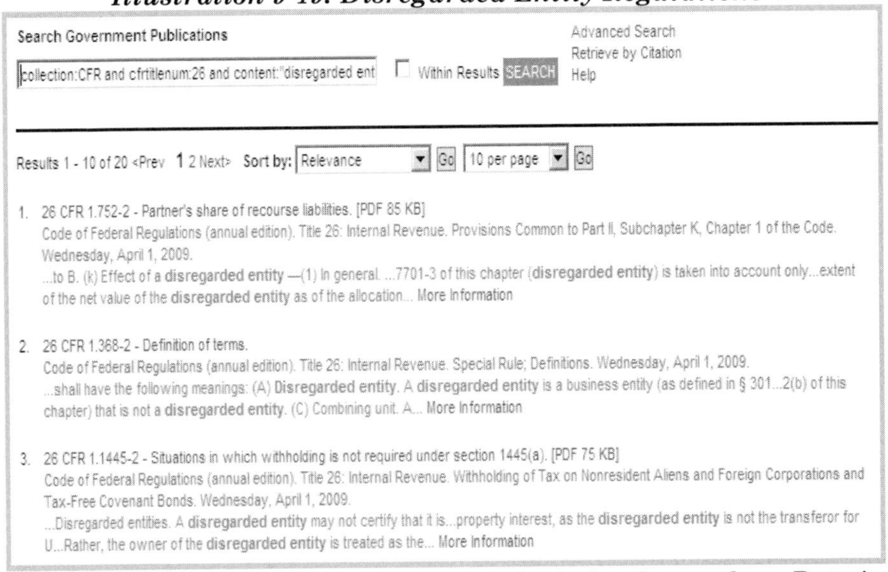

→You can sort results by relevance, alphabetical order, or date. Date is particularly relevant if you are searching multiple years' volumes at once.

c. Subscription Services That Include Regulations

Checkpoint, IntelliConnect, LexisNexis, Westlaw, and other online services have databases covering regulations. These services also include access to Preambles that accompany regulations. DVD services, such as OnPoint and OneDisc, also include regulations. Because DVD services are issued only monthly, you may prefer web-based searching.

Illustration 9-20. Search in OnPoint for Proposed Regulations

Search by Section, Regulation Type -and/or- Keywords

| 999xircsec
9xircsec
caution
Circ230
FR
irsreg
Preamble
prop
reg
td
TR
uid :cir230;31
uid :propamnd;10.27
uid :propamnd;1.1001
uid :propamnd;1.1001
uid :propamnd;1.101 | Section(s) or TD Number

[   ]

[   ]

[   ]

Examples: Code: 402xircsec,
402(a)xircsec
Regulation: 1.402(a)-1, 1.401(a)-1(a) | Fill in one or more of the fields with the Code and/or Reg section number, subsection number or pragraph number. Or fill in the TD number. | Limit by Type or Types of Regulations. Fill in one or more fields with abbreviation(s).

[prop] [   ] [   ]

fr = Final Regulations
prop = Proposed Regulations
td = Treasury Decisions |

Keywords

[basis broker]

Partitions with hits - 10

basis - 3544 ─┐
broker - 188 ├& - 10
[prop] - 1194 ─┘

[OK]   [Cancel]   [Help]

→The OnPoint DVD search template lets you search by type of regulation, Code section number, regulations citation, T.D. number, or key words. You can search on combinations of these fields.

Illustration 9-21. Search Results in OnPoint

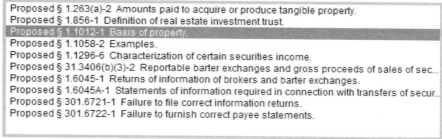

Proposed § 1.263(a)-2 Amounts paid to acquire or produce tangible property.
Proposed § 1.856-1 Definition of real estate investment trust.
Proposed § 1.1012-1 Basis of property.
Proposed § 1.1058-2 Examples.
Proposed § 1.1296-6 Characterization of certain securities income.
Proposed § 31.3406(b)(3)-2 Reportable barter exchanges and gross proceeds of sales of sec...
Proposed § 1.6045-1 Returns of information of brokers and barter exchanges.
Proposed § 1.6045A-1 Statements of information required in connection with transfers of secur...
Proposed § 301.6721-1 Failure to file correct information returns.
Proposed § 301.6722-1 Failure to furnish correct payee statements.

→If I had inserted 1012xircsec in the search screen shown in Illustration 9-20, I would have retrieved only the regulation I needed.

Looseleaf services, in particular United States Tax Reporter (USTR) and Standard Federal Tax Reporter (SFTR), include regulations text in their compilation volumes; Preambles are in separate volumes. USTR is available in print and on Checkpoint and Westlaw; SFTR is available in print and on IntelliConnect. Other tax-oriented services provide print versions of tax regulations. These include Mertens, Federal Tax Regulations, published in annual softbound volumes with updating throughout the year in a looseleaf Current Developments binder.

Looseleaf services frequently include proposed regulations in their compilation volumes along with temporary and final regulations. [See Illustration 9-22.] If a service instead files proposed regulations in a separate volume, it may arrange them by Federal Register date. Those services generally include a table that cross-references from the underlying Code or regulations section to the appropriate page, paragraph, or section in the looseleaf service. They are unlikely to have tables cross-referencing project numbers. If you use the service's electronic version, filing method is less important, as you can reach regulations using hyperlinks.

Illustration 9-22. United States Tax Reporter Regulations Listing

Select Top Line link type:

Regulations ▼

Filter Links

▶ Expl ▶ Annot ▶ FTC ▶ Regs ▶ Com Rpts ▶ Hist ▶ New Law Analysis

§ 1012 Basis of property—cost.

▤ Reg §1.1012-1 Basis of property.

▤ Prop Reg §1.1012-1 Basis of property.

▤ Reg §1.1012-2 Transfers in part a sale and in part a

→The proposed regulation from Illustrations 9-20 and 9-21 follows the existing final regulation in this looseleaf service.

3. Preambles

The Federal Register includes the Preambles for each proposed, temporary, and final regulation with the regulation text. Excerpts or full text also appear in the Internal Revenue Bulletin and Cumulative Bulletin.[180]

Tax-oriented looseleaf services don't publish Preambles with the regulations text. If they print the Preambles, they do so in separate volumes.[181] Mertens, Federal Tax Regulations, publishes Preambles for tax

---

[180] Preambles for proposed regulations were added to the C.B. in 1981.

[181] If a regulation was issued in both proposed and temporary format, a looseleaf service may carry only the Preamble to the temporary regulation.

regulations in looseleaf volumes. Coverage begins in 1985. Standard Federal Tax Reporter prints Preambles for proposed regulations in its U.S. Tax Cases Advance Sheets volume; it includes current year Preambles for T.D.s in the Regulations Status Table in its New Matters volume. United States Tax Reporter prints Preambles to proposed regulations in a separate volume for Preambles; it prints current year Preambles for T.D.s in the IRS Rulings section of its Recent Developments volume.

IntelliConnect includes the SFTR service, and Checkpoint includes USTR. If you use these looseleaf services online, simply use their Preamble option. Other electronic services may include Preambles as a separate database or in their Federal Register coverage. Illustrations 9-1 and 9-5 show excerpts from a Preamble.

4. Earlier Versions of Regulations

The discussion of the Federal Register and C.F.R. in this section listed services that covered earlier versions of those documents. This subsection continues that discussion.

a. 1954 and 1986 Codes

Prior language may be important for evaluating recent changes in a regulation or for research involving a completed transaction. If you need the language of a 1954 or 1986 Code regulation, you can find it in United States Code Congressional & Administrative News—Federal Tax Regulations. This service has separate volumes for each year since 1954 and prints regulations in effect on January 1 of the particular year. Electronic services such as Westlaw have "Prior" links that give access to earlier versions of the C.F.R. going back to the early 1980s.

If you need a regulation that was both issued and withdrawn within a single calendar year and thus might be omitted from a USCCAN or FDsys search for a single year, two other services may be of assistance. These services are Cumulative Changes and Mertens, Law of Federal Income Taxation. They are described later in this subsection.

If you lack access to a service that tracks regulations, make a list of T.D. numbers for the regulation you are tracing. Those numbers appear immediately after the particular regulation in C.F.R. and in most other versions of the regulations. The T.D.s are published in the Cumulative Bulletins, which your library is likely to carry.[182] The Cumulative Bulle-

---

[182] Finding Lists in the CCH and RIA citators indicate which volume of the Internal Revenue Bulletin or Cumulative Bulletin contains each T.D. For recent items, RIA is more likely to refer to the paragraph in United States Tax Reporter.

tin is also available online. LexisNexis begins coverage in 1954; HeinOnline and Westlaw include all volumes since 1919.

Note one limitation in using T.D. numbers to find older versions of regulations. The IRS republished many 1954 Code regulations that were issued before 1960 in T.D. 6498, 6500, or 6516. The USCCAN service ignores the pre-1960 publication in its history notes; Cumulative Changes omits the 1960 T.D. numbers but includes the pre-1960 T.D.s. If you use any service to find T.D. numbers, be sure you know how that service treats those early items.

(1) Cumulative Changes

Tables of amendments cover all regulations sections for each tax; individual sections do not have their own charts. Each table indicates the original and all amending T.D. numbers and filing dates and provides a Cumulative Bulletin or Internal Revenue Bulletin citation.

The 1986 service also includes cross-references to United States Tax Reporter. A numerically ordered Table of Amending TDs indicates the purpose, date, and C.B. or I.R.B. citation for each regulation issued.[183]

The tables follow the regulations part designations. As a result, they do not follow a strict Code section numerical sequence. The 1954 series includes tables for regulations that have been redesignated or replaced.

Immediately following the tables, the editors print prior versions of each regulation. Older materials note changes in italics and use footnotes to indicate stricken language; recent materials do not use this format. Cumulative Changes includes the T.D. number and the dates of approval and of filing for each version of a regulation.

(2) Mertens, Law of Federal Income Taxation

Until the mid-1990s, Mertens, Law of Federal Income Taxation, published a Regulations series. That series published all income tax regulations issued or amended within a given time span (two or more years per volume).

---

[183] Although T.D. 6500, a 1960 republication of existing income tax regulations is not formally included, Cumulative Changes does list the original pre-1960 T.D. A cautionary note warns the user to remember that pre-1960 regulations were republished in T.D. 6500. T.D. 6498 (procedure and administration) and T.D. 6516 (withholding tax) receive similar treatment. None of these T.D.s appears in the Cumulative Bulletin.

b. 1939 Code and Earlier

Early regulations don't follow the regulations format used elsewhere in this book. Initially they were issued with respect to individual revenue acts and divided into articles rather than section numbers. The first named set of regulations (Regulations Number 33) was issued in 1914.[184] The article numbers did not correspond to act section numbers.

The Federal Register became available online in 1994 and in print in 1936. Thus, it is not a good source for finding early regulations. Even for years it covers, it is tedious to search in print. In many libraries, the best source for 1939 Code and earlier regulations will be the Cumulative Bulletin. It began publication in 1919; the first T.D. it includes is 2836.

The Government Printing Office published Treasury Decisions–Internal Revenue from 1899 until 1942. It covers 1898 through July 9, 1942. The current T.D. numbering system began in 1900 with the third volume. Many early T.D.s look less like regulations and more like "public" private letter rulings.[185]

HeinOnline lets you browse the C.F.R. back to its 1938 edition. Its CFR Citation Locator lets you retrieve multiple years' regulations. You can search by title, part, or section.

Illustration 9-23. Searching C.F.R. in HeinOnline

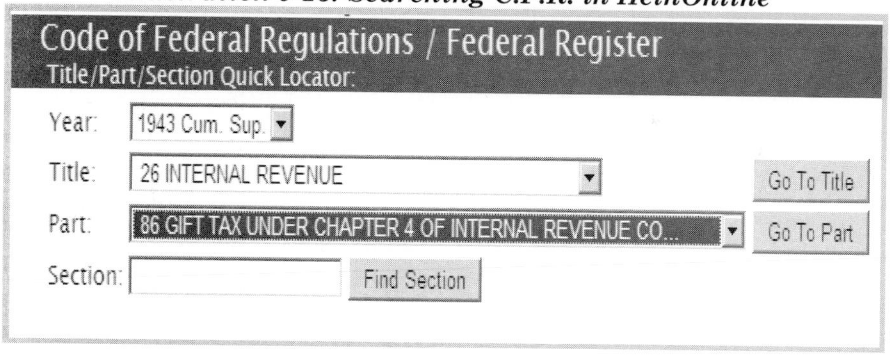

---

[184] See HENRY CAMPBELL BLACK, A TREATISE ON THE LAW OF INCOME TAXATION UNDER FEDERAL AND STATE LAWS § 71(2d ed. 1915). This treatise is included an online service, The Making of Modern Law: Legal Treatises 1800 – 1926.

[185] "SIR: In reply to a letter of inquiry addressed to this office on the 29th ultimo by Frederick D. Howe, treasurer and manager of the Warren Specialty Company, Auburn, N.Y., will you please inform him that the beverage (liqueur) called creme de menthe being, as it is understood, a compound of distilled spirits with other materials, any person manufacturing it for sale must be required to pay special tax as a rectifier ...." T.D. 33, 3 Treasury Decisions–Internal Revenue 32 (1900). This series is available in HeinOnline.

Illustration 9-24. 1943 Gift Tax Regulations in HeinOnline

Chapter I—Bureau of Internal Revenue   § 86.3

spouses is applicable regardless of varying local rules of apportionment, and State presumptions are not operative against the Commissioner.

§ 86.3 *Cessation of donor's dominion and control.* The tax is not imposed upon the receipt of the property by the donee, nor is it necessarily determined by the measure of enrichment resulting to the donee from the transfer, nor is it conditioned upon ability to identify the donee at the time of the transfer. On the contrary, the tax is a primary and personal liability of the donor, is an excise upon his act of making the transfer, is measured by the value of the property passing from the donor, and attaches regardless of the fact that the identity of the donee may not then be known or ascertainable.

As to any property or part thereof or time of enjoyment thereof. Thus, the creation of a trust the income of which is to be paid annually to the donee for a period of years, the corpus being distributable to him at the end of the period, and the power reserved by the donor being limited to a right to require that, instead of the income being so payable, it should be accumulated and distributed with the corpus to such donee at the termination of the period, constitutes a completed gift.

A donor shall be considered as himself having the power where it is exercisable by him in conjunction with any person not having a substantial adverse interest in the disposition of the transferred property or the income therefrom. A trustee, as such, is not a person having an adverse interest in the disposition of the trust property or its income.

5. Hearings Transcripts and Other Taxpayer Comments

Newsletters such as Daily Tax Report and Tax Notes report on testimony at hearings and taxpayer written comments. The Tax Notes Today file in LexisNexis includes texts of unofficial hearings transcripts and other taxpayer comments. You can also find these items in TaxCore.

Illustration 9-25. Hearing Reported in Daily Tax Report

Texts of SBSE-20-0709-016, dated Dec. 7, and SBSE-20-1209-058 and SBSE-20-1209-031, both dated Dec. 23, are in TaxCore.

Charitable Contributions

House Passes Haiti Tax Relief Bill As Senators Introduce Companion

The House Jan. 20 passed by voice vote a bill (H.R. 4462) allowing taxpayers to deduct charitable cash contributions made in 2010 to Haiti earthquake relief on their 2009 tax returns.

The expedited passage occurred under a suspension of the rules, which limits debate to 40 minutes, prohib-

Exempt Organizations

Witnesses United in Call to Vest Authority For Church Inquiries in IRS Deputy Director

A trio of witnesses at a Jan. 20 Internal Revenue Service hearing on proposed rules (REG—112756-09) on church tax inquiries said IRS should designate the deputy director for services and enforcement with the authority to begin church tax inquiries.

Marcus Owens, a former IRS exempt organizations director and current attorney with Caplin & Drysdale; Erik Stanley, senior legal counsel with the Alliance Defense Fund, a civil liberties law firm headquartered in

→TaxCore includes a transcript of the testimony at this hearing.

The Regulations.gov website lets you search for proposed and final rules and submit comments on proposed rules. It also gives you access to comments made by other taxpayers and their representatives.[186] Illustrations 9-26 through 9-28 cover written comments submitted with respect to the project described in Illustration 9-25.

Illustration 9-26. Search Options in Regulations.gov

→I decided to search for comments about REG-112756-09.

Illustration 9-27. Search for Comments in Regulations.gov

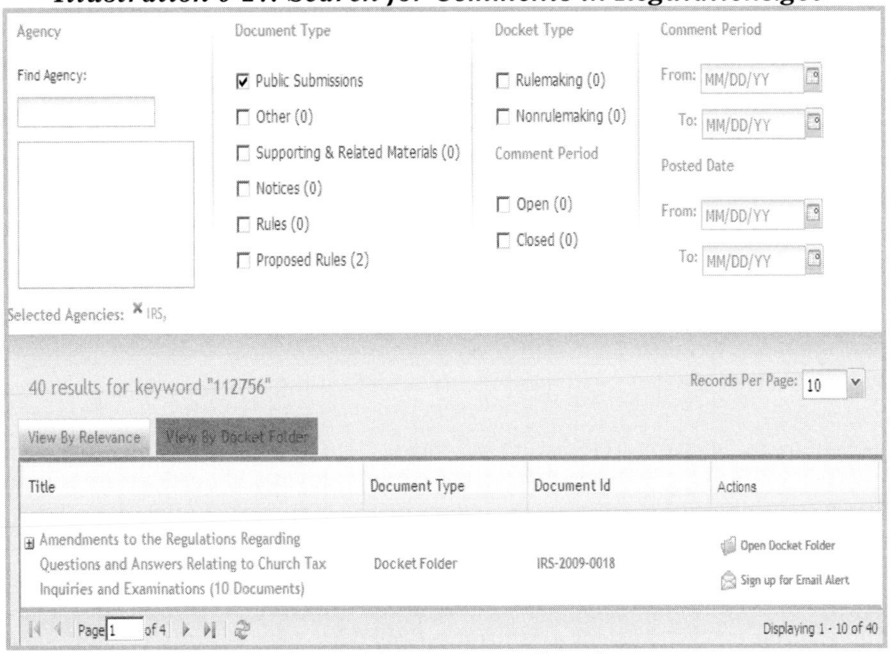

→I clicked on Open Docket Folder to view a list of comments.

---

[186] There may be a lag of several weeks before comments submitted through this website are actually posted.

Illustration 9-28. Partial List of Comments Received

Items in the Docket Folder					Records Per Page: 10	
Title	Document Type	Submitter Name	Organization	ID	Posted Date	View As...
Amendments to the Regulations Regarding Q & A Relating to Church Tax *Comments Due 11/03/09 11:59 PM ET*	PUBLIC SUBMISSIONS	Marcus Owens	Caplin & Drysdale	IRS-2009-0018-0007	10/14/09	
Amendments to the Regulations Regarding Q & A Relating to Church Tax *Comments Due 11/03/09 11:59 PM ET*	PUBLIC SUBMISSIONS	Marcus Owens	Caplin & Drysdale	IRS-2009-0018-0007.1	10/14/09	
Amendments to the Regulations Regarding Q & A Relating to Church Tax *Comments Due 11/03/09 11:59 PM ET*	PUBLIC SUBMISSIONS	Daniel Green	Covenant Family Church	IRS-2009-0018-0008	10/14/09	

→Marcus Owens testified at the hearing described in Illustration 9-25. Two more of his comments (not shown above) were posted on December 10, 2009.

When the IRS issues final regulations, the Preamble will summarize taxpayer comments made in response to the NPRM. The Preamble will also indicate whether the Service acted in response to those comments. [See Illustration 9-1.]

SECTION J. CITATORS FOR REGULATIONS

Regulations rarely keep pace with new legislative activity. Whenever a Code section changes, researchers must review existing regulations. They may no longer be relevant. They may even be totally invalid. If a regulation appears to contradict statutory language, check the date of its most recent T.D. to see if it predates the statutory change.

When an existing regulation affects a transaction, that regulation's success or failure in litigation is certainly relevant. The government is bound nationally by adverse decisions in the Supreme Court. It is effectively bound within a particular circuit by an adverse Circuit Court decision because trial courts follow the law of their circuit. The IRS is not bound in its dealings with taxpayers in circuits that have not addressed the regulation. Because the Supreme Court hears relatively few tax cases, the government may decide not to withdraw a regulation merely because the Tax Court or a single circuit court invalidates it.[187]

---

[187] Compare Western Nat. Mut. Ins. Co. v. Commissioner, 65 F.3d 90 (8th Cir. 1995), invalidating Treas. Reg. § 1.846-3(c), with Atlantic Mut. Ins. Co. v. Com-

A citator indicating judicial action on regulations is extremely useful for determining how courts ruled on challenges to particular regulations. Shepard's (LexisNexis) and KeyCite (Westlaw) serve that purpose. They allow you to check a particular regulation. The print and online citators provided by CCH and RIA are not as useful because they are based on T.D. number rather than regulation number. Because T.D.s often involve more than one regulations section, citators based on regulations section numbers are more likely to provide the desired information.

You can also search electronic services without using a citator by using the regulations section number and a variant of valid (or invalid) as your search terms. For example, I have two options for researching Treas. Reg. § 1.469-2 in Westlaw. I could enter the following in the Westlaw FTX-CS (Federal Taxation–Cases) database: 1.469-2 & valid invalid.[188] I could instead go directly to the regulation and use the KeyCite function. If I used a service that lacked a citator (or that had a citator that used T.D. instead of regulation numbers), my search would resemble the first option (modified to reflect that service's command structure).

SECTION K. JUDICIAL DEFERENCE

In determining the degree of deference they should give regulations, courts are guided by several Supreme Court decisions, the best-known of which is *Chevron*.[189] The *Chevron* Court held[190]

---

missioner, 111 F.3d 1056 (3d Cir. 1997), holding the regulation valid. The Supreme Court upheld the Third Circuit. See 523 U.S. 382 (1998).

[188] If I wanted to find decisions that used the term "validity," I could have refined my search by adding root expanders. Remember to check search terminology options when you use an electronic service.

[189] Chevron U.S.A. Inc. v. Natural Resources Defense Council, Inc., 467 U.S. 837 (1984). Other decisions that courts may cite when discussing deference include National Muffler Dealers Association v. United States, 440 U.S. 472 (1979), and National Cable & Telecommunications Association v. Brand X Internet Services, 545 U.S. 967 (2005).

[190] Id. at 842–43 (footnotes omitted). The Court added: "If Congress has explicitly left a gap for the agency to fill, there is an express delegation of authority to the agency to elucidate a specific provision of the statute by regulation. Such legislative regulations are given controlling weight unless they are arbitrary, capricious, or manifestly contrary to the statute.[12] Sometimes the legislative delegation to an agency on a particular question is implicit rather than explicit. In such a case, a court may not substitute its own construction of a statutory provision for a reasonable interpretation made by the administrator of an agency.[13]" Id. at 843–44 (footnotes omitted).

When a court reviews an agency's construction of the statute which it administers, it is confronted with two questions. First, always, is the question whether Congress has directly spoken to the precise question at issue. If the intent of Congress is clear, that is the end of the matter; for the court, as well as the agency, must give effect to the unambiguously expressed intent of Congress.[9] If, however, the court determines Congress has not directly addressed the precise question at issue, the court does not simply impose its own construction on the statute,[10] as would be necessary in the absence of an administrative interpretation. Rather, if the statute is silent or ambiguous with respect to the specific issue, the question for the court is whether the agency's answer is based on a permissible construction of the statute.[11]

Although *Chevron* is not a tax decision, it is cited in many tax cases and therefore appears if you enter *Chevron* into an electronic service. There are also tax cases involving the same company. This situation will also occur for other taxpayers that have been involved in significant non-tax litigation.

The excerpts below illustrate judicial approaches to deference. Two statements apply irrespective of the approach taken. First, the degree of deference accorded legislative or specific authority regulations is higher than that accorded interpretive or general authority regulations. Second, proposed regulations receive much less deference than do temporary or final regulations.

• While we do not defer to the trial court, an agency's interpretation of its own regulation is entitled to a level of deference even "broader than deference to the agency's construction of a statute, because in the latter case the agency is addressing Congress's intentions, while in the former it is addressing its own." *Cathedral Candle Co. v. U.S. Int'l Trade Comm'n*, 400 F.3d 1352, 1363–64 (Fed. Cir. 2005). That being said, "an agency's inconsistent interpretation of its regulation detracts from the deference we owe to that interpretation." *Gose v. U.S. Postal Serv.*, 451 F.3d 831, 837–38 (Fed. Cir. 2006) .... Abbot Laboratories v. United States, 573 F.3d 1327, 1330 (Fed. Cir. 2009).

• The agency's recent decision to adopt an alternative approach also does not mean that the regulations challenged here are incompatible with the statute. Either approach is permissible under the statute because the statute is silent on how LLCs should be taxed. Finally, the agency's decision to adopt a new approach does not strip it of Chevron deference. *See Natl. Cable & Telecomm. Ass'n v. Brand X Internet Svcs.*, 545 U.S. 967, 981 (2005) ("Agency inconsistency is not a basis for declining to analyze the agency's interpretation under the *Chevron* framework."). Kandi v. United States, 295 Fed. Appx. 873, 874 (9th Cir. 2008).

• To invoke these passages from our decisions for the general proposition that regulations may not add rules not found in the statute and not precluded by the statute is to misread them. Indeed, supplementation of a statute is a necessary and proper part of the Secretary's role in the administration of our tax laws. Hachette USA, Inc. v. Commissioner, 105 T.C. 234, 251 (1995).

• Although the difference between these two approaches [*Chevron* and *National Muffler*] is negligible at best—any regulation which is "based upon a permissible construction" of an ambiguous statute will almost always "implement the congressional mandate in some reasonable manner" and vice versa, the Ninth Circuit is correct to rely upon the more narrowly tailored holding of National Muffler. Bell Federal Savings & Loan Association v. Commissioner, 40 F.3d 224, 227 (7th Cir. 1994).

• If the regulations constituted a reasonable interpretation of [the statute], we would be compelled to uphold them even if [the taxpayer's] interpretation were more reasonable. Estate of Bullard v. Commissioner, 87 T.C. 261, 281 (1986).

• The reasonableness of each possible interpretation of the statute can also be measured against the legislative process by which [it] was enacted. Commissioner v. Engle, 464 U.S. 206, 220 (1984).

• "[L]egislative" regulations ... are entitled to even greater weight than regulations issued pursuant to the general authority granted by Congress under section 7805(a). Fife v. Commissioner, 82 T.C. 1, 15 (1984).

• Where the Commissioner acts under specific authority, our primary inquiry is whether the interpretation or method is within the delegation of authority. Rowan Cos., Inc. v. United States, 452 U.S. 247, 253 (1981).

• A regulation may have particular force if it is a substantially contemporaneous construction of the statute by those presumed to have been aware of congressional intent.... Other relevant considerations are the length of time the regulation has been in effect, the reliance placed on it, the consistency of the Commissioner's interpretation, and the degree of scrutiny Congress has devoted to the regulation during subsequent reenactments of the statute.[191] National Muffler Dealers Ass'n, Inc. v. United States, 440 U.S. 472, 477 (1979) (footnotes omitted).

• [Proposed regulations] carry no more weight than a position advanced on brief .... F.W. Woolworth Co. v. Commissioner, 54 T.C. 1233, 1265 (1970).

---

[191] At one time courts invoked a "re-enactment doctrine" if a regulation had been in effect through several revenue acts and Congress did not override it. Now that Congress amends specific provisions rather than re-enacting the entire Code, this doctrine is of questionable value.

Section L. Problems

1. What regulation was authorized by the listed Code section?

    a. 56(f)(2)(H)

    b. 409(p)(7)

    c. 882(c)

    d. 6109(a)

2. List all T.D.s issued for the regulation listed below.

    a. 1.213-1

    b. 1.531-1

    c. 20.2039-2

    d. 25.2522(a)-1

3. Who drafted the T.D. listed below? In which Chief Counsel division did that attorney work?

    a. 9408

    b. 9208

    c. 9008

    d. 8808

4. Who drafted the most recent version (original or amended) of the Treasury regulations section listed below?

    a. 1.179-1

    b. 1.1041-2

    c. 1.1366-2

    d. 1.7520-1

5. Who drafted the proposed regulations covered by the Project Number listed below?

    a. REG-113289-08

    b. REG-138326-07

    c. REG-127270-06

    d. REG-160871-04

6. Your instructor will assign you a Code section that uses the term "the Secretary shall prescribe" regulations. Determine which status best describes those regulations.

   a. have been proposed

   b. have been issued as temporary or final regulations

   c. are in the most current version of the Priority Guidance Plan

   d. are not in any of the first three categories

7. List any items in the most recent Priority Guidance Plan relating to guidance for a topic selected by your instructor.

8. Your instructor will select a regulations project from the most recent Priority Guidance Plan. Find that project in the most recent Unified Agenda and indicate all relevant dates for guidance.

9. Find comments submitted on a proposed regulation selected by your instructor.

10. Draft comments on a proposed regulation selected by your instructor.

11. Locate the court decision described and determine which regulation is involved. These decisions do not necessarily involve the regulation's validity. Use the materials in Chapter 11 as necessary.

   a. a 2009 Tax Court decision involving whether an LLC that was disregarded for income tax purposes was also disregarded for gift tax purposes

   b. a 2006 Tax Court decision involving buyout equity in the marital residence and the deduction for alimony

   c. a 2005 Court of Federal Claims decision involving whether the taxpayer's lack of records to establish he was a real estate professional was excused because a notebook was seized by a U.S. attorney

   d. a 2003 Court of Appeals decision involving one brother who received grain income while the other brother paid the income tax

12. Locate the court decision described below and indicate which regulation is involved. These decisions involve whether a regulation is valid. Use the materials in Chapter 11 as necessary.

   a. a 2009 Court of Federal Claims decision involving retroactivity, partnerships, and contingent obligations

   b. a 2008 Court of Appeals decision involving the right of an unenrolled tax preparer to represent clients before the IRS

c. a 2007 District Court decision involving whether interest paid on an underpayment of income tax was nondeductible personal interest

d. a 2007 Tax Court decision involving the right to a collection due process hearing after an Appeals Office conference

CHAPTER 10. INTERNAL REVENUE SERVICE DOCUMENTS

SECTION A. INTRODUCTION

This chapter discusses guidance, other than regulations, issued by the Internal Revenue Service. These documents can be issued more quickly than regulations, in part because they are not subject to notice and comment procedures. In addition to describing the different types of guidance, this chapter indicates which can be cited as precedential and which constitute "substantial authority," concepts discussed in Chapter 2. It also discusses sources in which you can find these documents, the role of the Freedom of Information Act and other statutes affecting the release of IRS documents, and judicial deference to various IRS pronouncements.

Your goals for this chapter include learning which documents are available and where they can be found, determining their relative importance, and locating IRS and judicial action with respect to them.

SECTION B. TYPES OF IRS DOCUMENTS

There are several methods for categorizing IRS documents. Three such methods are their means of publication, their initial audience, and their status as precedent or as substantial authority.

1. Means of Publication

The IRS publishes several documents in the weekly Internal Revenue Bulletin. The most important of these are revenue rulings, revenue procedures, notices, and announcements. Items currently included in the I.R.B. are cumulated every six months and appear in the Cumulative Bulletin. The I.R.B. and C.B. are discussed and illustrated in Section J.

The IRS issues other types of guidance, such as private letter rulings and actions on decisions, which it does not publish in the I.R.B. Many of these items were released to the public following Freedom of Information Act (FOIA) litigation; others have been exempted from release by statute.

The discussion in Sections C through H categorizes IRS documents by their publication status: officially published in the I.R.B. or in other IRS publications; available because of FOIA or other release-related litigation; or exempted from release by statute.[192]

---

[192] Section I discusses items issued before the IRS Electronic Reading Room came into existence.

Sections C through G generally track the documents' placement in the Electronic Reading Room, which is part of the IRS website. There are some exceptions. First, forms and publications are officially published, but they do not appear on the Electronic Reading Room page; there is a search function for these items on the IRS site home page. Second, several documents were discontinued before the IRS began electronic publication or have been subsumed into other document titles. Discussion in this chapter indicates those exceptions.

Illustration 10-1. IRS Website

→The Freedom of Information Act link takes you to the FOIA page.

→The home page also includes a search function and links to forms and publications.

Illustration 10-2. FOIA Page Link to IRS Electronic Reading Room

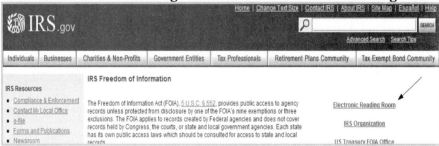

→The Electronic Reading Room link takes you to the page shown in Illustration 10-3.

Illustration 10-3. Electronic Reading Room

Published Tax Guidance

- Advance Releases
  Early distribution of some IRB materials before they are published in the IRB.
- Applicable Federal Rate (AFR) revenue rulings
- Final or Temporary Regulations (Treasury Decisions) and Proposed Regulations
- IRS Publications & Notices
- *Internal Revenue Bulletins (IRB)*
  Weekly compilations of Revenue Rulings, Revenue Procedures, Announcements, and Notices.
  ...PDF format (1996 to present)
  ...HTML format (July 7, 2003 to present)

Admin Manuals & Instructions

- Appeals Coordinated Issues (ACI)
- Chief Counsel (CC) Notices
- Internal Revenue Manual (IRM)
- LMSB Coordinated Issues
- LMSB Industry Director Guidance
- Recent Delegation Orders and Policy Statements
- Recent Interim Guidance to Staff
- Taxpayer Advocate Service Level Agreements

Program Plans & Reports

- Annual Performance Plan
- Art Appraisal Services Annual Summary Reports
- FOIA Annual Reports
- IRS Strategic Plan
- Priority Guidance Plan
- Privacy Impact Assessments
- Treasury Inspector General for Tax Admin. (TIGTA) Annual Audit Plans

Non-precedential Rulings & Advice

- Actions on Decisions (AOD)
- Appeals Settlement Guidelines
- Chief Counsel Bulletins
- Exempt Org. Field Memorandums
- General Counsel Memoranda
- Information Letters
- IRS Written Determinations
  Private Letter Rulings (PLR), Technical Advice Memorandum (TAM), & Chief Counsel Advice (CCA).
- Legal Advice Issued by Associate Chief Counsel
- Legal Advice Issued by Field Attorneys
- Legal Advice Issued to Program Managers

Training & Reference Materials

- Advance Pricing Agreement (APA) Training Materials
- CCA Check Training Material
- Chief Counsel Advice (CCA) Training Materials
- Disclosure & Privacy Law Reference Guide
- EO Tax Law Training Articles
- Market Segment Specialization Program (Audit Techniques Guides)

2. Initial Audience

Documents published in the Internal Revenue Bulletin are directed to all taxpayers and their representatives. Private letter rulings, on the other hand, are directed to a specific taxpayer; the IRS makes them available to other readers after deleting identifying material. Still other documents are written for government personnel. Many of them, such as Legal Advice Issued by Associate Chief Counsel, are publicly available.

3. Status as Precedent or Substantial Authority

Items printed in the Internal Revenue Bulletin constitute authority for avoiding the substantial understatement penalty discussed in Chapter 2. These documents can be cited as precedent, and the IRS considers itself bound by them in its dealings with taxpayers whose facts are the same as those discussed in the documents. As discussed in Section N, the degree of deference they receive from courts is mixed.

Items that are not published in the I.R.B. fall into two categories. A few of them are not precedential but nevertheless constitute authority for avoiding the substantial understatement penalty. Others are neither precedential nor authority for avoiding the penalty. Even though these documents are not precedential, courts occasionally cite them.

SECTION C. OFFICIALLY PUBLISHED IRS DOCUMENTS

The first four items discussed below are part of the Published Tax Guidance section of the Electronic Reading Room.

1. Revenue Rulings (Rev. Rul.)

a. Background

The IRS issues rulings designed to apply the law to particular factual situations. Unlike regulations, rulings do not first appear in proposed form for public comment. Rulings fall into two categories—revenue rulings and letter rulings. If the IRS determines a topic is of general interest, it may publish guidance in the Internal Revenue Bulletin (and later in the Cumulative Bulletin) as a **revenue ruling** rather than initiating a regulations project.

Although a revenue ruling is not as authoritative as a Treasury regulation, any taxpayer whose circumstances are substantially the same as those described in the ruling can rely upon it.[193] Revenue rulings also constitute authority for avoiding the substantial understatement penalty. Subject to the limitations in Code section 7805(b), revenue rulings can apply retroactively unless their text indicates otherwise. [See Illustration 4-17 for an excerpt from a revenue ruling.]

Although the number varies from year to year, there have been relatively few revenue rulings issued in recent years.[194] Many of those actually issued represent regularly scheduled guidance rather than rulings on new topics.

b. Numbering System

The IRS numbers revenue rulings chronologically.[195] The ruling number has two segments separated by a hyphen; the first indicates the year and the second indicates the ruling number for that year. Beginning in 2000, the Service began using all four digits to indicate the year; it previously used only the last two digits. The ruling number does not indicate which Code or regulations section is involved.

---

[193] Although it happens rarely, the IRS has issued adverse rulings based on a set of facts encountered in an audit and then asserted the ruling as authority when the taxpayer litigated. See Rev. Rul. 79-427, 1979-2 C.B. 120, discussed in Niles v. United States, 710 F.2d 1391, 1393 (9th Cir. 1983).

[194] The IRS issued more than 700 revenue rulings in 1955; it issued 40 in 2009.

[195] The first ruling issued in 2010 is Rev. Rul. 2010-1. Each week's rulings are numbered sequentially, often in Code section order.

The IRS began issuing numbered revenue rulings in 1953 and adopted the current numbering system in 1954. Earlier rulings, with different names, appeared in pre-1953 Cumulative Bulletins.

Table 10-1. Pre-1953 Titles of Published Rulings

A.R.M.	Committee on Appeals and Review Memorandum
A.R.R.	Committee on Appeals and Review Recommendation
A.T.	Alcohol Tax Unit; Alcohol and Tobacco Tax Division
C.L.T.	Child-Labor Tax Division
C.S.T.	Capital-Stock Tax Division
C.T.	Carriers Taxing Act of 1937; Taxes on Employment by Carriers
D.C.	Treasury Department Circular
Dept. Cir.	Treasury Department Circular
E.P.C.	Excess Profits Tax Council Ruling or Memorandum
E.T.	Estate and Gift Tax Division or Ruling
Em.T.	Employment Taxes
G.C.M	Chief Counsel's Memorandum; General Counsel's Memorandum; Assistant General Counsel's Memorandum
I.T.	Income Tax Unit or Division
L.O.	Solicitor's Law Opinion
MS.	Miscellaneous Unit or Division or Branch
M.T.	Miscellaneous Division or Branch
Mim.	Mimeographed Letter; Mimeograph
Mim.	Solicitor's Law Opinion
O.	Office Decision
Op. A.G.	Opinion of Attorney General
P.T.	Processing Tax Decision or Division
S.	Solicitor's Memorandum
S.M.	Solicitor's Memorandum
S.R.	Solicitor's Recommendation
S.S.T.	Social Security Tax and Carriers' Tax; Social Security Tax; Taxes on Employment by Other than Carriers
S.T.	Sales Tax Unit or Division or Branch
Sil.	Silver Tax Division
Sol. Op.	Solicitor's Opinion
T.	Tobacco Division
T.B.M.	Advisory Tax Board Memorandum
T.B.R.	Advisory Tax Board Recommendation
Tob.	Tobacco Branch

c. Format

Revenue rulings begin by indicating the regulations section involved; the Code section number also appears. Most recent revenue rulings contain five segments: Issue; Facts; Law; Analysis; and Holding. Other sections that may appear include Effect on Other Documents (for rulings that revoke, modify, obsolete, or otherwise affect a prior holding) and Effective Date. Rulings also indicate the IRS employee who drafted them or who can be contacted if the taxpayer has questions; Internal Revenue Bulletins issued before 1998 omit drafting information.

2. Revenue Procedures (Rev. Proc.) and Procedural Rules

a. Background

Revenue procedures are published statements of IRS practices and procedures. These documents are published in the Internal Revenue Bulletin and Cumulative Bulletin. Procedures of general applicability may also be added to the IRS Statement of Procedural Rules and published in the Code of Federal Regulations.

Several revenue procedures are issued each year to provide guidance on how to obtain rulings and other IRS advice. [See Table 10-2.] For example, the first procedure each year (e.g., Rev. Proc. 2010-1) provides procedures for obtaining rulings, determination letters, and closing agreements. It also includes a sample ruling request format and a schedule of user fees.

Revenue procedures constitute authority for avoiding the substantial understatement penalty.

b. Numbering System

Revenue procedures have been numbered chronologically since 1955. Beginning in 2000, the Service began using all four digits to indicate the year. The procedure number does not indicate the Code or regulations section involved.

Items included in the IRS Statement of Procedural Rules are part of 26 C.F.R. and are numbered as Treasury regulations. Their prefix is 601.

c. Format

Revenue procedures include several subdivisions. The number of subdivisions generally reflects the procedure's scope and complexity. The following subdivisions are commonly used: Purpose; Background; Scope; Effective Date; Effect on Other Documents; and Drafting Information. In appropriate cases, the procedure will also include sections such as Record Keeping, Request for Comments, and Paperwork Reduction Act.

Table 10-2. Regularly Issued Revenue Procedures[196]

3. Notices

The IRS issues **notices** to provide guidance before revenue rulings and regulations are available. As noted in Chapter 9, notices can describe future regulations in a manner that will pass muster under the Code section 7805(b) rules on retroactivity.[197]

Notices are numbered by year in the same manner as revenue rulings and revenue procedures. The number does not indicate the Code or regulations section involved. Notices constitute authority for avoiding the substantial understatement penalty.

Notices may be subdivided into parts similar to those used for revenue rulings and procedures. Shorter notices may not have subdivisions.

4. Announcements (Ann.)

Announcements alert taxpayers to a variety of information but are somewhat less formal than revenue rulings, revenue procedures, and no-

---

[196] The Appendix to the Priority Guidance Plan includes a month-by-month listing of Regularly Scheduled Publications; this list includes notices and revenue rulings in addition to revenue procedures.

[197] The Service may instead issue an announcement to provide information and elicit comments about regulations it is drafting. See, e.g., Ann. 2002-9, 2002-7 I.R.B. 536 (treatment of costs associated with intangible assets).

tices. Information provided in announcements includes corrections to previously published regulations,[198] lists of organizations classified as private foundations, and extensions of time to file forms. Announcements constitute authority for avoiding the substantial understatement penalty.

Announcements are numbered by year; the numbering does not indicate the underlying Code or regulations section. These I.R.B. documents were added to the Cumulative Bulletin in 1998.

Illustration 10-4. Excerpt from Notice 2009-89

Part III. Administrative, Procedural, and Miscellaneous

New Qualified Plug-in Electric Drive Motor Vehicle Credit

Notice 2009-89

Section 1. PURPOSE

This notice sets forth interim guidance, pending the issuance of regulations, relating to the new qualified plug-in electric drive motor vehicle credit under § 30D of the Internal Revenue Code, as in effect for vehicles acquired after December 31, 2009. Specifically, this notice provides procedures for a vehicle manufacturer (or, in the case of a foreign vehicle manufacturer, its domestic distributor) to certify to the Internal Revenue Service ("Service") both:

(1) That a motor vehicle of a particular make, model, and model year meets certain requirements that must be satisfied to claim the new qualified plug-in electric drive motor vehicle credit under § 30D; and

January 1, 2010, is provided in Notice 2009–54, 2009–26 I.R.B. 1124. This notice also amplifies Notice 2009–54 and Notice 2009–58, 2009–30 I.R.B. 163 (relating to the plug-in electric vehicle credit under § 30) to provide that a vehicle is considered "acquired" when title to that vehicle passes under state law.

Section 2. BACKGROUND

Section 30D provides for a credit for certain new qualified plug-in electric drive motor vehicles. The credit is equal to the sum of: (1) $2,500, plus (2) for a vehicle which draws propulsion energy from a battery with at least 5 kilowatt hours of capacity, $417, plus an additional $417 for each kilowatt hour of battery capacity in excess of 5 kilowatt hours. Under § 30D(b)(3), that portion of the credit determined by battery capacity cannot exceed $5,000. Therefore, the total amount of the credit allowed for a vehicle is limited to $7,500. The new qualified plug-in

(2) Are acquired by the taxpayer after December 31, 2009; and

(3) Otherwise meet the requirements of § 30D.

Section 4. MEANING OF TERMS

The following definitions apply for purposes of this notice:

.01 *In General.* Terms used in this notice and not defined in this section 4 have the same meaning as when used in § 30D.

.02 *Clean Air Act Regulations.* The Clean Air Act regulations are the regulations prescribed by the Administrator of the Environmental Protection Agency for purposes of the administration of Title II of the Clean Air Act (42 U.S.C. §§ 7521, *et. seq.*).

.03 *Battery Capacity.* Battery capacity is the quantity of electricity that a battery is capable of storing, expressed in kilowatt hours, as measured from a 100 percent state of charge to a zero percent state of charge.

5. Other Documents Published in the Internal Revenue Bulletin

The weekly Bulletins contain other information, much of which is issued by the IRS. IRS information includes disbarment notices, delegation orders (Del. Order) announcing delegations of authority to various IRS offices, and **notices of acquiescence** and **nonacquiescence** (acq.; nonacq.).[199] Those notices are important because they indicate if the IRS will continue to litigate an issue it has lost in a judicial proceeding. IRS litigation plans are discussed further in Subsection D.3.

---

[198] For example, Ann. 2010-8, 2010-7 I.R.B. 408, announced a correction to a final regulations.

[199] Most, but not all, I.R.B. items were cumulated every six months in the Cumulative Bulletin. Since 1998, the C.B. reprints all I.R.B. items. See Section J for a discussion of the C.B.

Non-IRS material includes Executive Orders issued by the President, Treasury regulations, new treaty documents, and Supreme Court decisions. These materials can also be found in sources other than the I.R.B. and are discussed in other chapters.

6. Other IRS Documents

The IRS publishes tax return forms, accompanying instructions, and explanatory booklets. These documents contain few, if any, citations to authority, and they do not indicate if the IRS position has been disputed. Even if they are misleading, taxpayers who rely on them cannot cite them as authority against a contrary IRS position.[200] These documents are not authority for avoiding the substantial understatement penalty.

The numbering system for tax return forms and explanatory booklets does not indicate the underlying Code or regulations section number. In addition, the numbering systems for forms and booklets are not coordinated. For example, Code section 280A provides the rules governing deductions for an office in the taxpayer's home. IRS Form 8829 is used for computing that deduction. Publication Number 587 explains the deduction rules to the public.

These documents are not generally published in the Internal Revenue Bulletin or in the Cumulative Bulletin. Some forms do appear in the Bulletins if the IRS is specifying parameters for privately printed items.

SECTION D. NON-PRECEDENTIAL RULINGS AND GUIDANCE

Many of the documents discussed in this section are useful for determining the IRS position on relevant issues. Others provide information but are not informative about IRS positions.

Code section 6110(k)(3) prevents you from citing the documents described in this section as precedent. You can use several of them as authority for avoiding the substantial underpayment penalty discussed in Chapter 2. Litigation resulted in their release and in the enactment of statutes requiring or restricting taxpayer access. Documents issued since the IRS began electronic release appear in this section of the IRS website.

---

[200] See Osborne v. Commissioner, 97-2 U.S.T.C. ¶ 50,524, 79 A.F.T.R.2d 97-3011 (6th Cir. 1997). See also TAM 8350008, involving an IRS refusal to allow a taxpayer to claim reliance on a portion of the Internal Revenue Manual or on the 1982 version of IRS Publication 544. But see Gehl Co. v. Commissioner, 795 F.2d 1324 (7th Cir. 1986); AOD 1988-002 explains the decision not to seek certiorari.

1. FOIA Litigation and Section 6110

The lawsuit that first resulted in disclosure of unpublished documents involved private letter rulings and was brought under the Freedom of Information Act (FOIA).[201] That lawsuit resulted in the disclosure of rulings issued after October 31, 1976, and led to the enactment of Code section 6110, an IRS-specific disclosure statute.

Section 6110, which has been amended several times since its 1976 enactment, requires the release of written determinations and of background file documents related to those written determinations. The Code defines written determination as rulings, determination letters, technical advice memoranda, and **Chief Counsel advice**.[202] Chief Counsel advice (CCA; C.C.A.) is defined in Section 6110(i)(1)(A):

> (A) In general
> For purposes of this section, the term "Chief Counsel advice" means written advice or instruction, under whatever name or designation, prepared by any national office component of the Office of Chief Counsel which—
> (i) is issued to field or service center employees of the Service or regional or district employees of the Office of Chief Counsel; and
> (ii) conveys—
> (I) any legal interpretation of a revenue provision;
> (II) any Internal Revenue Service or Office of Chief Counsel position or policy concerning a revenue provision; or
> (III) any legal interpretation of State law, foreign law, or other Federal law relating to the assessment or collection of any liability under a revenue provision.

Revenue provisions include former or existing revenue statutes, regulations, revenue rulings and procedures, tax treaties, and other published or unpublished guidance.[203]

---

[201] Tax Analysts and Advocates v. Internal Revenue Service, 405 F. Supp. 1065 (D.D.C. 1975) (brought under 5 U.S.C. § 552).

[202] I.R.C. § 6110(a) & (b). Background file documents are "the request for that written determination, any written material submitted in support of the request, and any communication (written or otherwise) between the Internal Revenue Service and persons outside the Internal Revenue Service in connection with such written determination ... received before issuance of the written determination."

The IRS makes written determinations available in its FOIA Reading Room and on its website. It releases background documents only on written request; there are fees for finding these items, deleting confidential information, and duplicating them. Id. § 6110(e) & (k); Rev. Proc. 95-15, 1995-1 C.B. 523.

[203] I.R.C. § 6110(i)(1)(B).

Section 6110 provides timetables for disclosure by the Service. The disclosure date is later than the document's actual issue date to allow time for notifying taxpayers that rulings they have requested are being made public and redacting taxpayer-identifying information. Taxpayers have the opportunity to dispute whether redaction is sufficient but cannot prevent disclosure altogether.[204]

2. Numbering Systems

Unless a different system is indicated, the publicly released documents discussed in Section D use a common numbering system. The system is based on a multi-digit number (e.g., 84-37-084 or 200203010). Although citation manuals use the hyphens, the IRS does not use them for these documents. Abbreviations preceding the numbers indicate the type of document (e.g., private letter ruling, technical advice memorandum).

The hyphens are useful because they call attention to what the document number means. The digits preceding the first hyphen reflect the year the document was released; the next two digits indicate the week of release; the final digits are the document number for that week.

Although the document number does not reflect the underlying Code section, many documents also include Uniform Issue List (UIL) numbers. UIL numbers, which do reflect the underlying Code section, are discussed in Section L. The IRS website lets you sort documents by UIL number.

3. Items Categorized as Non-precedential Rulings and Guidance

a. Actions on Decisions (AOD; A.O.D.; Action on Dec.; Action on Decision)

The IRS uses several means for announcing future litigation information. One mechanism is the notice of acquiescence or nonacquiescence in cases it has lost. Those notices appear in the Internal Revenue Bulletin. Until early 1993, the Service issued those notices only for Tax Court Regular decisions. It now issues them for all trial and circuit courts.[205]

An **action on decision** indicates why the Service recommends (1) appealing or not appealing an adverse decision and (2) acquiescing or not acquiescing in that decision. These are separate recommendations. The

---

[204] Anonymous v. Commissioner, 134 T.C. No. 2 (2010).

[205] Although these notices should be the primary means of publishing this information in the Bulletin, the IRS may use other guidance for this purpose. See, e.g., Rev. Rul. 94-47, 1994-2 C.B. 18; Notice 96-39, 1996-2 C.B. 309; Notice 95-57, 1995-2 C.B. 337. AODs are the primary non-I.R.B. method.

Service may recommend not acquiescing and continuing to litigate an issue even though it decides not to appeal the particular case it lost. For example, AOD 1984-022, reproduced below, involved a question of fact. The appellate court would be unlikely to reverse for this reason, but the IRS was not willing to concede the underlying issue in future litigation. [See Illustration 4-28 for a more traditional AOD.]

Illustration 10-5. AOD 1984-022

ACTION ON DECISION CC-1984-022

CC:TL
Br2:DCFegan

Re: Harold L. and Temple M. Jenkins v.
Commissioner
    Venue: C.A. 6th
    Dkt. No.: 3354-79
    Dec. November 3, 1983
    Opinion: T.C. Memo 1983-667

Issue: Whether Conway Twitty is allowed a business expense deduction for payments to reimburse the losses of investors in a defunct restaurant known as Twitty Burger, Inc. 0162.01-17; 0162.29-00.

Discussion: The Tax Court summarized its opinion in this case with the following "Ode to Conway Twitty":

"Twitty Burger went belly up
But Conway remained true
He repaid his investors, one and all
It was the moral thing to do.

"His fans would not have liked it
It could have hurt his fame
Had any investors sued him
Like Merle Haggard or Sonny James.

"When it was time to file taxes
Conway thought what he would do
Was deduct those payments as a
business expense
Under section one-sixty-two.

"In order to allow these deductions
Goes the argument of the Commissioner
The payments must be ordinary and necessary
To a business of the petitioner.

"Had Conway not repaid the investors
His career would have been under cloud
Under the unique facts of this case
Held: The deductions are allowed."
Our reaction to the Court's opinion is reflected in the following "Ode to Conway Twitty: A Reprise":

Harold Jenkins and Conway Twitty
They are both the same
But one was born
The other achieved fame.

The man is talented
And has many a friend
They opened a restaurant
His name he did lend.

They are two different things
Making burgers and song
The business went sour
It didn't take long.

He repaid his friends
Why did he act
Was it business or friendship
Which is fact?

Business the court held
It's deductible they feel
We disagree with the answer
But let's not appeal.

Recommendation:
Nonacquiescence.

Unlike notices of acquiescence, AODs were never limited to Tax Court decisions. As is true for acquiescence notices, the IRS does not issue an AOD for every case it loses. Taxpayers can use AODs issued after March

12, 1981, as authority for avoiding the substantial understatement penalty.

AODs are numbered sequentially by year. The numbering system provides no information about the underlying case name or issue involved. The IRS website search function [Illustration 10-23] numbers each AOD by year and number within the year (e.g., 1997-01). Internally, several of these documents have slightly different numbering formats.[206]

Although the IRS refers to these documents as AOD without periods, citation systems use other formats. For example, The Bluebook uses action on dec.; TaxCite uses action on decision.

If a later AOD revokes an earlier one, the IRS removes the earlier item from its website; subscription services generally retain these items.

b. Appeals Settlement Guidelines (ASG)

This section of the website includes several **Industry Specialization Program Coordinated Issue Papers**. Items are categorized by topic and contain extensive discussion and citations to authority. These documents are not numbered.

Illustration 10-6. Appeals Settlement Guidelines Document

DRAFT
SETTLEMENT GUIDELINES
TAXATION OF UNIVERSAL SERVICE FEES
UIL: 61.40-01

STATEMENT OF ISSUE

Whether payments received by telecommunication service providers from Federal and state universal service programs constitute income under section 61 of the Internal Revenue Code or contributions to capital under section 118(a) of the Internal Revenue Code.

COMPLIANCE POSITION

The Federal Government asserts that the payments are contingent on the provision of services by the payee telecommunications company, and thus represent compensation for services which do not qualify for capital contribution treatment notwithstanding that a government entity made the payment and that some public benefit may accrue from the payment.

INDUSTRY/TAXPAYER POSITION

Taxpayer asserts that because the motive of the contributors (Federal and state governments) was to benefit the greater public good by providing enhanced telecommunications services throughout the United States and since the contributor

---

[206] For example, some documents include CC (Chief Counsel) in their number (e.g., CC-2002-02), while others have no number at all (e.g., the document numbered 2001-07 on the search wheel). In addition, sometimes a document uses two digits and sometimes three for the item number (e.g., CC-1997-005 versus 2000-05).

c. Chief Counsel Bulletins

The Electronic Reading Room currently includes links to three types of Chief Counsel bulletins: Criminal Tax Bulletins; Collection, Bankruptcy and Summonses Bulletins; and Disclosure Litigation Bulletins. These documents provide information to IRS employees about litigation in a variety of areas. None of them constitutes authority for avoiding the substantial understatement penalty.

Criminal Tax Bulletins (CTB; C.T.B.) compile cases pertaining to criminal tax matters. The IRS has used several numbering systems for these documents. In some cases, it uses one set of numbers on the website, but the document itself is numbered using a different system.

Documents issued between December 1998 and October 2001 have nine digit numbers (e.g., 200202063); the first four digits represent the year, the second two digits represent the week, and the last three digits represent the number for that week.[207] This system is used on both the website and the documents.

The next numbering system generally reflects the year and month that begins each compilation (e.g., 2001-12 and 2006-12).[208] The Bulletins themselves either don't show any numbers or are numbered using the nine-digit system described in the preceding paragraph. The nine-digit number is based on the document's release date, which may be in a later year than the year covered by its contents.

Since November 2007, website Bulletin numbering shows the first and last month covered by each Bulletin (e.g., 200711–200806 for November 2007 through June 2008). The actual Bulletins don't show any numbers.

Collection, Bankruptcy and Summonses Bulletins (CBS; C.B.S.) summarize recent court decisions. These documents were called **General Litigation Bulletins** through June 2000 (Bulletins 458 through 477 on the website). Although numbered in a separate series, these bulletins also share the common nine-digit numbering system. For example, Bulletin No. 490 is also numbered 200139029. The most recent bulletin posted on the IRS website in February 2010 was issued in January 2002 (Bulletin 496).

---

[207] The number for this October 2001 item begins with 2002 because October 2001 is the first month of the government's fiscal year 2002.

[208] The Bulletin covering June through August 2006 is numbered 2006-2, which is inconsistent with the other Bulletins for that year 2006-1 (January 2006 through April 2006) and 2006-12 (December 2006 through February 2007).

Disclosure Litigation Bulletins (DLB; D.L.B.) discuss litigation and other developments concerning FOIA and related litigation. They are numbered by year. The most recent bulletin posted on the IRS website in February 2010 was DLB 2000-3.

Tax Litigation Bulletins (TLB; T.L.B.) summarized recent court decisions and briefs. They also include recommendations for appellate action. These bulletins are numbered by year (e.g., TLB 96-5). They are not included on the IRS website.

d. Exempt Organization Field Memoranda

These documents are produced by the Director, Exempt Organization Rulings & Agreements. They discuss recent developments in the law and may indicate changes in the Internal Revenue Manual or other guidance. As of February 2010, there are nine items posted; the oldest is from 1999 and the most recent is from 2009.

Illustration 10-7. Exempt Organization Field Memorandum

Internal Revenue Service

memorandum

date: 05/11/07

to: Director, Exempt Organizations, Examinations   SE:T:EO:E
       Director, Exempt Organizations, Rulings & Agreements   SE:T:EO:RA

From: Director, Exempt Organizations   SE:T:EO
         /s/ *Lois G. Lerner*

subject: Hospitals Providing Financial Assistance to Staff Physicians Involving Electronic Health Records

The purpose of this memorandum is to provide a directive for handling examination and exemption application cases involving hospitals that provide physicians who have staff privileges at those hospitals ("medical staff physicians") with financial assistance to acquire and implement software that is used predominantly for creating, maintaining, transmitting, or receiving electronic health records ("EHRs") for their patients.

e. General Counsel Memoranda (GCM; G.C.M.; Gen. Couns. Mem.)

Just as actions on decisions provide the reasoning behind litigation decisions, **general counsel memoranda** indicate the reasoning and authority used in revenue rulings, private letter rulings, and technical advice memoranda. IRS personnel used them in formulating positions.[209] Taxpayers can use GCMs issued after March 12, 1981, as authority for avoiding the substantial understatement penalty.

GCMs are numbered sequentially (e.g., GCM 39278). The numbering system does not indicate the year of issue, the Code section, or the document about which they supply information. The number of GCMs declined markedly during the 1990s. Only two (39892 (2002) and 39893 (2007)) have been issued since 1997; both merely revoked prior GCMs.

The Service's website includes a GCM Index, which lists GCMs written by the Chief Counsel's office after December 24, 1981. It is arranged in Code section order and is subdivided within each Code section by UIL number.

f. IRS Information Letters (IIL; I.I.L.)

The national office issues information letters to taxpayers (and to members of Congress who request them) that provide statements of well-defined law; they do not apply these statements to particular facts. These letters are numbered by year (e.g., 2009-0255).[210] You can search for them by key word, letter number, or Uniform Issue List code.

g. IRS Written Determinations

This category currently includes three items: letter rulings (and determination letters), technical advice memoranda, and Chief Counsel advice. As discussed below, several items currently included within the Chief Counsel advice umbrella had their genesis in documents that were previously issued under other names.

(1) Private Letter Rulings (PLR; P.L.R.; Ltr. Rul.; Priv. Ltr. Rul.)

Private letter rulings are written in response to taxpayer requests for guidance as to a proposed transaction's tax consequence. In addition to the underlying facts, issues raised, and legal analysis, these rulings indicate which Chief Counsel's office division produced them.

Some private letter rulings are eventually formally published as revenue rulings, but most are available to the public only through the section

---

[209] Don't confuse these GCMs with revenue rulings issued before 1953, many of which were also called general counsel memoranda. [See Table 10-1.]

[210] IIL 2009-0255 responds to a request for the IRS to publish a standard mileage rate for business use of a motorcycle.

6110 disclosure procedure. Although the IRS is not bound by them in its dealings with other taxpayers,[211] letter rulings issued after October 31, 1976, constitute authority for avoiding the substantial understatement penalty.

(2) Determination Letters

Determination letters are similar to letter rulings but emanate from IRS district offices rather than the national office. District office personnel issue them only if they can be based on well-established rules that apply to the issues presented. Otherwise, the matter is appropriately handled by the national office.

(3) Technical Advice Memoranda (TAM; T.A.M.; Tech. Adv. Mem.) and Technical Expedited Advice Memoranda (TEAM; T.E.A.M.)

Technical advice memoranda are issued by the national office in response to IRS requests arising out of tax return examinations. Unlike letter rulings, which focus on proposed transactions, technical advice memoranda cover completed transactions. In contrast to field service advice, discussed in the materials on Chief Counsel advice, technical advice requests generally involve both the taxpayer and the IRS. Memoranda issued after October 31, 1976, constitute authority for avoiding the substantial understatement penalty.

In mid-2002, the IRS announced a pilot project for a new form of guidance. **Technical expedited advice memoranda**, which would initially be available only for matters under the jurisdiction of the Associate Chief Counsel (Income Tax & Accounting), would result in a streamlined process for technical advice. Both the taxpayer and IRS would be involved in the process. The procedures for obtaining both TAMS and TEAMS are announced in the second revenue procedure each year.[212]

---

[211] But see Ogiony v. Commissioner, 617 F.2d 14, 17–18 (2d Cir. 1980) (Oakes, J., concurring). Although commenting that they had no precedential force, the Supreme Court has cited private letter rulings as evidence of IRS inconsistent interpretation. See Rowan Cos., Inc. v. United States, 452 U.S. 247, 261 n.17 (1981).

[212] In CC-2006-013 (May 5, 2006), the Case Specific Advice Task Force recommended eliminating TEAMs. Although CC-2006-013 no longer appears as a separate document on the IRS website, you can locate it in subscription services such as Westlaw.

(4) Other Chief Counsel Advice Items

a. Field Service Advice (FSA; F.S.A.)

IRS field attorneys, revenue agents, and appeals officers requested national office advice if a case presented a significant legal question of first impression and no guidance existed as to the Chief Counsel's legal position or policy.[213] Field personnel could seek **field service advice** instead of a technical advice memorandum and could do so without the taxpayer's knowledge. Field service advice does not constitute authority for avoiding the substantial understatement penalty. Field service advice has not been issued as a separately titled item since early 2004.

b. Service Center Advice (SCA; S.C.A.)

The national office issued **service center advice** with regard to tax administration responsibilities. The Service began using the common numbering system for these documents in 1999. It used a separate numbering system in 1997 and 1998. SCAs do not constitute authority for avoiding the substantial understatement penalty.

c. IRS Legal Memoranda (ILM; I.L.M.)

Legal memoranda provide information about taxpayers to IRS field or service center personnel. These documents may respond to a field office query or they may provide information to the field (e.g., notice that a taxpayer's request to change accounting method has been denied). These documents do not constitute authority for avoiding the substantial understatement penalty. Although these documents use the common numbering system, different services call them by different names. Searching by number yields the same results irrespective of system; searching by title may not.[214]

d. Litigation Guideline Memoranda (LGM; L.G.M.)

Litigation guideline memoranda discuss variations on fact patterns and tactical approaches that IRS field personnel might use in litigation. In mid-1999, the Service released memoranda issued between January 1, 1986, and October 20, 1998. LGMs are now released using the timetable

---

[213] In CC-2006-013 (May 5, 2006), the Case Specific Advice Task Force noted that the IRM no longer provided procedures for FSAs. The Task Force noted that the IRM provides options other than TAMs for requesting advice from the national office. See IRM 33.1.2.2.3.2 (Aug. 11, 2004).

[214] Depending on the publisher, these documents may be referred to as Chief Counsel advice, Chief Counsel advisories, or IRS legal memoranda (ILM).

set forth in section 6110. The numbering system initially reflected the IRS division involved (e.g., INTL-1 involved the foreign tax credit). Later items use the common numbering system (e.g., LGM 200018050).

e. IRS Technical Assistance (ITA; I.T.A.)

The national office provides **technical assistance** to other IRS offices. Technical assistance issued to district and regional offices, Chief Counsel field offices, and service centers is subject to disclosure. These documents are not authority for avoiding the substantial understatement penalty.

Technical assistance documents use the common numbering system (e.g., 200211042 dealt with whether the recipient of a transferable state remediation tax credit had gross income). Although Tax Analysts indexes these documents as ITAs, LexisNexis, Westlaw, and the IRS website classify them as Chief Counsel advice or advisory.

f. Additional Items

Guidance is subject to disclosure even if it takes relatively little time to produce. For example, even advice prepared in less than two hours and transmitted by email, is subject to disclosure.[215] Since 2003, redacted versions of revocations and denials of tax-exempt status have also been subject to release.[216]

The name given the particular item is generally unimportant because most Chief Counsel advice is numbered using a common system, can be searched based on Code sections, and with few exceptions does not constitute substantial authority for avoiding the section 6662(d) penalty.

h. Legal Advice Issued by Associate Chief Counsel

These documents are issued to IRS national program executives and managers to assist them in administering their programs; they are signed by executives in the national office of Chief Counsel. The legal advice in these documents often relates to industry-wide issues. The items described in this subsection and those following are often referred to as generic legal advice or non-taxpayer specific legal advice.

These documents are numbered by year and begin with the prefix AM (e.g., AM-2009-012, which deals with whether Liechtenstein Anstalts and Stiftungs are properly treated as business entities or trusts for United States tax purposes). This series begins in 2006.

---

[215] Tax Analysts v. Internal Revenue Service, 495 F.3d 676 (D.C. Cir. 2007).

[216] Tax Analysts v. Internal Revenue Service, 350 F.3d 100 (D.C. Cir. 2003).

i.Legal Advice Issued by Field Attorneys

These documents are issued to assist field or service center employees. Their numbering reflects the year and week of release and ends with an F (e.g., 201000901F, which deals with whether sales of gift cards by a disregarded entity are treated as sales of goods by the taxpayer if the goods are actually sold by the entity's parent). Some publishers refer to these documents as field attorney advice or Non Docketed Service Advice Reviews. This series begins in 2003.

j.Legal Advice Issued to Program Managers

These documents are similar in purpose to legal advice issued by Associate Chief Counsel; they are signed by attorneys in the national office of Chief Counsel. These documents are numbered by year and begin with the prefix PMTA (program manager technical assistance). For example, PMTA-2009-155 concerns whether publishing notices of revocation of exempt status on www.irs.gov satisfies the requirements of Code sections 6033(j) and 7428(c). This series begins in 2007.

The website listing includes UIL numbers for PMTA documents; it does not do so for legal advice issued by Associate Chief Counsel or legal advice issued to field attorneys.

SECTION E. ADMINISTRATIVE MANUALS & INSTRUCTIONS

1. Appeals Coordinated Issues (ACI)

Issues are selected for **appeals coordinated issue** status because they require uniformity of treatment on a national basis. Items selected may apply to an entire industry, a large number of partners, shareholders, or creditors, or a nationwide tax avoidance scheme. The list of issues appears in alphabetical order on the ACI page. Some of the listings include links to redacted versions of the Service's appeals settlement guidelines for those issues.

2. Chief Counsel Notices (CCN; C.C.N.)

These documents notify personnel of changes in policies or procedures, litigating positions, or other administrative information. Many of them are eventually added to the **Chief Counsel Directives Manual** and deleted as separate entries on the IRS website. Chief Counsel notices do not constitute authority for avoiding the substantial understatement penalty.

Since fiscal 2001, these documents are numbered by year with CC as a prefix. Some include UIL numbers. For example, CC-2009-004 instructed

Chief Counsel attorneys about determining whether a taxpayer who filed an action for damages had exhausted his administrative remedies. This document's cancellation date was set as the date on which the information was incorporated into the CCDM.[217]

3. Internal Revenue Manual (IRM; I.R.M.)

Your research may involve IRS operating policies. For example, you may want to determine IRS procedures for appeals or for dealing with rewards to informants. The **Internal Revenue Manual** is an excellent source of information about Service policies. It does not constitute authority for avoiding the substantial understatement penalty.

Illustration 10-8. Excerpt from IRM Table of Contents

Part 30	Administrative
Part 31	Guiding Principles
Part 32	Published Guidance and Other Guidance to Taxpayers
Part 33	Legal Advice
Part 34	Litigation in District Court, Bankruptcy Court, Court of Federal Claims, and State Court

Illustration 10-9. Excerpt from IRM Subdivisions

Part 32. Published Guidance and Other Guidance to Taxpayers

Chapter 3. Letter Rulings, Information Letters, and Closing Agreements

Section 2. Letter Rulings

32.3.2 Letter Rulings

- 32.3.2.1 Authority to Issue Letter Rulings
- 32.3.2.2 Refusal to Rule or Deferral of Letter Ruling Pending Issuance of Published Guidance
- 32.3.2.3 General Procedures for Handling Requests for Letter Rulings
- 32.3.2.4 Conferences
- 32.3.2.5 Coordination with Other Offices
- 32.3.2.6 Coordination with Other Federal Departments and Agencies
- 32.3.2.7 Referral of Copies of Letter Rulings to the Appropriate Service Official
- 32.3.2.8 Representation of Taxpayers
- Exhibit 32.3.2-1 Letter 1690
- Exhibit 32.3.2-2 Letter 1690 (Version 2): Accounting Method Change Letter
- Exhibit 32.3.2-3 Letter Ruling to Taxpayer
- Exhibit 32.3.2-4 Letter Ruling to Taxpayer's Representative
- Exhibit 32.3.2-5 Rulings, Determination Letters, Information Letters, and Closing Agreements
- Exhibit 32.3.2-6 Sample Format for Recommendation of Application or Rejection of Section 7805(b)(8) Relief
- Exhibit 32.3.2-7 Conference Report

---

[217] CCDM is the Chief Counsel Directives Manual, parts 30 through 39 of the IRM.

The IRM uses numerous decimals for subdivisions. Illustration 10-9 shows a portion of Part 32. The number after the first decimal is the chapter (3). The next number is the section (2). Items 1 through 8 are the next level. After you open the links, you are likely to find even more subdivisions (e.g., IRM 32.3.2.3.2.2.1).

4. LMSB Coordinated Issues

These documents provide guidance to field examiners on complex industry-wide issues. They are reviewed by Chief Counsel office personnel before LMSB issues them. Documents are generally grouped alphabetically by industry (and also alphabetically within an industry group). Issues that affect multiple industries appear before the separate industry listings. A list of so-called "listed transactions," which the Service has determined are structured with tax avoidance or evasion as the significant purpose—and for which it will issue a coordinated issue paper—appears at the end of the industry listings.

Illustration 10-10. Partial Listing of Coordinated Issues

ALL INDUSTRIES (Cross All Industry Lines)

- The Applicable Recovery Period under § 168(a) for Open-Air Parking Structures - 07-31-2009

- "Basis Shifting" Tax Shelter - 12-03-2002

- Contingent Liabilities - 04-04-2003

→Click on a listing to read the issue and the IRS analysis and conclusion.

→Several of these documents include LMSB numbers (e.g., LMSB-04-0208-005) or UIL numbers, which do not appear on the website listing.

5. LMSB Industry Director Guidance

These documents are issued to provide guidance to LMSB examiners to ensure consistent tax treatment. The website lists documents by date and topic. The listing indicates those issues that LMSB has designated as Tier I, II, or III issues.[218]

---

[218] Tier I (issues of high strategic importance); Tier II (issues of significant compliance risk); Tier III (issues of highest compliance risk for a particular industry). The LMSB Issue Tiering Fact Sheet provides more information. See http://www.irs.gov/businesses/corporations/article/0,,id=200574,00.html.

6. Recent Delegation Orders and Policy Statements

This page contains documents covering recent delegation within the Service and policy statements that have been approved but not yet added to the Internal Revenue Manual.

7. Recent Interim Guidance to Staff

The documents in this section are arranged by Internal Revenue Manual part. Because they often supplement the IRM, you should check this part of the website when you are working with a particular IRM section.

8. Taxpayer Advocate Service Level Agreements

The documents in this series cover agreements between the Taxpayer Advocate Service (TAS) and operating units within the IRS (e.g., appeals, criminal investigation, LMSB). They cover the procedures and responsibilities for processing TAS casework when the authority to complete a case transaction lies with the other unit.

F. PROGRAM PLANS & REPORTS

This section includes documents issued by the IRS or other entities within the Treasury Department. They include:

• IRS Performance Plan (a lengthy summary of IRS goals and accomplishments; the most recently posted item is for fiscal 2004)

• A link to a web page describing Art Appraisal Services

• FOIA Annual Reports (covering requests that were received and processed by agencies within the Treasury Department)

• IRS Strategic Plan (issued in June 2004)

• Priority Guidance Plans (this series begins in 1999 and is discussed in Chapter 9)

• Privacy Impact Assessments (covering information the IRS collects from the public)

• TIGTA Audit Plans (this series begins in 1999)[219]

G. TRAINING & REFERENCE MATERIALS

The documents in this section are training materials for IRS personnel. They include the following items:

---

[219] The Treasury Inspector General for Tax Administration's audit reports may give rise to changes in IRS procedures or even to legislation.

• APA Training Materials (training related to Code section 482 and transfer pricing)

• CCA Check Training Material (training related to a program that captures emailed Chief Counsel advice that may be subject to disclosure)

• Disclosure & Privacy Law Reference Guide (history and discussion of disclosure and privacy statutes related to taxpayer information)

• EO Tax Law Training Articles (materials to help the public understand how the IRS administers the tax law provisions applied to exempt organizations)[220]

• Market Segment Specialization Program (Audit Technique Guides)

The **Audit Technique Guides** are prepared to assist auditors who examine companies in a particular market segment (e.g., child care, farming, retail). Many of these documents include glossaries of terms a researcher can use to become familiar with a particular industry.[221]

SECTION H. UNRELEASED DOCUMENTS

1. Advance Pricing Agreements (APA)

Advance pricing agreements are made between taxpayers and the IRS regarding income allocation between commonly controlled entities. Companies that segment their operations between countries with different tax rates and structures can enter into APAs with both the United States and the other country if the two countries have a tax treaty. Code section 6110(b)(1)(B) exempts APAs from release to the public. The IRS does issue an annual report concerning APAs.[222]

2. Closing Agreements

Closing agreements memorialize the parties' agreement regarding specific taxpayer–IRS disputes. As a condition of the agreement, the IRS has occasionally forced publication of certain closing agreements with exempt

---

[220] Documents include continuing education program (CPE) materials (1979–2004), 2009 training materials, and determinations guide sheets related to particular topics (e.g., donor advised funds).

[221] For example, a Guide for the poultry industry explains terms such as grow out house and protein plant.

[222] Ann. 2009-28, 2009-15 I.R.B. 760, covers 2008. On March 30, 2010, the IRS announced that the report for 2009 would be published in Ann. 2010-21 and would appear in 2010-15 I.R.B. on April 12, 2010.

organizations. Code section 6110(b)(1)(B) exempts closing agreements from release to the public.

Section I. Documents That Are Not Available on IRS Website

If a document was released before the Electronic Reading Room began, you probably will not find it on the IRS website. This is true for older I.R.B. items and documents that reflect Freedom of Information Act or other statutory disclosure requirements. Some documents have never appeared on the IRS website because they were eliminated before there was an Electronic Reading Room. Technical Memoranda (TM; T.M.; Tech. Mem.) fall into this category. These documents provided background information on regulations. Much of their content is reflected in the Preambles to T.D.s and NPRMs.

Although you can find current documents on the IRS website, you will have to locate earlier documents from other sources. Services such as LexisNexis, Westlaw, Checkpoint, and IntelliConnect carry both I.R.B. items and other documents.

Section J. Print Internal Revenue Bulletin and Cumulative Bulletin

The IRS website is convenient because it includes information that the IRS publishes in the Internal Revenue Bulletin, other information that is available in the Electronic Reading Room, and miscellaneous information (e.g., publications and tax forms). But, as is true for most government websites, coverage before the mid-1990s is virtually nonexistent.

Although you may have to obtain non-I.R.B. items from subscription services, you can probably find print versions of the I.R.B. or at least of its semiannual compilation—the Cumulative Bulletin. Even if your library has retained only the semiannual Cumulative Bulletins, you will have access to most I.R.B. material.

This section covers the I.R.B. and C.B. It also includes a discussion of the Bulletin Index-Digest System, which the I.R.S. stopped publishing after the 1993/94 edition.

1. Internal Revenue Bulletin

The weekly **Internal Revenue Bulletin** (I.R.B.) has four parts. Part I prints the text of all revenue rulings, final regulations, and Supreme Court tax decisions issued during the week; publication is in Code section order. Part II covers treaties, including Treasury Department Technical Explanations (Subpart A), and used to include tax legislation (Subpart

B). Part III contains notices and revenue procedures, while Part IV, "Items of General Interest," is varied in content. Its coverage includes disbarment notices, announcements, and notices of proposed rulemaking. Federal Register dates and comment deadlines are provided in addition to the Preambles and text of proposed regulations. The I.R.B. also prints notices of IRS acquiescence or nonacquiescence for judicial decisions against the government.

Illustration 10-11. Internal Revenue Bulletin Cover Page

Internal Revenue

bulletin

Bulletin No. 2009-46
November 16, 2009

**HIGHLIGHTS
OF THIS ISSUE**

These synopses are intended only as aids to the reader in identifying the subject matter covered. They may not be relied upon as authoritative interpretations.

EMPLOYEE PLANS

REG–159704–03, page 632.
Proposed regulations contain proposed amendments to 20 CFR part 901 relating to the enrollment of actuaries under section 3042 of the Employee Retirement Income Security Act of 1974 (ERISA). The proposed amendments would update the eligibility requirements for performing actuarial services for ERISA-covered employee pension benefit plans, including the continuing education requirements, and the standards for performing such actuarial services. The proposed amendments would affect employee pension benefit plans and the actuaries providing actuarial services to those plans.

Notice 2009–86, page 629.
Further extension of effective date of normal retirement age regulations for governmental plans. This notice announces the intent to further extend the final effective date of the final regulations under section 401(a) of the Code relating to distributions from a pension plan upon attainment of Normal Retirement Age for governmental plans, as described in section 414(d). The regulations were published in the Federal Register as T.D. 9325, 2007–1 C.B. 1386 (72 FR 28604) on May 22, 2007. In Notice 2008–98, the effective date for governmental plans was extended to plan years beginning on or after January 1, 2011. Taking into account this extension, the NRA regulations will be effective for a governmental plan (as defined in § 414(d) of the Code) for plan years beginning on or after January 1, 2013. This notice does not change the

EXEMPT ORGANIZATIONS

Announcement 2009–80, page 646.
The Service has revoked its determination that Elimidebt Management Systems, Inc., of Orlando, FL and Hallandale, FL; and Richard & Jane Pater Charitable Foundation of Salt Lake City, UT, qualify as organizations described in sections 501(c)(3) and 170(c)(2) of the Code.

TAX CONVENTIONS

Announcement 2009–79, page 628.
Mutual Agreement on Share Attribution under Belgium Treaty. A copy of the Competent Authority Agreement released by the Deputy Commissioner (International) [U.S. Competent Authority] on October 15, 2009, is set forth.

ADMINISTRATIVE

Notice 2009–87, page 630.
This notice invites public comments on possible modifications to the conditions established in Rev. Proc. 80–59, 1980–2 C.B. 855, under which a trustee of a blind trust that meets the requirements of section 102(f)(3) of the Appendix to Title 5 of the United States Code (or any successor provision of the

Each I.R.B. was separately paginated until mid-1999. The I.R.B. is now paginated successively over a six-month period.

Each issue contains a Numerical Finding List for each type of item. A Finding List of Current Action on Previously Published Items indicates IRS, but not judicial, action. The Finding Lists lack any tie-in to Code sections and cover no more than six months. The quarterly subject area indexes also lack Code section information.

The Bulletin is best used to locate material for which you already have a citation[223] or as a tool for staying abreast of recent developments.

Illustration 10-12. Finding List of Current Actions in 2010-7 I.R.B.

Finding List of Current Actions on Previously Published Items[1]

Bulletins 2010–1 through 2010–7

Announcements:

2010-4
Corrected by
Ann. 2010-10, 2010-7 I.R.B. *410*

Notices:

2005-88
Superseded by
Notice 2010-13, 2010-4 I.R.B. *327*

2008-41
Modified by
Notice 2010-7, 2010-3 I.R.B. *296*

Revenue Procedures— Continued:

2008-14
Updated by
Rev. Proc. 2010-15, 2010-7 I.R.B. *404*

2009-1
Superseded by
Rev. Proc. 2010-1, 2010-1 I.R.B. *1*

2009-2
Superseded by
Rev. Proc. 2010-2, 2010-1 I.R.B. *90*

2009-3
Superseded by
Rev. Proc. 2010-3, 2010-1 I.R.B. *110*

2009-4
Superseded by
Rev. Proc. 2010-4, 2010-1 I.R.B. *122*

2. Cumulative Bulletin

Every six months the material in the I.R.B. is republished in a hardbound **Cumulative Bulletin** (C.B.). The C.B. began publication in 1919. Volumes initially were given Arabic numerals (1919–1921). Although volume spines may show Arabic numerals, the IRS used Roman numerals for 1922 through 1936 volumes. Since 1937, volumes have been numbered by year (e.g., 1937-1). With the exception of 1943–1945, there have been two volumes annually (with occasional extra volumes for extensive legislative history material)[224] since 1920; the -1, -2 numbering system for each year began in 1922.

The C.B. format has varied over time. Before 1998, it largely followed that of the weekly service with three exceptions. First, major tax legislation and committee reports generally appeared in a third volume rather

---

[223] You can locate citations in citators, looseleaf services, periodical articles, and newsletters.

[224] The I.R.S. stopped publishing the -3 volume after 2003-3 C.B. You can obtain the legislative history material previously included in these volumes using the services covered in Chapter 7.

than in the two semiannual volumes.[225] Second, only disbarment notices and proposed regulations appeared from Part IV.[226] Finally, rulings appeared in the C.B. in semiannual Code section order; this bore no relation to their numerical order.

Table 10-3. Cumulative Bulletin Format Changes

Year	Numbering	Other Major Changes
1919	1, 2, 3	
1922	I-1, I-2, II-1	Rulings divided by type of tax
1937	1937-1, 1937-2	
1939		Committee reports added
1953		End of separate table of contents by type of tax
1974		End of separate sections for 1939 Code
1981		Proposed Regulations added
1993		Acquiescences no longer limited to Tax Court regular decisions
1998		Six-month rearrangement of I.R.B. items ceased
2003		Last C.B. to include legislative materials

In 1998, the IRS ceased recompiling items in the C.B. Instead, C.B.s are simply bound versions of the individual I.R.B.s. If an item appears in the I.R.B., it will also appear in the C.B. Successive pagination for the I.R.B.s began in mid-1999.

When the C.B. changed format, it added a Code Sections Affected by Current Actions listing. Although this provides additional assistance in using six-month's worth of material, it does not make searching over longer periods of time any easier. The other C.B. indexes and finding lists are as difficult to use as are their counterparts in the I.R.B.

3. Bulletin Index-Digest System

The IRS issued the **Index-Digest** in four services: Income Tax; Estate and Gift Tax; Employment Tax; and Excise Tax. The Income Tax service, which is the focus of this discussion, was supplemented quarterly; the other services received semiannual supplementation. The last cumulation covered 1954–1993 for income tax and 1954–1994 for the other taxes.

---

[225] Committee reports for 1913 through 1938 appear in 1939-1 (pt. 2) C.B. Committee reports for the 1954 Code's enactment never appeared in the C.B.

[226] These are printed in Part III or immediately following it through 1997. Proposed regulations, which appear as a separate category, were added in the 1981-1 volume. The C.B.'s format differed from the above description until the 1974-2 volume.

The Index-Digest provided I.R.B. or C.B. citations for revenue rulings and procedures, Supreme Court and adverse Tax Court decisions, Public Laws, Treasury Decisions, and treaties. It also digested the rulings, procedures, and court decisions.

Illustration 10-13. C.B. Code Sections Affected by Current Actions

Code Sections Affected by Current Actions

Section 34.—Certain Uses of Gasoline and Special Fuels
Notice 2007-37, *1002*

Section 40A.—Biodiesel and Renewable Diesel Used as Fuel
Notice 2007-37, *1002*

Section 42.—Low-Income Housing Credit
Rev. Rul. 2007-2, *266*
Rev. Rul. 2007-5, *378*
Rev. Rul. 2007-9, *422*
Rev. Rul. 2007-15, *687*
Rev. Rul. 2007-23, *889*
Rev. Rul. 2007-25, *956*
Rev. Rul. 2007-29, *1223*
Rev. Rul. 2007-36, *1339*

Section 61.—Gross Income Defined
Rev. Proc. 2007-11, *261*   Rev. Rul. 2007-7, *468*

The following paragraphs explain using the final (1954–1993/94) Index-Digest to locate citations and digests.

a. Statutes and Regulations

Specific Code and regulations sections that were added or amended appear in the Finding Lists for Public Laws and Treasury Decisions. A C.B. citation is given for the first page of each Public Law involved.

Another Finding List, "Public Laws Published in the Bulletin," provides committee report citations and popular names for the various revenue acts. It is in Public Law number order.

b. Rulings and Procedures

The Finding Lists for Revenue Rulings, Revenue Procedures, and Other Items can be used in various ways to locate relevant rulings and procedures. These items appear in Code and regulations section order in the "Internal Revenue Code of 1986" section, and in ruling and procedure number order in the "Revenue Rulings" and "Revenue Procedures" sections. The Index-Digest lists revenue rulings and procedures involving treaties by country in the "Revenue Rulings and Revenue Procedures under Tax Conventions" section. The service covers both 1954 and 1986 Code items.

Instead of C.B. citations, the Finding Lists cite to a digest of each item in the Index-Digest itself; the C.B. citation follows the digest. The two-step format frequently saves time; a glance through the digest may indicate the item is not worth reading in full text.

Illustration 10-14. Excerpt from Bulletin Index-Digest System

Allowances	22.47 Rental; minister; traveling	nished by the National Guard to officers and
they are not ordained, commissioned, or licensed as ministers of the gospel. §1.107-1. (Sec. 22(b), '39 Code; Sec. 107, '86 Code.) Rev. Rul. 59-270, 1959-2 C.B. 44	evangelist. An ordained minister, who performs evangelistic services at churches located away from the community in which he maintains his permanent home may exclude	enlisted personnel while on active duty is not includible in the gross income of the recipients. §1.61-2 (Sec. 61, '86 Code.) Rev. Rul. 60-65, 1960-1 C.B. 21.

→The Index-Digest lists digest numbers (e.g., 22.47) after Code and regulations sections. The digests appear in a separate Index-Digest section.

Because the digests are arranged by subject matter, you can locate pertinent rulings even if you do not know the underlying Code or regulations section. The subject matter divisions are so numerous that the same item may be digested under several different headings.

If a particular ruling or procedure was modified or otherwise affected by subsequent IRS action, the information appears in the "Actions on Previously Published Revenue Rulings and Revenue Procedures" section of the Finding Lists. Judicial decisions affecting a ruling are not indicated. The IRS provided a C.B. citation for updating material if a subsequent ruling affected an earlier one.

c. Judicial Decisions

The Finding Lists for Revenue Rulings, Revenue Procedures, and Other Items listed all Supreme Court decisions and adverse Tax Court decisions in which the IRS acquiesced or nonacquiesced.

Supreme Court decisions appear alphabetically in the "Decisions of the Supreme Court" section of the Finding Lists. They are listed by an IRS-assigned Court Decision (Ct. D.) number in the "Internal Revenue Code of 1986" materials, arranged according to the applicable Code and regulations sections.

Tax Court decisions are listed alphabetically in the "Decisions of the Tax Court" section of the Finding Lists; they are listed by T.C. citation in the "Internal Revenue Code of 1986" materials.

As with rulings and procedures, references to Supreme Court decisions in the Finding Lists give only the digest number.[227] The official and Cumulative Bulletin citations follow the case digest. Because the digests follow a subject matter format, you can locate decisions by digest topic without first consulting the Finding Lists.

SECTION K. LOCATING IRS DOCUMENTS

1. Documents Published in Internal Revenue Bulletin

a. Finding Lists

You can find citations to these documents using print or electronic sources. Print sources include Code-based looseleaf services, such as Standard Federal Tax Reporter and United States Tax Reporter. You can also use topic-based looseleaf services such as Federal Tax Coordinator 2d and Rabkin & Johnson, Federal Income, Gift and Estate Taxation. Both types of looseleaf service are discussed in detail in Chapter 13. Another print source is the Bulletin Index-Digest System (Section J), although it is useful only for 1954–1993/94 material.

Because revenue rulings and procedures, notices, and announcements carry numbers that don't correspond to Code or regulations sections, CD/DVD and online services are excellent tools for locating them. You can search many electronic databases by topic, Code or regulations section, or prior ruling. Use case citators to find acquiescences.

b. Digests

Unlike finding lists, digests provide descriptions that help you decide if an item is likely to be useful. Keep in mind that a digest's usefulness is a function of its compiler's expertise and its frequency of supplementation.

You can locate digests in a looseleaf service such as United States Tax Reporter, in newsletters such as Tax Notes, and in the Service's Bulletin Index-Digest System (1954–1993/94 material only).

---

[227] Tax Court citations appear in both the Finding Lists and the digests. The Finding Lists indicate acquiescences; the digests provide citations for them.

c. Texts

Several services provide texts of Internal Revenue Bulletin items. Most of those listed below are available in both print and electronic formats.

Looseleaf services such as Standard Federal Tax Reporter and United States Tax Reporter include the text of current year rulings in their print services; electronic services may include older rulings or provide links to them on other databases. The Rulings volumes of Mertens, Law of Federal Income Taxation include full text of revenue rulings and procedures since 1954 but do not carry other Internal Revenue Bulletin documents.

Print versions of daily newsletters such as Daily Tax Report carry Internal Revenue Bulletin items as they are released; electronic versions include prior releases.

The print versions of the Internal Revenue Bulletin and Cumulative Bulletin (Section J) include text of all items issued for a particular week (or six-month period). Electronic services that carry these items include:

- Checkpoint (I.R.B. items since 1954)

- HeinOnline (C.B. since 1919)

- IntelliConnect (I.R.B. items since 1954)

- LexisNexis (I.R.B. items since 1954)

- Westlaw (I.R.B. items since 1954)

d. A Note on Searching in Electronic and Print Sources

In using electronic sources, you must differentiate between those that allow searching by topic and those that include the relevant information but do not provide a means to find it using word or Code section searches. This distinction is particularly important for online services. If you can't find the item without knowing its citation, the source is less valuable than one that allows access based on Code sections or other search terms.

Illustrations 10-15 through 10-20 illustrate searching for a revenue ruling discussing loan repayment assistance programs (LRAPs). I conducted this search in the IRS website, but I could have instead used a subscription service. The item I will find is Rev. Rul. 2008-34.

The IRS website includes a page that gives access to the Internal Revenue Bulletins. That page does not provide a tool to search for individual items if you don't know which Bulletin you want. Alternatively, you might try using the Advanced Search function, on another page of the IRS site, and search for "LRAP" or "loan repayment assistance program."

Illustration 10-15. *Internal Revenue Bulletin List on IRS Website*

Internal Revenue Bulletins

Instructions:

The Internal Revenue Bulletin (IRB) is the authoritative instrument for announcing official rulings and procedures of the IRS and for publishing Treasury Decisions, Executive Orders, Tax Conventions, legislation, court decisions, and other items of general interest.

1. Enter a term in the Find Box.
2. Select a category (column heading) in the drop down.
3. Click Find.

Find [2008-34]   in [Bulletin ▼]   Find   Find Help

1 - 100 of 742 files   Show per page: 25 50 **100** 200

Bulletin ♦ ⊘	Published ♦ ⊘
Internal Revenue Bulletin 2010-10	03/04/2010
Internal Revenue Bulletin 2010-09	02/26/2010
Internal Revenue Bulletin 2010-08	02/20/2010

→A search for 2008-34 will yield I.R.B. 2008-34, not Revenue Ruling 2008-34 or any other document numbered 2008-34.

→You can sort the Bulletin list in chronological order or reverse chronological order. The Published sort option gives misleading results. Even items from the 1990s bear Published dates of 2000 or later.

Illustration 10-16. *Advanced Search Option on IRS Website:* "*Exact Phrase*"

Advanced Search Options

[SEARCH]

Find Results

With all of the words:		in the body ▼
With the exact phrase:	LRAP ⇐———	in the body ▼
With any of the words:		in the body ▼
Without the words:		in the body ▼

Limit Search To

☐ Entire Site	☐ Individuals	☐ Internal Revenue Manual
☐ Forms and Instructions	☐ Businesses	☐ Tax Statistics
☐ Publications	☐ Charities & Non-Profits	☐ e-file
☐ Notices	☐ Government Entities	☐ Español
☑ IR Bulletins	☐ Tax Professionals (Includes Tax Regulations)	☐ FAQs

→The Advanced Search option also lets you specify dates, number of items shown per page (up to 500), sort order, and document format.

Illustration 10-17. Search Results on IRS Website: "Exact Phrase"

Search Results

"LRAP"	SEARCH	Advanced Search
		Search Tips

6 results found   Summaries: **Show** | Hide

Sort by: **Relevance** | Date   Results: 1-6

Results ⊙

IRB 2008-28 (Rev. July 14, 2008)   10 Jul 08
Internal Revenue Bulletin   Highlight Term(s)
Bulletin No. 2008-28 July 14, 2008 HIGHLIGHTS OF THIS ISSUE These synopses are intended only as aids to the reader in
identifying the subject matter covered. They may not be relied upon as authoritative ...
http://www.irs.gov/pub/irs-irbs/irb08-28.pdf - 2498.1KB

IRB 2008-52 (Rev. December 29, 2008)   24 Dec 08
Internal Revenue Bulletin   Highlight Term(s)
Bulletin No. 2008-52 December 29, 2008 HIGHLIGHTS OF THIS ISSUE These synopses are intended only as aids to the
reader in identifying the subject matter covered. They may not be relied upon as authoritative ...
http://www.irs.gov/pub/irs-irbs/irb08-52.pdf - 788.2KB

IRB 2008-47 (Rev. November 24, 2008)   23 Nov 08
Internal Revenue Bulletin   Highlight Term(s)
Bulletin No. 2008-47 November 24, 2008 HIGHLIGHTS OF THIS ISSUE These synopses are intended only as aids to the
reader in identifying the subject matter covered. They may not be relied upon as authoritative ...
http://www.irs.gov/pub/irs-irbs/irb08-47.pdf - 893.3KB

→The hit list doesn't provide information about the items.

Illustration 10-18. Advanced Search Option on IRS Website:
"All of the Words"

Advanced Search Options

SEARCH

Find Results

With all of the words:	LRAP ⟵	in the body ▾
With the exact phrase:		in the body ▾
With any of the words:		in the body ▾
Without the words:		in the body ▾

Limit Search To

☐ Entire Site	☐ Individuals	☐ Internal Revenue Manual
☐ Forms and Instructions	☐ Businesses	☐ Tax Statistics
☐ Publications	☐ Charities & Non-Profits	☐ e-file
☐ Notices	☐ Government Entities	☐ Español
☑ IR Bulletins	☐ Tax Professionals	☐ FAQs
	(Includes Tax Regulations)	

Illustration 10-19. Search Results on IRS Website:
"All of the Words"

Search Results

+LRAP	SEARCH	Advanced Search
		Search Tips

6 results found   Summaries: **Show** | Hide

Sort by: **Relevance** | Date   Results: 1-6

Results ⦿

IRB 2008-28 (Rev. July 14, 2008) 📄   10 Jul 08
Internal Revenue Bulletin   Highlight Term(s)
... This ruling clarifies that a law school loan made under a Loan Repayment Assistance Program (**LRAP**) generally satisfies
the requirements of section 108(f)(1) of the Code, and is ...
http://www.irs.gov/pub/irs-irbs/irb08-28.pdf - 2498.1KB

IRB 2008-52 (Rev. December 29, 2008) 📄   24 Dec 08
Internal Revenue Bulletin   Highlight Term(s)
Bulletin No. 2008-52 December 29, 2008 HIGHLIGHTS OF THIS ISSUE These synopses are intended only as aids to the
reader in identifying the subject matter covered. They may not be relied upon as authoritative ...
http://www.irs.gov/pub/irs-irbs/irb08-52.pdf - 788.2KB

IRB 2008-47 (Rev. November 24, 2008) 📄   23 Nov 08
Internal Revenue Bulletin   Highlight Term(s)
Bulletin No. 2008-47 November 24, 2008 HIGHLIGHTS OF THIS ISSUE These synopses are intended only as aids to the
reader in identifying the subject matter covered. They may not be relied upon as authoritative ...
http://www.irs.gov/pub/irs-irbs/irb08-47.pdf - 893.3KB

→The first item appears promising. I should read each item because the results screen doesn't give adequate information about most of them. Note the Highlight Terms option, which I can use in each document.

Illustration 10-20. Summary of Revenue Ruling 2008-34

Section 108.—Income From Discharge of Indebtedness

Law school loan repayment assistance programs. This ruling clarifies that a law school loan made under a Loan Repayment Assistance Program (LRAP) generally satisfies the requirements of section 108(f)(1) of the Code, and is a "student loan" within the meaning of section 108(f)(2).

Rev. Rul. 2008–34

→This ruling appears promising. Even though it is recent, I should use a citator to make sure it is still valid.

The IRS website includes two I.R.B. versions. Illustration 10-15 covers the PDF search screen for these documents. There is also an HTML option, which has hyperlinks. The HTML screen offers both HTML and PDF options. The PDF search screen occasionally includes the most recent I.R.B. before the HTML search screen does. The IRS website has PDF versions since 1996; its HTML coverage begins in July 2003.

Illustration 10-21. HTML Listing for I.R.B.s

IRB Title	Publication Date
IRB 2010-10 html pdf	March 8, 2010
IRB 2010-9 html pdf	March 1, 2010
IRB 2010-8 html pdf	February 22, 2010
IRB 2010-7 html pdf	February 16, 2010

Illustration 10-22. HTML Version of I.R.B. 2008-28

Table of Contents

- Highlights of This Issue
    - INCOME TAX
        - Rev. Rul. 2008-34
        - Rev. Rul. 2008-37
        - REG-101258-08
        - Notice 2008-56
        - Notice 2008-57
        - Notice 2008-58
        - Rev. Proc. 2008-32
        - Rev. Proc. 2008-33
        - Announcement 2008-63
    - EMPLOYMENT TAX
        - Rev. Proc. 2008-32
        - Rev. Proc. 2008-33
    - ADMINISTRATIVE
        - Announcement 2008-64
- Preface
    - The IRS Mission
    - Introduction
- Part I. Rulings and Decisions Under the Internal Revenue Code of 1986
    - Rev. Rul. 2008-34
        - ISSUE
        - FACTS
        - LAW
        - ANALYSIS
        - HOLDING
        - DRAFTING INFORMATION

→If you want to go directly to a particular segment within the ruling, the HTML version makes that easy.

Instead of using the IRS website, I could have used a subscription service (e.g., LexisNexis or Westlaw) with the same search terms. Alternatively, I might have used a the looseleaf services to find annotations dealing with loan repayment assistance programs (LRAPs).

2. Other Officially Published Documents

You can also find IRS forms, instructions, and explanatory publications using the IRS website. You can use a word search similar to that shown in the preceding illustrations if you don't know the name or number of the form or publication you seek. The IRS site includes these documents in full text. Commercial services also make them available.

3. Publicly Released Documents

Because the IRS issues so many of these documents, your library is more likely to provide access to them electronically than through a print service. If your library has a print service, you may prefer to find items electronically even if you ultimately read them in print.

Although the IRS website provides free access to publicly released documents, its home page does not indicate where to find them. To find publicly available documents, click on Freedom of Information Act, which appears on the bottom of the home page. Then click on Electronic Reading Room. You will reach a screen that shows the types of documents currently available for you to search. [See Illustrations 10-1 through 10-3.]

The link for IRS Written Determinations covers those documents discussed in Section D that follow a common numbering system. Documents such as AODs, which have their own numbering system, have their own search tools. Most of the items listed in the other Electronic Reading Room categories do not have search screens on the IRS site.

Texts of publicly released documents are included in numerous electronic research sources. These include OneDisc, LexisNexis, Westlaw, Checkpoint, IntelliConnect, and TaxCore. You can search these services by Code section or by phrases describing the issue you are researching.

With one exception, electronic services operate the same way for publicly released documents as they do for documents published in the I.R.B. That exception relates to the numbering system. As noted in Section D, commercial services may assign their own names to documents issued by the Chief Counsel's office. If you are not sure what name a particular service uses for Chief Counsel items, search across all possible databases rather than limiting yourself to a single database. Fortunately, all publishers use the same names for the most common items: letter rulings, technical advice memoranda, and actions on decisions.

The illustrations below compare search tools on the IRS website with options available in commercial services. Remember that the IRS website does not include items before the mid-1990s; commercial services generally begin their coverage with each item's first public release.

When using a commercial service, consider two important questions. First, does it have the most recent items? Second, does it include all types of Chief Counsel advice? For the former question, an online service is usually preferable to a CD/DVD service. For the latter, make sure you compare available items if you have access to more than one service.

Illustration 10-23. *IRS Website AOD Finding List*

Find		in Number ▾	Find	Find Help	

1 - 25 of 84 files　　　　　　Show per page: 25 50 100 200　　　　　　« Previous | 1 2 3 4 | Next »

Number ▼ ⓐ	Decision ⬍ ⓐ	Issue ⬍ ⓐ	Released ⬍ ⓐ
2009-01	Cox v. Comm., 514 F.3d 1119 (10th Cir. 2008), rev'g 126 T.C. 367	Whether indirect consideration of a tax liability in conjunction with evaluating collection alternatives raised in a collection due process hearing for an earlier tax year disqualifies an appeals offi	05/07/2009
2008-01	Herbert V. Kohler, Jr. et al. v. Comm.; T.C. Memo. 2006-152	Whether Sec. 2032 allows a discount for transfer restrictions and a purchase option ("restrictions") imposed on closely-held corporate stock pursuant to a post-death taxfree reorganization in determin	03/03/2008
2007-05	Roosevelt Wallace v. Comm., 128 T.C. No. 11 (April 16, 2007).	The Service will no longer litigate whether payments made by the Department of Veterans Affairs under the compensated work therapy program described in 38 U.S.C. section 1718 are tax exempt. RELEASE	10/18/2007
2007-04	U.S. v. Roxworthy, 457 F.3d 590 (6th Cir. 2006).	Whether a company should have been required to produce an accounting firm's opinion letters in response to an IRS summons. RELEASE DATE: Septemember 25, 2007	09/25/2007

→The IRS finding list sorts by AOD number, Decision, Issue, and Release date. This Finding List covers AODs issued since 1997.

Illustration 10-24. *Checkpoint Listing of AODs*

Checkpoint Contents
　　Federal Library
　　　　Federal Source Materials
　　　　　　IRS Rulings & Releases
　　　　　　　　Private Letter Rulings & TAMs, FSAs, SCAs, CCAs, GCMs, AODs & Other FOIA Documents
　　　　　　　　☐ Currently in: **Actions on Decisions (1967 to Present)**

+ ☐ **2009**
− ☐ **2008**
　📄 🔖 **AOD 2008-001 -- IRC Sec(s). 2032, 3/4/2008**
− ☐ **2007**
　📄 🔖 **AOD 2007-005 -- IRC Sec(s). 61; 140, 10/18/2007**
　📄 🔖 **AOD 2007-004 -- IRC Sec(s). 7602, 10/1/2007**
　📄 🔖 **AOD 2007-003 -- IRC Sec(s). 6103; 7431, 07/25/2007**
　📄 🔖 **AOD 2007-002 -- IRC Sec(s). 6320; 6330; 7122, 2/27/2007**
　📄 🔖 **AOD 2007-001 -- IRC Sec(s). 3111; 3401, 1/18/2007**
+ ☐ **2006**

→The Table of Contents indicates the Code section. Searching by key word, Code section, or taxpayer name is also possible.

Commercial services often include documents that predate release mandated by litigation. For example, Checkpoint covers AODs issued since 1967. The LexisNexis AOD file includes documents from 1963. Both predate the year (1981) for which the IRS was required to release these documents to the public.

Illustration 10-25. IRS Document Search Options in LexisNexis

Taxation > Find Federal Administrative Materials > **Agency Decisions** (Remove "Taxation" tab)

- ☐ IRS Bulletins, Letter Rulings & Memoranda Decisions, Combined ⓘ
- ☐ IRS General Counsel Memos, Actions on Decisions, & Technical Memos ⓘ
- ☐ IRS Cumulative Bulletin, IRB, Letter Rulings, & Technical Advice Memos ⓘ
- ☐ IRS Advance Releases ⓘ
- ☐ IRS Actions on Decisions ⓘ
- ☐ IRS Chief Counsel Advice ⓘ
- ☐ IRS Cumulative Bulletin and Internal Revenue Bulletin ⓘ
- ☐ IRS Field Service Advice Memorandums ⓘ
- ☐ IRS Chief Counsel Notices ⓘ
- ☐ IRS General Counsel Memoranda ⓘ

- ☐ IRS Generic Legal Advice Memoranda ⓘ
- ☐ IRS Private Letter Rulings and Technical Advice Memoranda ⓘ
- ☐ IRS Service Center Advice ⓘ
- ☐ IRS Technical Memoranda ⓘ
- ☐ Litigation Guideline Memorandums ⓘ
- ☐ Department of Labor ERISA Opinion Letters ⓘ
- ☐ Pension Benefit Guaranty Corporation Opinion Letters ⓘ
- ☐ TNT Applicable Federal Rates ⓘ
- ☐ TNT IRS ISP and MSSP ⓘ
- ☐ IRS Non-Taxpayer Specifics in Formal CCA ⓘ

→LexisNexis offers the type of electronic search options available from nongovernment services. I can search one or more databases and can do so by Code section or key word.

Illustration 10-26. IRS Website Written Determination Finding List

Find [＿＿＿＿＿] in [Number ▼] [Find] Find Help

1 - 25 of 39,387 files   Show per page: 25 50 100 200   « Previous | 1 2 3 4 5 6 7 8 9

Number ▼ ❓	UILC ⬍ ❓	Subject ⬍ ❓	Released ⬍
200952069	509.03-00	Continuation of Private Foundation Status	12/25/2009
200952068	412.00-00	Minimum Funding Standards	12/25/2009
200952067	408.03-00	Rollover Contributions	12/25/2009
200952066	408.03-00	Rollover Contributions	12/25/2009

→You can sort documents classified as written determinations based on document number, UIL number, Subject, or Release date.

→The website does not indicate whether the document is a letter ruling, technical advice memorandum, or other Chief Counsel document.

SECTION L. UNIFORM ISSUE LIST (UIL)

The **Uniform Issue List** is a Code-section-based index of issues. The IRS assigns UIL numbers to documents released to the public pursuant to Code section 6110, which is discussed in Section D. This list is prepared by Chief Counsel office personnel.[228] AOD 1984-022 [Illustration 10-5] includes two UIL numbers, both involving section 162. The IRS once published a UIL list in Publication 1102; its listing in the Catalog of U.S. Government Publications shows a November 1998 revision date.

The IRS varies in the terminology used for UIL numbers. The terms UIL, UILC, or Index may precede the actual UIL number in a document.

SECTION M. CITATORS FOR IRS DOCUMENTS

The IRS reviews its pronouncements for continued relevance. In addition, some IRS rulings have been subjected to judicial scrutiny. The status of these items can be determined from CD/DVD and online services and from the citators illustrated in Chapter 12.[229] You can also use Mertens, Law of Federal Income Taxation—Rulings (since 1954), or the IRS Bulletin Index-Digest System (1954–1993/94 only).

Citators include judicial action and cover both I.R.B. documents and publicly available IRS determinations. [See Illustrations 4-20 through 4-23 and additional illustrations in Chapter 12.] They are better-suited for determining continued relevance than are the Mertens and IRS services. The Mertens and IRS services have several limitations. First, they include only IRS action. Second, they cover only revenue rulings and procedures. Third, there is a risk that a revoked item was removed from the database. Because the IRS service is no longer published, it should be considered an updating service of last resort and only for historical research.[230]

SECTION N. JUDICIAL DEFERENCE

The items discussed in this chapter receive less government and public review than do Treasury regulations. As indicated by the excerpts below, judges vary in the amount of deference paid these pronouncements. Although items released as a result of FOIA litigation are not precedential, many courts take note of their holdings.

---

[228] IRM 30.7.1.4 (Oct. 5, 2005).

[229] Shepard's, KeyCite, RIA, and CCH citator services all cover IRS documents.

[230] The I.R.B. Current Actions on Previously Published Items is not cumulated over multiple years.

Decisions giving deference to rulings and other IRS documents must be judged in light of the Supreme Court's *Mead* decision, which involved a Customs Service ruling letter. The Court held: "We agree that a tariff classification has no claim to judicial deference under *Chevron*, there being no indication that Congress intended such a ruling to carry the force of law, but we hold that under *Skidmore v. Swift & Co.*, 323 U.S. 134 (1944), the ruling is eligible to claim respect according to its persuasiveness."[231]

In addition to judicial deference issues, the IRS must also take its own published guidance into account. In *Rauenhorst v. Commissioner*, the Tax Court criticized the IRS for taking a litigating position that conflicted with a published revenue ruling.[232]

1. Officially Published Documents

• Revenue rulings are not binding precedent, but are entitled to some weight, as reflecting an interpretation of the law by the agency entrusted with its interpretation. Such rulings, however, do not require this court to apply a mistaken view of the law to a particular taxpayer. In particular, Supreme Court precedent makes clear that if a revenue ruling is found to be unreasonable or contrary to law, it is binding neither on the Commissioner nor this court, based on the rationale that the Congress, and only the Congress, has the power to make law. Vons Companies, Inc. v. United States, 51 Fed. Cl. 1, 12 (2001).[233]

• We note that, in any event, revenue rulings are not entitled to any special deference. Bhatia v. Commissioner, 72 T.C.M. (CCH) 696, 699 n.5 (1996).

---

[231] United States v. Mead Corp., 533 U.S. 218, 221 (2001). See Chapter 9 for a brief discussion of *Chevron*. You may also encounter citations to Bowles v. Seminole Rock & Sand Co., 325 U.S. 410 (1945), and Auer v. Robbins, 519 U.S. 452 (1997). These decisions involve deference to an agency's interpretation of its own rules.

[232] 119 T.C. 157 (2002). The IRS response is contained in a Chief Counsel notice, CC-2003-014, clarifying and superseding CC-2002-043. This document provides the rules that govern the requirement that IRS attorneys follow published guidance.

[233] The court later revised the first two sentences to read as follows: "Taxpayers generally may rely on a revenue ruling to support their interpretation of a provision of the Code, provided the ruling is unaffected by subsequent legislation, regulations, cases or other revenue rulings. Such rulings do not require this court to apply a mistaken view of the law to a particular taxpayer." 89 A.F.T.R.2d 2002-301 (2001). The court also stated its view regarding letter rulings, technical advice memoranda, and general counsel memoranda.

• Revenue rulings represent the official IRS position on application of tax law to specific facts. ... They relate to matters as to which the IRS is the "primary authority." ... Revenue rulings are accordingly entitled to precedential "weight." Salomon Inc. v. United States, 976 F.2d 837, 841 (2d Cir. 1992).

2. Other IRS Documents

• Nor are we persuaded by the preamble or technical advice memorandum upon which petitioners rely. In addition to the obvious fact that these documents also are not items of legislative history, these documents are afforded little weight in this Court. Allen v. Commissioner, 118 T.C. 1, 17 n.12 (2002).

• The interpretation of Rev. Proc. 71-21 contained in the General Counsel Memorandum and the IRS decision under the Revenue Procedure is not reflected in a regulation adopted after notice and comment and probably would not be entitled to *Chevron* deference. See *Mead*, ... Here, however, as noted above, we are not dealing with an agency's interpretation of a statute and issues of *Chevron* deference, but with the IRS's interpretation of an ambiguous term in its own Revenue Procedure. In such circumstances, substantial deference is paid to an agency's interpretations reflected in informal rulings.... In the context of tax cases, the IRS's reasonable interpretations of its own regulations and procedures are entitled to particular deference. American Express Co. v. United States, 262 F.3d 1376, 1382–83 (Fed. Cir. 2001).

• Such private letter rulings "may not be used or cited as precedent," § 6110(j)(3), and we do not do so. It does not follow that they are not relevant here. Transco Exploration Co. v. Commissioner, 949 F.2d 837, 840 (5th Cir. 1992).

• Although this ruling cannot be cited as precedent under 26 U.S.C. § 6110(J)(3) [sic], it highlights the confusion this section has engendered at the IRS. More importantly, the fact that the IRS has done an about face since 1986 makes us even more reluctant to adopt their interpretation of this statute without an understandable articulation of a tax policy supporting it. Estate of Spencer v. Commissioner, 43 F.3d 226, 234 (6th Cir. 1995).

• In *Herrmann*, the court would not rely on the GCM to interpret the plan involved because the GCM was fact specific to the plan for which it was written. The court, however, did rely on its interpretation of the Code section involved because it assumed the IRS would insist upon a uniform interpretation of the section. Here, where there is no case law in point, it is arguably permissible to use GCMs to instruct the court on how the IRS itself interprets § 501(c)(5), since they constitute the only real guidance as to what the IRS considers a labor organization for the purposes of a

§ 501(c)(5) exemption. Morganbesser v. United States, 984 F.2d 560, 563 (2d Cir. 1993).

• While recognizing that the IRM does not represent law and is in no way binding upon this court, the court believes that the manual reflects the more reasonable interpretation of the Revenue Code's mandate in this instance. Thus, the manual's agreement with the court's own independent reading of the statute bolsters the court's conclusion. Anderson v. United States, 71 A.F.T.R.2d 93-1589, 93-1591, 93-1 U.S.T.C. ¶ 50,249, at 87,958 (N.D. Cal. 1993), rev'd, 44 F.3d 795, 799 (9th Cir. 1995) ("But the IRS correctly concedes that its internal agents' manual does not have the force of law, see *Schweiker v. Hansen*, ..., and makes no *Chevron* argument for deference to this language from its manual, not promulgated as a regulation.")

3. IRS Litigating Positions

• We now hold that the IRS' position in the amicus brief was an informal agency policy pronouncement not entitled to *Chevron* deference. Matz v. Household International Tax Reduction Investment Plan, 265 F.3d 572, 574 (7th Cir. 2001).

SECTION O. PROBLEMS

1. Who drafted the IRS document listed?

   a. Rev. Rul. 97-2

   b. Rev. Rul. 2001-14

   c. Rev. Proc. 2007-9

   d. Notice 2010-2

2. What is the most recent revenue ruling referring to the Code section listed?

   a. 132

   b. 223

   c. 1041

   d. 2042

3. What is the most recent revenue ruling referring to the Treasury regulation section listed?

   a. 1.162-1

   b. 1.451-1

   c. 1.513-1

   d. 1.1035-1

4. What is the status of the item listed? What later pronouncement effectuated the status change?

   a. Rev. Rul. 77-440

   b. Rev. Rul. 73-511

   c. Rev. Proc. 80-55

   d. Rev. Proc. 98-18

5. List all current year revenue procedures indicating matters on which the IRS will not grant a ruling.

6. What is the most recent revenue procedure providing information about the issue set forth below?

   a. Code sections for which the IRS will treat the child of divorced parents as a dependent of both parents

   b. classification of Indian tribal entities that the IRS recognizes as Indian Tribal Governments

   c. guidelines for excluding a prize from gross income when the taxpayer designates that it be transferred to a charity

7. Which IRS publication number has the title listed below?

   a. Basis of Assets

   b. Determining the Value of Donated Property

   c. Installment Sales

   d. Tax Guide for Seniors

8. Indicate what type of document the item listed below is.

   a. 199930006

   b. 200549007

   c. 200952005

   d. 201003018

9. What is the most recent PLR or TAM referring to the Code section listed?

   a. 152

b. 280B

c. 1091

10. What is the status of the item listed? What later pronouncement effectuated the status change?

a. TAM 8210014

b. PLR 8327090

c. PLR 200709065

11. Locate the document asked for below and indicate the Code section(s) involved; indicate the most recent if you locate more than one.

a. a 2008 PLR citing to Rev. Rul. 90-74

b. a 2006 PLR citing to Notice 87-18

c. a 2009 CCA citing to Rev. Rul. 64-40

d. a 1978 TAM citing to Rev. Rul. 72-617

12. Your instructor will assign an IRM segment. Prepare a full list of subdivisions for that segment.

13. Locate a PLR involving the following facts and indicate its holding. If you find more than one, provide the most recent.

a. whether an exchange of real property for development rights qualifies as a like-kind exchange

b. whether acquisition of 100% of the interests in a partnership constituted acquisition of its assets and could qualify as a like-kind exchange

c. whether a doctor who defrauded health insurers could deduct restitution payments as a business loss

d. whether an estate tax deduction was allowable for a bequest of paintings to a public museum in a foreign city

14. Locate a TAM involving the following facts and indicate its holding. If you find more than one, provide the most recent.

a. whether marijuana held for sale was includible in the taxpayer's gross estate

b. whether gain a utility realized from selling six power plants, pursuant to a state public utilities commission order to voluntarily divest assets, was gain from an involuntary conversion

c. whether income a credit union received from selling checks was substantially related to its exempt purpose

d. whether a charity engaged in research would jeopardize its exempt status if it performed research for a corporation that was engaged in business

15. Locate each AOD involving the following decision and indicate its holding:

a. Exxon v. Commissioner (1999 Tax Court)

b. McNamara v. Commissioner (2000 Eighth Circuit)

c. North Dakota State University v. United States (2001 Eighth Circuit)

d. Estate of Neisen v. Commissioner (1987 Tax Court)

16. Provide a citation to the revenue ruling indicating IRS agreement or disagreement or other litigation plans based on the decision listed below.

a. Sachs v. United States (1976 District Court)

b. Walker v. Commissioner (1993 Tax Court)

c. Cloutier v. United States (1983 Seventh Circuit)

d. St. Luke's Hospital of Kansas City v. United States (1980 District Court)

e. Auburn Packing Co. v. Commissioner (1973 Tax Court)

17. Locate a non-I.R.B. document other than a letter ruling or technical advice memorandum involving the following facts. Provide the citation and holding:

a. the date a self-produced animal is treated as being placed in service for purposes of depreciation

b. whether the IRS could seize a taxpayer's right to renew season tickets and sell it to satisfy tax liability

c. under what conditions a self-employed person could qualify for the Code section 72(t)(2)(D) exception and avoid paying the 10% additional tax for early withdrawals from an individual retirement plan

d. whether a partner could combine his share of partnership wagering gains with his personal wagering losses in computing the limitation on deductions for wagering losses

18. You have been assigned several clients for whom you expect to do tax controversy work. Locate and print out the first page of the following documents.

a. Audit Technique Guide for the hardwood timber industry

b. Audit Technique Guide for ministers

c. Audit Guide for new vehicle dealerships

d. Audit Guide for structured settlement factoring

19. Find the most recent judicial decision you can locate regarding deference to the IRS document listed. What did the court say?

a. revenue rulings

b. private letter rulings

c. field service advice

d. IRS publications

20. Congress occasionally rejects an IRS interpretation by amending the Code (or by trying to do so in a bill that does not get enacted). Find the Code section or introduced bill that appears to reject the IRS ruling listed below. Note that the congressional response may cover the original Code section or a related section.

a. Rev. Rul. 86-63

b. PLR 200941003

21. Courts may be called on to decide cases in which the IRS had already issued a ruling or other disclosed advice. Locate the judicial decision that appears to involve the taxpayer who received (or was the subject of) the item listed. What was the outcome of the litigation?

a. FSA 200242008

b. CCA 200603025

CHAPTER 11. JUDICIAL REPORTS

SECTION A. INTRODUCTION

This chapter discusses the courts that decide tax cases, both initially and on appeal, and the reporter services in which you can locate judicial opinions. It also lists name changes for several courts and indicates when each court began hearing tax cases.

Your goals for this chapter include locating pertinent decisions, judging their relevance in a particular jurisdiction, and updating your research to include cases that are working their way through the litigation and appeals processes. Because Congress can usually "overrule" a judicial decision it dislikes by amending the statute, remember to check recently passed and pending legislation before deciding that you can rely on a particular case as precedent. In addition, you must also check IRS litigating positions because the IRS may announce it will not follow an adverse lower court decision.

SECTION B. COURT ORGANIZATION

1. Trial Courts

Four courts serve as trial courts for most tax disputes: District Courts; the Court of Federal Claims; the Tax Court; and Bankruptcy Courts. Other bodies may also be relevant. The United States Court of International Trade hears cases involving tariffs and related tax matters.[234] In addition, as indicated in Chapter 8, disputes between governments may be heard by the World Trade Organization or other international tribunal. This chapter focuses on the four primary trial courts.

If litigation is contemplated, you must consider two questions. Which trial courts have jurisdiction over the matter?[235] If more than one court has jurisdiction, what factors are relevant in deciding where to litigate?

a. United States District Courts

Because District Courts are courts of general jurisdiction, their judges rarely develop as high a level of expertise on tax law questions as do

---

[234] See, e.g., Princess Cruises, Inc. v. United States, 22 Ct. Int'l Trade 498 (1998). Many, but not all, CIT cases also appear in Federal Supplement. Appeals go to the Court of Appeals for the Federal Circuit.

[235] Rules concerning jurisdiction appear in the Internal Revenue Code and in other titles of United States Code, particularly Title 28.

judges of the Tax Court or even of the Court of Federal Claims. Taxpayers must pay the amount in dispute and sue for a refund as a condition to litigating in District Court, the only tribunal where a jury trial is available.

A significant number of District Court decisions are not published in Federal Supplement. You may be able to find them in other reporter services.[236]

b. United States Court of Federal Claims

Although the Court of Federal Claims does not hear tax cases exclusively, the percentage of such cases it hears is likely to be greater than that heard in the average District Court. As in the District Court, a taxpayer must first pay the disputed amount before bringing suit.

Before October 1, 1982, this court was called the United States Court of Claims and the Court of Claims of the United States. Trials were conducted by a trial judge (formerly called a commissioner), whose decisions were reviewed by Court of Claims judges. Only the Supreme Court had jurisdiction over appeals from its decisions. Between October 1, 1982, and October 28, 1992, this court was called the United States Claims Court.

Table 11-1. Names Used by Tax Court and Court of Federal Claims

Tax Court	Court of Federal Claims
United States Tax Court (since 1970)	United States Court of Federal Claims (since Oct. 29, 1992)
Tax Court of the United States (October 22, 1942–1969)	United States Claims Court (Oct. 1, 1982–Oct. 28, 1992)
Board of Tax Appeals (1924–October 21, 1942)	United States Court of Claims (1948–Sept. 30, 1982)
	Court of Claims of the United States (1863–1948)

c. United States Tax Court

Because Tax Court judges hear only tax cases, their expertise is substantially greater than that of judges in the other trial courts. Tax Court cases are tried by one judge, who submits an opinion to the chief judge for consideration. The chief judge can allow the decision to stand or refer it

---

[236] These include American Federal Tax Reports (A.F.T.R.) and U. S. Tax Cases (U.S.T.C.), discussed in Subsection D.2, and various electronic services. Freedom of Information Act litigation forced the Justice Department to make all District Court tax opinions available to the public. United States Department of Justice v. Tax Analysts, 492 U.S. 136 (1989).

to the full court for review.[237] The published decision indicates if it has been reviewed; dissenting opinions, if any, are included.

In some instances, special trial judges hear disputes and issue opinions.[238] When the amount in dispute exceeds $50,000, the special trial judge does not issue the final opinion. The opinion is issued by a Tax Court judge. Before rule changes in 2005, the judge writing the opinion indicated that he or she adopted the special trial judge's report. The Tax Court did not separately release the trial judge's report to taxpayers. In 2005, the United States Supreme Court held that withholding the trial judge's report violated the Tax Court's own rules.[239]

There are three types of Tax Court decisions, two of which can result in appeals. The government printing office publishes **Regular** (or **Reported**) **Opinions**; these present important legal issues. Other publishers print **Memorandum Opinions**, which involve well-established legal issues and are primarily fact-based.[240]

The Tax Court also has a **Small Cases** division that taxpayers can elect to use for disputes of $50,000 or less. The **Summary Opinions** issued in those cases cannot be appealed or used as precedent. Until 2001, they were not published in any reporter service or on the Tax Court website.[241] Although Tax Court judges do hear cases brought in the Small Case division, these cases are likely to be heard by special trial judges.

A taxpayer can sue in the Tax Court without paying the amount in dispute prior to litigating. Taxpayers also had this privilege in the Tax Court's predecessor, the Board of Tax Appeals.

---

[237] "Court review is directed if the report proposes to invalidate a regulation, overrule a published Tax Court case, or reconsider, in a circuit that has not addressed it, an issue on which we have been reversed by a court of appeals." Mary Ann Cohen, *How to Read Tax Court Opinions*, 1 Hous. Bus. & Tax L.J. 1, 5–6 (2001).

[238] The Supreme Court upheld this practice in Freytag v. Commissioner, 501 U.S. 868 (1991). The special trial judges were called commissioners until 1984.

[239] See Ballard v. Commissioner, 544 U.S. 40 (2005). The taxpayers in this case had reason to believe the special trial judges' report varied significantly from the Tax Court's published opinion. The Tax Court has since modified its Rule 183.

[240] Memorandum decisions have been appealed as far as the Supreme Court. See, e.g., Commissioner v. Duberstein, 363 U.S. 278 (1960).

[241] I.R.C. § 7463(b). The increase to $50,000 in 1998 is likely to increase the percentage of taxpayers using this litigation route. The previous limit was $10,000. A typical citation is Hill v. Commissioner, T.C. Summ. Op. 2009-188.

d. United States Bankruptcy Courts

Bankruptcy Courts came into existence in 1979. Before that, bankruptcy trustees appointed by District Court judges administered bankruptcy cases.[242]

In addition to deciding priority of liens and related matters, United States Bankruptcy Courts may issue substantive tax rulings. District Court judges, Bankruptcy Appellate Panels, or Courts of Appeals review Bankruptcy Court decisions.[243]

As a general rule, each circuit decides if it will use a Bankruptcy Appellate Panel (BAP) and whether the BAP will hear all cases. Direct appeal to a Court of Appeals has been authorized since 2005, but only in limited situations.[244]

Bankruptcy cases often have two captions. One caption begins with "In re." The other follows the format used for most cases "Plaintiff v. Defendant." If you are looking for a particular bankruptcy case, note both the debtor and the trustee's names so that you can find the case no matter which case reporter or citator service you are using. Table 11-2 shows how a Bankruptcy Court case involving Guardian Trust Company (Henderson, Trustee) is captioned in three reporter services.[245]

Table 11-2. Case Captions for Bankruptcy Court Decisions

Reporter Service	Caption
Bankruptcy Reporter	In re Guardian Trust Co., 242 B.R. 608 (Bankr. S.D. Miss. 1999)
U.S. Tax Cases	In re Guardian Trust Company, 99-2 U.S.T.C. ¶ 50,819 (Bankr. S.D. Miss. 1999)
American Federal Tax Reporter	Henderson v. United States, 84 A.F.T.R.2d 99-5940 (Bankr. S.D. Miss. 1999)

---

[242] See Pub. L. No. 95-598, § 201(a), 92 Stat. 2549, 2657 (1978). Bankruptcy judges are currently appointed by Court of Appeals judges. 28 U.S.C. § 152(a).

[243] See, e.g., In re Michaud, 199 B.R. 248 (Bankr. D.N.H. 1996), aff'd, Michaud v. United States, 206 B.R. 1 (D.N.H. 1997); In re Mosbrucker, 220 B.R. 656 (Bankr. D.N.D. 1998), aff'd, 227 B.R. 434 (B.A.P. 8th Cir. 1998), aff'd, 99-2 U.S.T.C. ¶ 50,883, 84 A.F.T.R.2d 99-6457 (8th Cir. 1999)(unpublished opinion).

[244] Bankruptcy Abuse Prevention and Consumer Protection Act of 2005, Pub. L. No. 109-8, 119 Stat. 23 (2005), § 1233, amending 28 U.S.C. 158(d)(2).

[245] Even if each reporter uses the same case caption for the initial proceeding, they may use different captions for appellate decisions. See, e.g., In re Harvard Industries, Inc., 568 F.3d 444 (3d Cir. 2009); Harvard Secured Creditors Liquidation Trust v. Internal Revenue Service, 103 A.F.T.R.2d 2009-2701 (3d Cir. 2009).

2. Courts of Appeals

When your research uncovers trial court decisions, you should trace them to the appellate court level. This is particularly important if decisions conflict with each other and none comes from your jurisdiction.

Decisions of District Courts and the Tax Court are appealed to the Court of Appeals for the taxpayer's geographical residence[246] and from there to the Supreme Court. Even if the Tax Court disagrees with a particular Circuit Court precedent, it will follow it if that court would hear the appeal. This is the *Golsen* rule.[247] After appellate reversal in several circuits, the Tax Court is likely to change its position for future litigation.[248]

Two Courts of Appeals are of relatively recent vintage. The Eleventh Circuit was carved out of the Fifth Circuit in 1981. If you represent a taxpayer who lives in the Eleventh Circuit, you should also consider Fifth Circuit decisions issued before October 1, 1981.[249]

The second recently established court is the Court of Appeals for the Federal Circuit, which was formed in 1982 to review decisions of what is now the Court of Federal Claims. Because the Supreme Court reviews so few Court of Appeals decisions, the Court of Federal Claims–Federal Circuit route offers a forum-shopping opportunity. Taxpayers can avoid adverse appellate court decisions from their "home" circuits by suing in the Court of Federal Claims.[250]

The Court of Appeals for the Federal Circuit also hears appeals from the United States Patent and Trademark Office and from District Court decisions involving patents. Because the USPTO has approved business methods patents, including patents relevant to tax strategies, tax plan-

---

[246] From 1924 to 1926, appeals from the Board of Tax Appeals (the Tax Court's predecessor) were heard in District Court. Revenue Act of 1924, ch. 234, § 900(g), 43 Stat. 253, 336; Revenue Act of 1926, ch. 27, § 1001(a), 44 Stat. 9, 109.

[247] Golsen v. Commissioner, 54 T.C. 742 (1970).

[248] See, e.g., Fazi v. Commissioner, 102 T.C. 695 (1994).

[249] See, e.g., Estate of Kosow v. Commissioner, 45 F.3d 1524, 1529 (11th Cir. 1995), citing a 1972 Fifth Circuit decision. Because the Tenth Circuit was split from the Eighth Circuit in 1929, you are unlikely to find Eighth Circuit precedent relevant to research involving the Tenth Circuit. Splitting the Ninth Circuit into two or even three circuits has been proposed many times. See, e.g., H.R. No. 191, 111th Cong., 1st Sess. (2009).

[250] See Ginsburg v. United States, 184 Ct. Cl. 444, 396 F.2d 983 (1968), for a discussion of this phenomenon in the court's predecessor, the Court of Claims.

ning research may involve checking to see if a particular strategy is patented.[251] Litigation involving a business methods patent was pending at the Supreme Court when this book went to press.[252] The outcome of that controversy is likely to affect the patentability of various business (including tax) strategies.

In December 1989, the Federal Courts Study Committee recommended abolishing the present system for resolving tax controversies. The Committee recommended substituting a single trial court—the Tax Court— with appeals going to a specialized appellate court.[253] That suggestion, or variants using other courts, occasionally resurfaces.[254]

3. Supreme Court

As noted above, decisions from the Circuit Courts can be appealed to the United States Supreme Court. The Supreme Court hears cases involving both constitutional challenges and those involving statutory interpretation. The Court is unlikely to grant certiorari in a case involving only statutory interpretation unless there is a conflict between two or more circuits.

SECTION C. LOCATING DECISIONS

Your strategy for locating decisions depends on whether you are compiling a list of decisions to read or whether you are simply trying to locate a decision whose caption or citation you already have.

---

[251] See http://www.uspto.gov/patft/class705_sub36t.html for lists of patents and applications involving tax strategies. See generally Staff of the Joint Committee on Taxation, Background and Issues Relating to the Patenting of Tax Advice (JCX-31-06) (2006).

[252] In re Bilski, 545 F.3d 943 (Fed. Cir. 2008), cert. granted sub nom. Bilski v. Doll, 129 S. Ct. 2735 (2009), oral argument sub nom. Bilski v. Kappos held Nov. 8, 2009.

[253] Federal Courts Study Comm., Tentative Recommendations for Public Comment (1989). Earlier in 1989, an ABA committee had proposed assigning trial court jurisdiction to the Tax Court. ABA Standing Comm. on Federal Judicial Improvements, The United States Court of Appeals: Reexamining Structure and Process After a Century of Growth (1989).

[254] "If Congress decides to centralize tax appeals, the Federal Circuit provides a readily available forum for that purpose, one that already adjudicates appeals in tax cases coming to it from the Court of Federal Claims, and whose docket would be capable of absorbing appeals from the Tax Court or the district courts or both." Commission on Structural Alternatives for the Federal Courts of Appeals, TENTA-TIVE DRAFT REPORT (Oct. 1998), excerpted in Tax Notes today file on LexisNexis at 98 TNT 234-78.

1. Compiling Finding Lists

If you need to find judicial decisions involving a particular statute, treaty, regulation, or ruling, you can compile a preliminary reading list using one of the annotated looseleaf services and treatises discussed in Chapter 13. You can also use one of the citators discussed in Chapter 12. Finally, you can simply search in an electronic database using the item as a search term.

2. Locating Cases by Party Name

If you know the name of a party, but not the reporter citation, you have several options for locating the decision. Electronic services are particularly helpful because you can include facts and issues in your search request.[255] These services may include screens in which you can enter party names, judge names, or other information and retrieve a case. [See Illustrations 3-1, 3-3, 3-5, 11-1, and 11-2.] In addition to subscription services (e.g,, LexisNexis, Westlaw, Checkpoint, and IntelliConnect), your options include court websites, free websites maintained by law schools and other entities, and—more recently—Google.[256]

You also have print service options for locating case citations. If you know the taxpayer's first name and last names, you can use the RIA and CCH print citators; both list taxpayers alphabetically. The United States Tax Reporter looseleaf service also includes a Table of Cases. If you lack the taxpayer's first name, but do know the jurisdiction, you might instead consult the alphabetical list of parties in West's Federal Practice Digest 4th. That service does not include the Tax Court.

If you know who the other party is, you can narrow your search among various tax reporter services. As a general rule, cases that began in Tax Court are captioned "Taxpayer v. Commissioner," and cases that arose in District Court or Court of Federal Claims are captioned "Taxpayer v. United States."[257] Cases whose captions include "In re" often began in

---

[255] Web-based services are more likely than CD/DVD services to include citations for case reporter services.

[256] Google Scholar's Advanced Search function has a "Search only US federal court opinions" option.

[257] Knowing where to start is particularly useful if you use print reporter services and lack access to the CCH and RIA citators and electronic services. If the case arose in the Tax Court, you can use the CCH Tax Court Reporter's Table of Decisions, including the Current and Latest Additions supplements to ascertain the CCH Decision Number. You can obtain a citation by cross-referencing those numbers to the official reports or the CCH Tax Court Memoranda service using cross-reference tables in Volume 2 of this service. You can locate cases originating

Bankruptcy Court, but reporter services differ in their captioning of bankruptcy cases. [See Table 11-2.]

Illustration 11-1. Get a Document in LexisNexis

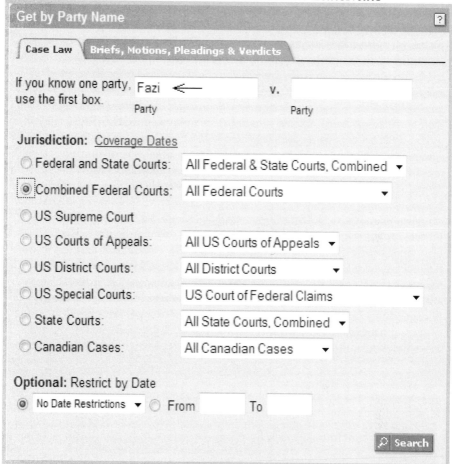

→I knew only the taxpayer's name. If I had known the court, I could have searched only in that court. *Fazi* is a Tax Court decision. Because I ran this search as if I didn't have that information, I used the Combined Federal Courts search option. If I knew the citation or docket number, I could have used those features instead of searching by name.

→Bankruptcy Court, Court of Federal Claims, and Tax Court are options in the US Special Courts selection.

---

in other trial courts, as well as all appeals court decisions, through A.F.T.R.'s Table of Cases, which is cumulated throughout each five-year period in the A.F.T.R. volumes.

Illustration 11-2. Using Find a Case by Citation in Checkpoint

Search All Federal Cases by Case Name
Example: Redlark

Case Name: Fazi ⟵   [Search]

American Federal Tax Reports
Example: 97 AFTR 2d 2006-1626   ⟋

[   ] [AFTR 2d ▼] [   ]   [Search]

Example: Fickling | AFTR 2d |
                    | S. Ct. |
Case Name: [| F. 3d |]   [Search]
                    | F. |
Tax Court Report| F. Supp |
Example: 126 TC 9 | USTC |
                    | AFTR | [Search]
[   ]   T | U.S. |
Example: Swallows | F. 2d |
                    | F. Supp. 2d |
Case Name: [| Fed Appx |]   [Search]

Tax Court Memo   ons
Example: TC Memo 2006-17

[   ]   [Search]

Example: Motsko

Case Name: [   ]   [Search]

Tax Court Summary Opinions
Example: TC Summary Opinion 2001-129

[   ]   [Search]

Example: Fred F. Humble

Case Name: [   ]   [Search]

→Checkpoint includes search by name and search by citation functions in one screen.

→The box for searching AFTR2d has a pull-down menu allowing searches in several reporter services. Neither Bankruptcy Reporter nor Federal Claims is a listed option, so you would need their parallel A.F.T.R. or U.S.T.C. citation.

Westlaw has a function similar to that for LexisNexis (Find a Case by Party Name), but it does not include a date restriction option. Westlaw includes Bankruptcy Courts, Court of Federal Claims, and Tax Court in its Specialized Courts option.

The IntelliConnect Citations search function lists case citations rather than names. If you enter a case name in the Search Selected Content box you will retrieve all cases that include that name of the party, whether or not the case involved that party.

3. Locating Cases by Citation

Online services let you find decisions by citation. In many cases, you don't need to worry about periods or spacing in reporter service abbreviations.[258] Services such as Checkpoint [Illustration 11-2] and IntelliConnect use templates for citation format.

Tax Court Regular and Memorandum Opinions can present problems. The Government Printing Office officially publishes Regular Opinions, but it does not paginate them successively until it compiles them into a volume. Instead, it gives them opinion numbers. For example, *Fazi v. Commissioner*, the decision I searched for in Illustrations 11-1 and 11-2, was initially released as 105 T.C. No. 29 (1995) and later became 105 T.C. 436 (1995). If you have a citation to a fairly recent Tax Court Regular Opinion, be sure to note whether your citation is to a page number or a decision number.

The CCH and RIA services discussed in Section D do not use the same format for citing Tax Court Memorandum Opinions. For example, *Derby v. Commissioner* is reported on the Tax Court website as T.C. Memo. 2008-48; CCH cites it as 95 T.C.M. (CCH) 1177 (2008); RIA cites it as either T.C.M. (RIA) 2008-045 or 2008 RIA TC Memo 2008-045. Table 11-4 contains more information about CCH and RIA citation formats for Tax Court and other courts covered by their reporter services.

4. Digests of Decisions

Digests are useful for locating decisions and for deciding which of them to read first. They may be less important if you are using online services that give an overview of each "hit" or if you search online services by Key Number.

Warren, Gorham & Lamont publishes several specialized digests. These include Corporate Tax Digest, Pass-Through Entity Tax Digest, Real Estate Tax Digest, and Tax Procedure Digest.

Services such as Standard Federal Tax Reporter and United States Tax Reporter digest cases in their compilation and updating volumes or in their newsletters. Newsletters such as Tax Notes and Daily Tax Report include case digests, but these are not cumulated over time.

---

[258] You may also be able to search by docket number, which could be preferable to searching by name if the taxpayer has a common name (e.g., Smith).

SECTION D. CASE REPORTERS

Discussion in this section covers print reporter services that focus on taxation because you may not have encountered them in the basic legal research course. You can generally find the same materials electronically using subscription and free services. In some instances, electronic services will be your only option; Tax Court Summary Opinions are an example of that category.

Online and CD/DVD services may have limited retrospective coverage; remember to check when each service began including a court's decisions. Your library may also carry microform services that include judicial decisions; these services may have extensive retrospective coverage but lag other services in covering current material.

1. Tax Court Decisions

Coverage of Tax Court decisions varies.[259] The government published Regular decisions by the Tax Court's predecessor, the Board of Tax Appeals in the Board of Tax Appeals Reports (B.T.A.). The government did not publish B.T.A. Memorandum decisions. Prentice-Hall printed both Regular and Memorandum decisions. RIA, which acquired the Prentice-Hall services, also makes Tax Court decisions available.

The government also publishes Tax Court Regular decisions in Tax Court of the United States Reports and United States Tax Court Reports; both are cited as T.C. It does not officially publish Tax Court Memorandum decisions or Tax Court Summary decisions. The Tax Court website includes Regular and Memorandum Opinions since 1995 and Summary Opinions since 2001.

Commerce Clearing House currently publishes Tax Court decisions in a three-volume looseleaf service. Volume 1 contains Memorandum decisions and Volume 2 contains Regular decisions. Volume 3 contains information about pending litigation. Volume 1 has an alphabetical Table of Decisions, while Volume 2 provides cross-references to CCH case numbers.

HeinOnline includes Tax Court and Board of Tax Appeals Regular Opinions (but not Memorandum or Summary Opinions) in its U.S. Federal Agency Documents, Decisions, and Appeals Library.

---

[259] Table 11-1 lists relevant dates and court names for the Tax Court and Board of Tax Appeals. Although the Board began in 1924, it did not issue Memorandum decisions until 1928.

2. Decisions of Other Courts

With the exception of Tax Court decisions, you can locate federal court decisions involving taxation in the sets listed in Table 11-3. Most of those sets are published by the Government Printing Office or by West and are used the same way for tax research as for nontax research.

Table 11-3. Print Reporter Services Other Than Tax Court[260]

Court/ Service	Supreme Court	Court of Appeals	District Court	Bankr. Court	Federal Claims
U.S.	1796–				
S. Ct.	1882–				
L. Ed.	1796–				
A.F.T.R.	1796–	1880–	1882–	1979–	1876–
U.S.T.C.	1913–	1915–	1915–	1979–	1924–
F.		1880–	1882–1932		1929–1932 1960–1982
Fed. Appx.		2001–			
F. Supp.			1932–		1932–1960
Ct. Cl.					1863–1982
Cl. Ct.					1982–1992
Fed. Cl.					1992–
Bankr.				1979–	

→Several reporters are in second or third series (e.g., F., F.2d, F.3d).

→Only A.F.T.R. and U.S.T.C. print cases from all these courts.

→A.F.T.R. volumes 1–4 reprint cases by reporter service (e.g., Federal Reporter, United States Reports) and not in strict chronological order.

→Until 1912, so-called Circuit Courts decided cases; reports are found in Federal Cases and Federal Reporter.

The sets published by Research Institute of America (American Federal Tax Reports) and Commerce Clearing House (U.S. Tax Cases) differ enough from the others to warrant further discussion. These sets are available in print and as part of their respective publishers' online services: Checkpoint and IntelliConnect.

You can use these sets alone or in conjunction with each publisher's looseleaf reporting service, A.F.T.R. with RIA United States Tax Reporter

---

[260] The Cumulative Bulletin has included Supreme Court decisions since 1920; it calls them Court Decisions (Ct. D.) Early Bulletins included lower federal court decisions either as Ct. D.s or as Miscellaneous Rulings. Because the disparate labels make these items virtually impossible to locate, I have omitted them from the table and from the discussion of case reporter services.

and U.S.T.C.[261] with CCH Standard Federal Tax Reporter. Each service publishes decisions from all courts except the Tax Court, and each includes "unpublished" decisions omitted from Federal Supplement and Federal Reporter.[262]

a. Locating Decisions

A.F.T.R. and U.S.T.C. first include decisions in an Advance Sheets volume of the related looseleaf reporting service. This initial publication in conjunction with the looseleaf services results in recent decisions being available in print on a weekly basis. While both services are supplemented weekly, each occasionally prints decisions before the other does.

These cases also appear in the listings of new material in the services' update volumes (Recent Developments for United States Tax Reporter; New Matters for Standard Federal Tax Reporter). The listings appear in Code section order and are cross-referenced to discussions in the services' compilation volumes. As a result, you can locate a recent case when you know the Code section involved but not the taxpayer's name, and you can immediately find a discussion of the topic in the compilation volumes. Daily and weekly newsletters, which are probably the only more current print source of these cases, often print only partial texts or digests and don't provide full-year cumulative indexes.

The reference method is important if you use these services. CCH cites decisions in the U.S.T.C. advance sheets and bound volumes by paragraph number (e.g., 88-1 U.S.T.C. ¶ 9390). RIA cites to decisions in A.F.T.R. by page number (e.g., 62 A.F.T.R.2d 88-5228).

The bound volumes include all types of tax cases—income, estate and gift, and excise; the individual Advance Sheets volumes do not. The different types of cases appear in Advance Sheets sections accompanying each publisher's looseleaf service for the particular area of tax law.

b. Citation Format

Citation formats for the services published by CCH and RIA vary depending upon whether you follow the guidelines in The Bluebook, ALWD,

---

[261] The earliest volumes of this service print all Supreme Court decisions and those lower court decisions of "genuine precedent value ...." Foreword to 1 U.S.T.C. (1938). When CCH began issuing two volumes per year, it expanded coverage.

[262] See, e.g., Alexander v. United States, 88-1 U.S.T.C. ¶ 9390, 62 A.F.T.R.2d 88-5228 (N.D. Ga. 1988); Estate of McLendon v. Commissioner, 96-1 U.S.T.C. ¶ 60,220, 77 A.F.T.R.2d 96-666 (5th Cir. 1995) (unpublished opinion).

or TaxCite.[263] Depending on the format adopted, you are likely to encounter any of the Table 11-4 citation formats.

Table 11-4. Citation Formats for CCH and RIA Reporters

Reporter Service	Possible Citation Formats
American Federal Tax Reports	AFTR; A.F.T.R.; A.F.T.R. (P-H); A.F.T.R. (RIA); AFTR2d; A.F.T.R.2d; A.F.T.R.2d (RIA)
U.S. Tax Cases	USTC para.; U.S.T.C. ¶; U.S. Tax Cas. (CCH)
Tax Court Reports	T.C.R. (CCH) Dec.; T.C.R. Dec. (P-H) ¶; T.C.R. Dec. (RIA) ¶; Tax Ct. Rep. (CCH); Tax Ct. Rep. Dec. (P-H); Tax Ct. Rep. Dec. (RIA)
Tax Court Memorandum Decisions	T.C. Memo; TCM; para. #, P-H memo T.C.; T.C.M. (CCH); T.C.M. (P-H) ¶; T.C.M. (RIA) ¶; T.C.M. (P-H); T.C.M. (RIA)
Board of Tax Appeals Memorandum Decisions	B.T.A. Mem. Dec. (P-H) ¶; B.T.A.M. (P-H)

3. Parallel Citations

Online and CD/DVD services make cases accessible without regard to reporter service. Online services are more likely to include citations than are CD/DVD services.

If you use bound volumes for your research, you may find that the volume for which you have a citation is not on the library shelf. Because so many case reporters cover each court level, you may be able to find that case in another set. All you need is the correct citation for the other reporter service.

Because general reporter services print nontax as well as tax decisions, numerous volumes cover each year's cases. Looking up the case name in several volumes is a tedious method of finding another printing. You can accomplish this task more quickly by locating the case citation in a citator obtaining a parallel citation to the same decision in another reporter.

SECTION E. BRIEFS AND PETITIONS

Briefs are relevant in determining which arguments the taxpayers and government have raised for court consideration. Westlaw's Federal Taxation Briefs (FTX-BRIEF) file covers selected briefs filed with the Supreme

---

[263] Although the ABA Section of Taxation is one of TaxCite's participants, ABA publications often use formats other than those listed in TaxCite. Because Tax-Cite has not been updated since 1995, it omits many of the IRS documents discussed in Chapter 10.

Court, Circuit Courts, and the Tax Court. Westlaw also has a Tax Court Briefs and Petitions file (FTX-TCBRIEF). In addition, judicial decisions available on Westlaw often include links to the relevant briefs. Lexis has files for U.S. Supreme Court Briefs, All Federal Briefs and Motions, and All Federal Pleadings. Its Tax Analysts file covers briefs and petitions included in the Tax Analysts database; despite its title, it is not limited to Tax Court filings. It is unlikely that these services will provide full coverage for every trial court action.

SECTION F. EVALUATING DECISIONS

1. In General

Courts must determine how much weight to give opinions in cases cited by the taxpayer or government. An individual court, whether Tax Court, District Court, or Court of Federal Claims, will give its own decisions far more deference than it will give decisions of the other trial courts.

If a Court of Appeals has ruled, that opinion will be binding precedent for District Court, Bankruptcy Court, and Tax Court cases that will be appealed in that circuit. Otherwise, the opinion will be persuasive precedent. Supreme Court decisions are binding precedent for all courts.

2. Headnotes and Syllabus Numbers

Judicial decisions often include headnotes or syllabus numbers, which relate to the points of law involved. Publishers use these numbers in compiling digests and in other case-finding tools, including citators. You should not be surprised that publishers don't use the same numbering systems for these items. If you read a case in one publisher's reporter, you are likely to have problems using its headnote numbers in another publisher's digest or citator system.

3. Unpublished Opinions

There is a difference between an unpublished opinion and an opinion to which you cannot get access. Many services include decisions issued under no-publication rules. You may want to find these decisions, as they shed light on the court's thinking. In the past, some circuits allowed citations to those opinions; other circuits barred the citations. On April 12, 2006, the Supreme Court approved Federal Rule of Appellate Procedure 32.1, allowing citation to those opinions in all circuits. Note that the

Court's ruling relates to citing the opinions; it does not mandate whether a court must treat them as precedent.[264]

4. Officially Published Opinions

There is also a difference, as noted earlier in this chapter, between an officially published opinion and one available through other reporter services. Unless it was designated by court or statute as not precedential, you can cite any opinion as precedential or persuasive authority.

Unofficial reporters may include official pagination, but they do not have to do so. If you need to cite official pagination, you must use reporters that provide that information. If courts abandon the requirement of citing to print page numbers, and more decisions are posted online, the distinction between official and other publication sources will diminish for items other than headnotes.

5. Government Litigation Plans

If a court ruled against the government position, and the IRS issues a notice of acquiescence, the precedential value of the decision is further enhanced. Instead of acquiescing, the IRS announcement may issue a notice of nonacquiescence, an action on decision [Illustration 4-28], or other document indicate it will continue litigating and why it will do so. These IRS documents are discussed in Chapter 10.

Keep geographical limitations in mind; the government might indicate that it will continue to litigate only in courts outside the circuit in which it lost on appeal.

6. Changes in Code or Regulations

If Congress disagrees with a particular court decision, it may amend the Code and change the result for future years.[265] The IRS may also issue a new regulation, or amend an existing one, for the same purpose.[266] If you find a decision that appears relevant, make sure that the Code and regulations applied in that case are still in effect.

---

[264] This rule went into effect because Congress did not vote to reject it. See http://www.supremecourtus.gov/orders/courtorders/frap06p.pdf for the Court's transmittal of the proposed rule.

[265] An example involving the Supreme Court's decision in *Gitlitz v. Commissioner* appears in Chapter 6, Section F.

[266] Administrative agencies can change their interpretations, and the outcome of future litigation, if the ruling in the *Brand X* case (cited to in Chapter 9, Section K), applies.

7. Statements Regarding Deference

If no appeals have been taken, you may be tempted to accord greater weight to a Tax Court decision than to a decision of another trial court. Although the Tax Court judges have specialized knowledge, the degree of deference their decisions receive is not necessarily greater than that given decisions from other trial courts.

The items below illustrate statements regarding deference to decisions.

• We review the Tax Court's construction of the tax code de novo.... Although we presume that the Tax Court correctly applied the law, we give no special deference to the Tax Court's decisions. Best Life Assur. Co. of Calif. v. Commissioner, 281 F.3d 828, 830 (9th Cir. 2002).

• The Commissioner also argues that a sufficient explanation had been provided, relying upon an older body of case law that purports to grant great deference to the Tax Court.... In these cases, however, the Tax Court provided some justification for its conclusions in a manner that allowed us to understand and reconstruct the Tax Court's rationale. In the case at hand, the Tax Court merely announced the discount it applied to the Estate's stock without any explanation. Estate of Mitchell v. Commissioner, 250 F.3d 696, 703 n.6 (9th Cir. 2001).

• A finding is clearly erroneous when, although there is evidence to support it, a review of the entire record leaves the reviewing court with the definite and firm conviction that a mistake has been made.... This standard of review requires that we accord great deference to the values established by the tax court, but it does not render us a mere rubber stamp. Gross v. Commissioner, 272 F.3d 333, 343 (6th Cir. 2001).

• For the following reasons, pursuant to 28 U.S.C. § 1334(c)(1), we voluntarily ABSTAIN: (1) This adversary proceeding involves a classic two-party dispute, the outcome of which will have little or no effect on the estate;3 (2) there is litigation currently pending before the United States Tax Court, Docket # 4516-88; (3) the litigation requires the resolution of complex issues of tax law, some of which are unsettled or are questions of first impression; (4) there is a specialized forum for hearing this kind of dispute (i.e., the United States Tax Court); and (5) resolution of the issues would require this Court to interpret decisions of the United States Tax Court.4 .... In the circumstances, and in deference to its expertise in the subject matter of the litigation, this adversary proceeding is transferred to the United States Tax Court for hearing and adjudication. In re Williams, 209 B.R. 584, 585 (Bankr. D.R.I. 1997) (footnotes omitted).

SECTION G. CITATORS

1. Subsequent Judicial Action

There are four commonly used citators for judging the relative authority of any tax decision, and many libraries own or have online access to all of them. The four are Shepard's, KeyCite, RIA Citator, and CCH Citator. KeyCite is an online service. The others are available in print and online (but the RIA Citator has more retrospective coverage in its print version). All four are discussed in detail in Chapter 12.

You can use a citator for several purposes. First, you can determine if a trial court decision has been affirmed or reversed on appeal. Second, you can find other decisions that approve of, or disagree with, the earlier case but do not affirm or reverse it. The later cases may be from the same jurisdiction, but distinguishable in some particular, or they may be from another jurisdiction altogether. Third, you can find IRS citations to the decision. Fourth, some citators list treatises, law review articles, and other secondary sources that discuss the decision.

If you are using an online case reporter service, you don't have to leave the case to use its citator function. You may be able to click an accompanying link to find the decision's subsequent history [Illustrations 11-3 and 11-4, both of which involve the *Mitchell* decision from Table 11-5].

Illustration 11-3. Case Status and Other Options in Westlaw

▷ Some negative history but not overruled   KeyCite

Full History

Direct History
(Graphical View)

Citing References

Monitor With KeyCite Alert

Illustration 11-4. Link to Shepard's in LexisNexis

More Like This | More Like Selected Text | Shepardize® | TOA

ESTATE OF PAUL MITCHELL v. COMMISSIONER OF INTERNAL REVENUE, 250 F.3d 696 (Copy w/ Cite)

Warning: Negative treatment is indicated. Click to Shepardize®

250 F.3d 696, *; 2001 U.S. App. LEXIS 7990, **

2. Headnotes and Syllabus Numbers

There is one caveat regarding using different reporter services. As noted in Subsection F.2, each reporter service makes its own decision regarding the headnotes or syllabus numbers it assigns a case. If you read a case in one service and are interested in a particular issue, make sure the citator you use is keyed to that service.

Table 11-5 indicates how many headnotes appear in various reporter services for *Estate of Mitchell*, decided by the Ninth Circuit in 2001. Illustrations 11-5 through 11-8 show excerpts from the headnotes in four reporter services. Although Federal Reporter and Westlaw are commonly owned, the print and electronic services differ in format.

Table 11-5. Headnote Numbers in Estate of Mitchell

Service	Citation	Headnotes
Federal Reporter	250 F.3d 696	10
Westlaw	250 F.3d 696	10
LexisNexis	2001 U.S. App. Lexis 7990	9
A.F.T.R.	87 A.F.T.R. 2d 2001-2043	2
U.S.T.C.	2001-1 U.S.T.C. ¶ 60,403	0

Illustration 11-5. Federal Reporter Headnotes

1. Internal Revenue ⟜4708

Whether notice of tax deficiency is timely presents mixed question of law and fact, which is reviewed de novo. 26 U.S.C.A. § 6501(a).

2. Internal Revenue ⟜4474

Statute under which postmark stamped on return, claim, or statement mailed to Internal Revenue Service (IRS) is deemed to be date of delivery applies only when document would otherwise be considered untimely filed. 26 U.S.C.A. § 7502(a).

3. Internal Revenue ⟜4474

Where prescribed due date for estate's return fell on a Saturday, return was timely filed when received on following Monday, as next succeeding day that was not a Saturday, Sunday, or legal holiday. 26 U.S.C.A. § 7503.

Illustration 11-6. Westlaw KeyCite Headnotes

[1] ☑ KeyCite Citing References for this Headnote

➡ 220 Internal Revenue
   ➡ 220XXI Assessment of Taxes
      ➡ 220XXI(F) Review of Tax Court Decisions
         ➡ 220XXI(F)4 Scope and Extent of Review
            ➡ 220k4706 Review Dependent on Whether Questions Are of Law or of Fact
               ➡ 220k4708 k. Mixed Questions of Law and Fact. Most Cited Cases

Whether notice of tax deficiency is timely presents mixed question of law and fact, which is reviewed de novo. 26 U.S.C.A. § 6501(a).

[2] ☑ KeyCite Citing References for this Headnote

➡ 220 Internal Revenue
   ➡ 220XIX Returns and Reports
      ➡ 220k4474 k. Time for Making. Most Cited Cases

Statute under which postmark stamped on return, claim, or statement mailed to Internal Revenue Service (IRS) is deemed to be date of delivery applies only when document would otherwise be considered untimely filed. 26 U.S.C.A. § 7502(a).

[3] ☑ KeyCite Citing References for this Headnote

➡ 220 Internal Revenue
   ➡ 220XIX Returns and Reports
      ➡ 220k4474 k. Time for Making. Most Cited Cases

Where prescribed due date for estate's return fell on a Saturday, return was timely filed when received on following Monday, as next succeeding day that was not a Saturday, Sunday, or legal holiday. 26 U.S.C.A. § 7503.

Illustration 11-7. LexisNexis Headnotes

LEXISNEXIS® HEADNOTES   ⊟ Hide

Civil Procedure > Appeals > Standards of Review > De Novo Review 🔊
Governments > Legislation > Statutes of Limitations > General Overview 🔊
HN1 🔽 Mixed question of law and fact are reviewed de novo. More Like This Headnote | *Shepardize:* Restrict By Headnote

Tax Law > Federal Tax Administration & Procedure > Administration > Tax Payment & Tax Return Requirements (IRC secs. 6071-6091, 6151-6167) > General Overview 🔊
HN2 🔽 See 26 U.S.C.S. § 7502(a)(1).

Tax Law > Federal Tax Administration & Procedure > Administration > Tax Payment & Tax Return Requirements (IRC secs. 6071-6091, 6151-6167) > General Overview 🔊
HN3 🔽 See 26 U.S.C.S. § 7503.

Tax Law > Federal Tax Administration & Procedure > Administration > Tax Payment & Tax Return Requirements (IRC secs. 6071-6091, 6151-6167) > General Overview 🔊
HN4 🔽 26 U.S.C.S. § 7502(a) is intended to make the date of mailing the date of delivery only where a document would otherwise be considered untimely filed. More Like This Headnote

Illustration 11-8. A.F.T.R.2d Headnotes on Checkpoint

HEADNOTE

1. Timely-mailing-as-timely-filing rules—application to return due on Saturday—effect on assessment limitations period. Tax Court properly rejected estate's claim that Code Sec. 7502 's timely-mailing provisions applied to establish return's filing date, and corresponding 3-year assessment limitations period's trigger, as early mailing date: Code Sec. 7502 wasn't applicable to timely-mailed return; and, because statutory deadline fell on Saturday, Code Sec. 7503 applied to extend due date, and thus limitations period's trigger, to following Monday. Also, even if Code Sec. 7502 applied, Code Sec. 6501 's early return filing rules established filing date as last day of statutory period; so, deficiency notice sent within 3 years of return's Saturday deadline and Monday *delivery* dates was timely under either statutory scheme.

Reference(s): USTR Estate & Gift Taxes ¶75,085.01(10). ¶ 75,025.01(45) ; ¶ 65,015.03(40) ; ¶ 75,035.01 Code Sec. 6501 ; Code Sec. 7502 ; Code Sec. 7503 ; Code Sec. 7508

2. Gross estate—valuation—closely- held stock—burden of proof—expert opinions. Tax Court improperly failed to shift burden of proving estate tax deficiency to IRS where IRS own experts' testimony and valuations showed assessment was arbitrary and excessive, and thus not entitled to presumption of correctness. Also, propriety of Court's valuation of decedent's stock in closely-held co. wasn't determinable where Court didn't adequately clarify how it arrived at valuation, which widely diverged from experts on which it allegedly relied: Court didn't explain use of contradictory acquisition and publicly traded values as start values; or how it arrived at 35% combined lack-of- [pg. 2001-2044] marketability and minority-interest discount that wasn't supported by experts' estimates.

Reference(s): USTR Estate & Gift Taxes ¶20,315.12(5); 20,315.06(10); 66,625.01 ¶ 74,536.1426(90) ; ¶ 74,536.1428 (37) Code Sec. 2031 ; Code Sec. 6662

3. IRS Action

IRS action with regard to cases it has lost can be located in the Bulletin Index-Digest System (1954–1993/94) (Chapter 10) or in a service covering IRS documents. You will probably find it easier to locate IRS action using either the IRS website or a commercial service. Commercial services have more extensive retrospective coverage. Do not be surprised if a commercial service cites to a notice of acquiescence or nonacquiescence but not to an action on decision or vice versa. [See Illustrations 11-9 through 11-11.] You can easily find both by searching in the service's databases covering the Internal Revenue Bulletin (or Cumulative Bulletin) and actions on decisions.

Illustration 11-9. RIA Citator Results for Mitchell Decision

Select Top Line link type:

Citator ▼

Filter Links

📄 FUJIEKI, PATRICK T. v. COM., 93 AFTR 2d 2004-362, (CA9, 12/29/2003)

📄 MITCHELL, PAUL, EST, 2002 RIA TC Memo ¶2002-098

📄 MITCHELL, PAUL, EST OF, 1997 RIA TC Memo ¶97,461

📄 MITCHELL, PAUL, EST OF, v. COM., 87 AFTR 2d 2001-2043, 250 F3d 696, 2001-1 USTC ¶60,403, (CA9, 5/2/2001)

📄 MITCHELL, PAUL, EST. OF, 103 TC 520, ¶103.30 TCR

📄 AOD 2005-001, 2005 USTR ¶86,273

→The RIA Citator on Checkpoint cites to AOD 2005-001.

Illustration 11-10. KeyCite Results for Mitchell Decision

History

(Showing All Documents)

Direct History

SELECT TO PRINT, EMAIL, ETC.

☐ ▶1 Estate of Mitchell v. Commissioner of Internal Revenue, T.C. Memo. 1997-461, 1997 WL 6254 T.C.M. (RIA) 97,461, 1997 RIA TC Memo 97,461 (U.S.Tax Ct. Oct 09, 1997) (NO. 21805-93)

Affirmed in Part, Vacated in Part, Remanded by

☐ ➡2 KeyCited Citation:
Estate of Mitchell v. C.I.R., 250 F.3d 696, 87 A.F.T.R.2d 2001-2043, 2001-1 USTC P 60,40£ 3453, 01 Cal. Daily Op. Serv. 4238, 2001 Daily Journal D.A.R. 4253 (9th Cir. May 02, 2001) (N (May 21, 2001)

On Remand to

☐ H 3 Estate of Mitchell v. C.I.R., T.C. Memo. 2002-98, 2002 WL 531148, 83 T.C.M. (CCH) 1524, T RIA TC Memo 2002-098 (U.S.Tax Ct. Apr 09, 2002) (NO. 21805-93)

AND Nonacq.,

☐ H 4 2005-23 I.R.B. 1152, 2005 WL 1318362 (IRS ACQ Jun 06, 2005)

AND Nonacquiescence Recommended by

☐ H 5 AOD- 2005-01, 2005 WL 1331108 (IRS AOD Jun 07, 2005)

→KeyCite cites to both the AOD and the nonacquiescence.

→Shepard's on LexisNexis (not illustrated) cites to the AOD.

Illustration 11-11. CCH Citator Results for Mitchell Decision

• **CA-9**-- (aff'g, vac'g and rem'g TC) 2001-1 USTC ¶60,403 , 250 F3d 696

Trompeter Est. CA-9, 2002-1 USTC ¶60,428 , 279 F3d 767

Dunia Est. TC, Dec. 55,643(M) , 87 TCM 1353 , TC Memo. 2004-123

Harper Est. TC, Dec. 54,745(M) , 83 TCM 1641 , TC Memo. 2002-121

Sp. Rul. 6-7-2005, June 7, 2005Sp. Rul. 6-7-2005, June 7, 2005

→The CCH Citator on IntelliConnect refers to a "Sp. Rul.," which is probably a citation to the AOD, but does not provide a link.

SECTION H. PROBLEMS

1. Indicate the names of the parties, court involved, and year, for the decision listed below. How many headnotes does the case have in this service?

  a. 2009-2 U.S.T.C. ¶ 50,517

  b. 2009 WL 1287255

  c. 2010 U.S. Tax Ct. LEXIS 4

2. Give the preferred citation for any decisions involving the taxpayer listed below. Use a citation to LexisNexis or Westlaw only if you cannot locate a citation to a reporter service.

  a. Glenn Gaffey

  b. Marlene Johansen

  c. Alicia Garnett

  d. Sally-Ann Nash

3. Was the lower court affirmed or reversed on appeal?

  a. 127 T.C. 96

  b. 503 F. Supp. 2d 1164

  c. 366 F. Supp. 253

  d. 83 Fed. Cl. 291

4. In which case does the following language appear?

a. "The debtor, on the other hand, tells a very different tale. He portrays himself as in effect parading out of bankruptcy, but closely pursued by vigilant taxing authorities holding a lien on everything he owns—including the shirt on his back. That lien, curiously enough, does not grant the IRS the right to seize the debtor's clothes."

b. "The eye of the IRS, to paraphrase the psalmist, is only at that moment open 'upon those who fear him, upon those that hope in his mercy.' Or at least upon those asking for a CDP hearing."

c. "To paraphrase *Wilkinson*: We cannot believe that a romp down the yellow brick road of subchapter K can yield these absurd results."

d. "Suffice it to say, however, the text of (b)(3) and the examples are extremely generous to teachers. To paraphrase Gertrude Stein in Sacred Emily (1913), 'teacher is a teacher is a teacher is a teacher.'"

5. Locate judicial decisions involving the following issues.

a. a 2008 Circuit Court decision involving statutory flush language and a wrongful levy

b. a 2008 Circuit Court decision involving whether the Tax Court was a court that can transfer cases to a District Court

c. a 2007 Tax Court decision involving the meaning of the term i.e., which is an abbreviation for "id est"

d. a 2007 Tax Court decision involving whether a taxpayer who filed a joint return, but whose spouse already had a wife and six children, qualified for section 6015 relief

6. Provide the citation for the judicial decisions involving the facts below, including both trial court and any appeals.

a. a pathological gambling disorder and a definition taken from Wikipedia

b. imputing a bankrupt taxpayer's misconduct to the bankruptcy trustee for purposes of Code section 1341

c. in vitro fertilization expenses incurred by a fertile male

d. a taxpayer who was tape recorded by an IRS agent at a tax-avoidance seminar in Belize saying that taxes above 10% were confiscation

7. Provide the citation for judicial decisions, including both trial court and any appeals, involving the tax consequences of the following celebrities or individuals who interacted with them.

a. divorce-related expenses of Doris Day's son

b. estate tax deductions by the estate of the creator of The Muppets

c. income tax deductions by the estate of the woman on whom the female companion in the movie Citizen Kane was allegedly based

d. tax collection action against the "Queen of the Blues"

CHAPTER 12.CITATORS

SECTION A. INTRODUCTION

This chapter discusses features of citators that were illustrated in earlier chapters. It makes appropriate references to illustrations in those chapters (and to illustrations in Chapter 14, dealing with periodical articles).

As illustrated in other chapters, you can use citator services to determine if a particular statute, regulation, ruling, or judicial decision has been criticized, approved, or otherwise commented upon in a more recent proceeding. And as shown in Illustrations 14-3, 14-4, 14-6, and 14-7, Shepard's and KeyCite let you determine if a judicial opinion has cited a particular periodical article or if an article has cited a particular decision.

Goals for this chapter include determining coverage and format differences for each citator. The chapter focuses primarily on online versions of each citator. The online versions are easier to use, are generally updated more frequently, and provide hyperlinks to the citing material.

SECTION B. TERMINOLOGY

This chapter discusses four citator services. Print citators group documents in a particular format (for example, by year of decision, alphabetically, or by type of tax). Each item is followed by a list of later items that cite to it. Online versions of some citators also group cited items, but format is largely irrelevant when using an online citator.

A later item may merely cite the earlier item as authority or it may discuss the earlier item and indicate agreement or disagreement with its holding. The discussion may center on the earlier item as a whole or on a particular issue involved in that item.

In this chapter, the earlier material is referred to as the **cited** item; any later material that refers to it is a **citing** item. Subdivisions such as headnote or syllabus numbers, which refer to issues, are referred to by either term throughout this book.

SECTION C. CITATOR FORMAT AND COVERAGE OVERVIEW

This section provides a brief overview of differences in citator format and coverage. Detailed descriptions appear in Sections D through G.[267]

---

[267] These descriptions cover each cited authority in the same order.

Three of the four citators described in this chapter are available in both print and online formats. Because of updating frequency and the ability to search the equivalent of multiple print citator volumes, electronic citators are superior if you can find the same material in both formats. As noted above, this chapter focuses primarily on online citators.

1. Arrangement

a. Cited Items in Print Citators

The manner in which cited items are arranged is relevant only if you use a print citator and need to locate the correct citator volume. Arrangement is irrelevant for an electronic citator. Print citators follow a variety of format conventions, the most important of which relate to judicial decisions. The major distinction is between citators that arrange cases by reporter service citation and those that arrange them alphabetically. A second distinction relates to the overall arrangement of multivolume services.

The Shepard's print citators arrange cited cases by numerical reporter citations. The Commerce Clearing House (CCH) and Research Institute of America (RIA) citators arrange them by taxpayer name. Noting the taxpayer's first name can make your search easier, particularly if the taxpayer has a common last name. Alphabetization rules, particularly for names that begin with numbers are also important (e.g., 21 West Lancaster precedes Twenty Mile Joint Venture in RIA but not in CCH).

Each service uses a different method for classifying items into citator volumes. CCH divides its citator service to correspond to its separate income, estate and gift, and excise tax services. Shepard's uses separate volumes for different courts and reporter services. RIA does neither.

b. Citing Items in Online Citators

The arrangement for citing items is important no matter what type of citator you use. When listing citing items for judicial decisions, RIA subdivides citing cases by headnote or syllabus number. Within each number, it arranges items by rank of court; within each rank, it lists the earliest items first. Shepard's electronic service arranges citing items by circuit and then by rank of court. KeyCite arranges citing judicial decisions by category (e.g., positive, cited, mentioned); within each category, it lists them by court. Shepard's and KeyCite list the most recent items first. CCH lists appellate cases before lower court cases. It is important to keep distinctions in mind if you use more than one citator so that you don't overlook an item because you are used to a different arrangement.

2. Headnote/Syllabus Number and Judicial Commentary

Shepard's, KeyCite, and RIA use syllabus numbers to indicate issues and words or letter symbols to indicate commentary (e.g., distinguished, explained); CCH does neither. If you use CCH, you avoid the risk of an editor's coding error, but you also receive no guidance as to whether citing references tend to be positive or negative.

3. Miscellaneous Differences

CCH uses fewer citing cases than do the others; it limits its coverage to citing cases that affect the cited case's "effectiveness as precedent." The online Shepard's and KeyCite include secondary sources as citing items. All services (including the online Shepard's) are more likely than the general Shepard's print service to include Tax Court (particularly Memorandum decisions) and IRS material as citing items.

SECTION D. SHEPARD'S CITATIONS

Because of its long history, Shepard's is the best-known citator. It is available in print and electronically through LexisNexis.

Shepard's publishes a general version and a Shepard's Federal Tax Citator version. The print versions of Shepard's, both the general and the tax services, are divided both chronologically and by cited authority into hardbound and softbound volumes [Table 12-1]. As a result, searches using the print Shepard's take longer than those using another system.

Table 12-1. General Shepard's Volumes

Cited Item	Shepard's Volumes
Constitution	Federal Statute Citations
Statutes	Federal Statute Citations
Treaties	Federal Statute Citations (until 1995)
Regulations	Code of Federal Regulations Citations
Revenue Rulings	Not Covered
District Court	Federal Citations
Federal Claims	Federal Citations
Bankruptcy Court	Bankruptcy Citations
Court of Appeals	Federal Citations
Supreme Court	United States Citations

Shepard's uses color-coded signals to alert you to how the citing item treated the cited item. A letter I in a blue circle (🛈) means that citing information is available.

Table 12-2. Shepard's Analysis Definition Codes

Color	Symbol	Meaning
Red	●; ⓘ	Warning: Negative treatment indicated
Orange	Q	Questioned: Validity questioned by citing references
Yellow	△	Caution: Possible negative treatment indicated
Green	◆	Positive treatment indicated
Blue	Ⓐ	Cited and neutral analysis indicated

Shepard's citing items appear in this order: legislative history (citations in statutes); cases; IRS material; and articles and other secondary source material. Supreme Court decisions appear before Courts of Appeals. Within each circuit, opinions of the Circuit Court come first, followed by District Court (or Court of Federal Claims), followed by Bankruptcy Court opinions. Tax Court opinions (Regular and Memorandum, grouped together) are the last federal judicial decisions; they are followed by state decisions. The most recent items appear first.

You can choose to find all citing references (Full option) or those for which Shepard's provides analytical notations (KWIC option). Shepard's provides pinpoint citations to the exact page. It also has hyperlinks to the cited items, so that you can read them online.

1. Constitution, Statutes, and Treaties

If a constitutional provision has been cited by a federal or state court, or by the IRS, Shepard's includes it in a list of citing references [Illustration 12-1]. Shepard's also includes citations in secondary materials.

Illustration 12-1. Shepard's Citations to Constitution

View: Index | KWIC | Full
Display Options ▶

⬅ 1101 - 1150 of 1,614 Total Cites ➡
Save As *Shepard's Alert*® | Unrestricted | All Neg | All Pos | FOCUS™- Restrict By
Shepard's® U.S. Const. amend. 16

IRS AGENCY MATERIALS

☐ 1112. **Cited by:**
Rev. Proc. 2010-1, 2010 IRB LEXIS 30, 2010-1 I.R.B. 1, Rev. Proc. 2010-1 (I.R.S. 2010) △

2010 IRB LEXIS 30
Rev. Proc. 2010-1

☐ 1113. **Cited by:**
Rev. Proc. 2010-2, 2010 IRB LEXIS 26, 2010-1 I.R.B. 90, Rev. Proc. 2010-2 (I.R.S. 2010) Ⓐ

2010 IRB LEXIS 26
Rev. Proc. 2010-2

☐ 1114. **Cited by:**
Chief Couns. Adv. Mem. 200947055, IRS CCA 200947055, 2009 IRS CCA LEXIS 274 (I.R.S. 2009)

Shepard's accords the same treatment to statutes and indicates if the statute's validity has been passed upon. Shepard's also indicates any subsequent congressional amendments or repeals of statutory material. As shown in Illustration 12-2, Shepard's does not limit itself to citing material. It includes other information you may find useful, including the statute's history and online links to the relevant Public Laws.

Illustration 12-2. Shepard's Citations to I.R.C. § 221

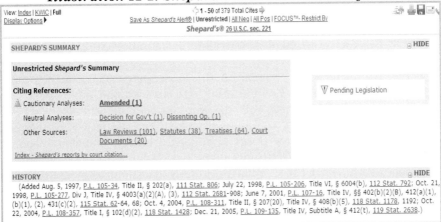

→Shepard's includes information you may find useful in narrowing your search.

The print Shepard's stopped covering treaties in 1995. The online Shepard's does not currently include a "Shepardize" tab with its treaties

2. Regulations and IRS Documents

The online Shepard's lets you Shepardize both regulations sections and IRS documents. Illustration 4-21 shows the results from Sheperdizing Revenue Ruling 87-22, which is discussed and illustrated in Chapter 4.

Illustration 12-3. Shepard's Citations to Treas. Reg. § 1.104-1

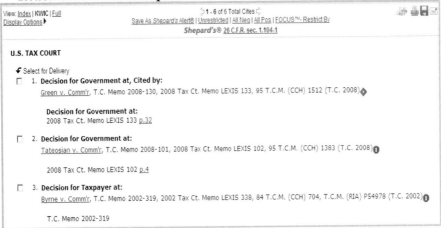

3. Judicial Decisions

The electronic version indicates both the first page of the citing decision and the page where the citation to the earlier item appears. Instead of West's Key Numbers, the online version of Shepard's uses LexisNexis headnote numbers.

Illustration 12-4. Shepard's Citations to Huntsman

View: KWIC | Full
Display Options
1 - 50 of 54 Total Cites
Save As Shepard's Alert® | Unrestricted | All Neg | All Pos | FOCUS™- Restrict By
Shepard's® Huntsman v. Commissioner, 905 F.2d 1182 (TOA)

14. **Distinguished by:**
Cao v. Commissioner, T.C. Memo 1994-60, 1994 Tax Ct. Memo LEXIS 61, 67 T.C.M. (CCH) 2171, T.C.M. (RIA) P94060, 94 TNT 33-6 (T.C. 1994)

T.C. Memo 1994-60

15. **Distinguished by:**
Dodd v. Commissioner, T.C. Memo 1992-341, 1992 Tax Ct. Memo LEXIS 362, 63 T.C.M. (CCH) 3141, T.C.M. (RIA) P92341 (T.C. 1992)

T.C. Memo 1992-341

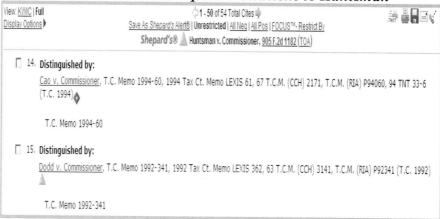

→Note that Shepard's uses different symbols (positive treatment; caution) for cases that both distinguish the cited decision.

→The KeyCite results for this decision appear in Illustration 4-27.

4. Other Materials

As noted in the preceding paragraphs, Shepard's lists law review articles that cite to primary source authorities. In addition, you can use Shepard's to obtain citations to law review articles. Illustration 12-5 shows the citing references to one of the articles that cited Revenue Ruling 87-22. Illustration 14-7 shows judicial citations to an article.

Illustration 12-5. Citations to 80 Ky. L.J. 431 in Shepard's

(CITATION YOU ENTERED):
ARTICLE: My Home, My Debt: Remodeling the Home Mortgage Interest Deduction, 80 Ky. L.J. 431 (1992)

LAW REVIEWS AND PERIODICALS (13 Citing References)

Select for Delivery

1. ARTICLE: The Bankruptcy of Haig-Simons? The Inequity of Equity and the Definition of Income in Consumer Bankruptcy Cases, 10 Am. Bankr. Inst. L. Rev. 765 (2002)

2. ARTICLE: The (Not So) Little House on the Prairie: The Hidden Costs of the Home Mortgage Interest Deduction, 32 Ariz. St. L.J. 1347 (2000)

SECTION E. KEYCITE

When LexisNexis acquired full ownership of Shepard's, Westlaw substituted its KeyCite system for Shepard's citators. Unlike the other three citators, KeyCite is available only online. After you locate a primary source on Westlaw, you click the KeyCite icon to obtain citations to later materials included in the Westlaw database. Alternatively, if you already have a citation, you can go directly to KeyCite and enter that citation.

You can use KeyCite, to obtain all references (neutral, positive, and negative along with secondary materials) to the cited item, or you can limit yourself to negative references. KeyCite provides hyperlinks to the citing material.

KeyCite uses color-coded symbols to indicate how the citing item treated the cited item. Green "depth of treatment" stars (★) indicate how extensively a cited case or administrative decision has been discussed by the citing case. Purple quotation marks (") indicate that the citing case or administrative decision directly quotes the cited case.

Table 12-3. KeyCite Citing Reference Codes

Color	Symbol	Meaning
Red	▶	Severe negative treatment
Yellow	▷	Negative treatment indicated
Green	C	Citing references
Blue	H	Direct history

Citing material is arranged by treatment (e.g., positive, negative) and within each treatment group by category (e.g., Discussed, Cited, Mentioned). Within categories, judicial decisions are arranged by level of court. Within each level, the most recent material is listed first. KeyCite indicates both the first page and the citing page for later material. If the number of citing sources is large enough, categories may be subdivided into topics.

1. Constitution, Statutes, and Treaties

KeyCite provides citations to cases that have interpreted constitutional provisions. It also lists articles and other secondary source materials. KeyCite also provides citations to cases and IRS materials that have interpreted statutes and to cases that have discussed the constitutionality of statutes. Cases are arranged by topic or issue.[268]

KeyCite alerts you to pending legislation and provides information about prior amendments to the statute. It does not cover treaties.

Illustration 12-6. Citing References to Constitution in KeyCite

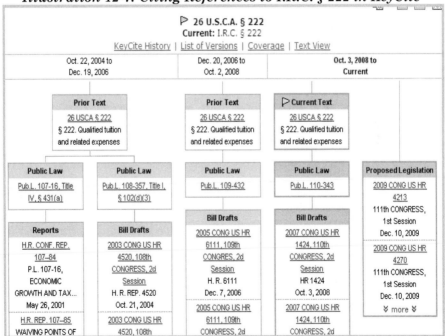

→KeyCite doesn't list District Court decisions immediately following the relevant Court of Appeals.

Illustration 12-7. Citing References to I.R.C. § 222 in KeyCite

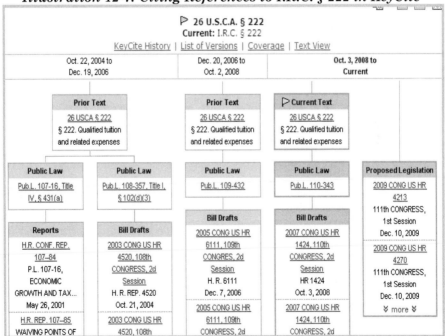

---

[268] Because the service includes pre-1954 Code cases, you may retrieve some irrelevant material. For example, KeyCiting 26 USC 213 or IRC 213 (medical expenses) yields decisions citing section 213 of pre-Code revenue acts.

2. Regulations and IRS Documents

KeyCite provides citations to judicial decisions, officially published and publicly available IRS documents, and secondary sources interpreting regulations and IRS documents [Illustration 4-22]. KeyCite provides T.D. numbers and dates for regulations. It provides dates and Cumulative Bulletin cites (if any) for IRS documents.

3. Judicial Decisions

KeyCite indicates both the first page of the citing decision and the page where the citation to the earlier item appears. It indicates the headnote covered by the citing material. [See Illustration 4-27.]

4. Other Materials

As was true for Shepard's, KeyCite indicates if a judicial decision has cited an article and if an article has mentioned a judicial decision.

Illustration 12-8. Citing References for Article in KeyCite

```
  C                                    74 SCALR 5
                              Southern California Law Review
                           THE ECONOMIC SUBSTANCE DOCTRINE
                                     November, 2000

FOR EDUCATIONAL USE ONLY
                                   Citing References

                               (Showing 84 documents)


                               Citing Cases (U.S.A.)

  SELECT TO PRINT, EMAIL, ETC.

                                  ★ ★   Cited

  ☐  H 1  U.S. v. Fletcher, 562 F.3d 839, 842, 103 A.F.T.R.2d 2009-1674, 2009-1674, 2009-1 USTC P
          50,334, 50334 (7th Cir.(Ill.) Apr 10, 2009) (NO. 08-2173)

  ☐  H 2  Rogers v. U.S., 281 F.3d 1108, 1115+, 89 A.F.T.R.2d 2002-1115, 2002-1115+, 2002-1 USTC
          P 50,240, 50240+ (10th Cir.(Kan.) Feb 22, 2002) (NO. 00-3013, 00-3030)
```

→Illustration 14-7 shows results for the same article in Shepard's.

SECTION F. RIA CITATOR

The RIA Citator began as the Prentice-Hall print citator. It is still available in print and is also carried online in both RIA Checkpoint and in Westlaw. The earlier volumes are available only in the print version. The online services limit themselves to RIA Citator 2d. Unless you need earlier material, the online versions will be easier to use than the print version because you will not have to use multiple volumes.[269] If you do

---

[269] The first series covers federal tax cases from 1796 to 1954.

need earlier materials, and the choice is between the RIA and CCH print citators, RIA is likely to provide more extensive results.

The discussion below covers using the RIA Citator in Checkpoint.

1. Constitution, Statutes, and Treaties

The RIA Citator does not cover the Constitution, statutes, or treaties.

2. Regulations and IRS Documents

RIA covers both regulations and IRS documents, but it is not the best source for finding to citations to regulations. It lists cited regulations in T.D. (rather than regulations section) number order; this is not the best method for finding regulations, as a single T.D. may cover several sections. Illustrations 12-9 through 12-11 cover searching for citations to Revenue Ruling 84-108.

Illustration 12-9. Citator Option in Checkpoint

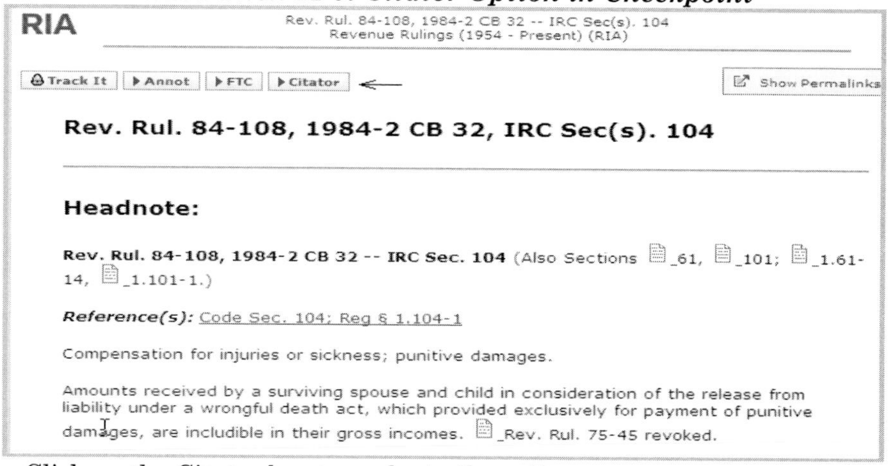

RIA
Rev. Rul. 84-108, 1984-2 CB 32 -- IRC Sec(s). 104
Revenue Rulings (1954 - Present) (RIA)
Track It
Annot
FTC
Citator
Show Permalinks
Rev. Rul. 84-108, 1984-2 CB 32, IRC Sec(s). 104
Headnote:
Rev. Rul. 84-108, 1984-2 CB 32 -- IRC Sec. 104 (Also Sections _61, _101; _1.61-14, _1.101-1.)
Reference(s): Code Sec. 104; Reg § 1.104-1
Compensation for injuries or sickness; punitive damages.
Amounts received by a surviving spouse and child in consideration of the release from liability under a wrongful death act, which provided exclusively for payment of punitive damages, are includible in their gross incomes. _Rev. Rul. 75-45 revoked.

→Click on the Citator box to evaluate the ruling.

Illustration 12-10. RIA Citator Link

Contents
Search Tools
Document List
Links
Outline
Select Top Line link type:
Citator
Filter Links
REVR 84-108, 1984-2 CB 32

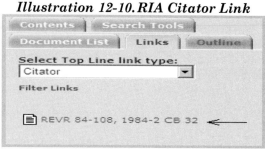

Click on the link to get the results.

Illustration 12-11. RIA Citator Results

Rev Rul 84-108, 1984-2 CB 32, ,

Judicial History

Revoking : Rev Rul 75-45 , 1975-1 CB 47 , ,

Cited In

Cited without Comment: O'Gilvie, Kevin M. v. U.S., <u>78 AFTR 2d 96-7456</u> , 96-7460, 519 US 83 , 89, 117 S Ct 455 *(US, 12/10/1996)*

Cited favorably : Miller, Bonnie; Comm. v, <u>66 AFTR 2d 90-5624</u> , 914 F2d 591 *(CA4, 9/21/1990)*

Cited without Comment: Reese, Elizabeth, A., v. U.S., <u>73 AFTR 2d 94-2014</u> , 24 F3d 235 *(CA Fed Cir, 5/16/1994)*

3. Judicial Decisions

RIA arranges citing cases according to the pertinent RIA syllabus number of the cited case. Within syllabus groupings, RIA lists cases by rank of the citing court, starting with the Supreme Court. Within each group of courts, the earliest cases generally appear first. Geographical jurisdiction is indicated for cited and citing decisions, but District Court subdivisions are not indicated.

Citations are given for both the first page and the citing page. Case citations are given to the official and West services in addition to RIA services.[270]

RIA also includes citations to IRS action with respect to the cited decision. Citations for revenue rulings and procedures are given to the appropriate volume and page of the Internal Revenue Bulletin or Cumulative Bulletin or to United States Tax Reporter; letter rulings and T.D.s are cited by number, followed by a reference to United States Tax Reporter.

----

[270] The print RIA uses letters to indicate whether or not subsequent decisions follow the cited decision. Citations to subsequent decisions indicate the page where the cited case is mentioned, not the first page of the citing material.

Illustration 12-12. RIA Citator Results for Polone v. Commissioner

RIA   POLONE, GAVIN, 2003 RIA TC Memo ¶2003-339
Citator 2nd (RIA)

Affirmed: Polone, Gavin v. Com., <u>100 AFTR 2d 2007-6277</u> *(CA9, 10/11/2007)*

Cited In

Cited favorably : Long Term Capital Holdings, et al. v. U.S., <u>94 AFTR 2d 2004-5701</u> , 330 F Supp 2d 166 —167 *(DC CT, 8/27/2004) [See 2003 RIA TC Memo 2003-1957]*

Cited favorably : Murphy, Marrita et al. v. I.R.S. et al., <u>95 AFTR 2d 2005-1509</u> *(DC Dist Col, 3/22/2005) [See 2003 RIA TC Memo 2003-1959]*

Cited favorably 1: HIE Holdings Inc, et al, 2009 <u>RIA TC Memo 2009-1051</u> *(6/8/2009)*

Cited favorably 2: Stadnyk, Daniel J. & Brenda J., 2008 <u>RIA TC Memo 2008-1579</u> *(12/22/2008)*

Cited without Comment3: Voelker, Frank T. v. Nolen, Catherine M. et al., <u>93 AFTR 2d 2004-1995</u> , 365 F3d 582 *(CA7, 4/23/2004)*

→See Table 6-1 for the timeline in *Polone*.

4. Other Materials

The RIA citator does not cover law review articles.

SECTION G. CCH STANDARD FEDERAL TAX REPORTER—CITATOR

The CCH print citator service is actually three separate services. Standard Federal Tax Reporter—Citator is a two-volume service that covers the income tax. The CCH Federal Estate and Gift Tax Reporter and Federal Excise Tax Reporter have their own citator sections, which cover those taxes. [271] The three services combined have fewer volumes than does the full RIA Citator service.[272] If you access the CCH Citator online through CCH IntelliConnect, you avoid having to use separate citator services.

---

[271] Although the SFTR citator volumes list non-Tax Court cases involving estate and gift taxes and excise taxes, actual citations to those cases appear only in the Citator sections of Federal Estate and Gift Tax Reporter and Federal Excise Tax Reporter.

[272] While its compactness makes it the easiest print citator to use, the CCH citator has the fewest useful features and omits, through editorial selection, many citing cases. It does provide paragraph cross-references to discussion in the SFTR compilation volumes.

1. Constitution, Statutes, and Treaties

The CCH Citator does not cover the Constitution, statutes, or treaties.

2. Regulations and IRS Documents

CCH covers both regulations and IRS documents. It lists cited regulations in T.D. number order. This is not the best method for finding regulations, as a single T.D. may cover several sections.

Citations for decisions include citations to CCH case reporter services; many citations include the official and West publications. CCH Decision numbers are given for Tax Court materials. The editors provide no indication as to how non-IRS citing material dealt with the cited material.

CCH shows a cited ruling's location in the Cumulative Bulletin or Internal Revenue Bulletin. It lists citing items issued by the IRS only by number. Illustrations 12-13 through 12-15 show the results obtained using CCH Citator for citations to Rev. Rul. 84-108 in IntelliConnect.

Illustration 12-13. Rev. Rul. 84-108

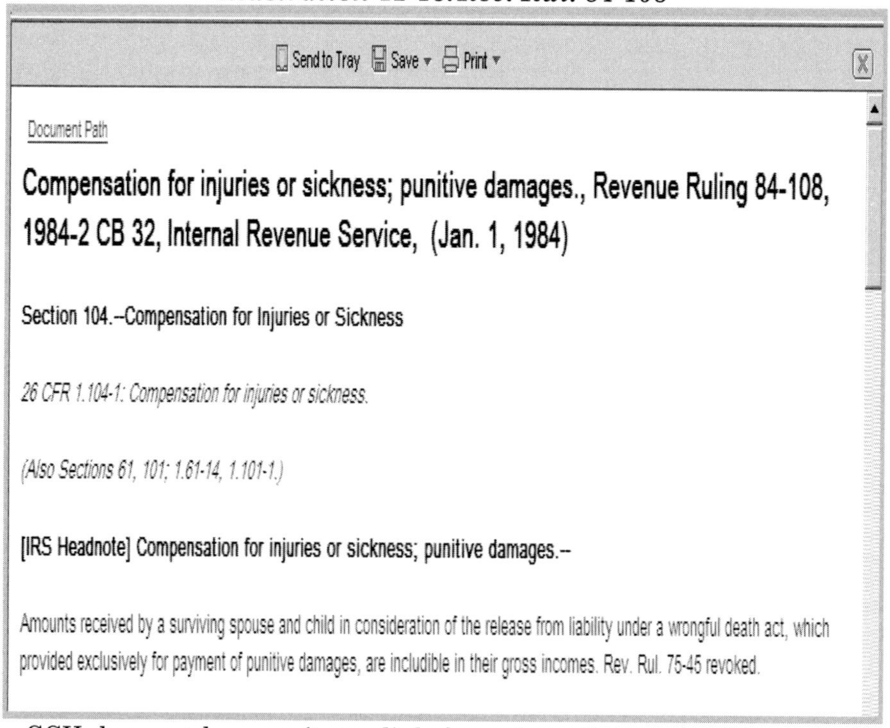

☐ Send to Tray ☐ Save ▾ ☐ Print ▾   ⊠

Document Path

Compensation for injuries or sickness; punitive damages., Revenue Ruling 84-108, 1984-2 CB 32, Internal Revenue Service, (Jan. 1, 1984)

Section 104.--Compensation for Injuries or Sickness

26 CFR 1.104-1: Compensation for injuries or sickness.

(Also Sections 61, 101; 1.61-14, 1.101-1.)

[IRS Headnote] Compensation for injuries or sickness; punitive damages.--

Amounts received by a surviving spouse and child in consideration of the release from liability under a wrongful death act, which provided exclusively for payment of punitive damages, are includible in their gross incomes. Rev. Rul. 75-45 revoked.

→CCH does not have a citator link from the ruling, so I will search directly in the citator.

Illustration 12-14. Searching in CCH Citator

Citator
Revenue Ruling 84 - 108 Go
Special Ruling Go

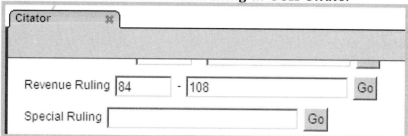

Illustration 12-15. Results in CCH Citator

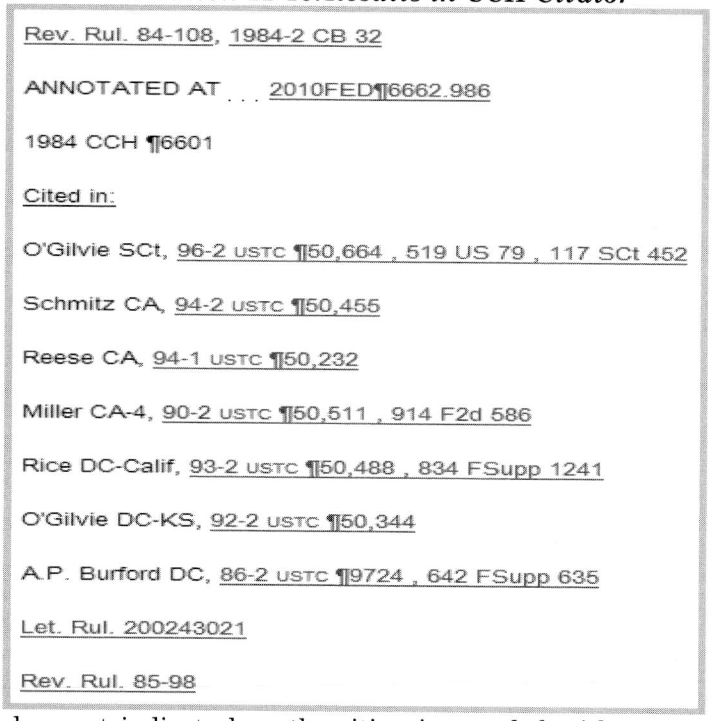

Rev. Rul. 84-108, 1984-2 CB 32
ANNOTATED AT . . . 2010FED¶6662.986
1984 CCH ¶6601
Cited in:
O'Gilvie SCt, 96-2 USTC ¶50,664 , 519 US 79 , 117 SCt 452
Schmitz CA, 94-2 USTC ¶50,455
Reese CA, 94-1 USTC ¶50,232
Miller CA-4, 90-2 USTC ¶50,511 , 914 F2d 586
Rice DC-Calif, 93-2 USTC ¶50,488 , 834 FSupp 1241
O'Gilvie DC-KS, 92-2 USTC ¶50,344
A.P. Burford DC, 86-2 USTC ¶9724 , 642 FSupp 635
Let. Rul. 200243021
Rev. Rul. 85-98

→CCH does not indicate how the citing item ruled with respect to the cited item.

3. Judicial Decisions

CCH limits itself to cases commented on or cited in SFTR. It does not indicate which syllabus number is involved in the citing case; likewise, it does not indicate whether the citing material follows or distinguishes the cited decision. Its case citations refer to the CCH case reporters and to the official and West services. Citations to subsequent decisions in services other than U.S.T.C. indicate the first page of the citing case, not the page where reference is made to the cited material.[273]

CCH includes numerical citations to revenue rulings, letter rulings, and revenue procedures discussing the cited decision. It indicates IRS acquiescence or nonacquiescence in adverse judicial decisions.

4. Other Material

The CCH citator does not cover law review articles. It does provide references to the Standard Federal Tax Reporter (or appropriate CCH service covering estate and gift or excise taxes if the cited item does not involve an income tax issue).

Illustration 12-16. CCH Citator Results for Polone v. Commissioner

Federal Tax Citator, 2010FED, Main Citator Table, Polone, Gavin

Polone, Gavin

ANNOTATED AT 2010FED¶2900.31, ¶6662.521, ¶29,226.528, ¶39,652.38, ¶42,520.10

• **CA-9**-- (withdrawing prior CA; aff'g TC) 2007-2 USTC ¶50,729 , 505 F3d 966

HIE Holdings, Inc. TC, Dec. 57,847(M) , 97 TCM 1672 , TC Memo 2009-130

Stadnyk TC, Dec. 57,625(M) , 96 TCM 475 , TC Memo 2008-289

• **CA-9**-- (withdrawing prior CA; aff'g TC) 2007-1 USTC ¶50,392 , 479 F3d 1019

• **CA-9**-- (aff'g TC) 2006-1 USTC ¶50,367

• **TC**-- Dec. 55,375(M) , 86 TCM 698 , TC Memo. 2003-339

Polone CA-9, 2007-1 USTC ¶50,392 , 479 F3d 1019

Polone CA-9, 2006-1 USTC ¶50,367

Murphy DC-DC, 2005-1 USTC ¶50,237

Long Term Capital Holdings DC-CT, 2004-2 USTC ¶50,351 , 330 FSupp2d 122

Ziegler TC, Dec. 56,983(M) , 93 TCM 1418 , TC Memo 2007-166

Allum TC, Dec. 56,100(M) , TC Memo. 2005-177 , 90 TCM 74

---

[273] Citations to U.S.T.C. are to the paragraph number assigned the case, not to the U.S.T.C. page number.

SECTION H. PROBLEMS

1. Your instructor will assign you a primary source item to check in as many citators as are available to you. Make a list of differences in citing documents and a list of any differences in treatment. If you find differences in treatment, go to the actual citing material to determine which citators were correct.

2. Several of the problems in other chapters are easily completed with a citator. If you initially completed a problem using a particular citator, redo it using a different publisher's service and compare your results.

CHAPTER 13. LOOSELEAF SERVICES, ENCYCLOPEDIAS, AND TREATISES

SECTION A. INTRODUCTION

You may wish to consult explanatory materials early in the research effort, perhaps even before you read the relevant statutes.[274] If so, you are likely to use a looseleaf service, encyclopedia, or treatise. Those texts provide insight into the problem being researched. In addition, you can draw upon their liberal use of citations for a preliminary reading list of cases and administrative pronouncements. Each is updated at frequent intervals, and most have at least one related newsletter.

While general research texts would list some of these materials as looseleaf services and others as legal encyclopedias or treatises, those classifications are less significant in this context than are classifications based upon their formats. Most of them take a subject matter approach, but two of the best-known services are arranged in Code section order.

SECTION B. CODE SECTION ARRANGEMENT

The Commerce Clearing House[275] and Research Institute of America[276] looseleaf services take essentially the same approach. Each service's compilation volumes print the full texts of Code sections and Treasury regulations along with editorial explanations. An annotation section listing cases and rulings follows each section. Users wanting ready access to the text of the law alongside explanatory material will appreciate this format.

Because of the arrangement described above, problems involving multiple Code sections do not receive comprehensive discussion. Although the publishers supplement their looseleaf materials with newsletters and other aids, Code-based services are not as suited as are subject-based services for learning about issues involving multiple Code sections.

---

[274] In appropriate cases you can use these textual materials to ascertain which statutes are involved. In addition, you should consult these materials whenever you desire additional textual information.

[275] Standard Federal Tax Reporter (income tax); Federal Estate and Gift Tax Reporter; Federal Excise Tax Reporter.

[276] United States Tax Reporter—Income Taxes; United States Tax Reporter—Estate & Gift Taxes; United States Tax Reporter—Excise Taxes. RIA also publishes a subject matter format service, Federal Tax Coordinator 2d.

Although each service is arranged in Code section order, all materials are assigned paragraph numbers. A "paragraph" can be the size of a traditional paragraph, but it might be several pages long. Unless noted otherwise, each service cross-references between paragraph numbers, not between page numbers.

These services have subject matter indexes; their format makes Code section indexes unnecessary. New material arrives weekly for insertion in the compilation volumes or in a separate updating volume. These new developments are indexed according to the paragraph in the main compilation to which they relate, i.e., in Code section order.

Libraries often carry both services in print or online, and users eventually develop a preference for one or the other. As each service's annotations are editorially selected, using both can reduce the risk that you will miss a valuable annotation. Using both may substantially increase research time, and the extra material obtained rarely justifies the additional time involved.

1. Standard Federal Tax Reporter

The discussion of this CCH looseleaf service follows the format in which it is arranged. Several volumes, such as the Citator, are discussed in greater detail elsewhere in this book; appropriate cross-references to those discussions appear here. A Taxes on Parade newsletter provides cross-references to SFTR.

SFTR is available online on IntelliConnect, and the illustrations in this chapter are taken from that version. If you are using the online version, you do not need to know volume numbers because online links let you navigate between materials. The print and online versions are also somewhat different in their general layout. There is additional discussion of the IntelliConnect version at the end of the SFTR discussion.

a. Code Volumes. These volumes print, in Code section order, all provisions involving income, gift and estate, employment, and excise taxes as well as procedural provisions. A brief explanation of amendments since 1954 (including the Public Law number and section and effective dates) follows each Code provision. These explanations include information about prior statutory language. These volumes are updated at intervals following Code amendments.

Volume I's Source Notes and Finding Lists section covers a variety of useful legislative history information.[277] Tables I and II provide cross-references between the 1939 and 1954 Codes. Table III indicates sections of the 1986 Code that refer to other sections. Because the Code itself is not fully cross-referenced, this table is valuable for researching an unfamiliar area. Table III does have limitations. First, as shown in Illustration 6-12, it is not revised as frequently as statutes are enacted. Second, it does not include references in other titles of United States Code. Finally, because related Code sections may not refer to each other at all, it omits many "relationships." Fortunately, you can use the annotated materials discussed in this chapter to familiarize yourself with interrelated Code sections.

A Legislative History Locator Table lists committee reports and dates for acts that affected the Code since 1954. This Table includes the act name and number, bill number, report numbers, and any Cumulative Bulletin citation. Another set of lists, which begins with 1971 legislation, covers Acts Supplementing the 1954 and 1986 Codes. These lists provide the Public Law number, bill number, date, and Statutes at Large citation for each act; they include popular names for several acts. These lists are in Public Law number order. Each act is arranged in act section order; the list indicates every Code section affected by an act section.[278] These lists do not indicate how the particular Code sections were affected.

Volume I also includes a Public Laws Amending the Internal Revenue Code section. It lists Public Law number, popular name (if any), and enactment date. These materials begin in mid-1954 and are in Public Law number order.

Volume I includes both a Topical Index and a Table of Contents listing all Code sections in order.

Volume II prints the text of non-Code statutory provisions affecting federal taxes in the Related Statutes section that begins in 1939. Volume II also includes subject matter and Code section lists of 1954–1966 amendments to the 1939 Code. The Code section list includes Public Law number and Congress, act section, and SFTR paragraph number.

b. Index Volume and Compilation Volume 1. Both volumes provide useful tables and other reference material. Because it covers the annota-

---

[277] The Volume I listings are not as up to date as other parts of the service. In March 2010, some of the lists described here were current only through 2004 while others did reflect current developments.

[278] Some libraries may have retained a special 1971 SFTR publication covering earlier acts.

tions in addition to the Code, the topical index in the Index volume is far more detailed than the index in Code volume I. The Index volume also includes:

- Tax calendars
- IRS Service Center mailing addresses
- Exemption and Standard Deduction Amounts since 1998
- Tax rates since 1909
- Withholding tables
- Depreciation tables—class life ADR; MACRS
- Annuity tables, including valuation for life estates and remainders
- Savings bond redemption tables
- Interest rate tables
  applicable federal rates since 1984
  uniform tables and procedures for compounding interest
  interest on overpayments/underpayments
- Low income housing credit rates and recapture information
- Per diem rates
- Checklists
  for completing tax returns
  income and deductions
  medical expenses—summary of rulings and cases
  real property tax dates by state
  tax elections
  information return filing
  disaster areas declared in current and preceding year
- Tax terms—explanatory definitions of commonly used jargon

Compilation volume 1 includes the following reference material:

- Tax planning by topic—e.g., impact of divorce; retirement
- Inflation adjustments for several years—by topic and Code section
- Return preparer information
- Who Is the Taxpayer?—discussion and annotations
- Constitutional and tax protest materials, including annotations

c. Compilation Volumes. Volumes 1–18 contain, in Code section order, the full text of the Code, proposed, temporary, and final regulations, and digest-annotations of revenue rulings and revenue procedures, letter rulings and other publicly available IRS documents, and judicial decisions. [Illustrations 13-1 through 13-4.] An alphabetical index is provided if the annotations section is lengthy. CCH provides an editorial explanation, including citations to the annotations, for each Code provision.

Immediately after each Code section, the editors indicate which Public Laws have amended it and print text of, or citations to, committee reports; a brief T.D. history also follows regulations sections. The pre-amendment text is omitted in the historical notes for both Code and regulations sections.

Regulations follow the Code section material. If a regulation does not reflect Code amendments, SFTR indicates that fact at the top of each regulations page. Because regulations are printed in Code section order, regulations from different parts of 26 C.F.R. (or even from other titles of C.F.R.) appear together. [See Illustration 13-1.] Because regulations from other C.F.R. titles follow their own prefix system, it is critical that your citation indicate Treas. Reg. (or 26 C.F.R.) for Treasury regulations and the other C.F.R. title for other regulations. See, e.g., 40 C.F.R. § 20.1, which appears in SFTR with Code section 169. If this were a Treasury regulation, the prefix 20 would indicate an estate tax regulation and the 1 following it would indicate Code section 1 (which covers income tax rates).

Illustration 13-1. SFTR Grouping of Regulations for Section 169

1. ☐ Regulation: Standard Federal Income Tax Reporter, §1.169-1. Amortization of pollution control facilities

2. ☐ Regulation: Standard Federal Income Tax Reporter, §1.169-2. Definitions

3. ☐ Regulation: 2010 Standard Federal Income Tax Reporter, §1.169-3. Amortizable basis

4. ☐ Regulation: Standard Federal Income Tax Reporter, §1.169-4. Time and manner of making elections

5. ☐ Regulation: Standard Federal Income Tax Reporter, §20.1. Applicability

6. ☐ Regulation: Standard Federal Income Tax Reporter, §20.2. Definitions

7. ☐ Regulation: Standard Federal Income Tax Reporter, §20.3. General provisions

→The regulations list does not indicate that §§20.1 through 20.3 are from 40 C.F.R. That information does appear if you click on each regulation's hyperlink.

The compilation volume covering taxation of foreign income also includes summaries of United States tax treaties.

Repealed tax provisions may be re-enacted in whole or part. Volume 18 includes annotations arising under expired laws, such as excess profits taxes. These will be useful for historical research as well as in the event of re-enactment.

Volume 18 also lists IRS and Tax Court forms (numerically and alphabetically), IRS publications (numerically), Treasury and IRS personnel, IRS procedural rules, and Circular 230.

Illustration 13-2. SFTR Compilation Volume Contents

- Sec. 1001. DETERMINATION OF AMOUNT OF AND RECOGNITION OF GAIN OR LOSS
- Legislative History
- §1.1001-1. Computation of gain or loss
- §1.1001-1. Computation of gain or loss, REG-141901-05, 10/18/2006.
- §1.1001-2. Discharge of liabilities
- §1.1001-3. Modifications of debt instruments
- §1.1001-4. Modifications of certain notional principal contracts
- §1.1001-5. European Monetary Union (conversion to the euro)
- §1.1002-1. Sales or exchanges
- §1.1001-6. Sales or exchanges, REG-143686-07, 1/19/2009 (corrected 3/5/2009).
- [¶29,225] Computation of Gain or Loss - Explanations
- Computation of Gain or Loss - Annotations
- [¶29,226] Sales or Exchanges - Explanations
- Sales or Exchanges - Annotations
- Current Developments

→The print looseleaf uses a separate volume for Current Developments.

Illustration 13-3. SFTR Explanation

2010 Standard Federal Income Tax Reporter--
Explanations, 29,225.022 , Computation of Gain or Loss: Sale or Disposition of Property Defined: Transactions treated as sales or dispositions

Related Information

The following transactions, while not sales in the strict sense, nonetheless are treated as dispositions on which gain is realized.

Transfers to creditors. A property transfer to a creditor in satisfaction of a debt is a sale or exchange on which gain or loss is realized (*Peninsula Properties Co.*, 47 BTA 84, Dec. 12,522, and *W.R. Kenan, Jr.*, CA-2, 40-2 USTC ¶9635; ¶29,226.1104). As with foreclosures, the amount realized depends upon whether the debt satisfied by the transfer is recourse or nonrecourse. If the loan is nonrecourse (situations when the debtor is not personally liable), the full amount of remaining debt is the amount realized, even if debt exceeds basis (*J.F. Tufts*, SCt, 83-1 USTC ¶9328, and *J. Delman Est.* Dec. 36,380; ¶29,225.1033). If the debt is recourse, the amount realized is the property's fair market value. The resulting gain is not income from the discharge of debt under Code Sec. 61(a)(12) and, therefore, is not excludable from income even though the debtor was insolvent at the time the property was transferred. If the debt satisfied exceeds the property's fair market value, the excess is debt discharge income which may be excludable under Code Sec. 108(a) (*J.S. Danenberg*, Dec. 36,459; ¶29,225.1019).

→Online looseleaf services provide hyperlinks to primary sources and to other documents. The paragraph numbers are more important when using the print service.

Illustration 13-4. SFTR Annotations

2010 Standard Federal Income Tax Reporter, 29,225.101 Computation of Gain or Loss: Allocation of sales price

Related Information

The basis of improvements should not have been included in the computation of gain on the sale of land because the seller retained title to them.

R.A. Waldrep, CA-5, 70-2 USTC ¶9485, 428 F2d 1216.

The IRS acted arbitrarily in allocating to a covenant not to compete the difference between the amount allocated by an "asset purchase agreement" to "personal property and agreements not to compete" and the book value of the assets.

Fulton Container Co., Inc., CA-9, 66-1 USTC ¶9177, 355 F2d 319.

On remand from CA-9, a $250,000 excess of sale price over basis was allocated equally to a covenant not to compete and to goodwill.

Fulton Container Co., Inc., DC, 68-1 USTC ¶9277.

→Each group of annotations has a paragraph number.

→Note the links to each decision's text in U.S. Tax Cases.

d. New Matters Volume. The compilation volumes' annotations receive little updating during the year involved. Instead, recent material is indexed in the New Matters volume (volume 19). Because the Cumulative Index (including a Latest Additions supplement) is based on the paragraph numbers used in the compilation volumes, it is easy to use the New Matters volume to find recent developments. If you use the online version, you can go directly to the Current Developments section for each Code section.

SFTR reproduces updating material as follows:

• New Matters volume—texts of revenue rulings and procedures; digests of Tax Court Regular and Memorandum Opinions

• U.S.T.C. Advance Sheets volume—texts of decisions rendered by all other courts

• Compilation volumes—Code and regulations.

The New Matters volume has several other helpful features. In addition to a Topical Index of current year developments, there are sections devoted to highlights of important new developments (CCH Comments). These items, which are covered in the Topical Index, also contain cross-references to the compilation volumes.

The New Matters volume digests a limited number of publicly available IRS documents. It also includes Preambles for current year Treasury Decisions and indicates where final and temporary regulations appear in the SFTR service.

A Case Table (including a supplement for Latest Additions) lists each year's decisions alphabetically. It indicates (1) which trial court is involved and where the decision appears in the U.S.T.C. Advance Sheets or SFTR New Matters volumes;[279] (2) appeals by either side and IRS acquiescence or nonacquiescence in unfavorable decisions; and (3) outcome at the appellate level.

A Supreme Court Docket, which also lists cases alphabetically, includes a brief digest of the issues involved and their disposition. This table includes cases in which the Court denies certiorari.

A Finding List of Rulings cross-references current year IRS documents to the appropriate paragraphs in volume 19. Consult this list in addition to the Finding Lists in the SFTR Citator when checking the status of IRS items.

e. U.S. Tax Cases (U.S.T.C.) Advance Sheets Volume. This volume contains the Preambles to proposed income tax regulations. Lists of proposed income tax regulations appear in both topical and Code section formats; the topical format is arranged chronologically rather than alphabetically.

This volume also contains the texts of income tax decisions rendered by courts other than the Tax Court.[280] You can locate these items using the Cumulative Index in the New Matters volume. Decisions appear in the order in which they are received rather than in Code section order. These decisions will later be issued in hardbound volumes as part of the U.S.T.C. reporter service discussed in Chapter 11.

---

[279] It may not indicate the state for District Court and lists only decisions covered in SFTR. Bankruptcy Court cases are listed as BC-DC (Bankruptcy Court-District Court).

[280] Preambles and recent court decisions involving estate and gift taxes or excise taxes appear in the CCH services covering those topics. Court decisions involving all taxes appear in the U.S.T.C. hardbound volumes.

f.Citator. You can use these volumes, which list decisions alphabetically, to determine if subsequent decisions have affected earlier items. The Citator also covers revenue rulings, revenue procedures, other IRS items, and Treasury Decisions. The Citator provides cross-references to discussions of cases and rulings in the compilation volumes. The online version of this Citator is discussed in Chapter 12.

The final item in the second volume is a list of Cumulative Bulletin citations to committee reports for sections amending the 1986 Code. These materials are in Code section order. Because Cumulative Bulletin coverage of legislation ended in 2003, these lists are unlikely to reflect recent legislation.

g. IntelliConnect. CCH recently switched from the Tax Research NetWork to IntelliConnect (discussed further in Chapter 19) as the platform for SFTR and other services. The IntelliConnect version of the SFTR does not track the format of the print version as closely as do the online versions of other looseleaf services described in this chapter, so you may have some initial difficulty transitioning from the print service or the previous electronic version.

Illustration 13-5. IntelliConnect Search for Gold and 1031

| Search | all content | ▽ | for | gold AND 1031 | ▽ | Go |

→You can search IntelliConnect across different types of authority.

Illustration 13-6. IntelliConnect Search Results

All results [257]

⊟ by Document Type [257]

    News [2]

    Explanations [6]

    Journals [10]

    Annotations [5]

  ⊟ Laws and Legislative Documents [92]

      Enacted [7]

      Proposed Legislation [57]

      Committee Reports [28]

  ⊟ Regulations [5]

      Final and Temporary [5]

    Cases [50]

  ⊞ IRS Materials [58]

  ⊞ Government Rulings and Procedures [62]

    Other Document Types [5]

→You can sort your results by relevance or date. You can also limit the document types you want to read.

Illustration 13-7. IntelliConnect Search Results: "News"

1. ☐ News: CCH Federal Tax Weekly, ¶7, Supply Contracts Transferred In Gold Mine For Coal Mine Swap Qualify As Like-Kind Property, Not Taxable Boot, (May 11, 2006)
   - ...Supply Contracts Transferred In **Gold** Mine For Coal Mine Swap Qualify...operating coalmine in a Code Sec. **1031** like-kind exchange was not...kind exchanges under Code Sec. **1031**. • Comment. The general rule...court also noted that Code Sec. **1031** requires only like kind and not...

2. ☐ News: CCH Federal Tax Weekly, ¶6, IRS Rejects Like-Kind Patent Exchange; Trademarks And Trade Names Not Like-Kind Under Code Sec. 1031, (Jan. 26, 2006)
   - ...Like-Kind Under Code Sec. **1031** TAM 200602034 Arecent technical Advice...determined that $20 U.S. **gold** coins, which are numismatic...like-kind under Code Sec. **1031**. Other issues The IRS also determined...Like-Kind Under Code Sec. **1031**

2. United States Tax Reporter—Income Taxes

Prentice-Hall revamped its Federal Taxes service in 1990, improving the layout to make the materials easier to locate and read. Research Institute of America continued the new format when it acquired and renamed this service.

The discussion of USTR follows the format in which it is arranged. Several of its volumes, and the RIA Citator, are discussed and illustrated in greater detail elsewhere in this book; this section includes appropriate cross-references to those discussions. Illustrations of USTR are taken from the online version on Checkpoint.[281] Volume numbers aren't critical if you use the online version; you can navigate using hyperlinks.

a. Code Volumes. The two Code volumes print, in Code section order, all provisions involving income, gift and estate, employment, and excise taxes as well as procedural provisions.[282] Historical information follows Code provisions that have been amended. Historical material includes the Public Law number, the Public Law section number, and the effective date of any amendments. Prior statutory language is provided for several sections.

Volume I contains a Topic Index to the Code [Illustrations 4-2 through 4-5] and a listing of all Code sections. Volume I also contains an Amending Acts section. This section includes Public Law number, date, act title

---

[281] USTR is also available on Westlaw.

[282] Repealed Code sections are included in the Code and compilation volumes.

or subject, and Cumulative Bulletin or Statutes at Large citation for acts since 1954. This section is not separately indexed and does not list the Code sections amended.

b. Index Volume. Volume 1 contains an extensive index (main and supplementary sections), using paragraph numbers, to the material in the compilation volumes discussed below. This index uses different type-faces to denote Code section numbers and locations, location of topical discussions, and location of regulations text. Volume 1 also includes a Glossary, which provides succinct definitions of terms (both words and phrases) used by tax practitioners.

c. Tables Volume. Volume 2 contains main, supplementary, and current Tables of Cases and main and supplementary Tables of Rulings. These tables cross-reference cases and rulings to the appropriate discussions in the compilation volumes or in the Weekly Alert newsletter.[283] RIA provides case citations to several different reporter services in addition to A.F.T.R. Special notations indicate paragraph numbers for decisions printed in RIA's Tax Court Memorandum Decisions service. A Supreme Court docket listing indicates petitions filed and their status.

The case tables are not citator supplements. The main table merely lists cases discussed in USTR. The supplementary and current tables indicate appeals action and IRS acquiescences for cases previously reported in the main table. The rulings tables, which cover both Internal Revenue Bulletin and other documents, do indicate prior or subsequent IRS action; they do not indicate judicial action. This volume also includes withholding, tax rate, per diem, and interest tables.

d. Compilation Volumes. Volumes 3–15A contain, in Code section order, the full text of the Code; final, temporary and proposed regulations; and digest-annotations of revenue rulings, letter rulings and other IRS releases, and judicial decisions. Texts of committee reports (or Cumulative Bulletin citations) are also included. Paragraph numbers assigned to these materials correspond to the Code section involved.

If a regulation does not reflect a Code amendment, that information appears at the beginning of the regulation. There is an extensive editorial explanation, and citations to the annotations, for each Code provision.

e. Recent Developments Volume. The Recent Developments Volume (volume 16) contains a Cross Reference Table that cross-references from USTR paragraphs to updating material. Use this table to determine if a recent ruling or decision has been issued in any area of interest.

---

[283] Weekly Alert has cross-references to Federal Tax Coordinator and USTR.

USTR reproduces the updating material in the Recent Developments volume (IRS rulings and procedures), the A.F.T.R.2d Decisions Advance Sheets volume (texts of decisions rendered by courts other than the Tax Court), or the Weekly Alert newsletter (digests of Tax Court decisions). The Recent Developments volume provides Public Law number, title or subject, and introduction and signing dates for recent acts. There are also tax calendars and lists of IRS publications.

f.A.F.T.R.2d Decisions Advance Sheets Volumes. Volumes 17 and 17A contain the texts of recent income tax decisions from all courts except the Tax Court.[284] You can locate these items by Code section using the Cross Reference Table in the Recent Developments volume. Decisions appear in the order they were received rather than in Code section order. Decisions printed in this volume will later be issued in hardbound volumes as part of the A.F.T.R. reporter service discussed in Chapter 11.

g. Federal Tax Regulations Volume. Volume 18 prints the Preambles to proposed regulations. Coverage is chronological. A Finding List is in Code section order. Regulations whose numbers do not correspond to a Code section appear before traditionally numbered regulations. This list indicates Federal Register publication date.

h. Citator. The RIA Citator is not part of USTR and does not cross-reference to it. You can use this citator with any looseleaf service to determine the status of both judicial decisions and IRS items. The online version of the RIA Citator is discussed in Chapter 12.

Illustration 13-8. USTR Compilation Topic

```
Checkpoint Contents
  Federal Library
    Federal Editorial Materials
      United States Tax Reporter
        Income (USTR)
          Gain or Loss on Disposition of Property §§1001-1111
            Determination of Amount Of and Recognition of Gain or Loss §§1001-1002
              ☐ Currently in: §1001 Determination of amount of and recognition of gain or loss

📄 🔖 §1001 Determination of amount of and recognition of gain or loss.
 + ☐  Committee Reports for Code Sec. 1001
 + ☐  Regulations for Code Sec. 1001
 + ☐  Explanations for Code Sec. 1001
 + ☐  Advance Annotations for Code Sec. 1001
 + ☐  Annotations for Code Sec. 1001
```

→I reached this page by doing a search for section 1001.

---

[284] Recent decisions involving estate and gift taxes or excise taxes appear in the RIA services covering these topics. Decisions for all taxes appear in the A.F.T.R. hardbound volumes.

Illustration 13-9. USTR Explanation

> **EXP ¶10,014.16 Gain or loss on taxable exchanges.**
>
> The amount realized on an exchange is usually composed of the fair market value of the property received, ¶10,014.17 — ¶10,014.18, but it may also include cash and the value of notes received, as well as liens transferred with the property. ¶10,014.02. The amount realized is reduced by any cash and the face amount of notes given by the taxpayer for the exchange, as well as by liens outstanding against property received from the exchange. The gain or loss on the exchange is the difference between the amount realized and the taxpayer's basis for the property surrendered in the exchange. Rules governing valuation of property are explained at ¶10,114.21 et seq.

→Note the links to annotations, Code, etc., at the top of the online page.

Illustration 13-10. USTR Annotations

> 📄 ANN ¶10,015.13(37) Rescission.
>
> 📄 ANN ¶10,015.13(40) Change in terms of life insurance policy.
>
> 📄 ANN ¶10,015.13(45) Time for reporting gain. ←——
>
> 📄 ANN ¶10,015.13(47) Determination of actual seller.
>
> 📄 ANN ¶10,015.13(50) Proof.
>
> 📄 ANN ¶10,015.13(55) Gain on sale of business.

→If you used the print version, you could see more than one annotation topic on the same page.

Illustration 13-11. Annotation ¶ 10,015.13(45)

> **Ann ¶ 10,015.13(45). Time for reporting gain.**
>
> 1989 deficiency resulting from erroneously claimed capital gains deduction was upheld against taxpayer who reported gain from '86 property sale under installment method: gain was recognized on each installment payment in year of receipt and not in year of sale; and gain was taxable under laws in effect in year of receipt, so claimed Code Sec. 1202 deduction was erroneous because law was no longer effective in 1989.
>
> *Sanford, Chapman v. Com.*, (1995, CA5) 76 AFTR 2d 95-5585.
>
> In computing AMTI, cash method potato farmers had to treat FMV of deferred payment obligation on sales as amount realized in year payment was received: Code Sec. 56(a)(6) prohibits use of installment method of income reporting for AMT purposes. Also, payment obligation's FMV was ascertainable: under 9th Cir. caselaw, taxpayers' contractual obligation didn't have to be evidenced by negotiable debt; and fact that contracts didn't specify purchase price was irrelevant because buyers obligation to pay fixed amount arose when potatoes were delivered and accepted.
>
> *IRS Letter Ruling 9640003 (TAM).*

Illustration 13-12. USTR Advance Annotation

▶ Expl ▶ Annot ▶ IRC ▶ Regs ▶ Com Rpts ▶ Hist Show Permalinks

Ann ¶ 10,015.13(45). Time for reporting gain.

Govt. was granted summary judgment on its complaint to recover erroneous refund issued to cash method taxpayers/tax firm's consulting partner and wife in connection with firm merger/stock transfer transaction: taxpayers' amended return claim to delay recognition of restricted stock that was allocated to husband and placed in escrow upon closing of transaction was rejected where overall facts and circumstances showed that husband constructively received stock in transaction year. Taxpayers' argument that restrictions on stocks' alienability and/or various forfeiture provisions precluded inclusion in gross income for transaction year failed in face of facts that such restrictions were temporary and contingencies that would cause forfeiture were entirely within husband's control; and, lack of alienability didn't affect whether shares were in his control but rather affected only discount applicable thereto, which he was foreclosed from challenging in light of fact that he specifically agreed to same. Also, arguments that husband didn't intend to enter into transaction and/or that he did so under duress were unsupported and belied by fact that he never sought to invalidate transaction.

U.S. v. Nackel, (2009, DC CA) 105 AFTR 2d 2010-474 .

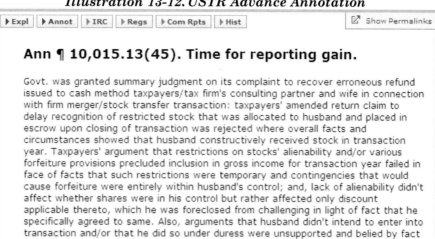

→I clicked the AdvAnnot tab [indicated by an arrow in Illustration 13-11] to reach the most current item for this annotation.

Illustration 13-13. USTR Explanation in Westlaw

P 10,014 Gain or loss determination

P 10,014.16 GAIN OR LOSS ON TAXABLE EXCHANGES.

The amount realized on an exchange is usually composed of the fair market value of the property received, P 10,014.17--P 10,014.18, but it may also include cash and the value of notes received, as well as liens transferred with the property. P 10,014.02. The amount realized is reduced by any cash and the face amount of notes given by the taxpayer for the exchange, as well as by liens outstanding against property received from the exchange. The gain or loss on the exchange is the difference between the amount realized and the taxpayer's basis for the property surrendered in the exchange. Rules governing valuation of property are explained at P 10,114.21 et seq.

→The links at the top of the page in Checkpoint [Illustration 13-9] are at the bottom of the page in Westlaw.

SECTION C. SUBJECT ARRANGEMENT: MULTIPLE TOPICS

This section covers four subject-based services. Many libraries lack at least one of them or carry others not discussed here. Each covers a wide range of topics using a subject matter arrangement. Each is available in print and online versions.

If you use several services, you will get quicker access to relevant items in the second (or later) service by using tables for cases and other primary sources. Once you have obtained these items from one service, you can use them to locate relevant discussion in the other service. If the second service lacks these tables,[285] you can enter it from its topical or Code section index.

1. Federal Tax Coordinator 2d

This weekly service contains excellent discussions of all areas of taxation, with minimal coverage of employment taxes. Federal Tax Coordinator identifies most items by paragraph number. It identifies the text of Code, regulations, and treaties by page number. The Weekly Alert newsletter provides cross-references to both Federal Tax Coordinator and United States Tax Reporter.

Material in each volume is discussed in the following paragraphs. Illustrations are from the online version in Checkpoint; Federal Tax Coordinator 2d is also available on Westlaw. Volume numbers are not important when using the online versions.

a. Topic–Index Volume. This volume contains an extensive Topic Index, which you can use to locate appropriate discussion in the text volumes. There are main and current sections.

b. Finding Tables Volumes. Volume 1 includes several Finding Tables that indicate where items are discussed in the text volumes. These tables cover the Internal Revenue Code, Public Laws since 1991, other United States Code titles, temporary and final regulations, Treasury Decisions for the past six months, Labor regulations, and proposed regulations. There is also a table of Code sections that indicates the relevant volumes and chapters covering them.

Volume 1 also includes a Law–Regulation Table. It provides a list of Code sections for which the regulations do not reflect the most recent Code amendment. This table is in Code section order and includes the relevant acts amending that Code section.

Volume 2 contains a Rulings and Releases Table giving cross-references to discussions in the text volumes or an indication that the ruling has been revoked or otherwise modified. The table arranges each type of IRS document chronologically. Letter rulings are included.

Volume 2 also includes an alphabetical list of cases with cross-references to discussions in the text volumes. This list includes citations to various case reporter services, often including both A.F.T.R. and U.S.T.C. in addition to reporters such as Federal Reporter.

---

[285] For example, Tax Management Portfolios lack case and rulings tables. They have excellent Code and topical indexes.

A Supreme Court Docket and a Court of Appeals Docket indicate where discussion of pending cases appears in the text volumes.

c. Practice Aids Volume. Volume 3 includes sample letters to clients on a wide variety of topics. [See Illustration 15-3.] It also includes planning checklists, tax tables, a tax calendar, interest and annuity tables, and tables showing where tax return forms are discussed in the text. Other reference items, such as applicable federal rates and per diem amounts, appear in the text volumes.

Volume 3 has a Current Legislation Table, which lists acts since 1993 by Public Law number, subject, committee reports, and relevant dates.

d. Text Volumes. The text volumes (4–26, including some additional volumes such as 10A, 12A, 12B, and 14A) are arranged by chapters using a subject matter approach. Discussions in each chapter include liberal use of citations and analysis of as yet unresolved matters.

Each chapter has the following arrangement: a Detailed Reference Table for topics included; cross-references to topics of potential relevance discussed in other chapters; discussion of each topic, including extensive footnote references; and text of Code and regulations sections applicable to the chapters being discussed. Chapters are subdivided into topics, and then into paragraphs.

Treaties are covered in two chapters. Volume 20A contains the texts of United States income, estate, and gift tax treaties and textual material dealing with the treaties. United States and OECD model treaties are also included. Volume 20A prints only treaties currently in effect. Volume 20 discusses the treaties. Volume 20 also includes a list of treaties awaiting ratification or exchange of instruments of ratification.

Illustration 13-14. Federal Tax Coordinator 2d Contents

- ☐ Federal Tax Coordinator 2d
  - ☐ Chapter A Individuals and Self-Employment Tax
  - ☐ Chapter A-7000 Alternative Minimum Tax
  - ☐ Chapter B Partnerships
  - ☐ Chapter C Income Taxation of Trusts, Estates, Beneficiaries and Decedents
  - ☐ Chapter D How Corporations Are Taxed.
  - ☐ Chapter D-2500 Accumulated Earnings Tax; Personal Holding Company Tax
  - ☐ Chapter D-3900 Exempt Organizations, Private Foundations
  - ☐ Chapter E Special Corporations and Organizations: Consolidated Returns

Illustration 13-15. Federal Tax Coordinator 2d Text

¶I-3058. Compensation for services.

If property is received as compensation for services rendered, there is no "reciprocal" transfer (¶ I-3054). Thus, there was no exchange for purposes of the like- kind exchange rules where a tenant (a partnership) arranged to have its mineral lease cancelled and replaced by a different lease from the lessor to a corporation from which the partnership would receive an overriding royalty on coal mined under the lease. The overriding royalty interest was compensation to the partnership for its services in arranging for cancellation of its mineral lease. [35]

---

[35]

Badgett, Bentley v. U.S., (1959, DC KY) 3 AFTR 2d 973 , 175 F Supp 120 , 59-1 USTC ¶9336 .

For deferred like-kind exchanges involving transfers in exchange for services (including production services), see ¶ I-3111 et seq.

→Federal Tax Coordinator uses paragraphs for most cross-references.

→The online version provides hyperlinks to other paragraphs and to the relevant primary source material. Full text is provided for judicial decisions in the online version. The print version does not include the text of decisions.

Illustration 13-16. Federal Tax Coordinator 2d
Online Topic Search

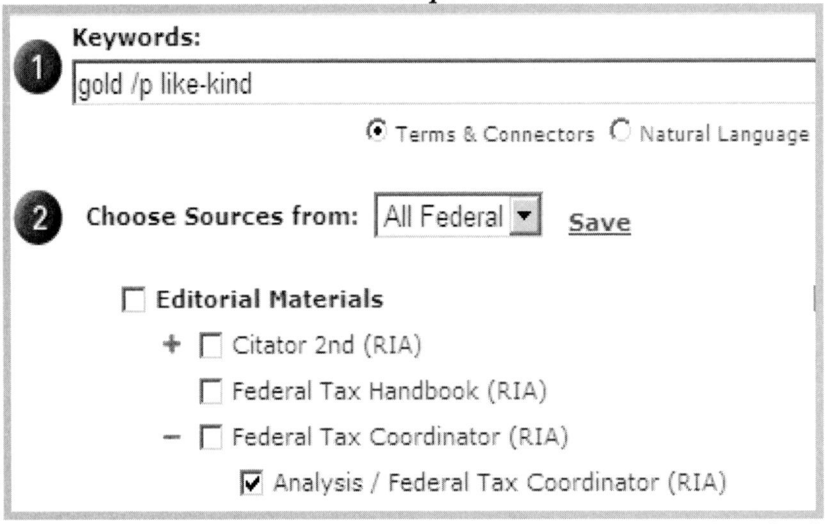

Keywords:

1 gold /p like-kind

⊙ Terms & Connectors ○ Natural Language

2 **Choose Sources from:** All Federal ▾ Save

☐ **Editorial Materials**

+ ☐ Citator 2nd (RIA)

☐ Federal Tax Handbook (RIA)

− ☐ Federal Tax Coordinator (RIA)

☑ Analysis / Federal Tax Coordinator (RIA)

→I can search for topical coverage using terms. This search is for "gold" in the same paragraph as "like-kind."

→I could also conduct a term search in the index.

Illustration 13-17. Results of Topic Search

Source: Analysis / Federal Tax Coordinator (RIA)

☐ 📄 I-3066 How the like-kind test has been applied to exchanges of personal property.
Analysis / Federal Tax Coordinator (RIA)

☐ 📄 I-3070 Duration of interests or rights in real property for purposes of determining whether exchanges of real property are like-kind.
Analysis / Federal Tax Coordinator (RIA)

☐ 📄 I-3076 Safe harbor treating leaseholds of at least 30 years as like-kind to a fee interest in real property.
Analysis / Federal Tax Coordinator (RIA)

☐ 📄 I-3079 Oil, gas, coal, timber, water, and other interests in natural resources—whether the exchange of interests are like-kind.
Analysis / Federal Tax Coordinator (RIA)

→Item I-3076 actually contains a reference to gold.

e. Proposed Regulations. Volumes 27 and 27A contain proposed regulations reproduced in the order in which they were issued, along with Preambles and Federal Register citations. A cross-reference table lists the proposed regulations in Code section order. Proposed regulations issued as temporary regulations are reproduced in the Text Volumes instead of the Proposed Regulations Volumes.

f. Internal Revenue Bulletin. Volume 28 contains reprints of the weekly Internal Revenue Bulletin. Because the material in volume 28 is not indexed by Code section or by subject matter anywhere in this service, it will be difficult to locate a particular item without an Internal Revenue Bulletin citation.

2. Tax Management Portfolios

BNA issues three series of Tax Management Portfolios: U.S. Income; Foreign Income; and Estates, Gifts, and Trusts. Each series is subdivided into several softbound booklets that cover narrow areas of tax law in great depth. [286] Each Portfolio refers to other Portfolios containing information relevant to a particular problem. BNA offers the Portfolios in print and online. An online version is illustrated in this chapter.

In addition to a Table of Contents, each Portfolio includes a Detailed Analysis section (Section A) with extensive footnoting. A Worksheets section (Section B) includes checklists, forms that can be used as models in drafting documents, and texts of relevant congressional and IRS materials. A Bibliography and References section (Section C) includes cita-

---

[286] Subdivisions are so narrow that several portfolios may cover one Code section.

tions to regulations, legislative history, court decisions, and rulings. It also includes lists of books and articles.

BNA supplements the Portfolios with Changes & Analysis sheets, or completely revises them, whenever warranted by new developments.

The looseleaf Portfolio Index includes a Portfolio Classification Guide and a detailed Master Subject Index for each series. A Master Code Section Index covers all series; if there is a primary Portfolio on point, it indicates it as "Main discussion." Numerical IRS Forms and IRS Publications Finding Tables are cross-referenced to appropriate Portfolios.

Illustration 13-18. Topic from Compensation Planning Index

⊟ **ADOPTION**

Adoption assistance programs

—Cafeteria plans, TM 397.IV.G; TM 397.IV.K.6

—Contingent workers, TM 399.III.E.6

—Definition, TM 399.III.E.6

—Eligibility, TM 397.IV.G.4.b; TM 399.III.E.6

—Exclusion from gross income, TM 373.IV.B.9; TM 397.II.J; TM 397.IV.G.2; TM 397.IV.G.4.c; TM 399.III.E.6

—Inflation adjustments re expenses, TM 373.IV.B.9; TM 397.IV.G.2

—Qualifying expenses, TM 397.IV.G.4.a

→The Index above is from BNA's Practice Center; it includes only Portfolios related to compensation and benefits topics.

Illustration 13-19. Discussion in Portfolio 397-3rd

⊟ G. Adoption Assistance
1. General Description
⊞ 2. Tax Treatment in Gener
⊞ 3. Advantage of Inclusion
⊞ 4. Requirements of §137
⊞ H. Section 401(k) Cash or De
I. Post-Retirement Group Life
J. Vacation Days
⊞ K. Qualified Cafeteria Plan Be
V. Benefits Not Available Under a
A. Nonqualified Benefits
B. Consequences of Includin
C. Deferred Compensation
VI. Nondiscrimination Rules for (

Related Code Sections: 137(c)

b. Adoption Assistance Program

An adoption assistance program is a nondiscriminatory plan of an employer under which the employer provides employees with adoption assistance. 644 An adoption assistance program is not required to be funded. 645 In addition, an employer is not required to apply to the IRS for a determination that the plan is a qualified program. The basic requirements for an adoption assistance program are discussed below.

644 §137(c). An adoption reimbursement program operated under 10 USC §1052 (relating to the armed forces) or 14 USC §514 (relating to members of the Coast Guard) is treated as an adoption assistance program for purposes of §137.

645 1996 Blue Book, p. 203; §§137(c)(2) and 127(b)(5).

(1) Separate Written Plan

An adoption assistance program must be a separate written plan of an employer for the exclusive benefit of employees. 646

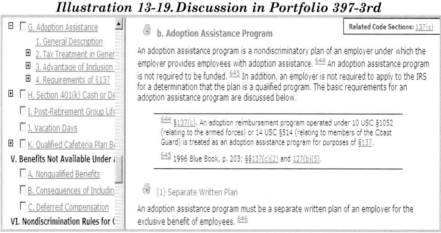

→ Footnotes are at the bottom of the page in the print version.

→I chose to show both the Table of Contents and text, an option when using the Portfolios online.

The Tax Management Memorandum provides analysis of current developments, unsettled problems, and other significant items. It includes cross-references to discussions in the Portfolios

3. Mertens, Law of Federal Income Taxation

The original Mertens service contained five sets of volumes: treatise; rulings; Code; Code commentary; and regulations. Only the treatise and rulings materials have continued in their original format. Many libraries retain the original materials, which may still be useful for historical research. Mertens is available in print and on Westlaw.

a. Treatise. The treatise volumes closely resemble general encyclopedias such as Am. Jur. 2d and C.J.S. in format.[287] Material is presented by subject matter with extensive footnoting. Treatise materials are supplemented monthly; supplements are cumulated semiannually. Supplemental material appears at the beginning of each volume rather than at the beginning of each chapter. Tables and indexes are updated quarterly.

Discussions include extensive historical background information. Because its discussions are so thorough, Mertens is often cited in judicial decisions.[288] Its thoroughness can be a drawback; using the treatise materials for background knowledge can be very time-consuming.

The Tables Volume contains tables indicating where primary source materials are discussed in the treatise volumes. These include the Internal Revenue Code, other United States Code titles, Treasury regulations, other Code of Federal Regulations titles, and IRS materials. IRS materials covered include items printed in the Cumulative Bulletin, letter rulings, and technical advice memoranda. Two other tables provide Cumulative Bulletin citations for revenue rulings and revenue procedures. The Table of Cases Volume has similar cross-references for judicial decisions. These tables are unnecessary in the online version because you can search by citation.

The Index Volume contains a detailed topic index. The monthly Developments & Highlights newsletter in the Current Materials Volume includes lists of recent tax articles.

b. Rulings. The Rulings volumes contain the texts of revenue rulings and procedures. Notices, announcements, and other IRS items are ex-

---

[287] These encyclopedias cover a wide variety of topics. Discussions of taxation appear in separate volumes within each service. A tax-oriented looseleaf service or treatise will probably provide more extensive information.

[288] See, e.g., Speltz v. Commissioner, 124 T.C. 165, 178 (2005).

cluded. Each volume covers a particular time period and includes rulings in numerical order, followed by procedures in numerical order. Mertens adds current items monthly.

The looseleaf current volume has Code–Rulings and Code–Procedures Tables, which provide chronological listings of every revenue ruling or procedure involving income tax Code sections or subsections.[289] There are separate tables for the current year and for prior years (beginning with 1954).

A Rulings Status Table lists the most recent revenue ruling or procedure affecting the validity of a previously published item. Mertens indicates the effect on the earlier item (e.g., modified, revoked). A separate section of this volume includes Cumulative Bulletin citations for revenue rulings and procedures. The Code–Rulings and Rulings Status Tables are not always as current as the rest of the service; citators are likely to provide more accurate information.

c. Code. Each Code volume contained all income tax provisions enacted or amended during a particular time period (one or more years). Textual notations (diamond shapes and brackets) indicate additions and deletions. A historical note indicates Act, section, and effective date and can be used to reconstruct the prior language. The subject matter index in the looseleaf current volume cross-references each topic to applicable Code sections. This material does not cover the 1986 Code.[290]

d. Code Commentary. Looseleaf volumes of Code Commentary initially provided useful short explanations of statutory provisions as well as cross-references to the discussions in the treatise materials. More recent items are limited to references to statutory changes or to recent cases or rulings for the particular Code section.

e. Regulations. Regulations materials have undergone change since the mid-1990s. In a separate service, but using the Mertens name, the publisher currently issues a softbound set of regulations in force (volumes 1 through 6) and proposed regulations (volume 7). Regulations appear in Code section order; there is also a subject matter index. New matter issued during the year is filed in a looseleaf Current Developments and Status Table binder. The service also includes looseleaf volumes containing the Preambles issued since 1995 to proposed, temporary, and final regulations.

---

[289] Although this is an income tax service, these tables do cover estate and gift tax rulings. However, that coverage does not extend back to 1954.

[290] Mertens currently publishes softbound Code volumes, but they are not cross-referenced to the Law of Federal Income Taxation service.

The volumes in the discontinued regulations service included the texts of all income tax regulations issued or amended during a particular time period (two or more years). Publication was in Code section order.

The discontinued volumes have several useful features. Textual notations (diamond shapes and brackets) indicate deletions, additions, and other changes in amended regulations. A historical note, from which you can determine the regulation's prior wording, follows. This facilitates research into early administrative interpretations. Each volume also contains a section reproducing the Preamble to the Treasury Decision or Notice of Proposed Rulemaking announcing each proposed and final regulation.

Illustration 13-20. Discussion in Mertens

◀ Previous Section **MERTENS § 20B:29** Next Section ▶
§ 20B:29. Same taxpayer requirement
Approx. 4 pages

West's Key Number Digest

West's Key Number Digest, Internal Revenue ⟺3184

Although it is not explicitly stated in Section 1031, the same taxpayer that disposed of the relinquished property must acquire the replacement property to satisfy the exchange requirement.[FN1]

Spouses

If the relinquished property is held by a husband and wife as tenants in the entirety or as community property, the replacement property should also be held in the same manner.[FN2] If the relinquished property is held as a spouse's separate property, the replacement property should also be held as his or her separate property. A gift of the replacement property can be made later tax free under Section 1041 after the exchange is "old and cold."[FN3]

Death of Taxpayer

If a taxpayer dies during the exchange period and the exchange is not completed with the acquisition of replacement property by the personal representative or testamentary trust of the taxpayer, the disposition of the relinquished property would be taxable to either the taxpayer on his or her final income tax return, or to the estate or testamentary trust as income with respect to a decedent. If the exchange is completed, then the exchange will be valid and the estate or heirs of the deceased taxpayer will receive a stepped up tax basis in the replacement property.[FN4]

→Mertens includes links to West Key Number Digest references.

4. Rabkin & Johnson, Federal Income, Gift and Estate Taxation

Rabkin & Johnson originally had three segments: treatise; Code and Congressional Reports; and Regulations. Only the treatise materials are currently being updated. Supplementation is monthly, with New Matter pages appearing near the beginning of each volume rather than at the beginning of each chapter. This service is also available on LexisNexis.

a. Treatise. The treatise materials consist of explanatory materials and two volumes of reference material designed to facilitate research in the remainder of the set. It is arranged in chapters; each chapter is divided into sections that use chapter numbers in their prefixes. Cross-referencing is done by section number.

The first two volumes (1 and lA) contain tables and other user aids. Volume 1 includes the following indexes and tables, which cross-reference to discussions in the treatise volumes: topical Index; Table of Statutory References (Internal Revenue Code and other parts of United States Code); Table of Cases; and Table of Regulations, Rulings and Releases (publicly available IRS materials in addition to revenue rulings). The Table of Cases indicates discussion in both text and footnotes.

Volume 1A includes a detailed User's Guide to using Rabkin & Johnson. This volume also contains tax calendars and checklists of deductions (arranged by the tax form involved). Tax forms are listed numerically; IRS publications are listed alphabetically. In addition to rates, the Tax Rates section includes imputed interest rates, annuity valuation tables, depreciation tables, and similar helpful tables. Tax Court and IRS Practice Rules also appear in this volume.

Volumes 2 through 5 contain textual discussion of the law. While discussions are thorough, they do not purport to cover all types of authority. Letter rulings are rarely discussed or cited as authority "[b]ecause they lack precedential value."[291]

b. Code and Congressional Reports. Volumes 6 through 7B contain the text of the Code in Code section order.[292] You can use the Legislative History notes following each Code subsection to determine how amendments changed prior statutory language. These notes indicate the act, section, and date for amendments, but they do not provide a citation to Statutes at Large.

The legislative history notes refer to congressional committee reports explaining each provision. Relevant excerpts from these reports, including full citations, appear at the end of each Code section. These materials cover only the 1954 Code.

Volume 6 contains a topical index to the Code materials. Volume 7B (Appendix) includes tables cross-referencing 1939 and 1954 Code sections. Because these tables were printed in 1963, they miss section number changes that occurred after 1963.

---

[291] 1A Rabkin & Johnson, FEDERAL INCOME, GIFT AND ESTATE TAXATION § G 1.03[6].

[292] This service omits miscellaneous excise taxes other than those involving registration required obligations, public charities, private foundations, qualified pension plans, real estate investment trusts, and the crude oil windfall profit tax.

c. Regulations. Volumes 8 through 12 print 1954 Code regulations. Regulations appear in numerical order and are preceded by T.D. numbers and dates for the original version and amendments.[293] There is no list of regulations in T.D. number order. Regulations sections are cross-referenced to subject matter discussions in the treatise volumes.

Volume 12A printed selected proposed regulations in numerical order. That volume's Table of Contents contains a numerical list of included provisions. Both the Table of Contents and the heading for each proposed regulation indicate the Federal Register date and a cross-reference to treatise discussion. The volumes do not include Preambles.

Illustration 13-21. Discussion in Rabkin & Johnson

CHAPTER 48 Tax-Deferred Like-Kind Exchanges

3B-48 Federal Income, Gift and Estate Taxation § 48.20

§ 48.20 Computation of Gain or Loss

[1] In General

No realized gain or loss is recognized if a taxpayer receives only qualifying like-kind property in exchange for qualifying property.[388] Any gain or loss that is not recognized because of Section 1031 is simply deferred. That gain or loss is preserved in the taxpayer's basis in the replacement property received in the exchange.[389]

[2] Exchanges Not Solely in Kind; Boot

[a] Gain

Since it is unusual for two properties being exchanged to be exactly equal in value, an exchange of real property is likely to also involve a transfer of cash or other nonqualifying (that is, non-like-kind) property to equalize the transaction. This nonqualifying property, whether cash or other property, is referred to as "boot." If a taxpayer receives boot in an exchange in addition to qualifying like-kind property, any realized gain is recognized, but only to the extent of the amount of money and the fair market value of any non-cash boot received. This rule allows taxpayers to enjoy at least a partial deferral of gain under IRC Section 1031.[390] The partial gain attributable to the boot that is recognized in the exchange is added to the taxpayer's basis in the replacement property.[391]

→There are hyperlinks to primary source items in the online version.

Table 13-1. Cross-Referencing in Print Looseleaf Services

Service	Method	Location of Updates
SFTR	¶	New Matters; USTC Adv. Sheets
USTR	¶	Compilations; Recent Dev.; AFTR Adv. Sheets; Weekly Alert
Fed. Tax Coordinator	¶	Inserted in chapter
Tax Mgt Portfolios	Page	Beginning of Portfolio; Weekly Report
Mertens	§	Beginning of volume
Rabkin & Johnson	§	Beginning of volume

---

[293] Federal Register dates are instead given for IRS procedural rules. These materials do not include the text of a regulation's prior versions.

Section D. Subject Arrangement: Limited Scope

Various publishers issue textual materials discussing a limited number of Code sections, such as those covering S corporations.[294] These texts are extremely useful for research involving very complex areas of tax law. In recent years the number of texts covering a particular topic, and the number of topics covered, have both grown explosively. You can locate at least one text on almost any topic, from tax problems of the elderly to estate planning for farmers. While these materials are periodically supplemented, their updating is rarely as frequent as that for the services in sections B and C.

The following materials are a representative sample.

• Bittker & Eustice, Federal Income Taxation of Corporations and Shareholders

• Blankenship, Tax Planning for Retirees

• Fried, Taxation of Securities Transactions

• Hardesty, Electronic Commerce: Taxation & Planning

• McKee, Nelson & Whitmire, Federal Taxation of Partnerships and Partners

• Schneider, Federal Income Taxation of Inventories

Other potential sources include law school casebooks or textbooks, which may include copious notes. CLE providers such as Practising Law Institute regularly publish softbound volumes of course materials. Finally, the multivolume Bittker & Lokken, Federal Taxation of Income, Estates and Gifts, provides thorough treatment of difficult issues.

Section E. Problems

1. Using SFTR, locate the paragraph reference in the compilation volumes assigned by your instructor. Then use the New Matters updating materials to find all updating references to the original item. Provide a citation to each new item that includes its location in SFTR and its "official" location (e.g., I.R.B. for a revenue ruling).

Your instructor may ask you to use the print SFTR, the online version, or both.

2. Repeat problem 1 using USTR and its Recent Developments feature.

---

[294] Form books (Chapter 15) may also include extensive textual material.

3. Indicate the Tax Management Portfolios concerned with the Code section listed below. Your instructor will tell you whether to indicate the Portfolio titles, numbers, or authors.

a. 32

b. 221

c. 1045

d. 2058

4. Indicate who authored or revised

a. Tax Management Portfolio: Earnings and Profits

b. Tax Management Portfolio: Real Estate Leases

c. Mertens chapter: Section 1244 Stock

d. Mertens chapter: Estates and Trusts

5. Indicate if there a Tax Management Portfolio covering

a. Austria

b. Norway

c. Pakistan

d. Vietnam

CHAPTER 14.LEGAL PERIODICALS AND NONGOVERNMENTAL REPORTS

SECTION A. INTRODUCTION

This chapter provides information about periodical literature. It covers methods for locating both citations to articles and the articles themselves. It also discusses determining if a judicial opinion has cited an article or if an article has cited a judicial opinion or other authority.

Although periodical literature is a secondary source, and articles cannot be used as authority for avoiding the substantial understatement penalty, they are still important research tools. Because articles written for practitioner-oriented journals (or posted online before their actual publication in peer-reviewed or student-edited law reviews) may appear more quickly than do treatise supplements, they are valuable tools for learning about new or amended Code sections, regulations, and judicial decisions. In addition, articles may provide citations to primary source materials that you can use as authority.

This chapter also briefly covers reports issued by nongovernmental organizations. These include professional groups and think tanks. Reports issued by these groups (or testimony by their representatives at congressional or Treasury Department hearings) may affect legislation or regulations.

SECTION B. CATEGORIZING PERIODICALS

Commentary on particular tax problems appears in various legal periodicals. These include general focus, student-edited law reviews, publications that focus on a broad variety of tax-related topics, and publications that specialize in a particular area of taxation.

Although general focus, student-edited law reviews occasionally include tax articles, other sources generally carry a larger number of relevant items.[295] These other sources include law school-based law reviews (student-edited or peer-reviewed[296]) that focus on taxation, tax-oriented periodicals published by professional groups or commercial entities, and tax-oriented newsletters. Although not technically periodicals, tax insti-

---

[295] See William J. Turnier, *Tax (and Lots of Other) Scholars Need Not Apply: The Changing Venue for Scholarship*, 50 J. LEGAL EDUC. 189 (2000).

[296] Peer-reviewed publications may have student editors, who edit work that was accepted after review by faculty members or practitioners.

tute proceedings contain useful information and are covered by several periodical indexes.

Table 14-1. Representative Periodical Titles

Category	Title
Student-edited	Akron Tax Journal
Student-edited	Houston Business & Tax Law Journal
Student-edited	Virginia Tax Review
Peer-reviewed	Florida Tax Review
Peer-reviewed	Tax Law Review
Peer-reviewed	The Tax Lawyer
General tax focus	Journal of Taxation
General tax focus	TAXES–The Tax Magazine
Specialized focus	Real Estate Taxation
Newsletter	Tax Notes (Chapter 16)
Institute	Heckerling Institute on Estate Planning
Institute	NYU Institute on Federal Taxation

SECTION C. CITATIONS TO PERIODICALS

Your search for relevant publications may begin in a variety of sources. For example, looseleaf services such as Tax Management Portfolios include lists of articles. Citators may also provide citations to articles. Other publications digest articles. Digests may cover a particular topic or a general range of topics; they generally cover fewer articles than do the other tools.

Although the materials mentioned in the preceding paragraph are useful, periodical indexes are the most comprehensive sources for compiling lists of articles. This section divides indexes into three categories—general legal indexes, specialized indexes, and other indexes.

General legal periodical indexes such as Index to Legal Periodicals and Current Law Index cover all areas of law. Two specialized indexes, Federal Tax Articles and Index to Federal Tax Articles, cover only tax-related materials. The third category of indexes covers areas related to law (such as political science, economics, and history) and nontax specialized legal topics (such as indexes to articles published in other countries).

The tax-oriented and general indexes differ in their indexing methods, publication frequency, and lists of publications covered. All are available in print versions; the general indexes are also available in electronic formats. Law-related indexes are available in a variety of formats.

Section F illustrates searching for articles in several sources discussed in this chapter. Those illustrations cover electronic searches for articles written by Professor Christopher Pietruszkiewicz. I conducted each search on March 6, 2010. I searched in Legal Resource Index (LRI) and Index to Legal Periodicals (ILP) on both Westlaw and LexisNexis and then expanded my Westlaw and LexisNexis searches to their law reviews and journals databases. I also searched in HeinOnline, WilsonWeb, SSRN, bepress, Google Scholar, and the author's own web page. The different results I obtained illustrate the risks involved in compiling a bibliography from a single source.

Publications discussed below are categorized by type, beginning with periodicals indexes.

1. General Legal Periodicals Indexes

a. Current Law Index; Legal Resource Index; LegalTrac

Current Law Index (CLI) indexes articles by subject, author/title, case name, and statute. Its Table of Statutes includes a heading for Internal Revenue Code. Because that section lists articles in Code section order, CLI is the most convenient print-based general index for researching articles by Code section.

CLI covers more publications than does Index to Legal Periodicals. It includes several tax-oriented publications, including Tax Notes. It began publication in 1980, limiting its usefulness to more recent materials. It is published monthly and cumulated quarterly and annually.

An online version, Legal Resource Index (LRI), is available through Westlaw and LexisNexis. The publisher also offers an electronic version, LegalTrac, online through InfoTrac Web. The online versions also cover material indexed since 1980, and they are updated more frequently than the print volumes.

b. Index to Legal Periodicals & Books; WilsonWeb; WilsonDisc

Index to Legal Periodicals[297] includes tax articles in its subject matter listings. It indexes articles by subject/author, case name, and act name. Because it indexes by statute, you cannot search the print version by Code section.

---

[297] ILP began covering books in 1994.

ILP indexes fewer tax-related publications than do the other indexes, and it imposes page minimums for indexed material.[298] Because ILP began publication in 1908, it is more useful than CLI for historical research.[299] ILP is published monthly and cumulated quarterly and annually.

Both Westlaw and LexisNexis carry ILP. Wilson also offers its own online service, WilsonWeb. WilsonDisc is a CD-ROM product. Because Wilson's electronic offerings cover material indexed since mid-1981, they allow rapid searching for current material but not for earlier items. WilsonWeb also offers Index to Legal Periodicals Retrospective: 1908–1981. This tool supplements the online information available on LexisNexis and Westlaw. Although this service begins in 1908, initial coverage dates vary by periodical. For example, coverage of Tax Law Review begins in 1945 (volume 1); coverage of The Tax Lawyer begins in 1967 (volume 21).

The CD-ROM version is cumulated monthly. WilsonWeb is updated daily. The Westlaw and LexisNexis versions are updated at least weekly.

2. Tax-Oriented Periodicals Indexes

a. Federal Tax Articles

This looseleaf reporter contains summaries of articles on federal taxes appearing in legal, accounting, business, and related periodicals. It also covers proceedings and papers delivered at major tax institutes.

Contents appear in Code section order; each item receives a paragraph cross-reference number. The service is published monthly; contents are cumulated at six-month intervals. The articles receive new paragraph numbers when they are cumulated. There is a cross-reference table linking the old and new numbers. There are topic and author indexes.

Federal Tax Articles is cumulated into multiyear volumes at regular intervals. As of December 2009, those volumes covered 1954–67, 1968–72, 1973–78, 1979–84, 1985–89, 1990–96, and 1997–2003. The current looseleaf volume contains the most recent material.

Federal Tax Articles has advantages and disadvantages. It is relatively timely, covers a wide array of publications, and its use of Code sections facilitates searching. However, its use is limited to 1954 and later mate-

---

[298] ILP has steadily reduced its page minimums. The minimum was five pages in volume 38, two pages in volume 39, and one-half page in volume 42.

[299] Renumbering of ILP volumes occurred in 1926. A related series was published between 1888 and 1908.

rials, and coverage in recent volumes does not appear as broad as that of other indexes. Searching through its multivolume format is more time-consuming than searching electronically, but it is not available in an electronic format.

Illustration 14-1. Excerpt from Federal Tax Articles

525 5-2006

¶ 10,183   Imposition of Fraud Penalty (Code Sec. 6663)

2006 Article Summaries

¶ 10,183.02 IRS Clarifies Foreign Bank and Financial Accounts Report Penalty. Lyubomir G Georgiev. 17 Journal of International Taxation 5, May 2006, p. 61.

Refers to a Chief Counsel Advice that explains willful violation in the context of the offshore credit card program and the last chance compliance issues. Notes that counsel's guidance concluded that the IRS could impose a foreign bank and financial accounts report (FBAR) penalty on taxpayers who failed to cooperate. Explains that the FBAR penalty is not a tax or a penalty imposed by Title 31, not Title 26 of the U.S. Code.

→The author index cross-references articles by paragraph number to the Code section listing. The author index does not separately list articles.

b. Index to Federal Tax Articles

This multivolume work covers tax literature contained in legal, specialized tax, accounting, and economics journals, and nonperiodical publications. It includes comprehensive coverage of nontax journals.

Contents appear in topical order. There are separate topical and author indexes but no Code section index. The most recent entry appears first in each listing of articles.

Coverage begins with 1913. Volumes I–III cover through mid-1974. There are cumulation volumes for 1974–81, 1982–83, 1984–87, 1988–92, 1993–96, and 1997–2004. Subsequent material appears in the quarterly cumulative supplement volume. This index is updated less frequently than the other indexes and is available only in a print version.

Because Index to Federal Tax Articles begins coverage with 1913 and covers a wide array of publications, it is an excellent source for locating discussions of early developments in taxation. Although you cannot search by Code section, searching by topic may yield more generalized information. Depending on your familiarity with an area, that can be an advantage or disadvantage. Because it is a multivolume print service, searches take more time than those done with electronic services.

Illustration 14-2. Excerpt from Index to Federal Tax Articles

SUMMER 2006 CUMULATIVE SUPPLEMENT

Prizes and Awards—*Cont'd*
Scholarships and Fellowships—*Cont'd*
Extreme Makeover Home Edition, Brian Hirsch, 73 University of Cincinnati Law Review No. 4, 1665 (2005)

The Interaction of Broad-Based State Scholarship Programs with Federal Education Credits, Craig G. White and James R. Hamill, 109 Tax Notes No. 4, 515 (2005)

3. Other Periodicals Indexes

Representative titles in this category include Business Periodicals Index, Index to Periodical Articles Related to Law, and Social Sciences Index. If your problem involves another country, indexes such as Index to Foreign Legal Periodicals and European Legal Journals Index may be useful. As Table 14-2 illustrates, many nonlaw publications print articles relevant to taxation.

Table 14-2. Examples of Tax-Related Articles in Nonlaw Journals

Andrew D. Cuccia & Gregory A. Carnes, *A Closer Look at the Relation Between Tax Complexity and Tax Equity Perceptions*, 22 J. ECON. PSYCHOL. 113 (2001)
Thomas W. Hanchett, *U.S. Tax Policy and the Shopping Center Boom of the 1950s and 1960s*, 101 AM HIST. REV. 1082 (1996)
John T. Scholz & Neil Pinney, Duty, Fear, and Tax Compliance: *The Heuristic Basis of Citizenship Behavior*, 39 AM. J. POL. SCI. 490 (1995)
Leo Lawrence Murray, *Bureaucracy and Bi-Partisanship in Taxation: The Mellon Plan Revisited*, 52 BUS. HIST. REV. 201 (1978)
James A. Mirrlees, *An Exploration in the Theory of Optimum Income Taxation*, 38 REV. ECON. STUD. 175 (1971)

4. HeinOnline, SSRN, bepress, and Google Scholar

You can use these services to compile lists of publications and gain direct access to their texts. HeinOnline has the largest database of publications. This service is publication-based; its database includes many law reviews in full text back to their inception. HeinOnline is discussed further in Section D, covering full text.[300]

The Legal Scholarship Network is a subdivision of Social Science Research Network (SSRN). Unless an author (or the journal itself) posts an

---

[300] HeinOnline's government databases are covered in earlier chapters.

article or work in progress to SSRN, the work will not be in its database. As its name implies, SSRN is not limited to law. Thus, you can also use it to locate recent law-related literature relevant to tax. In many cases, you can download items posted to SSRN or read them online.

Authors can also post their work to Berkeley Electronic Press (bepress) and many authors use both SSRN and bepress. Bepress also hosts online journals in law and in law-related topics (e.g., economics and political science). Bepress has the same limitation as SSRN; it is dependent on material being posted. As is true for SSRN, it is likely to include works in progress in addition to work that has already been published.

Google Scholar lists articles and indicates if they are available online in other sources (e.g., HeinOnline, bepress).

5. Citators

You can use Shepard's and KeyCite to compile lists of articles discussing such primary sources as statutes and cases.[301] Secondary source materials generally follow the primary source citations to the cited item.

Illustration 14-3. Shepard's Search for Articles Citing a Case

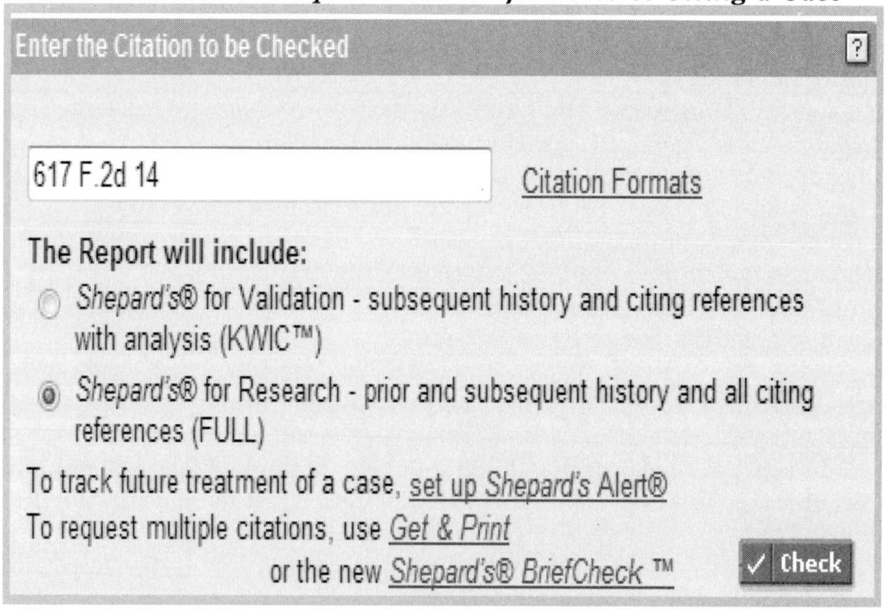

Enter the Citation to be Checked   [?]

617 F.2d 14   Citation Formats

The Report will include:
○ _Shepard's®_ for Validation - subsequent history and citing references with analysis (KWIC™)
◉ _Shepard's®_ for Research - prior and subsequent history and all citing references (FULL)
To track future treatment of a case, _set up Shepard's Alert®_
To request multiple citations, use _Get & Print_
or the new _Shepard's® BriefCheck_ ™   ✓ Check

→I searched on Ogiony v. Commissioner, 617 F.2d 14 (2d Cir. 1980).

---

[301] The CCH and RIA citators discussed in Chapter 12 do not include citations to articles.

Illustration 14-4. Excerpt from List of Articles Retrieved

LAW REVIEWS AND PERIODICALS (11 Citing References)

31. 84 Taxes 7

    84 Taxes 7 p.12

32. NOTE: CONSTITUTIONAL LIMITS ON STATE TAX JURISDICTION., 87 Colum. L. Rev. 1238 (1987)

33. ATTRIBUTING THE ACTIVITIES OF CORPORATE AGENTS UNDER U.S. TAX LAW: A FRESH LOOK FROM AN OLD PERSPECTIVE, 38 Ga. L. Rev. 143 (2003)

    38 Ga. L. Rev. 143 p.143

34. Article: SECTION 10.35(b)(4)(ii) OF CIRCULAR 230 IS INVALID (BUT JUST IN CASE IT IS VALID, PLEASE NOTE THAT YOU CANNOT RELY ON THIS ARTICLE TO PENALTIES), 7 Hous. Bus. & Tax L.J. 293 (2007)

35. ARTICLE: Fog, Fairness, and the Federal Fisc: Tenancy-by-the-Entireties Interests and the Federal Tax Lien, 60 Mo. L. Rev. 839 (1995)

36. NOTE: ONE-MAN PERSONAL SERVICE CORPORATIONS: SINGING A NEW FOGLESONG, 58 Notre Dame L. Rev. 652 (1983)

    58 Notre Dame L. Rev. 652 p.652

37. ARTICLE: Should Courts Require the Internal Revenue Service to be Consistent?, 40 Tax L. Rev. 411 (1985)

    40 Tax L. Rev. 411 p.425

38. ARTICLE: DOES THE INTERNAL REVENUE SERVICE HAVE A DUTY TO TREAT SIMILARLY SITUATED TAXPAYERS SIMILARLY?, 74 U. Cin. L. Rev. 531 (2005)

→Among the articles citing this decision was one (indicated by the arrow) written by Professor Pietruszkiewicz.

6. Looseleaf Services

Two of the looseleaf services discussed in Chapter 13 include lists of articles, but they do so in different ways.

Tax Management Portfolios include Bibliography sections after the textual material. These sections include lists of articles related to the topic of the particular Portfolio.

Mertens, Law of Federal Income Taxation, lists current articles by topic in the Recent Tax Articles section of its monthly Developments & Highlights newsletter. Although Mertens is an income tax service, the lists include articles on estate planning. The monthly lists are not cumulated.

7. Miscellaneous Sources

a. Institutes

The New York University Institute on Federal Taxation has published Consolidated Indexes of its proceedings at irregular intervals. These indexes are arranged by subject, author, title, case name, statute, regulation, and ruling. The second volume of each annual Institute includes current indexes and tables. Institutes other than NYU's include those conducted by the University of Miami (Heckerling Institute on Estate Planning) and the University of Southern California (Major Tax Planning). Other institutes also provide current indexes of their proceedings.

b. Bibliographies

Bibliographies compiled by a librarian or by another researcher may be available in the library's reference section or in law review symposium issues covering a particular area of law.

Tax Policy in the United States: A Selective Bibliography with Annotations (1960–84) was published by the Vanderbilt University Law Library in cooperation with the ABA Section of Taxation. This looseleaf covers articles, books, and government documents dealing with tax policy. Each item is explained briefly. There are author and subject indexes. Unfortunately, it does not cover developments since 1984.

c. Current Index to Legal Periodicals

CILP indexes law review articles on a weekly basis, but it is not cumulated. It is worth consulting because it may cover an article sooner than one or more of the indexes discussed above. Articles are listed both by topic and by law review in each CILP issue.

d. Author Web Pages

When you search for articles by a particular author, don't ignore the Internet. Authors often list publications in a resume or publications section posted on their own or their employer's website.

8. WG & L Tax Journal Digest

Previously published as the Journal of Taxation Digest, this service covers articles published in the Journal of Taxation and several other Warren, Gorham & Lamont publications. Coverage begins with 1977, and the publications covered have varied over time. Digests are arranged by topic. Cross-references are given to relevant articles digested under other topical headings. The digest is published annually.

SECTION D. TEXTS OF PERIODICALS

1. Print

If your library subscribes to publications printing articles you wish to read, you can easily locate them. Many libraries shelve all periodicals together in alphabetical order; a library with an alcove devoted to a particular subject area may shelve specialized periodicals in the alcove. No matter which shelving method it uses, the library is likely to keep a periodical's most current issues on reserve.

2. Online

If your library does not subscribe to a particular publication, or it is in use by another researcher, try locating it online in HeinOnline, LexisNexis, Westlaw, or Index to Periodicals Full Text. These services carry numerous publications in full text. In addition, some periodicals include full-text articles on their own websites.

If you search in LexisNexis or Westlaw, you can find articles on particular topics (e.g., Code sections or cases) by using those topics as search terms. Publications in LexisNexis and Westlaw include hyperlinks to other materials in the online service.

HeinOnline also provides full-text access. You can search it by author, title, or words in text and can use Boolean search terms. It allows direct access by citation, and includes an electronic table of contents for each volume. Each page is reproduced as originally published. As of early December 2009, it includes Akron Tax Journal Florida Tax Review, Pittsburgh Tax Review, Tax Law Review, Tax Lawyer, and Virginia Tax Review in its extensive list of journals.

Index to Legal Periodicals Full Text currently provides full-text articles in numerous publications. Retrospective coverage dates vary by periodical. The collection can be searched by topic, case or statute name.

Illustration 14-5. Excerpt from HeinOnline

Federal Courts As Makers Of Income Tax Law

ROBERT N. MILLER

> The income tax laws . . . ignore some things that either a theorist or a business man would take into account in determining the pecuniary condition of the taxpayer.
>
>   HOLMES, J., in *Weiss v. Wiener*,
>   279 U.S. 333, 335 (1929).

IT is not inadvertence on the part of Congress and its staff of tax experts that accounts for the divergencies between tax laws on the one hand and tax theories or business ideas on the other. Instead, most of these divergencies are solidly founded on the lessons of experience as to what kind of tax laws actually work best in maintaining a massive flow of revenue.

Much of the present confusion in interpreting and applying our income tax laws seems to stem from a failure on the part of some of our influential federal judges to recognize, as Mr. Justice Holmes so clearly did, these facts: that Congress at many points intends the tax law to deviate from theory and from business ideas, and that Congressional decisions

→HeinOnline reproduces actual pages. This page is from Tax Law Review, 1950-1951.

3. Microform

Before initiating HeinOnline, William S. Hein & Co., Inc., published many periodicals in microform. Libraries may purchase microform versions if space is at a premium or the print version is no longer available.

SECTION E. CITATORS FOR ARTICLES

As noted in Section C, you can use citators to find citations to articles discussing various primary source materials. You can also use citators to determine if any court has cited a particular article. To find this information, insert the article's citation in the citator's search box.

Illustration 14-6. Shepard's Search for Decisions Citing an Article

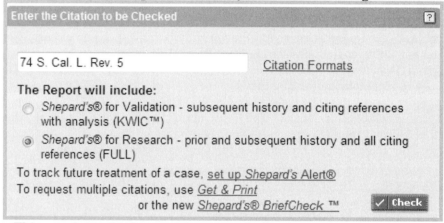

→This search involved an article written by Professor Joseph Bankman.

Illustration 14-7. Results of Search for Decisions

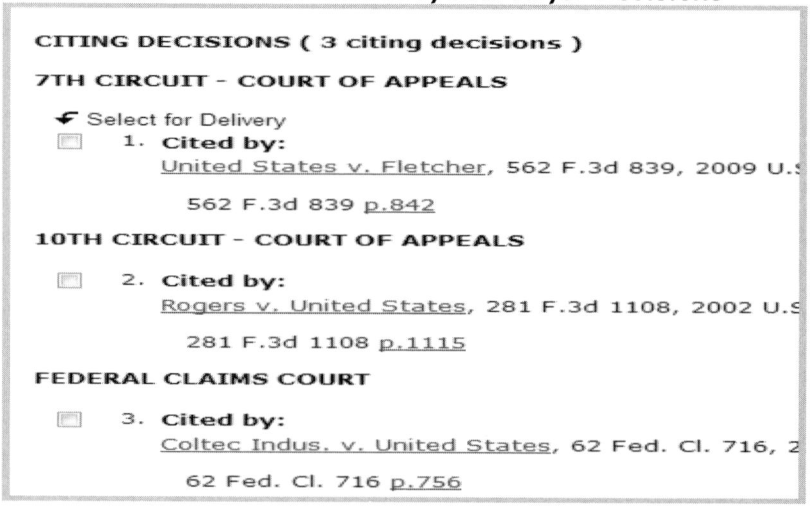

CITING DECISIONS (3 citing decisions)

7TH CIRCUIT - COURT OF APPEALS

✔ Select for Delivery
☐ 1. **Cited by:**
United States v. Fletcher, 562 F.3d 839, 2009 U.S
562 F.3d 839 p.842

10TH CIRCUIT - COURT OF APPEALS

☐ 2. **Cited by:**
Rogers v. United States, 281 F.3d 1108, 2002 U.S
281 F.3d 1108 p.1115

FEDERAL CLAIMS COURT

☐ 3. **Cited by:**
Coltec Indus. v. United States, 62 Fed. Cl. 716, 2
62 Fed. Cl. 716 p.756

SECTION F. ILLUSTRATIONS

I decided to check Professor Pietruszkiewicz's list of articles in as many databases as possible. I began by finding a list of publications in his CV. I then searched in the databases listed below. Because I used the same search in each service, I show the actual search only once per service.

• Westlaw: Index to Legal Periodicals (ILP); Legal Resource Index (LRI); Journals & Laws Reviews (JLR)

• LexisNexis: Index to Legal Periodicals (ILP); Legal Resource Index (LRI); US Law Reviews & Journals, Combined

• HeinOnline

• WilsonWeb

• SSRN

• bepress

• Google Scholar

Illustration 14-8. Articles Listed on Author's Web Page

LAW REVIEW PUBLICATIONS

Economic Substance and the Standard of Review
60 ALABAMA LAW REVIEW 339 (2009)

Conflating Standards of Review in the Tax Court: A Lesson in Ambiguity
44 HOUSTON LAW REVIEW 1337 (2007)

Discarded Deference: Judicial Independence in Informal Agency Guidance
73 TENNESSEE LAW REVIEW 1 (2006)

Does the Internal Revenue Service Have a Duty to Treat Similarly Situated Taxpayers Similarly?
74 UNIVERSITY OF CINCINNATI LAW REVIEW 531 (2005)

Of Summonses, Required Records, and Artificial Entities: Liberating the IRS from Itself
73 MISSISSIPPI LAW JOURNAL 921 (2004)

A Constitutional Cause of Action and the Internal Revenue Code: Can You Shoot (Sue) the Messenger?
54 SYRACUSE LAW REVIEW 1 (2004)

Noncontrolled Section 902 Corporation: Playing Field Leveled by TRA '97
U.S. TAXATION OF INTERNATIONAL OPERATIONS ¶6001 (August 1998)

The Taming of the Noncontrolled Section 902 Corporation Provisions: A Step Toward Subpart F
15 JOURNAL OF TAXATION OF INVESTMENTS 257 (1998)

→This list is included in Professor Pietruszkiewicz's CV. It is available on his web page, at http://faculty.law.lsu.edu/tax/.

Illustration 14-9. Search in ILP on Westlaw

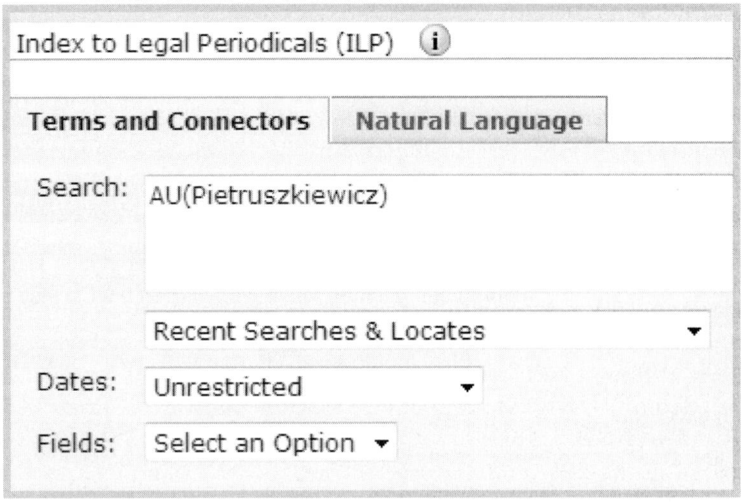

Index to Legal Periodicals (ILP) (i)

Terms and Connectors   **Natural Language**

Search: AU(Pietruszkiewicz)

Recent Searches & Locates   ▼

Dates: Unrestricted   ▼

Fields: Select an Option ▼

Illustration 14-10.Results from ILP on Westlaw

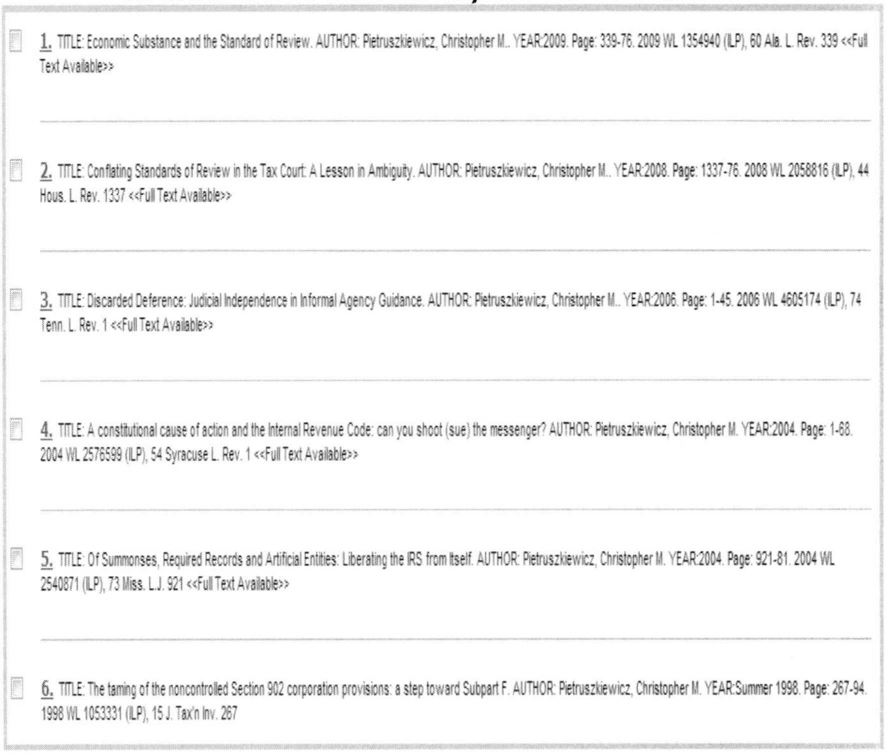

☐ **1.** TITLE: Economic Substance and the Standard of Review. AUTHOR: Pietruszkiewicz, Christopher M.. YEAR:2009. Page: 339-76. 2009 WL 1354940 (ILP), 60 Ala. L. Rev. 339 <<Full Text Available>>

☐ **2.** TITLE: Conflating Standards of Review in the Tax Court: A Lesson in Ambiguity. AUTHOR: Pietruszkiewicz, Christopher M.. YEAR:2008. Page: 1337-76. 2008 WL 2058816 (ILP), 44 Hous. L. Rev. 1337 <<Full Text Available>>

☐ **3.** TITLE: Discarded Deference: Judicial Independence in Informal Agency Guidance. AUTHOR: Pietruszkiewicz, Christopher M.. YEAR:2006. Page: 1-45. 2006 WL 4605174 (ILP), 74 Tenn. L. Rev. 1 <<Full Text Available>>

☐ **4.** TITLE: A constitutional cause of action and the Internal Revenue Code: can you shoot (sue) the messenger? AUTHOR: Pietruszkiewicz, Christopher M. YEAR:2004. Page: 1-68. 2004 WL 2576599 (ILP), 54 Syracuse L. Rev. 1 <<Full Text Available>>

☐ **5.** TITLE: Of Summonses, Required Records and Artificial Entities: Liberating the IRS from Itself. AUTHOR: Pietruszkiewicz, Christopher M. YEAR:2004. Page: 921-81. 2004 WL 2540871 (ILP), 73 Miss. L.J. 921 <<Full Text Available>>

☐ **6.** TITLE: The taming of the noncontrolled Section 902 corporation provisions: a step toward Subpart F. AUTHOR: Pietruszkiewicz, Christopher M. YEAR:Summer 1998. Page: 267-94. 1998 WL 1053331 (ILP), 15 J. Tax'n Inv. 267

→Note that Westlaw does not include full-text for the sixth item.

Illustration 14-11.Results from LRI on Westlaw

1. TITLE: Economic substance and the standard of review. AUTHOR: Pietruszkiewicz, Christopher M. YEAR: Publication Date: Winter 2009. Page: 339-376. 2009 WL 2438168 (LRI), 60 Ala. L. Rev. 339 <<Full Text Available>>

2. TITLE: Conflating standards of review in the tax court: a lesson in ambiguity. AUTHOR: Pietruszkiewicz, Christopher M. YEAR: Publication Date: Winter 2008. Page: 1337-1376. 2008 WL 1765184 (LRI), 44 Hous. L. Rev. 1337 <<Full Text Available>>

3. TITLE: Discarded deference: judicial independence in informal agency guidance. AUTHOR: Pietruszkiewicz, Christopher M. YEAR: Publication Date: Fall 2006. Page: 1-45. 2006 WL 4572107 (LRI), 74 Tenn. L. Rev. 1 <<Full Text Available>>

4. TITLE: Civil and criminal tax penalties.(Annual Report: Important Developments During the Year). AUTHOR: Abrams, Stuart E.; Rettig, Charles P.; Ungerman, Josh O.; Pietruszkiewicz, Christopher M. YEAR: Publication Date: Summer 2004. Page: 1001-1008. 2004 WL 3213711 (LRI), 57 Tax Law. 1001 <<Full Text Available>>

5. TITLE: A constitutional cause of action and the Internal Revenue Code: can you shoot (sue) the messenger? AUTHOR: Pietruszkiewicz, Christopher M. YEAR: Publication Date: February 2004. Page: 1-68. 2004 WL 3267658 (LRI), 54 Syracuse L. Rev. 1 <<Full Text Available>>

6. TITLE: Of summonses, required records and artificial entities: liberating the IRS from itself. AUTHOR: Pietruszkiewicz, Christopher M. YEAR: Publication Date: Winter 2004. Page: 921-981. 2004 WL 3168548 (LRI), 73 Miss. L.J. 921 <<Full Text Available>>

→Professor Pietruszkiewicz did not author the fourth article listed. He served as the editor for an article written by others.

Illustration 14-12. Results from JLR on Westlaw

Results: 6 Documents   Add Search to WestClip

SELECT TO PRINT, EMAIL, ETC.

1. 60 Ala. L. Rev. 339
Alabama Law Review 2009 Article ECONOMIC SUBSTANCE AND THE STANDARD OF REVIEW Christopher M. Pietruszkiewicz

2. 44 Hous. L. Rev. 1337
Houston Law Review Winter 2008 Article CONFLATING STANDARDS OF REVIEW IN THE TAX COURT: A LESSON IN AMBIGUITY Christopher M. Pietruszkiewicz

3. 74 Tenn. L. Rev. 1
Tennessee Law Review Fall, 2006 Articles DISCARDED DEFERENCE: JUDICIAL INDEPENDENCE IN INFORMAL AGENCY GUIDANCE Christopher M. Pietruszkiewicz

4. 74 U. Cin. L. Rev. 531
University of Cincinnati Law Review Winter 2005 Article DOES THE INTERNAL REVENUE SERVICE HAVE A DUTY TO TREAT SIMILARLY SITUATED TAXPAYERS SIMILARLY? Christopher M. Pietruszkiewicz

5. 73 Miss. L.J. 921
Mississippi Law Journal Winter 2004 Article OF SUMMONSES, REQUIRED RECORDS AND ARTIFICIAL ENTITIES: LIBERATING THE IRS FROM ITSELF Christopher M. Pietruszkiewicz

6. 54 Syracuse L. Rev. 1
Syracuse Law Review 2004 Articles A CONSTITUTIONAL CAUSE OF ACTION AND THE INTERNAL REVENUE CODE: CAN YOU SHOOT (SUE) THE MESSENGER? Christopher M. Pietruszkiewicz

Illustration 14-13. Search in ILP on LexisNexis

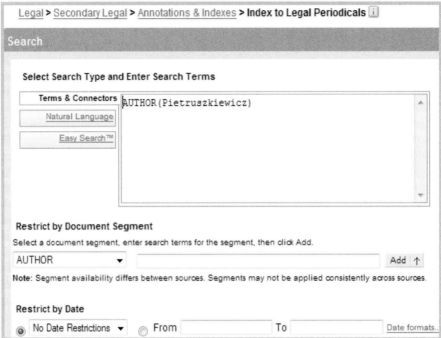

Illustration 14-14. Results from ILP on LexisNexis

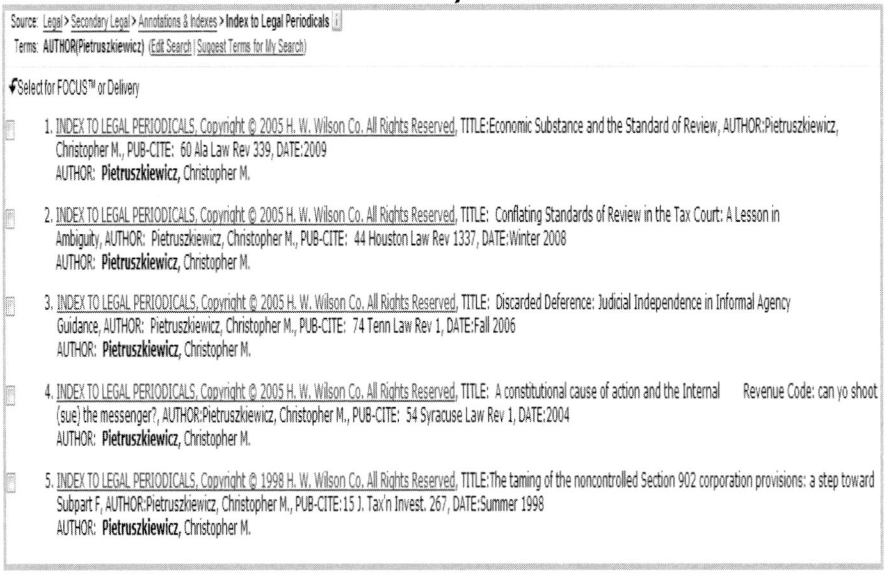

→Different services may yield different results for the same database. Compare these results to those in Illustration 14-10.

Illustration 14-15. Results from LRI on LexisNexis

Source: Legal > Secondary Legal > Annotations & Indexes > **Legal Resource Index**
Terms: AUTHOR(Pietruszkiewicz) (Edit Search | Suggest Terms for My Search)

✔Select for FOCUS™ or Delivery

1. LGLIND/LEGAL RESOURCE INDEX (TM) Copyright (c) 2009 Information Access Co., Pietruszkiewicz, Christopher M., Economic substance and the standard of review., Alabama Law Review, 60, 2, 339-376, University of Alabama, WINTER, 2009, 205303388

2. LGLIND/LEGAL RESOURCE INDEX (TM) Copyright (c) 2008 Information Access Co., Pietruszkiewicz, Christopher M., Conflating standards of review in the tax court: a lesson in ambiguity., Houston Law Review, 44, 5, 1337-1376, Houston Law Review Inc., WINTER, 2008, 177930564

3. LGLIND/LEGAL RESOURCE INDEX (TM) Copyright (c) 2007 Information Access Co., Pietruszkiewicz, Christopher M., Discarded deference: judicial independence in informal agency guidance., Tennessee Law Review, 74, 1, 1-45, Tennessee Law Review Association Inc., FALL, 2006, 164647963

4. LGLIND/LEGAL RESOURCE INDEX (TM) Copyright (c) 2005 Information Access Co., Pietruszkiewicz, Christopher M., Of summonses, required records and artificial entities: liberating the IRS from itself., Mississippi Law Journal, 73, 3, 921-981, University of Mississippi, WINTER, 2004, 128152300

5. LGLIND/LEGAL RESOURCE INDEX (TM) Copyright (c) 2005 Information Access Co., Pietruszkiewicz, Christopher M., A constitutional cause of action and the Internal Revenue Code: can you shoot (sue) the messenger?, Syracuse Law Review, 54, 1, 1-68, Syracuse University, 02/01/2004, 131388946

→Note that this search did not find the edited article found in Illustration 14-11 even though both searches were conducted in the LRI database.

Illustration 14-16. Results from US Law Reviews and Journals, Combined on LexisNexis

Source: Legal > Secondary Legal > Law Reviews & Journals > **US Law Reviews and Journals, Combined**
Terms: AUTHOR(Pietruszkiewicz) (Edit Search | Suggest Terms for My Search)

✔Select for FOCUS™ or Delivery

1. Copyright (c) 2009 University of Alabama Alabama Law Review, 2009, 60 Ala. L. Rev. 339, 17291 words Review, Christopher M. Pietruszkiewicz*

2. Copyright (c) 2005 University of Cincinnati Law Review University of Cincinnati Law Review, Winter, 20 INTERNAL REVENUE SERVICE HAVE A DUTY TO TREAT SIMILARLY SITUATED TAXPAYERS SIMILARLY?, (

3. Copyright (c) 2004 Florida Law Review Florida Law Review, January, 2004, 56 Fla. L. Rev. 1, 64051 wor AND THE PARTIAL PARADIGM SHIFT IN THE IRS RESTRUCTURING AND REFORM ACT OF 1998 , Bryan T.

4. Copyright (c) 2003 Georgia Law Review Association Georgia Law Review, Winter, 2003, 37 Ga. L. Rev. (INTERNAL REVENUE CODE , Donald B. Tobin *

5. Copyright (c) 2008 Houston Law Review Houston Law Review, Winter, 2008, 44 Hous. L. Rev. 1337, 16 TAX COURT: A LESSON IN AMBIGUITY, Christopher M. Pietruszkiewicz*

6. Copyright (c) 2009 University of Miami Law Review University of Miami Law Review, July, 2009, 63 U. M How Derivatives Changed the "Business of Banking", Saule T. Omarova+

7. Copyright (c) 2006 Minnesota Law Review Minnesota Law Review, June, 2006, 90 Minn. L. Rev. 1664, 2 Contracts, George S. Geis +

→In addition to articles by Professor Pietruszkiewicz, this search yielded eight articles authored by others, who acknowledged Professor Pietruszkiewicz's comments.

Illustration 14-17. Search in HeinOnline

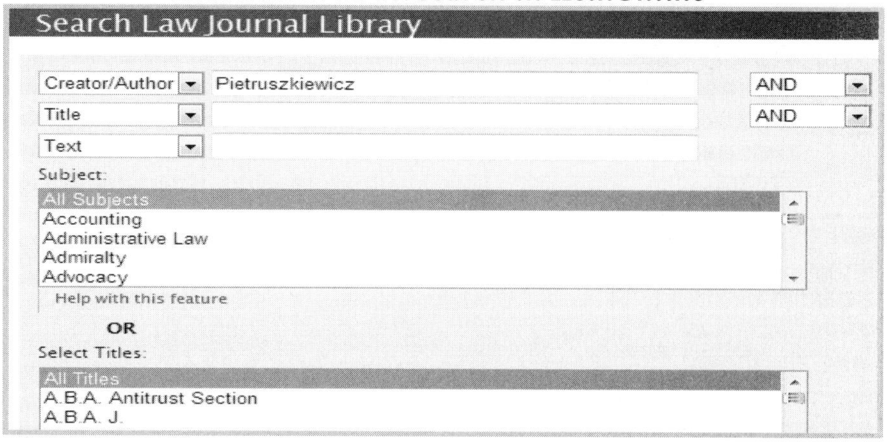

Illustration 14-18. Results from HeinOnline

→Click on any of the articles to read a full-text PDF version. You can also read the articles that cite any of these articles.

→HeinOnline also includes Professor Pietruszkiewicz's article in the Tennessee Law Review. It did not appear in the search results because his name is spelled incorrectly in the database.

Illustration 14-19. Search in WilsonWeb

| story | Print Email Save | Exporting / Citing | Journal Directory | My WilsonWeb |

⊟ **Close Database Selection Area**

☐ Database Description ☐ Mark All Databases ☐ Unmark Selected Databases ☐ Journal Directory

☐ Applied Science & Tech Retro	☐ Education Full Text	☐ Library Lit & Inf Full Text
☐ Applied Science Full Text	☐ Education Index Retro	☐ Library Lit & Inf Science Retro
☐ Art Full Text	☐ ERIC	☐ OmniFile Full Text Mega
☐ Art Museum Image Gallery	☐ Essay & General Lit	☐ Play Index
☐ Biological & Agr Index Plus	☐ General Science Full Text	☐ Readers' Guide Full Text
☐ Book Review Digest Plus	☐ Humanities & Social Sci Retro	☐ Readers' Guide Retro
☐ Book Review Digest Retro	☐ Humanities Full Text	☐ Short Story Index
☐ Business Full Text	☑ Legal Periodicals Full Text	☐ Social Sciences Full Text
☐ Business Periodicals Retro	☐ Legal Periodicals Retro	

Basic Search | Advanced Search

FIND	Pietruszkiewicz	**As:** Author, Personal ▾
and ▾		Keyword ▾
and ▾		Keyword ▾

Sort By: Relevance ▾

Clear   Start

→WilsonWeb is not limited to ILP or even to legal databases.

Illustration 14-20. Results from WilsonWeb

Pietruszkiewicz, C. M. Economic Substance and the Standard of Review. *Alabama Law Review* v. 60 no. 2 (2009) p. 339-76

▤ Full Text HTML ◀) ⬛ Full Text PDF ▤ Library Owns? ▦ Save to My WilsonWeb

Pietruszkiewicz, C. M. Conflating Standards of Review in the Tax Court: A Lesson in Ambiguity. *Houston Law Review* v. 44 no. 5 (Winter 2008) p. 1337-76

▤ Library Owns? FIND IT! Find It! ▦ Save to My WilsonWeb

Pietruszkiewicz, C. M. Discarded Deference: Judicial Independence in Informal Agency Guidance. *Tennessee Law Review* v. 74 no. 1 (Fall 2006) p. 1-45

▤ Full Text HTML ◀) ⬛ Full Text PDF ▤ Library Owns? ▦ Save to My WilsonWeb

Pietruszkiewicz, C. M. Does the Internal Revenue Service Have a Duty to Treat Similarly Situated Taxpayers Similarly?. *University of Cincinnati Law Review* v. 74 no. 2 (Winter 2005) p. 531-76

▤ Library Owns? FIND IT! Find It! ▦ Save to My WilsonWeb

Pietruszkiewicz, C. M. Of Summonses, Required Records and Artificial Entities: Liberating the IRS from Itself. *Mississippi Law Journal* v. 73 no. 3 (Winter 2004) p. 921-81

▤ Library Owns? FIND IT! Find It! ▦ Save to My WilsonWeb

Pietruszkiewicz, C. M. A constitutional cause of action and the Internal Revenue Code: can you shoot (sue) the messenger?. *Syracuse Law Review* v. 54 no. 1 (2004) p. 1-68

▤ Library Owns? FIND IT! Find It! ▦ Save to My WilsonWeb

Pietruszkiewicz, C. M. The taming of the noncontrolled Section 902 corporation provisions: a step toward Subpart F. *Journal of Taxation of Investments* v. 15 no. 4 (Summer 1998) p. 267-94

▤ Library Owns? FIND IT! Find It! ▦ Save to My WilsonWeb

→Note the articles for which HTML or PDF text is available. The service includes a Find It feature for other articles.

Illustration 14-21. Search in SSRN

SSRN eLibrary Database Search

Search Term(s):

Options: ⦿ Title Only   ○ Title, Abstract & Keywords | All Dates ▾ |

Author(s): | Christopher | | Pietruszkiewicz |

[Search]

Illustration 14-22. Results from SSRN

1. ☐ **Conflating Standards of Review in the Tax Court: A Lesson in Ambiguity**
   Houston Law Review, Vol. 44, No. 1337, 2008
   Christopher M. Pietruszkiewicz
   Louisiana State University, Baton Rouge - Paul M. Hebert Law Center
   Date Posted: April 5, 2007
   Last Revised: April 18, 2008
   Accepted Paper Series
   65 downloads

2. ☐ **Does the Internal Revenue Service have a Duty to Treat Similarly Situated Taxpayers Similarly?**
   University of Cincinnati Law Review, Vol. 74, p. 531, 2005
   Christopher M. Pietruszkiewicz
   Louisiana State University, Baton Rouge - Paul M. Hebert Law Center
   Date Posted: May 25, 2006
   Last Revised: September 11, 2006
   Accepted Paper Series
   65 downloads

3. ☐ **Discarded Deference: Judicial Independence in Informal Agency Guidance**
   Tennessee Law Review, Vol. 74, p.1, 2006
   Christopher M. Pietruszkiewicz
   Louisiana State University, Baton Rouge - Paul M. Hebert Law Center
   Date Posted: April 5, 2007
   Last Revised: April 21, 2008
   Accepted Paper Series
   58 downloads

4. ☐ **A Constitutional Cause of Action and the Internal Revenue Code: Can You Shoot (Sue) the Messenger?**
   Syracuse Law Review, Vol. 54, No. 1, 2004
   Christopher M. Pietruszkiewicz
   Louisiana State University, Baton Rouge - Paul M. Hebert Law Center
   Date Posted: June 14, 2004
   Last Revised: December 22, 2004
   Accepted Paper Series
   35 downloads

5. ☐ **Of Summonses, Required Record and Artificial Entities: Liberating the IRS from Itself**
   Mississippi Law Journal, Vol. 73, pp. 921-981, 2004
   Christopher M. Pietruszkiewicz
   Louisiana State University, Baton Rouge - Paul M. Hebert Law Center
   Date Posted: October 20, 2004
   Last Revised: October 20, 2004
   Accepted Paper Series
   28 downloads

6. ☐ **Economic Substance and the Standard of Review**
   Alabama Law Review, Vol. 60, p. 339, 2009

→SSRN shows the number of downloads and when the item was posted or revised. SSRN listed all six law review articles.

Illustration 14-23. Search in bepress

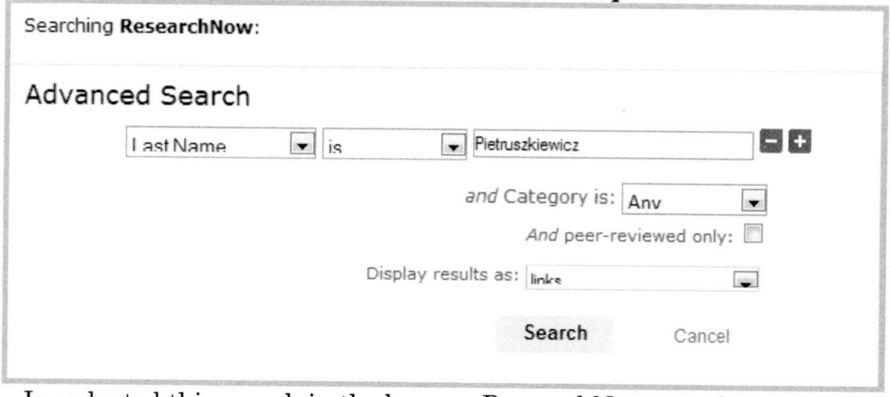

> Searching **ResearchNow**:
>
> ## Advanced Search
>
> | Last Name ▾ | is ▾ | Pietruszkiewicz | ▬ ✚ |
>
> *and* Category is: Anv ▾
>
> *And* peer-reviewed only: ☐
>
> Display results as: links ▾
>
> **Search**   Cancel

→I conducted this search in the bepress ResearchNow portal

Illustration 14-24. Results from bepress

> Sort by: **Year** ▾   Publication   Author   Title   Institution
>
> **Economic Substance and the Standard of Review**
> Author: Christopher M. Pietruszkiewicz
> Publication: The SelectedWorks of Christopher M. Pietruszkiewicz
> Date: 2008
> Instutution:
>
> **Economic Substance and the Standard of Review**
> Author: Christopher M. Pietruszkiewicz
> Publication: The SelectedWorks of Christopher M. Pietruszkiewicz
> Date: 2008
> Instutution:
>
> **REINTERPRETING THE ROLE OF SPECIAL TRIAL JUDGES THROUGH STANDARDS OF REVIEW**
> Author: Christopher M. Pietruszkiewicz
> Publication: The SelectedWorks of Christopher M. Pietruszkiewicz
> Date: 2007
> Instutution:
>
> **Discarded Deference: Judicial Independence in Informal Agency Guidance**
> Author: Christopher M. Pietruszkiewicz
> Publication: ExpressO
> Date: 2006
> Instutution:
>
> **Discarded Deference: Judicial Independence in Informal Agency Guidance**
> Author: Christopher M. Pietruszkiewicz
> Publication: ExpressO
> Date: 2006
> Instutution:

Illustration 14-25. Search in Google Scholar

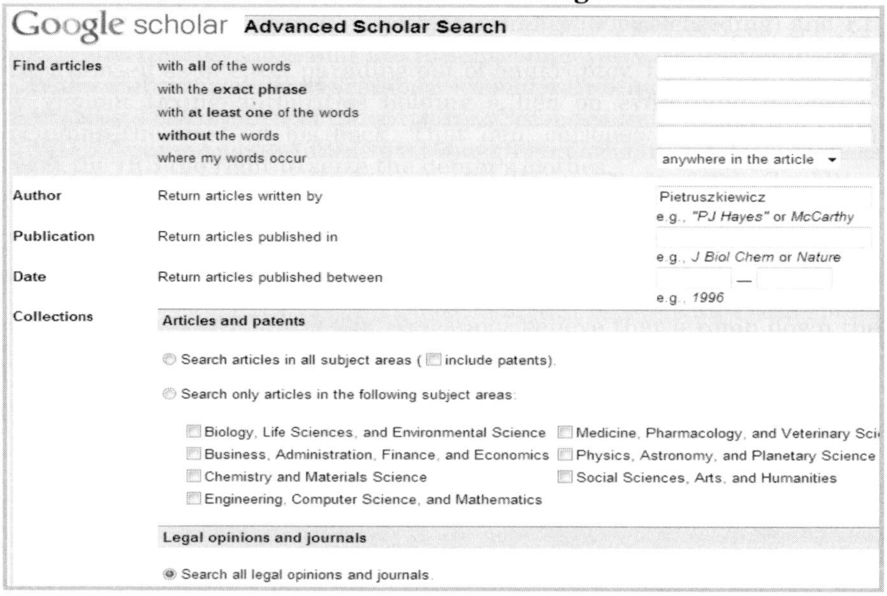

Google scholar **Advanced Scholar Search**

Find articles	with **all** of the words	
	with the **exact phrase**	
	with **at least one** of the words	
	without the words	
	where my words occur	anywhere in the article
Author	Return articles written by	Pietruszkiewicz e.g., *"PJ Hayes"* or *McCarthy*
Publication	Return articles published in	e.g., *J Biol Chem* or *Nature*
Date	Return articles published between	— e.g., *1996*
Collections	**Articles and patents**	

Search articles in all subject areas (include patents).

Search only articles in the following subject areas:

- Biology, Life Sciences, and Environmental Science
- Business, Administration, Finance, and Economics
- Chemistry and Materials Science
- Engineering, Computer Science, and Mathematics
- Medicine, Pharmacology, and Veterinary Sci
- Physics, Astronomy, and Planetary Science
- Social Sciences, Arts, and Humanities

Legal opinions and journals

Search all legal opinions and journals.

Illustration 14-26. Results from Google Scholar

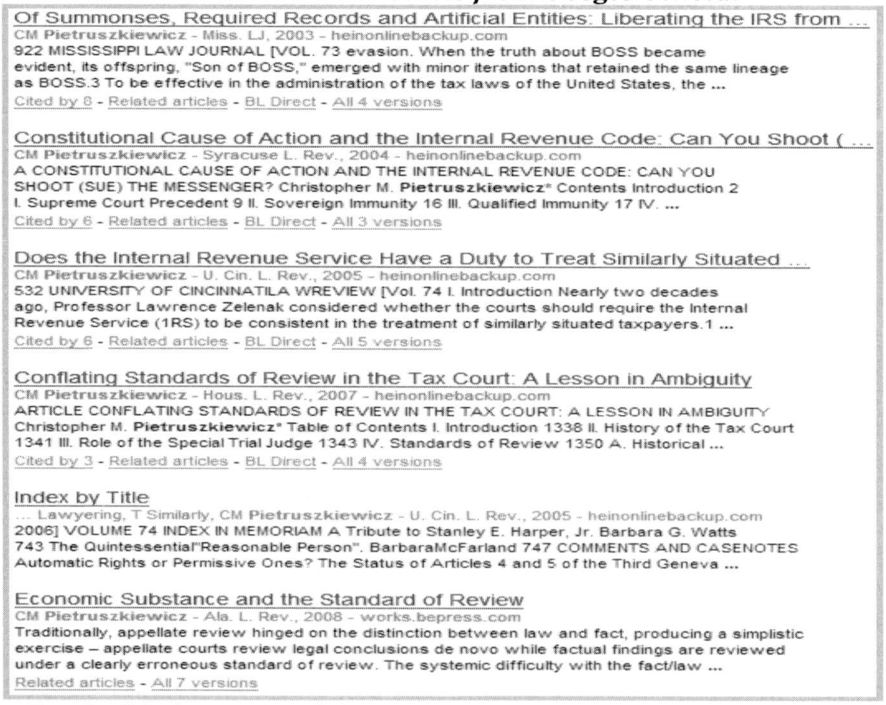

Of Summonses, Required Records and Artificial Entities: Liberating the IRS from ...
CM **Pietruszkiewicz** - Miss. LJ, 2003 - heinonlinebackup.com
922 MISSISSIPPI LAW JOURNAL [VOL. 73 evasion. When the truth about BOSS became evident, its offspring, "Son of BOSS," emerged with minor iterations that retained the same lineage as BOSS.3 To be effective in the administration of the tax laws of the United States, the ...
Cited by 8 - Related articles - BL Direct - All 4 versions

Constitutional Cause of Action and the Internal Revenue Code: Can You Shoot (...
CM **Pietruszkiewicz** - Syracuse L. Rev., 2004 - heinonlinebackup.com
A CONSTITUTIONAL CAUSE OF ACTION AND THE INTERNAL REVENUE CODE: CAN YOU SHOOT (SUE) THE MESSENGER? Christopher M. **Pietruszkiewicz*** Contents Introduction 2 I. Supreme Court Precedent 9 II. Sovereign Immunity 16 III. Qualified Immunity 17 IV. ...
Cited by 6 - Related articles - BL Direct - All 3 versions

Does the Internal Revenue Service Have a Duty to Treat Similarly Situated ...
CM **Pietruszkiewicz** - U. Cin. L. Rev., 2005 - heinonlinebackup.com
532 UNIVERSITY OF CINCINNATILA WREVIEW [Vol. 74 I. Introduction Nearly two decades ago, Professor Lawrence Zelenak considered whether the courts should require the Internal Revenue Service (1RS) to be consistent in the treatment of similarly situated taxpayers.1 ...
Cited by 6 - Related articles - BL Direct - All 5 versions

Conflating Standards of Review in the Tax Court: A Lesson in Ambiguity
CM **Pietruszkiewicz** - Hous. L. Rev., 2007 - heinonlinebackup.com
ARTICLE CONFLATING STANDARDS OF REVIEW IN THE TAX COURT: A LESSON IN AMBIGUITY Christopher M. **Pietruszkiewicz*** Table of Contents I. Introduction 1338 II. History of the Tax Court 1341 III. Role of the Special Trial Judge 1343 IV. Standards of Review 1350 A. Historical ...
Cited by 3 - Related articles - BL Direct - All 4 versions

Index by Title
... Lawyering, T Similarly, CM **Pietruszkiewicz** - U. Cin. L. Rev., 2005 - heinonlinebackup.com
2006] VOLUME 74 INDEX IN MEMORIAM A Tribute to Stanley E. Harper, Jr. Barbara G. Watts 743 The Quintessential"Reasonable Person". BarbaraMcFarland 747 COMMENTS AND CASENOTES Automatic Rights or Permissive Ones? The Status of Articles 4 and 5 of the Third Geneva ...

Economic Substance and the Standard of Review
CM **Pietruszkiewicz** - Ala. L. Rev., 2008 - works.bepress.com
Traditionally, appellate review hinged on the distinction between law and fact, producing a simplistic exercise – appellate courts review legal conclusions de novo while factual findings are reviewed under a clearly erroneous standard of review. The systemic difficulty with the fact/law ...
Related articles - All 7 versions

→Google Scholar retrieved both the article and table of contents from Cincinnati, which is why that journal is listed twice.

SECTION G. NONGOVERNMENTAL REPORTS

Many groups appear before Congress and the Treasury Department to testify at hearings that may lead to legislation or regulations.[302] These groups may also submit reports to individual legislators and executive branch officials, post them on their websites, or publish them in law reviews and newsletters.

As is true for periodical articles, these reports often include numerous citations to authority to support their policy analysis.

Table 14-3. Examples of Nongovernmental Groups

Group	Website
ABA Section of Taxation	www.abanet.org/tax
AICPA	www.aicpa.org
American Law Institute	www.ali.org
Cato Institute	www.cato.org
Citizens for Tax Justice	www.ctj.org
The Heritage Foundation	www.heritage.org
National Bureau of Economic Research	www.nber.org
National Taxpayers Union	www.ntu.org/main
Tax Policy Center	www.taxpolicycenter.org
Urban Institute	www.urban.org

SECTION H. PROBLEMS

Your instructor may assign one or more of the sources listed in this chapter for answering the questions below. If you have carte blanche to decide among sources, try using several sources so that you can compare their relative value. Unless you receive contrary instructions, your search can include articles in professional journals, newsletters, and institutes in addition to articles in law reviews.

1. Locate the text of the article below online or in its print version. What are the first five words of the article?

a. John J. Potts, *Did Your Law Professor Tell You Basis Means Cost? The Recognition Theory of Basis*, 22 VAL. U. L. REV. 233 (1988).

b. Shari Motro, *A New "I Do": Towards a Marriage Neutral Income Tax*, 91 IOWA L. REV. 1509 (2006).

c. Samuel A. Donaldson, *The Easy Case Against Tax Simplification*, 22 VA. TAX REV. 645 (2003).

---

[302] The TaxProf Blog (Chapter 19) includes an extensive list of organizations and provides hyperlinks to their sites.

d. David Elkins & Christopher H. Hanna, *Taxation of Supernormal Returns*, 62 TAX LAW. 93 (2008).

2. The articles listed below all appear in at least one online articles index. Add the author name and the law review information to complete the citation.

a. Making a List and Checking It Twice: Must Tax Attorneys Divulge Who's Naughty and Nice?

b. The Taming of the Shrewd: Identifying and Controlling Income Tax Avoidance

c. The Federal Income Tax Consequences of the Bobble Supreme Phenomenon

d. Sticks and Snakes: Derivatives and Curtailing Aggressive Tax Planning

3. The individual listed below will be speaking at your institution. Using whichever of the sources your instructor assigns from those illustrated in this chapter, compile a list of the last five articles he or she has published. Use the year of publication in determining which articles are the last five published.

a. Ellen Aprill

b. Adam Chodorow

c. Douglas A. Kahn

d. Francine Lipman

4. The articles below were published between 1940 and 1979. Add the author name and the law review information to complete the citation.

a. Cold War Taxation Policy

b. Limitations on the Use of Anti-Recessionary Tax Policy

c. Carrying Losses to a Different Taxpayer

d. Taxation of Unrealized Gains at Death—An Evaluation of the Current Proposals

5. The articles below were published before 1940. Add the law review information to complete the citation.

a. Arthur A. Ballantine, Corporate Personality in Income Taxation

b. Robert E. Cushman, Social and Economic Control Through Federal Taxation

c. Thomas C. Lavery, Some Phases of the Deduction for Depreciation under Long-Term Leases

d. John B. Martin, Jr., Taxation of Undistributed Corporate Profits

6. Provide a full citation to an article that includes the Code section listed below in its title. Unless your instructor tells you otherwise, find the most recent article you can.

a. 83

b. 355

c. 6015

d. 7872

7. Provide a full citation to an article involving federal taxation that includes the term listed below in its title. Unless your instructor tells you otherwise, find the most recent article you can.

a. tax gap

b. executive compensation

c. death tax

d. carbon tax

CHAPTER 15.FORM BOOKS, CHECKLISTS, AND IRS MODEL LANGUAGE

SECTION A. INTRODUCTION

The drafter's choice of language may determine the tax consequences of a contract, lawsuit settlement, or other legal matter. To avoid adverse consequences, you might consider adapting a form book's model language to your client's situation. The author's comments explain why particular language avoids tax problems. You can also use checklists to guide you in drafting your own form. The IRS occasionally provides model language in revenue procedures and other documents and even in tax return forms. The IRS language may not be mandatory, but it does provide a safe harbor. Illustrations in this chapter cover both commercially available and IRS materials.

SECTION B. FINDING FORMS AND OTHER DOCUMENTS

You can find drafting language relatively easily using a form book. Relevant forms or checklists will be listed by topic or Code section or will appear along with the topical discussion. You can also use the publication's table of contents or relevant tables of authority to locate forms. The method of publication, print or electronic, should not matter.

If you are interested in IRS model language, you can locate the relevant document through an electronic search. Use such search terms as "model language," "prototype language," or "sample language." Using only "form" as a search term is risky; it might produce a significant number of references to tax return forms.

1. Form Books Available

The following list illustrates the range of available materials. Forms are most useful if the author includes citations to authority as footnotes to the form or in a separate analysis section.

• Becker, Gibberman & Becker, Legal Checklists

• Cavitch, Tax Planning for Corporations and Shareholders – Forms

• Foster & Long, Tax-Free Exchanges Under Sec. 1031

• Mancoff & Steinberg, Qualified Deferred Compensation Plans – Forms

• McGaffey, Legal Forms with Tax Analysis

• Murphy's Will Clauses: Annotations and Forms with Tax Effects

• Rabkin & Johnson, Current Legal Forms with Tax Analysis

• Regan, Gilfix, Morgan & English, Tax, Estate & Financial Planning for the Elderly: Forms and Practice

• Rohan, Real Estate Financing – Text, Forms, Tax Analysis

In addition to using form books, you can find model language in loose-leaf services, articles,[303] and tax institute proceedings. For example, several Tax Management Portfolios include model language in their Worksheets section, and Checkpoint includes client letters with cross-references to explanatory material in Federal Tax Coordinator 2d.[304]

Internal Revenue Service documents that include model language appear in the Internal Revenue Bulletin, which is available in print, online through commercial services, and online through the IRS website. You do not need the actual citation to find these documents electronically.

In addition to model language that appears in the I.R.B., the IRS website also includes a section for tax forms and publications. Although many tax return forms simply provide information related to tax liability, others include the sort of language you might find in a form book. If you are researching a topic in a treatise or looseleaf service, you will probably encounter references to relevant IRS forms.

2. Publication Format

Although form books are available in print, materials published in electronic formats have an added advantage. Users can download forms and customize them for their clients' needs. In some instances, a CD/DVD may accompany a print form book. Many of the books listed above are available in multiple formats.

Westlaw and LexisNexis include form books in their databases (e.g., West's Legal Forms on Westlaw; LEXIS Clause Library – Estates, Gifts and Trusts on LexisNexis). The Tax Management Portfolios and Federal Tax Coordinator 2d are available in print and electronic formats.

As noted above, you can locate IRS forms and model language on the IRS website. Many of the PDF forms have fields that allow you to complete them electronically.

---

[303] See, e.g., James F. Gulecas, *Old Trusts—New Tricks (With Forms)*, PRAC. TAX LAW., Winter 2002, at 27.

[304] The Portfolios are described in detail in Chapter 13.

Illustration 15-1. Contents Section from Rabkin & Johnson, Current Legal Forms with Tax Analysis

Rabkin & Johnson - Current Legal Forms with Tax Analysis

Terms and Connectors Natural Language

Search: Full-text of source documents

Table of Contents (TOC) only

Search

Search Selected Only

Clear All Selections | Hide Book Headers

Illustration 15-2.Sample Form from BNA Portfolio 351-5th

Worksheet 12 Sample Deferral Opt-Out Form

[Plan Name]

DEFERRAL OPT-OUT FORM

Unless you opt out of participating, contributions in the amount of [rate]% of your base pay will begin being taken out of your paycheck on a pre-tax basis and contributed to the Plan effective as of the date shown below. If you wish to have a different percentage of your base pay contributed to the Plan, or if you do not wish to have any contributions made on your behalf to the Plan, you must complete this form. Please call [number] or log on to www.websiteaddress to direct how your contributions under the Plan will be invested. If you make no election, your contributions will be invested in the default funds as shown in the investment materials in this package. You may change your investment election at any time, in accordance with the procedures in this package.

In order for this deferral cancellation/change to be effective, this form must be received by Human Resources before 4:00 p.m. Central time on the date shown below.

Participation Date: [Date]

→In addition to being part of the U.S. Income Portfolio series, Portfolio 351-5th (Plan Qualification—Pension and Profit-Sharing Plans) is also available to subscribers to BNA's Benefits Practice Center.

Illustration 15-3. Excerpt from RIA Client Letters on Checkpoint

RIA

1121 Office at home for telecommuting employees
Client Letters (RIA)

Show Permalinks

¶1121 Office at home for telecommuting employees

Document Assembly

To the practitioner: When a taxpayer may deduct expenses of an office at home is discussed in RIA's Complete Analysis of the American Jobs Creation Act of 2004 ¶ 123 et seq.; United States Tax Reporter ¶ 280A4 . The convenience of the employer rule for employees is discussed at Federal Tax Coordinator ¶ L-1348 ; United States Tax Reporter ¶ 280A4.018 . For a sample client letter dealing with the treatment of the home offices of non-telecommuting employees, see ¶2351 . For a sample client letter dealing with the treatment of computers used at home, see ¶2435 . For a sample client letter dealing with the exclusion of gain on the sale or exchange of a principal residence, see ¶1340

Dear Client:

If you're an employee who "telecommutes"—that is, you work at home, and communicate with your employer mainly by telephone, e-mail, fax, electronic data transfer, express mail services, etc.—you should know about the strict rules that govern whether you can deduct your home office expenses.

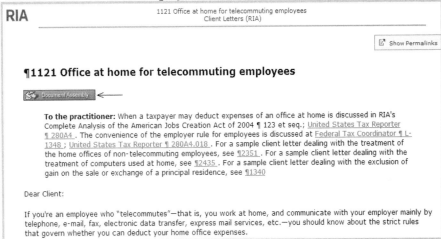

→The language above is the beginning of a sample client letter discussing tax consequences.

→Cross-references to topical discussions appear before the letter. The discussion materials include cross-references to the sample letters.

→After clicking on the Document Assembly box, users can add the client's name and address.

Illustration 15-4. Search for Model Language on IRS Website

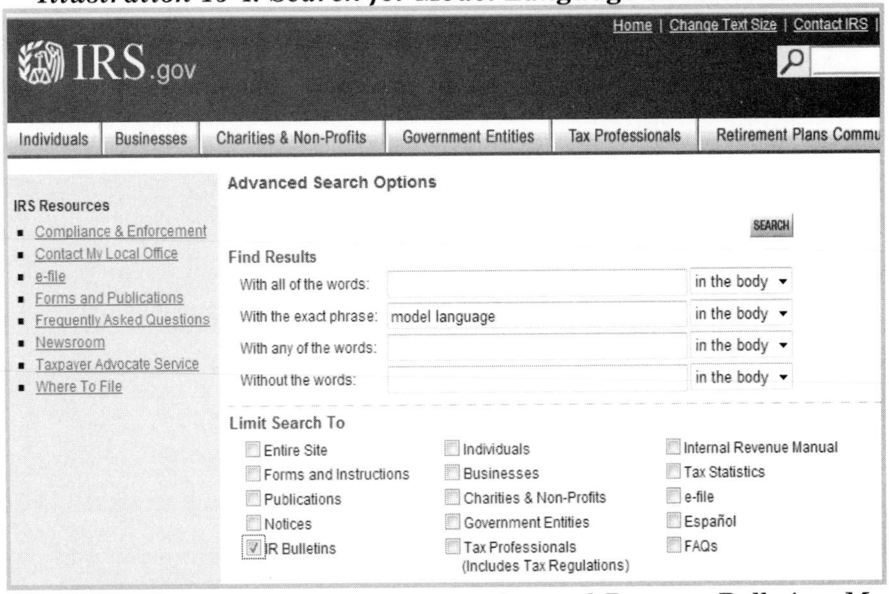

→I searched for an exact phrase in the Internal Revenue Bulletins. My search could miss relevant documents (e.g., those using "sample" instead of "model" and those in which the two words aren't adjacent).

Illustration 15-5. Results of Search on IRS Website

Search Results

"model language"   SEARCH | Advanced Search
                                Search Tips

15 results found   Summaries: **Show** | Hide

Sort by: **Relevance** | Date   Results: 1-10   ▷

Results ⓘ

IRB 2007-51 (Rev. December 17, 2007) 🗎   14 Dec 07
Internal Revenue Bulletin   Highlight Term(s)
Bulletin No. 2007-51 December 17, 2007 HIGHLIGHTS OF THIS ISSUE These synopses are intended only as aids to the
reader in identifying the subject matter covered. They may not be relied upon as authoritative ...
http://www.irs.gov/pub/irs-irbs/irb07-51.pdf - 844.1KB

Internal Revenue Bulletin 1996-50 🗎   19 Jul 07
INCOME TAX Rev. Rul. 96±57, page 5. Federal rates; adjusted federal rates; adjusted federal long-term rate, and the long-term Highlight Term(s)
exempt rate. For purposes of sections 1274, 1288, 382, and other sections of the Code, ...
http://www.irs.gov/pub/irs-irbs/irb96-50.pdf - 121.5KB

→My search yielded 15 items. If you redo the initial search using the "With all of the words" option, you will find more documents but many of them will not be relevant.

Section C. Problems

1. Locate a non-IRS-produced form or checklist covering tax consequences of a

   a. settlement for damages attributable to a personal injury

   b. formation of a family limited partnership

   c. designation of property in a deferred like-kind exchange

2. Locate the IRS model language described below.

   a. most recent IRS Announcement that includes model language for advance pricing agreements

   b. automatic contribution features for 401(k) plans (2009 Notice)

   c. declaration of trust for an inter vivos charitable lead unitrust (2008 Revenue Procedure)

3. What is the purpose of the IRS Form listed?

   a. 6847

   b. 8332

   c. 8498-EP

   d. 8893

   e. 13981

CHAPTER 16.NEWSLETTERS

SECTION A. INTRODUCTION

Researchers in any area must update their findings or risk citing obsolete sources. When the research involves taxation, the odds of change are extremely high and the number of sources to consult may appear endless. Although keeping current requires a significant time commitment, it pays off in the long run. Regular self-education ultimately reduces your research time.

Newsletters are convenient tools for keeping up with changes in the law. While they are no substitute for updating with a citator or the new matter section of a looseleaf service, they provide a means for reviewing material issued during a predetermined time period.

Several newsletters print texts or digests of primary source material. The publisher often maintains these materials on electronic databases. If your library has sufficient shelf space for print copies, or you have electronic access, you can also use newsletters to locate and read primary source materials. Electronic versions are generally better for this purpose. They are more likely—using hyperlinks—to provide access to full text. In addition, because print versions often lack cumulative indexes, electronic searches are more efficient.

SECTION B. CATEGORIZING NEWSLETTERS

Methods for categorizing newsletters include frequency of publication, subject matter, relation to looseleaf services, and publication format.

1. Frequency of Publication

Newsletters may appear daily, weekly, or even monthly. Daily and weekly newsletters either offer longer excerpts from cases and rulings than do their monthly counterparts or cover a wider range of topics. To avoid extraordinary length, monthly newsletters limit their breadth or depth of coverage. The IRS's practice of issuing advance revenue rulings and revenue procedures, notices, and announcements makes daily newsletters particularly attractive. They may carry these items weeks before they appear in the Internal Revenue Bulletin.

Online publication represents the ultimate in frequency. Because electronic databases can update their newsletter files daily, subscribers enjoy instant access while avoiding the library shelving problems associated with daily newsletters. Many newsletters are available online in addition to being published in print versions.

2. Subject Matter

Newsletters may be general in scope, covering all (or at least most) areas of tax. Unless a general purpose newsletter is relatively lengthy, or published very frequently, it gives limited attention to various areas or to particular types of authority. Other newsletters may limit coverage to a particular specialty, such as the estate tax or oil and gas taxation.

3. Relation to Looseleaf Services

Publishers of looseleaf services provide subscribers with pamphlet-type newsletters summarizing major events of the week or other relevant time period. Although their summaries may be short, many of these newsletters include cross-references to discussion in the relevant looseleaf. CCH and RIA publish newsletters associated with their looseleaf services.

In other instances, a looseleaf service subscription may not include a newsletter. Tax Management Weekly Report and Daily Tax Report fall into this category; neither is part of a subscription to the print version of Tax Management Portfolios. Even if it is not included in a subscription, a newsletter may include cross-references to a looseleaf service. For example, Tax Management Weekly Report includes updating material keyed to the Tax Management Portfolios.

Many newsletters have no relation to a looseleaf service. Some of these, including Tax Notes, provide cross-references to sources printing full texts of items digested in the newsletter. Others simply provide citations to the primary source material.

4. Publication Format

Newsletters are available in a variety of formats, but print and online are the most common. Disc or microform publication is useful if shelf space is limited and you want permanent access to the publication.

SECTION C. DESCRIPTIONS OF NEWSLETTERS

It is impossible to provide a detailed description of every available newsletter in this short a book. Although I limited this section to a handful of newsletters and publishers, you should not overlook other resources available in print or online. This is particularly important for relatively specialized areas.

Many newsletters are available on LexisNexis or Westlaw in addition to their publishers' website. Several professional law or accounting organizations, and individual law or accounting firms, publish newsletters for group members, clients, or even the general public; these are likely to be available electronically.

1. Bureau of National Affairs/Tax Management

BNA publishes daily and weekly newsletters. The Daily Tax Report is an invaluable aid in following current developments in the law. Each separately paginated issue includes a section describing congressional activity, including bills passed and introduced, committee hearings, and committee reports.

Daily Tax Report prints full texts or digests of judicial decisions; full texts of most revenue rulings and procedures; summaries of other IRS materials (e.g., private letter rulings); and texts of proposed, temporary, and final regulations. Newsletter subscribers can access full-text documents online using Tax Management's TaxCore.

Illustration 16-1. Excerpt from Daily Tax Report

> *Tax Policy*
>
> ## CRS Releases Issue Statements On Tax Gap, Investment Income Taxation
>
> The Congressional Research Service Jan. 21 released two issue statements dated Jan. 19 addressing taxation and the considerations the 111th Congress may undertake in its second session.
>
> The first, on the tax gap, Internal Revenue Service collection, and tax shelters, said Congress "may reconsider ... the acceptable level of the gross tax gap and the appropriate allocation of resources to achieve this tax gap."
>
> Most tax experts favor a comprehensive approach to reduce the gap that "would include collection resources, service to taxpayers, research, information technology, and new legislation," CRS said.
>
> The second, on investment income taxation, said the 111th Congress will turn toward a variety of often conflicting issues in its second session.
>
> "Using the tax system to achieve some goals could worsen the chances of achieving other goals," CRS said. "For example, tax incentives to increase investment and saving may improve long-term economic growth if they are effective, but reduces the progressivity of the tax system and could exacerbate problems associated with rising income inequality."
>
> *Texts of the documents, CRS Issue Statement on Tax Gap, IRS Collection, and Tax Shelters and CRS Issue Statement on Investment Income Taxation, are in TaxCore.*

→Daily Tax Report includes news reports in addition to primary source material. The excerpt above is from the January 22, 2010, print version.

The Weekly Report primarily serves as a digest rather than a full-text service for primary source material. It focuses on news and analysis of current issues. Short articles appear in its Focus section.

The Weekly Report covers court decisions, regulations, revenue rulings and procedures, private letter rulings, and other IRS material. It is particularly useful for subscribers to Tax Management Portfolios, as it includes cross-references and updating information for Portfolio material.

2. Tax Analysts

The weekly Tax Notes newsletter covers pending legislation, IRS and Treasury material, and court opinions. It also covers comments made by government representatives at tax conferences, comments by taxpayer representatives at public hearings on regulations, and comments the government receives on proposed regulations. Each issue of Tax Notes includes articles by practitioners or academics.

Full text of documents is available in Tax Notes Today. You can access both Tax Notes and Tax Notes Today on LexisNexis and on Tax Analysts' web-based service.

Illustration 16-2. Excerpt from Tax Notes

NEWS AND ANALYSIS

Insurance Practices Focus of Hearing on Physical Harm Awards

By Sam Young — syoung@tax.org

Insurance companies' practices in negotiating settlements with plaintiffs were the focus of an IRS hearing on proposed regulations on income exclusions for sums related to sickness or personal injuries, with government officials hearing from five speakers on that issue and other possible changes to the proposed regs, including per se exclusions for amounts received for sex abuse or long-term wrongful imprisonment.

The proposed regs, issued in September 2009, reflect changes to section 104(a)(2) made in the Small Business Protection Act of 1996. Most significantly, they eliminate the requirement that damages received from a lawsuit or settlement must be based on "tort or tort-type rights." (For REG-127270-06, see *Doc 2009-20411* or *2009 TNT 176-6*. For prior coverage, see *Tax Notes*, Sept. 21, 2009, p. 1187, *Doc 2009-20488*, or *2009 TNT 176-1*.)

→This report is from the March 1, 2010, print issue. Note the citations to primary source material and to earlier coverage in Tax Notes.

3. Commerce Clearing House

Federal Tax Day and Federal Tax Weekly are available online through CCH IntelliConnect. CCH includes links to primary source material discussed in these newsletters. There are also links to discussion in online versions of CCH looseleaf services.

Illustration 16-3. Excerpt from Federal Tax Day

Federal Tax Day - Current, W.1 President Signs IRS Funding and Aviation Excise Tax Bills, (Dec. 17, 2009)

President Obama on December 16 signed an omnibus spending bill (HR 3288) that includes fiscal year (FY) 2010 appropriations for the IRS. The Consolidated Appropriations Act, 2010, funds the Departments of Commerce, Defense, Education, Health and Human Services, Housing and Urban Development, Justice, Labor, State, Transportation, Treasury and Veterans Affairs and other agencies through the end of the government's fiscal year on September 30, 2010.

In addition, the president on December 16 signed the Fiscal Year 2010 Federal Aviation Administration Extension Act, Part II (HR 4217), which will extend through March 31, 2010, authorities to collect taxes that fund the Airport and Airway Trust Fund, make expenditures from the Airport and Airway Trust Fund and provide grants to airports under the Airport Improvement Program.

By Paula Cruickshank, CCH News Staff

→Note the hyperlinks to primary source materials.

Illustration 16-4. Excerpt from Federal Tax Weekly

Issue Number 50 www.CCHGroup.com December 17, 2009

Inside this Issue

Extenders, Estate Tax, Foreign Account Reporting, And More Await Passage

◆ *H.R. 4154, H.R. 4213*

As Congress' holiday recess approaches, lawmakers are scrambling to pass some "must-do" tax legislation. The House has approved a $31 billion package of extenders including heightened disclosure and reporting rules for foreign accounts. The House is also expected to pass a jobs bill before its holiday recess. Congress also approved a FY 2010 budget for Treasury and the IRS.

Extenders

The House bill extends a host of temporary tax incentives through December 31, 2010. Among the individual extenders are the state and local sales tax deduction, the additional standard deduction for state and local real property taxes, the higher education tuition deduction, and the teacher's classroom expense deduction. The House bill also extends the temporary provision for tax-free distributions from IRAs for charitable purposes.

■ ***Comment.*** "No inclusion of

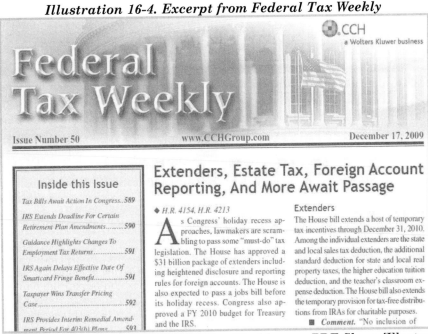

→Online users can access Federal Tax Weekly as a PDF file or [Illustration 16-4] as a text file with hyperlinks. Print users of Standard Federal Tax Reporter receive a similar publication, Taxes on Parade.

Illustration 16-5. Excerpt from Federal Tax Weekly

CCH Federal Tax Weekly, ¶2 IRS Extends Deadline One Year For *PPA* Plan Amendments, (Dec. 17, 2009)

Notice 2009-97

The IRS has extended for one year the deadline for amending qualified retirement plans to comply with certain requirements enacted in the *Pension Protection Act of 2006 (PPA)*. The deadline is extended to the last day of the first plan year that begins on or after January 1, 2010.

CCH Take Away. While many of the *PPA* provisions applied to plan years beginning after 2007, the *PPA* and Rev. Proc. 2007-44 provided a later deadline for adopting plan amendments to comply with the *PPA* and applicable regs. That deadline was the end of the first plan year beginning on or after January 1, 2009. The IRS is extending the deadline to provide more time to comply with recent and forthcoming final regs.

Extended deadline

In Notice 2009-97, the IRS extended the deadline for:

→Note the hyperlinks to primary source materials.

4. Research Institute of America

Federal Taxes Weekly Alert reports on major legislative, administrative, and judicial action. It also includes highlights of material covered in Warren, Gorham & Lamont journals. This newsletter is available electronically on the Checkpoint service in both PDF and text versions.

Illustration 16-6. Excerpt from Federal Taxes Weekly Alert

RIA

Federal Taxes

Weekly *Alert*

12/24/2009
Volume 55, Number 52

■ **Highlights** ■

IRS finalizes regs on D reorganizations without distributions IRS has finalized previously issued temporary and proposed regs allowing transactions to qualify as D reorganizations even though no stock and/or securities of the acquiring corporation is issued and distributed in the transaction. The final regs also provide guidance on basis determinations and controlled group transactions.

Proposed regs address basis and character reporting rules for securities acquired after 2010–Part II IRS has issued proposed regs explaining the complex basis and character reporting requirements for most stock acquired after 2010, for shares in a regulated investment company (RIC, i.e., a mutual fund) or stock acquired in connection with a dividend reinvestment plan (DRP) after 2011, and other specified securities acquired after 2012. This article, covering the proposed abolition of the double category method for determining RIC shares' basis, DRPs, and reporting of sales by S corporations, is the second installment of a multi-part article article on these complex new regs.

IRS issues W-4 Instructions for nonresidents aliens IRS has issued a notice that provides guidance to nonresi-

→Online users can access Federal Taxes Weekly Alert as a PDF file or [Illustration 16-7] as a text file with hyperlinks.

Illustration 16-7. Excerpt from Federal Taxes Weekly Alert

Full - Preview articles for the week of 12/24/2009 - Volume 55, No. 52
Federal Taxes Weekly Alert Newsletter

T.D. 9475, 12/17/2009 ; Reg. § 1.358-2 ; Reg. § 1.368-2 ; Reg. § 1.1502-13

IRS has finalized previously issued temporary and proposed regs allowing transactions to qualify as D reorganizations even though no stock and/or securities of the acquiring corporation is issued and distributed in the transaction. The final regs also provide guidance on basis determinations and controlled group transactions.

Background. The Code provides general nonrecognition treatment for reorganizations specifically described in Code Sec. 368(a) . Under Code Sec. 368(a)(1)(D) , a reorganization includes a transfer by a corporation (transferor corporation) of all or a part of its assets to another corporation (transferee corporation) if, immediately after the transfer, the transferor corporation or one or more of its shareholders (including persons who were shareholders immediately before the transfer), or any combination thereof, is in control of the transferee corporation; but only if stock or securities of the controlled corporation are distributed in pursuance of a plan of reorganization in a transaction that qualifies under Code Sec. 354 , Code Sec. 355 , or Code Sec. 356 .

Under Code Sec. 354(a)(1) , no gain or loss is recognized if stock or securities in a corporation a party to a reorganization are, in pursuance of the plan of reorganization, exchanged solely for stock or securities in such corporation or in another corporation a party to the reorganization. Code Sec. 354(a)(1) does not apply to an

CHAPTER 17. MICROFORMS

SECTION A. ADVANTAGES AND DISADVANTAGES

Microforms have three important advantages. The first relates to space. As primary and secondary source materials proliferate, libraries can use microforms to save shelf space. A second advantage relates to availability. Your library may be able to buy non-electronic versions of some historical materials only in microform. A third advantage relates to cost. Once the library has purchased materials in microform, it has no obligation to make further outlays to ensure its access to those materials.

There are several reasons why you may prefer other formats. These relate to availability, ease of searching, mobility, space, and security.

Availability may be the most critical factor. Many publishers are eliminating microform products and switching to electronic services. Even if a publisher no longer updates a microform service, these materials remain valuable for historical research.

Navigation and mobility are also important. Electronic sources are easier to navigate and permit word and phrase searching. Microforms are effectively used only if the compiler has indexed them well. In addition, electronic materials do not tie you to a fixed place. Microforms require a reader or reader-printer. If you have the appropriate computer configuration, you can use electronic materials anywhere.

Space and security are relevant factors for many libraries. Web-based systems require no library storage space; CD/DVDs require relatively little space. Although microforms require less space than their print counterparts, they do require more than the electronic versions. Finally, microforms share a problem with looseleaf services; the individual forms can be misfiled or stolen.

SECTION B. FORMAT

Microforms are available in a variety of formats, including microfilm, microprint, microcard, microfiche, and ultrafiche. You can use a reader-printer to produce a copy of materials you locate.

SECTION C. AVAILABLE MATERIALS

Government publications available in microform include Congressional Record, Statutes at Large, Federal Register, Code of Federal Regulations, and the Cumulative Bulletin. Other materials include Tax Court and Supreme Court case reporter services. Many libraries include briefs filed with the United States Supreme Court in their microform collections.

You are also likely to find legislative history materials available in microform. Publishers using this format include Congressional Information Service (part of LexisNexis) and William S. Hein & Co., Inc.

The CIS Microfiche Library includes committee hearings, reports, and prints and Public Laws since 1970. Libraries can customize their purchases to include only certain types of documents. The print CIS Index provides abstracts of publications and a separate index.[305]

Several series of Hein's Internal Revenue Acts of the United States (Chapter 7) are available in microform. These include the sets for 1909–1950, 1950–51, 1954, 1953–72, 1978, and 1984.

Some libraries may own ultrafiche copies of Tax Management Primary Sources–Series I (Chapter 7).

Law reviews and other periodicals may also be available in microform. Representative publications that Hein provided in microform include Akron Tax Journal, American Journal of Tax Policy, Tax Law Review, Tax Lawyer, and several tax institutes.[306]

Because the number of materials and the microform format used varies, always consult a librarian about microform access before concluding that your library lacks a particular resource.

---

[305] See http://academic.lexisnexis.com/cis/cis.aspx for a listing of CIS publications. Many of the CIS publications are now available online.

[306] HeinOnline has an extensive collection of law reviews and journals, which is discussed in Chapter 14.

CHAPTER 18. CD/DVD

SECTION A. ADVANTAGES AND DISADVANTAGES

Disc-based services store significant amounts of information yet require little storage space.[307] In many areas of research, CD/DVD and online services have supplanted microform as an alternative to print materials.

Although they may be updated less frequently than looseleaf services or other research tools are,[308] these services have offsetting advantages. The CD/DVD format lets you perform more efficient searches than can be accomplished using print services.

Most looseleaf services print recent developments in separate subdivisions, sometimes even in separate volumes. Update discs integrate new material directly into the original text. Because all material is on the same disc,[309] you don't have to worry about filing errors or stolen pages.

Discs are not a perfect substitute for print versions of primary source materials. A disc may not use the citation format you need for a brief or article; even if it does, it may not show page numbers for individual sections of text.

Obtaining the service's most current disc is critical. Some discs have an expiration date; you won't be able to access their contents after that date. Even the most current disc can be "stale" because its cut-off date for new matter ends before the month or other calendar period listed on the disc. And, while a publisher may update online material before it updates print material, it is less likely to do so for its CD/DVD version.

A major disadvantage of disc-based services relates to access. Unless the disc is networked, only one researcher can use it at a time. In contrast, several researchers can simultaneously use different volumes of a print reporter service. If they use an online service, they can search the same volumes simultaneously.

---

[307] Several publishers have migrated from CD-ROM to DVD because the latter format has more capacity.

[308] Several CD/DVD services offer updating options. Check the option in use (for example, monthly or quarterly) so that you don't erroneously assume your disc reflects the most recent changes in the law.

[309] Some services require multiple CD-ROMs. In that case, you will be prompted to insert the appropriate CD if your computer is not attached to a CD changer.

SECTION B. SEARCH STRATEGIES

1. Similarities to Searching Print Materials

You can use CD/DVD materials much as you would print items. In the case of treatises, for example, you can locate a topic in the table of contents and then review that text segment or download it for later reading.

As is true for other types of research, you must consider synonyms if your concept can be expressed in different ways.[310] In addition, just as print publishers use different cross-referencing methods, CD/DVD publishers may use different search commands. Table 18-1 lists search commands you may encounter.

2. Search Strategies Unique to Electronic Materials

A major difference between print and electronic services relates to the latter's use of hypertext links. When you click on a link, you go to other text sections or to primary source materials such as the Code or Treasury regulations. To return to the original text, you merely click on the appropriate command. Although the process appears similar to conducting a search using multiple print volumes, using links is not the same. Be careful to backtrack rather than exit the service if you want to retrace your steps later.

Another difference relates to your initial search strategy. Rather than using indexes or tables to find material, you can use electronic services to find primary source material directly. As shown in Illustration 18-6, these services offer several search fields and also let you specify words that must appear in the document.

Electronic services also allow more sophisticated searching. You can specify Boolean connectors (e.g., and, or, and not). You can also take advantage of wildcard symbols (e.g., deduct* for deduct, deducting, deduction, deducted, deductions, and deductible) to expand your search results.

Because search commands vary, be sure to read the user's guide for each service. If you regularly use CD/DVDs from different publishers, you might benefit from compiling a short command list for each service you use. Remember also to check the contents; electronic services often expand or contract their coverage based on market demand.

---

[310] Check to see if the CD/DVD includes a thesaurus feature. If you insert a $ sign at the end of a word on some services, your results will include synonyms. [See Illustration 18-10.]

3. Differences Between CD/DVD and Online Services

Online services are likely to include more primary and secondary sources than a single CD/DVD and are more likely to let you narrow searches by year or by dates within a year. Online services also use their own search command structure. If you use a particular service's disc version, don't be surprised if you must use different commands online. You are most likely to encounter different search commands if you use a general online service rather than one offered by the CD/DVD's publisher.

Table 18-1. Common CD/DVD Search Connectors and Wildcards

Term	Meaning
And	Both terms must appear
Or	Either term must appear (both terms may appear)
Not	Only the first term may appear
Xor	Only the first or only the second term may appear
/N	Second term must follow first by no more than N words
@N	First and second terms must be within N words of each other
?	Replaces a single character (used anywhere in word)
*	Replaces one or more characters (used at end of word)
%	Finds variations of word endings (used at end of word)
$	Finds synonyms for word (used at end of word)

→Check the CD/DVD service you are using to ascertain the search connectors and wildcard symbols.

→A publisher may use one set of symbols for its disc-based service and another for its online service.

Section C. Representative Materials

The discussion below focuses on two disc-based services, OneDisc Premium and OnPoint.

1. Tax Analysts OneDisc Premium

The OneDisc includes the Code, treaties, regulations, Internal Revenue Bulletin items, and other IRS publications (letter rulings and other Chief Counsel documents), and judicial decisions. It also covers new legislation and treaty histories. There is explanatory material (the Tax Analysts Baedeker) and useful tables of IRS information, including inflation adjustments and interest rates. You can search by text or Code section in multiple databases simultaneously.

The OneDisc Premium is a DVD service, for which you can select monthly or quarterly updates. An annual archive disc has no expiration date.

Illustration 18-1. OneDisc Premium Databases

Select All | Deselect All

Code and Regulations	IRS Documents	Chief Counsel Advice
Internal Revenue Code	Announcements	LTRs and TAMs 1998-present
Final and Temporary Regs	Notices	LTRs and TAMs 1980-1997
Treasury Decision Preambles	Revenue Rulings	Actions on Decisions
Proposed Regulations	Revenue Procedures	ISP and Settlement Guidelines
IRS Regulatory Agenda	IRS Publications	Market Segment Specialization Program
	Circular 230	Chief Counsel Notices
Explanations and Tables		Compliance Officer Memos
Federal Tax Baedeker	Internal Revenue Manual	Field Attorney Advice
Quick Reference Tables	US Tax Treaties	Field Service Advice
	US Tax Treaties	Information Letters
Court Opinions	Integrated US Treaty Text	Legal Memorandums
Tax Court Decisions 1972 - Present	Legislative History	Litigation Guideline Memos
Tax Court Decisions 1942 - 1971		Service Center Advice
BTA Decisions 1924 - 1942	Tax Legislation	Technical Assistance
Federal Court Tax Decisions 1972 - Present	New Tax Legislation	General Counsel Memos
Federal Court Tax Decisions 1913 - 1971	Public Laws List	
	JCT Blue Book	Miscellaneous Documents
		The Tax Directory of Federal and State Officials
		IRS Annotated Business Plan

[Word Search]   [Advanced Word Search]   [Code Section Search]

Illustration 18-2. Search Using OneDisc

Multiple Database | Advanced Word Search

Search for word or phrase:

`gold`   **HELP with this search**

- all the words
- ● exact phrase
- within `10` words of each other

● And ○ Or ○ Not ○ within `10` words of each other

Search for word or phrase:

`1031`

- all the words
- ● exact phrase
- within `10` words of each other

[Search] [Clear] [Cancel]

Thesaurus is: ○ On ● Off

→I searched in the databases covering revenue rulings, revenue procedures, notices, and announcements for documents containing both the
word "gold" and 1031. I did not turn on the Thesaurus function.

Illustration 18-3. Items Found Using OneDisc

(1-8 of 8 matches)			
	Document	Database	Heading
1	Rev. Proc. 2007-1	IRS Revenue Procedures	PROCEDURES REVISED FOR ISSUING LETTER RULINGS.
2	Rev. Proc. 2006-1	IRS Revenue Procedures	PROCEDURES REVISED FOR ISSUING LETTER RULINGS.
3	Rev. Proc. 2005-1	IRS Revenue Procedures	PROCEDURES REVISED FOR ISSUING LETTER RULINGS.
4	Rev. Proc. 2002-1	IRS Revenue Procedures	PROCEDURES REVISED FOR ISSUING LETTER RULINGS.
5	Rev. Rul. 82-166	IRS Revenue Rulings	
6	Rev. Rul. 82-96	IRS Revenue Rulings	
7	Rev. Rul. 79-143	IRS Revenue Rulings	
8	Rev. Rul. 76-214	IRS Revenue Rulings	

→The references in the revenue procedures are to "frivolous issues" involving the gold standard.

Illustration 18-4. Options Using Thesaurus

Hide Search Terms

Search Terms, Word Variations and Search Results are listed below. To Refine your search, select or deselect any of the terms and click on Refine Search.

(select | deselect all)   Refine Search

gold	"precious metal"	"wealth"	"riches"	"gold coin"	"heavy metal"
select all	none	"golden trinkets"	"beaten gold"	"gold alloy"	"gold plate"	"gold wire"
	"aurum"	"white gold"	"aurous metal"	"red gold"	"color"
	"deep yellow"	"flaxen"	"gold-colored"	"ochroid"	"aureate"
	"wheat-colored"	"yellow"	"dark yellow"	"tawny"	

→OneDisc offers several synonyms for gold.

2. Research Institute of America OnPoint

The OnPoint service offers several combinations of sources on DVD. Materials available include a variety of primary and secondary source materials. OnPoint includes a synonym option and search templates. This service is updated monthly; recent discs are labeled RIA Federal/WG&L rather than OnPoint.

Illustration 18-5. Excerpt from OnPoint Contents

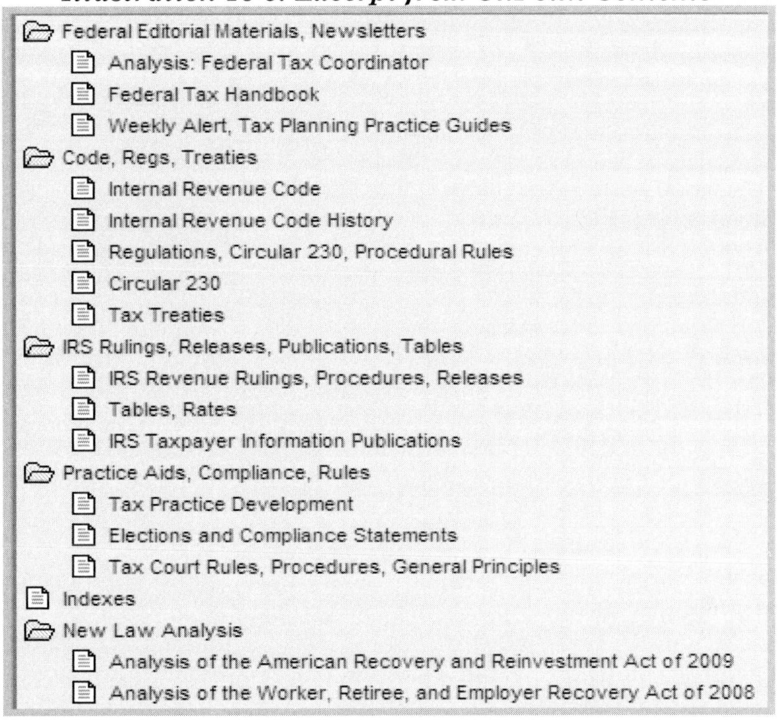

Federal Editorial Materials, Newsletters
Analysis: Federal Tax Coordinator
Federal Tax Handbook
Weekly Alert, Tax Planning Practice Guides
Code, Regs, Treaties
Internal Revenue Code
Internal Revenue Code History
Regulations, Circular 230, Procedural Rules
Circular 230
Tax Treaties
IRS Rulings, Releases, Publications, Tables
IRS Revenue Rulings, Procedures, Releases
Tables, Rates
IRS Taxpayer Information Publications
Practice Aids, Compliance, Rules
Tax Practice Development
Elections and Compliance Statements
Tax Court Rules, Procedures, General Principles
Indexes
New Law Analysis
Analysis of the American Recovery and Reinvestment Act of 2009
Analysis of the Worker, Retiree, and Employer Recovery Act of 2008

Illustration 18-6. Available Search Options in OnPoint

Search
Where to Search
Search Options
Search For:
How to Search
Keyword. All of the words, no strict order. Connectors optional.
Phrase. All of the words as an exact phrase.
Hints
Proximity. All of the words within
10
words of each other.
Natural Language. One or more of the words ranked by relevance.
Automatically find variations of the words.
How to View the Results
In a Contents & Docs display
Fully expanded.
In a Hit List & Docs display.
Search
View
Templates...
Stop Search
Clear All
Close
Help

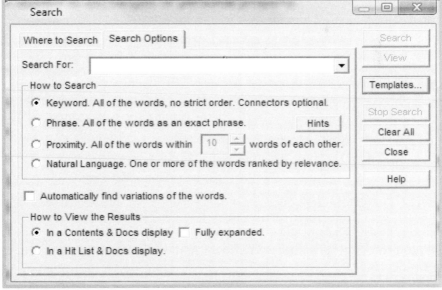

→Search options include searching by phrase or proximity and using word variants. You can also change how results are displayed.

Illustration 18-7. Search for IRS Documents in OnPoint

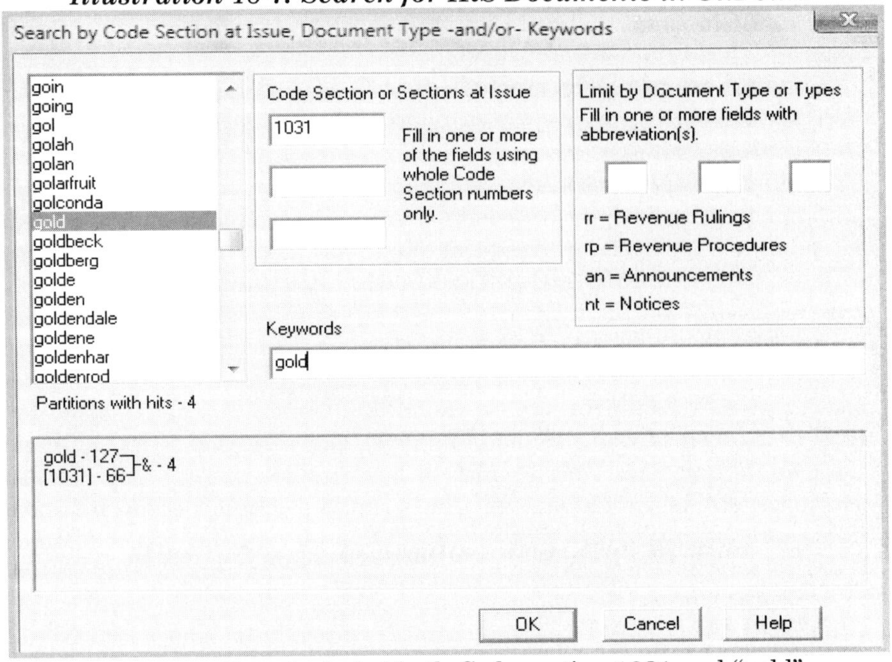

Search by Code Section at Issue, Document Type -and/or- Keywords

```
goin
going
gol
golah
golan
golarfruit
golconda
gold
goldbeck
goldberg
golde
golden
goldendale
goldene
goldenhar
goldenrod
```

Code Section or Sections at Issue

`1031`

Fill in one or more of the fields using whole Code Section numbers only.

Limit by Document Type or Types

Fill in one or more fields with abbreviation(s).

rr = Revenue Rulings

rp = Revenue Procedures

an = Announcements

nt = Notices

Keywords

`gold`

Partitions with hits · 4

gold · 127 ┐
         ├ & · 4
[1031] · 66 ┘

OK   Cancel   Help

→Four revenue rulings included both Code section 1031 and "gold"

Illustration 18-8. Search Results for Section 1031 and Gold

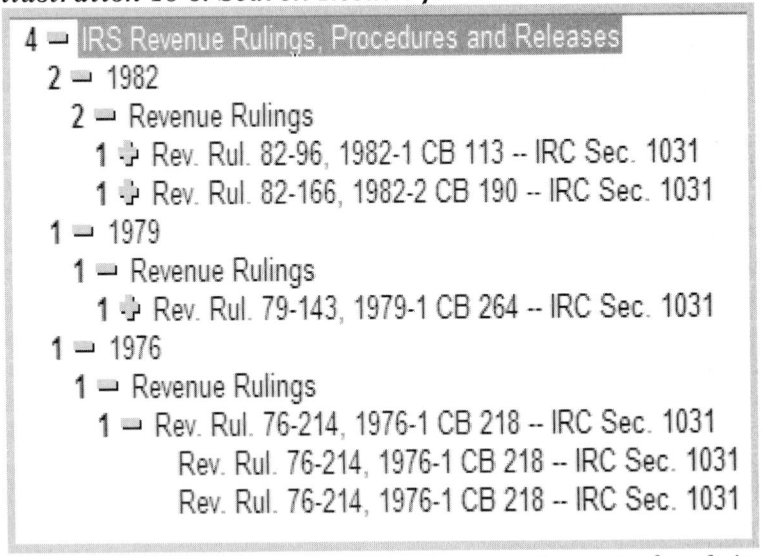

```
4 ▬ IRS Revenue Rulings, Procedures and Releases
   2 ▬ 1982
      2 ▬ Revenue Rulings
         1 ✦ Rev. Rul. 82-96, 1982-1 CB 113 -- IRC Sec. 1031
         1 ✦ Rev. Rul. 82-166, 1982-2 CB 190 -- IRC Sec. 1031
   1 ▬ 1979
      1 ▬ Revenue Rulings
         1 ✦ Rev. Rul. 79-143, 1979-1 CB 264 -- IRC Sec. 1031
   1 ▬ 1976
      1 ▬ Revenue Rulings
         1 ▬ Rev. Rul. 76-214, 1976-1 CB 218 -- IRC Sec. 1031
               Rev. Rul. 76-214, 1976-1 CB 218 -- IRC Sec. 1031
               Rev. Rul. 76-214, 1976-1 CB 218 -- IRC Sec. 1031
```

→You can use a split screen view, which shows the text of each item as you select it.

→You can link to Federal Tax Coordinator analysis for the items found.

→Compare these results to those obtained in Illustration 18-3.

Illustration 18-9. Analysis in Federal Tax Coordinator

Analysis: Federal Tax Coordinator
Chapter I Sales and Exchanges, Capital Gains and Losses, Cost Recovery Recapture, Depreciation Recapture
¶ I-3050 Like-Kind Exchanges.
  ¶ I-3066 How the like-kind test has been applied to exchanges of personal property.

26.1 IRS Letter Ruling 9612009

The following exchanges of personal property didn't qualify as like-kind exchanges under the like-kind test:

...U.S. currency for foreign currency or foreign currency for U.S. currency. 27

...Swiss francs for U.S. Double Eagle gold coins. Swiss francs are a medium of exchange in Switzerland, while U.S. Double Eagles are traded only by numismatists. Therefore, the taxpayer's economic position after the exchange was far different from its economic position beforehand. 28

...Gold bullion for silver bullion. While the metals have some similar qualities and uses, they are "intrinsically different metals and primarily are used in different ways. Silver is essentially an industrial commodity. Gold is primarily utilized as an investment in itself. An investment in one of the metals is fundamentally different from an investment in the other metal. Therefore, the silver bullion and the gold bullion are not property of like kind." 29

...Collector-type gold coins for bullion-type gold coins; for example, U.S. $20 gold coins for South African Krugerrands. The former are collector-type coins whose value is determined by such factors as rarity and aesthetics. The value of the latter is solely determined by their metal content. Hence, they are different kinds of investment. In so holding, IRS distinguished Rev Rul 76-214 (footnote 22) as having involved the exchange of coins that were both bullion-type coins. 30

...A truck for an automobile. 30.1

27 Rev Rul 74-7, 1974-1 CB 198
28 California Federal Life Insurance Co, (1981) 76 TC 107, affd (1982, CA9) 50 AFTR 2d 82-5271, 680 F2d 85, 82-2 USTC ¶9464
29 Rev Rul 82-166, 1982-2 CB 190
30 Rev Rul 79-143, 1979-1 CB 264.
30.1 IRS Letter Ruling 200241013; IRS Letter Ruling 200242009; IRS Letter Ruling 200240049.

Illustration 18-10. Search in OnPoint Using Synonyms

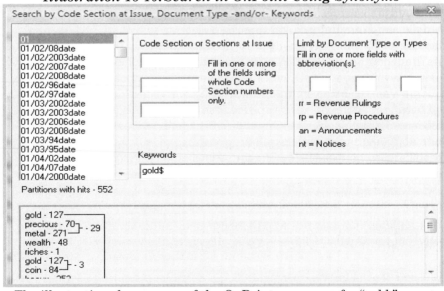

→The illustration shows some of the OnPoint synonyms for "gold."

CHAPTER 19. ONLINE LEGAL RESEARCH

SECTION A. INTRODUCTION

This chapter continues the discussion of electronic research begun in Chapter 3 and continued in several other chapters. In addition to discussing advantages and disadvantages of online research, it describes three types of service: general focus subscription services; tax-oriented subscription services; and other online services. [311] Government websites are separately covered in chapters dealing with particular types of material and are summarized in this chapter.

SECTION B. ADVANTAGES AND DISADVANTAGES

Online legal research systems have many useful features. First, they bring research materials together in one readily accessible location. Libraries with tax alcoves require several shelf ranges to house the relevant information; libraries without alcoves may shelve these items on several floors. An online system requires only a computer, a modem or other online access tool, and a printer or other means of memorializing your research. If you have wireless access and a good battery, you can conduct online research from virtually any location.

The Internet provides a quick means for transmitting and accessing both text and graphics. More important than the time saved in gathering the material is the ability to do searches that are virtually impossible to accomplish using print materials. Because the service responds to queries based on words appearing or not appearing in its database, you could easily use an online system to locate all opinions by a particular judge or all decisions rendered in 2010, at every court level, involving the medical expense deduction. Although CD/DVD searches can yield similar results, online services often include more material and are updated more frequently.

Given these advantages, why isn't research conducted solely online? That question was raised in Chapter 3, Section E, in comparing print and electronic services. As noted there, online services may be less suited than print materials for certain research tasks, such as using looseleaf services to familiarize yourself with a topic. Some older material may not be available online, and tax-specific articles indexes are not available in any online service. Publisher consolidation, discussed in Chapter 1, is

---

[311] See Katherine Pratt, Jennifer Kowal & Daniel Martin, *The Virtual Tax Library: A Comparison of Five Electronic Tax Research Platforms*, 8 FLA. TAX REV. 935 (2008). This article appeared before CCH changed its search platform.

also a factor. If you have access only to Westlaw, for example, you currently lack access to Shepard's and Tax Analysts publications. Even if an online service offers a particular source, your subscription option may not cover it.

Cost constraints may limit the time you can spend online. If your final product requires accurate page numbers, a final check of print sources may be necessary to assure yourself that you have made no citation errors. As the discussion in Chapter 3 indicates, there is no "best source" for tax research.

SECTION C. AVAILABLE MATERIALS

Some subscription-based services include tax materials in a general database. Others focus exclusively on taxation. Nonsubscription services vary in their coverage; they may include data from a variety of sources or may focus on a single type of information. They may provide links to relevant materials rather than including text in their databases.

Materials available online may also be available in print or on CD/DVD, often from the same publisher. Several publishers offer their own online services and also include their materials on services such as Westlaw or LexisNexis.

Keep three important rules in mind. First, you must check the time period covered for materials made available online. Don't assume a source included in an online service begins its coverage with the first print volume of that service. Coverage for many sources begins at a later date online than it does in print in both subscription and free services.

Second, remember that different systems use different search commands, rules for wildcard searches, or methods for indicating you want to use a Boolean search. You will not achieve the desired results unless you tailor your search to the rules imposed by the service you are using.[312]

Third, online systems are not static. They may add or eliminate databases or change their layout or search templates. In recent years, CCH has replaced Tax Research NetWork with IntelliConnect, Westlaw and LexisNexis have added tax-oriented search sites linked to their services (and are in the process of upgrading their overall services), and HeinOnline and Google have added new databases. Government services are also evolving; the migration from GPO Access to FDsys is a major example.

---

[312] We covered a print service analogy in Chapter 13, dealing with looseleaf services. Those services vary in using page, paragraph, and section numbers for categorizing and cross-referencing information.

D. Subscription Services—General Focus

1. Services Covered

This section covers three subscription services: LexisNexis, Westlaw, and HeinOnline. The first two have extensive tax databases within their overall coverage.[313] The third includes a significant amount of tax material, particularly material that is likely to be out of print. The discussion in this section begins with LexisNexis and Westlaw and concludes with HeinOnline. All three services have been discussed and illustrated in other chapters of this book.

2. LexisNexis and Westlaw: Introduction

Although they do not focus on tax, LexisNexis and Westlaw have extensive tax databases. You can complete many research tasks using the tax databases, but you may also need to use materials in the services' general databases.[314]

These services differ slightly in their coverage and search commands, but both offer the same type of search options. You can specify particular words that must appear or be absent in a document; if the words must be in a desired proximity, you can include that limitation. You can use these systems to locate decisions involving damages within five words of the term personal injury, or for decisions involving damages but not personal injury. You can limit your search to particular types of authority (e.g., only Tax Court) or to particular dates.

Before formulating a search query, you should become familiar with the search term symbols used on the system being accessed. In addition to each service's explanatory texts, other guides are available.

3. LexisNexis

a. Database Screens

LexisNexis offers two options in addition to its general Legal database. You can add a Taxation tab, or you can research in the LexisNexis Tax Center. Illustrations 19-1 and 19-2 show how each version currently looks. Each may change slightly as LexisNexis revamps its platform.

---

[313] This chapter does not cover two other general focus services, Loislaw and VersusLaw. Each includes fewer tax materials than LexisNexis or Westlaw. Loislaw is a Wolters Kluwer company; this chapter does cover another Wolters Kluwer service, CCH IntelliConnect.

[314] Some tools (e.g., articles indexes) may require searching in nontax libraries.

Illustration 19-1. LexisNexis Taxation Tab Screen

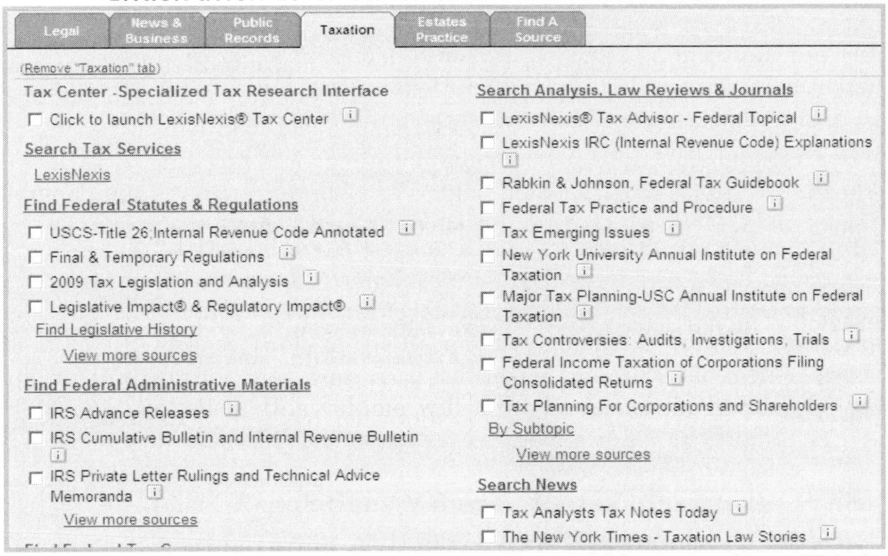

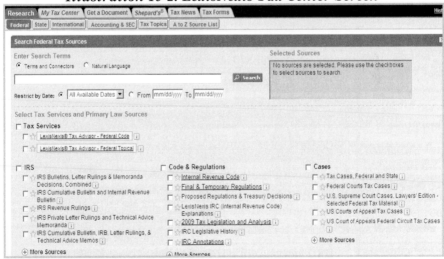

→LexisNexis lets you customize your opening page by area of law. This is a partial source list for the Taxation tab. The Estates Practice tab includes tax materials focused on estate planning.

→Click on the icon to obtain a contents list. Use the View more sources option if you don't see the particular service you want.

Illustration 19-2. LexisNexis Tax Center Screen

→You can customize within the Tax Center by clicking on the starred items. Only those items will appear when you select My Tax Center

→Click on the icon to obtain a contents list. Use the More Sources option if you don't see the particular service you want.

b. Database Files

The LexisNexis tax library, FEDTAX, is divided into files.[315] There are files for primary source material, for secondary source materials, and for various publishers. Because of this arrangement, you can access many items through multiple files. Primary source files include CASREL for judicial decisions and IRS material, TXLAWS for statutes and regulations), and OMNI, which combines most primary source material.

The icon ⓘ shown in Illustrations 19-1 and 19-2 provides dates of coverage for the particular source.

Secondary source files cover tax-oriented law reviews and treatises, Shepard's Citations, and services published by Matthew Bender (e.g., Rabkin & Johnson, Federal Income, Gift, and Estate Taxation) and Tax Analysts (including Tax Notes).

c. Connectors, Wildcard Characters, and Synonyms

LexisNexis uses several Boolean and proximity connectors:

Table 19-1. LexisNexis Connectors

Term	Meaning
And	Both terms must appear
Or	At least one of the terms must appear
and not	Only the first term may appear
w/N; /N	Terms must appear within N words of each other; either can appear first (N cannot exceed 255)
w/s; /s	Terms must appear within the same sentence
w/p; /p	Terms must appear within the same paragraph
w/seg	Terms must appear in the same segment (e.g., case caption, text)
pre/N	First term must precede second by no more than N words (N cannot exceed 255)

LexisNexis also lets you state proximity connectors in the negative (e.g., NOT w/s). You can exclude documents unless the term appears AT LEAST a stated number of times, and you can specify that the term must appear in all capital letters or only as a plural. If you use multiple words without a connector, LexisNexis treats them as a phrase.

LexisNexis lets you use an exclamation point (!) as a wildcard symbol to expand words by any number of letters following the !. You can use an

---

[315] You do not need to know library or file names to use LexisNexis.

asterisk (*) to add missing letters anywhere except at the beginning of the word. Each * represents a single missing letter. If you add three asterisks (***) following a letter, LexisNexis will include words that have zero, one, two, or three characters after that letter; it won't include words that have four or more characters.

LexisNexis does not automatically add synonyms to your search. If you use the Select terms for my search option, it suggests possible search terms based on those you have already selected. It also has a Check spelling option. Neither of these options appears on the Tax Center screen.

Illustration 19-3. Select Terms for My Search Results

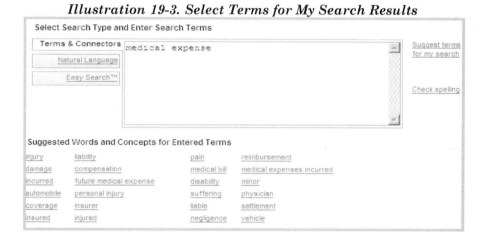

d. Segment and Date Restrictions

LexisNexis lets you specify the segment in which a word or phrase must appear. Segments vary by database. Segment options in a database covering judicial decisions include counsel, dissent, and outcome; options in a database covering IRS rulings include cite, number, and text. Searches in the Tax Center do not include segment options.

You can restrict your search by date. Options include no date restriction and previous week, month, six months, year, two years, five years, or ten years. Alternatively, you can enter from or to (or both) dates. Searches in the Tax Center include date options.

e. Search Method Options

LexisNexis has two search options in addition to using Boolean connectors (Terms & Connectors). The Natural Language search option lets you enter an issue to be searched; phrases must be enclosed in quotation marks. The Easy Search option is for searches involving only a few words; the service returns the results it considers most relevant. The Tax Center allows Terms & Connectors and Natural Language searches.

f. Citator

LexisNexis includes the Shepard's Citator, which is discussed in Chapter 12. Hyperlinked symbols to the left of cases or other items indicate that updating material is available. You can also enter citations directly into the citator.

4. Westlaw

a. Database Screens

Westlaw offers two options in addition to its general Law School database. You can add a Tax tab to the general database, or you can research in the Westlaw Tax option. Illustrations 19-4 through 19-6 show how each version currently looks. Each may change slightly when Westlaw moves to its WestlawNext platform.

Illustration 19-4. Westlaw Tax Tab Screen

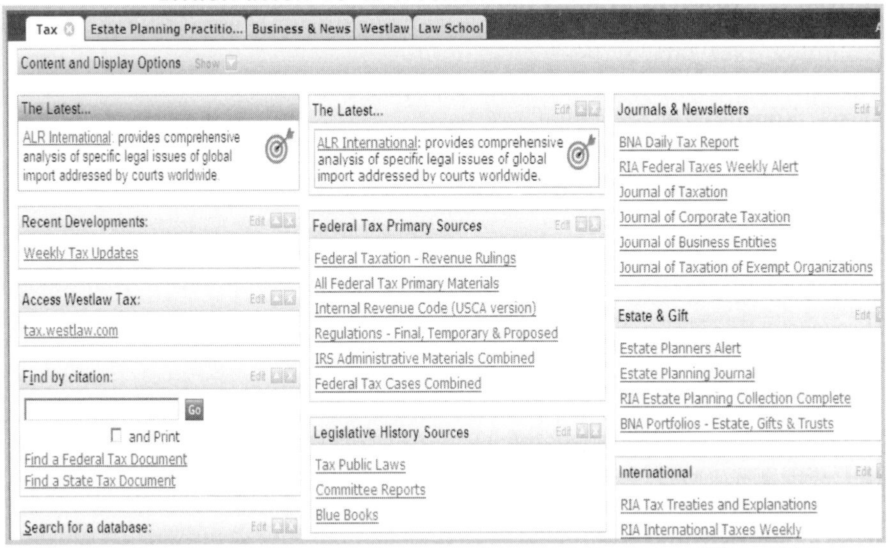

→Westlaw lets you customize your opening page by area of law. This is a partial source list for the Tax tab. The Estate Planning Practitioner tab includes tax materials focused on estate planning.

→The Westlaw Tax tab doesn't include an icon to click for a contents list. If you click on one of the links to reach a source, you will find an ⓘ icon.

Westlaw has an Edit option for each category. To add more sources to a category (or to rename the category), use the Edit option.

Illustration 19-5. Westlaw Tax Screen

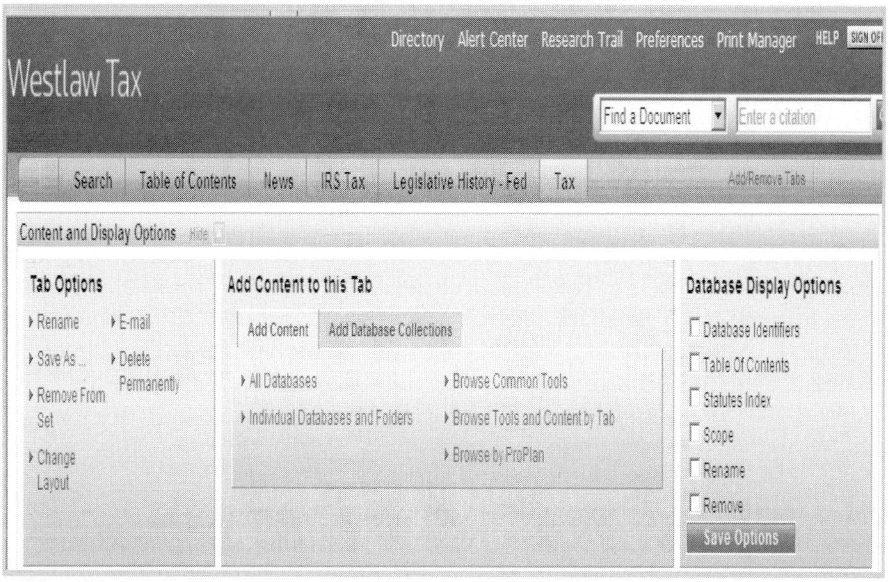

→The Westlaw Tax screen contents page initially resembles the Tax tab page on Westlaw. You can customize it using the Content and Display Options shown above.

→Note the separate display tabs for Search, Table of Contents, News, IRS Tax, and Legislative History. You can go directly to those tabs instead of selecting items from the main screen.

Illustration 19-6. Westlaw Tax Table of Contents Screen

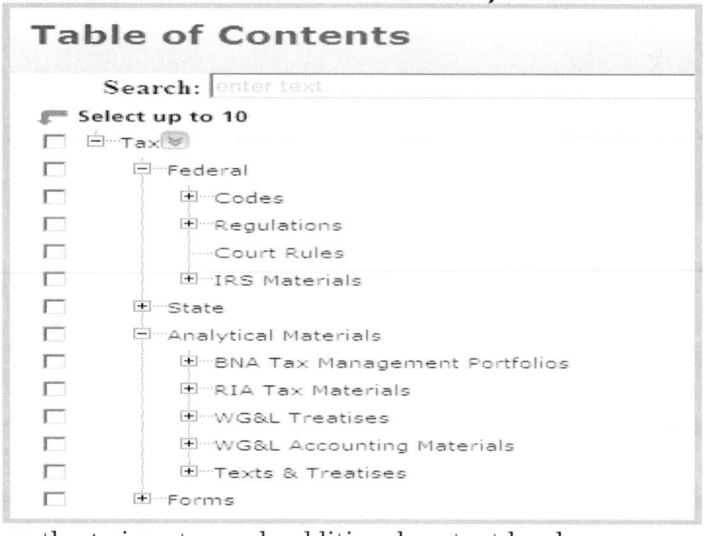

→Click on the + signs to reach additional content levels.

b. Database Files

The Westlaw tax database, FTX-ALL, is divided into separate files covering primary and secondary source materials.[316] Primary source files include FTX-CSRELS for judicial decisions and IRS material and FTX-CODREG for statutes and regulations.

Within each database, you can click on an icon to see dates of coverage.

Secondary source files cover tax-oriented law reviews, RIA Citator 2nd and West's KeyCite for Tax, and treatises and looseleaf services from Research Institute of America, Warren, Gorham & Lamont, and other West Group entities. Looseleaf services include United States Tax Reporter, Federal Tax Coordinator 2d, and Mertens, Law of Federal Income Taxation. BNA/Tax Management publications are available but are not included in every subscription option.

c. Connectors, Wildcard Characters, and Synonyms

Westlaw uses several Boolean and proximity connectors:

Table 19-2. Westlaw Connectors

Term	Meaning
&	both terms must appear
Space	at least one of the terms must appear
%	only the term before the % may appear
/n	terms must appear within n words of each other; either can appear first (n cannot exceed 255)
/s	terms must appear within the same sentence
/p	terms must appear within the same paragraph
+n	first term must precede the second by no more than n words (n cannot exceed 255)
+s	first term must precede the second in same sentence
+p	first term must precede the second in same paragraph
""	terms must appear in order (a phrase)

You can use a single exclamation point (!) as a wildcard symbol (root expander) to expand words by any number of letters following the !. An asterisk (*) adds missing letters anywhere but at the beginning of the word. Each * represents a single missing letter. Use a # sign to turn off automatic retrieval of plural forms. Westlaw Tax also uses connectors and universal characters.

---

[316] You do not need to know database names to use Westlaw.

Westlaw does not automatically add synonyms. If you use the Thesaurus option, it suggests search terms based on those you selected. Westlaw Tax doesn't show the Thesaurus.

Illustration 19-7. Westlaw Thesaurus

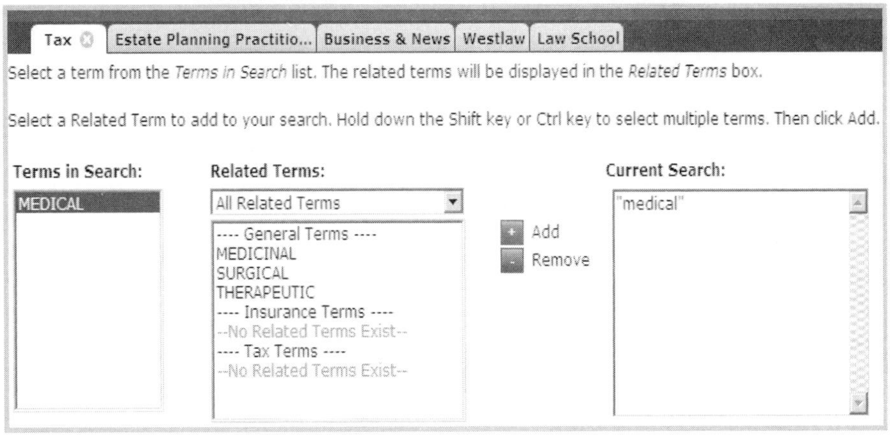

d. Field and Date Restrictions

Westlaw lets you specify the field in which a word or phrase must appear. Fields vary by database. Field options in a database covering judicial decisions include headnote, judge, and docket number; options in a database covering IRS rulings include citation and text. Searches in Westlaw Tax Center let you limit searches by all text, citation, or title.

You can restrict your search by date. Options include unrestricted and last 30, 60, or 90 days, year to date, this year and last year, last three years, and last ten years. Alternatively, you can enter after, before, between, specific, last, and today as date restrictions. Searches in Westlaw Tax include these date options.

e. Search Method Options

Westlaw offers Terms and Connectors, Natural Language, and Template search options. The Natural Language search allows fewer field restrictions than the Terms and Connectors search; it does allow date restrictions. Template searches limit you to the template items: Title of case, Synopsis & Digest, and Terms for a search in a case database.

Westlaw Tax offers Terms and Connectors and Natural Language search options. It also lets you select limitations, such as Code and regulations section cited, jurisdiction, and source being searched. You don't have to enter its search function by way of a particular database.

Illustration 19-8. Search Screen in Westlaw Tax

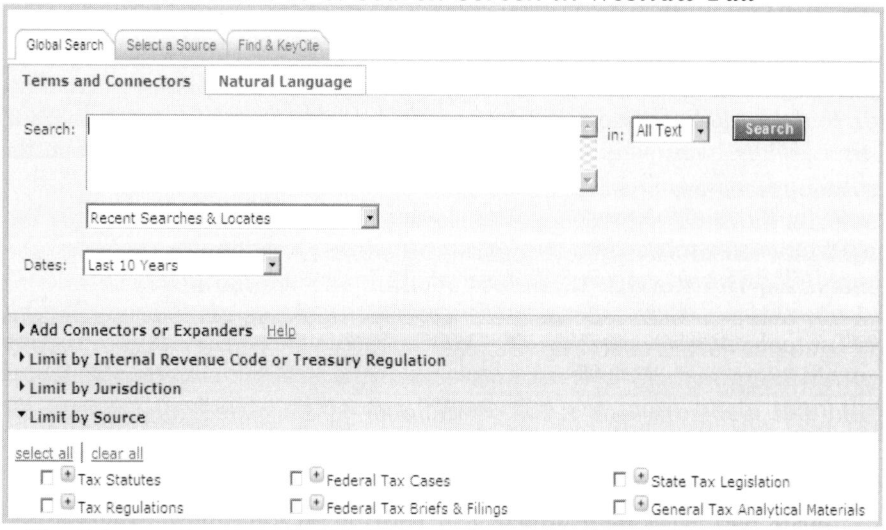

→The Select a Source option lets you select a single database.

f. Citator

Westlaw offers two citators, RIA 2nd Citator and KeyCite; both are discussed in Chapter 12. KeyCite is the default option when you find an item in one of the Westlaw or Westlaw Tax databases. You can also enter citations directly into either citator.

5. HeinOnline

HeinOnline was initially known as a site for finding old law review issues. It has since evolved into a significant source for finding full text of articles, legislative history materials, and other services. Items in this service were scanned from original documents. This feature gives you easy access to correct pagination.

a. Databases

HeinOnline databases relevant to tax research include:

• Law Journal Library

• Code of Federal Regulations (since 1938)

• Federal Register Library (since 1936)

• Taxation & Economic Reform in America: A Historical Archive, 1781–2009 (legislative history compilations and Seidman's and Barton's legislative history tracing materials)

• Treaties and Agreements Library (government and secondary sources)

• United States Code (since 1925)

• U.S. Congressional Documents (Congressional Record since 1873)

• U.S. Federal Agency Documents, Decisions and Appeals (Cumulative Bulletins since 1919; Board of Tax Appeals and Tax Court Reports since 1924)

• U.S. Statutes at Large (since 1789)

• U.S. Supreme Court Library (since 1754)

b. Browsing and Searching Options

HeinOnline lets you browse each database or search it for desired information. The browse option works much like a traditional table of contents. You can browse multiple titles within a database or limit yourself to a single title. When you locate an item that looks promising, you can reach it directly through hyperlinks.

Search options vary by library. In addition to doing a general word or phrase search, you can search many libraries by field, date, and title.

Illustration 19-9. Advanced Search Option
in Cumulative Bulletins

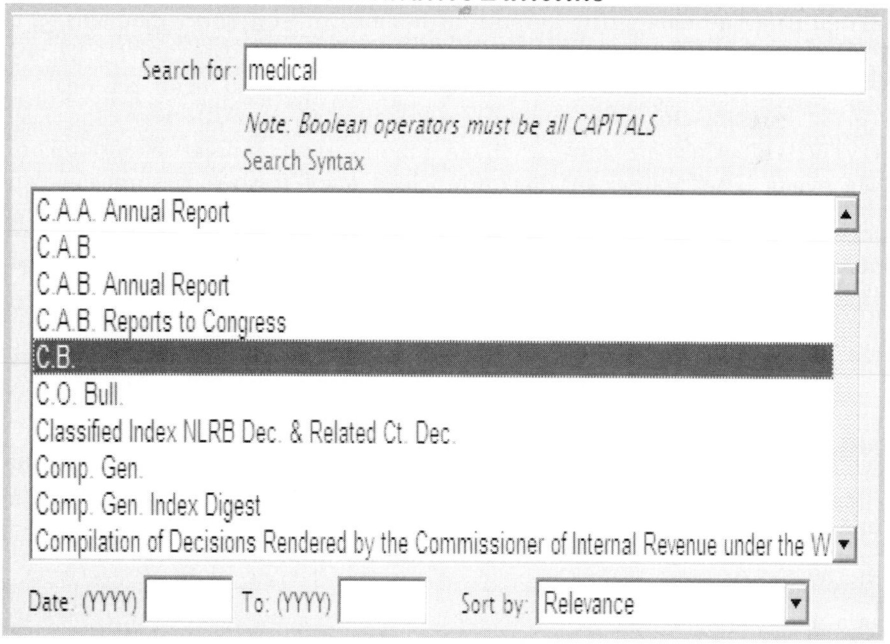

Illustration 19-10. *Results from Search in Cumulative Bulletins*

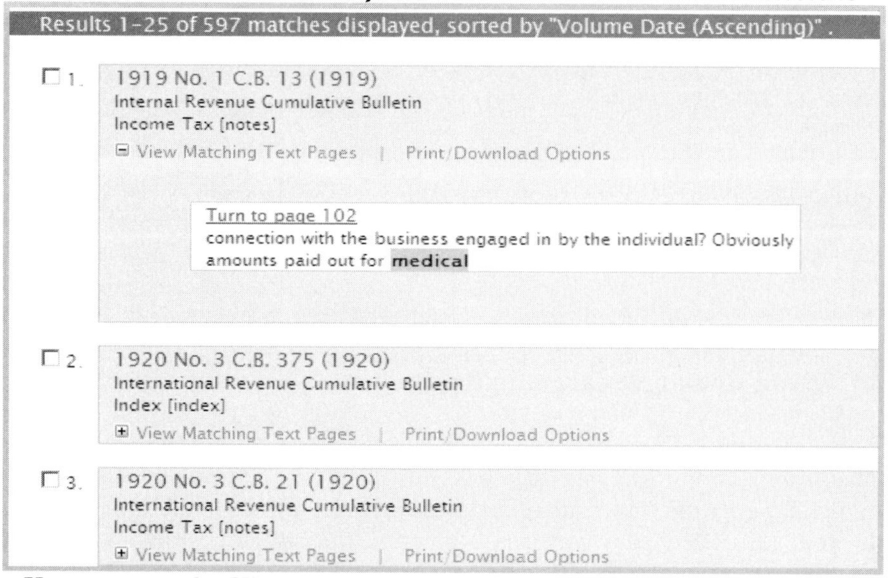

Results 1–25 of 597 matches displayed, sorted by "Volume Date (Ascending)".

☐ 1.   1919 No. 1 C.B. 13 (1919)
        Internal Revenue Cumulative Bulletin
        Income Tax [notes]
        ⊟ View Matching Text Pages | Print/Download Options

        Turn to page 102
        connection with the business engaged in by the individual? Obviously
        amounts paid out for **medical**

☐ 2.   1920 No. 3 C.B. 375 (1920)
        International Revenue Cumulative Bulletin
        Index [index]
        ⊞ View Matching Text Pages | Print/Download Options

☐ 3.   1920 No. 3 C.B. 21 (1920)
        International Revenue Cumulative Bulletin
        Income Tax [notes]
        ⊞ View Matching Text Pages | Print/Download Options

→You can use the View Matching Text Pages option to see your search term in each hit.

Several libraries have a Citation Navigator option. This is similar to the "get a document by citation" option offered in services such as Lexis-Nexis and Westlaw.

Illustration 19-11. *Citation Navigator for Federal Register*

Citation Navigator

Vol.   Page
75 (2010) ▾ Fed. Reg.

☐ open in new tab/window

Get Citation

By Date

Month Day Year
Jan ▾ 1 ▾ 2010 ▾ ☐ open in new
tab/window
Get Citation

c. Connectors and Wildcard Characters

HeinOnline uses several Boolean and proximity connectors:

Table 19-3. HeinOnline Connectors

Term	Meaning
AND; &&	both terms must appear
OR	at least one of the terms must appear
NOT; !	The term following NOT (or !) must not appear
+	the term immediately following the + must appear
−	The term immediately following the − must not appear
[TO]	Find all items within the range before and after TO
{ TO }	Find all items within the range before and after TO except the actual terms listed
" "~N	The words in the quotation marks must be within N words of each other

You can use a question mark (?) as a wildcard symbol for a single character anywhere but at the beginning of the word. You can use an asterisk (*) to expand words by one or more characters anywhere but the beginning of the word. If you place a tilde (~) at the end of a word, HeinOnline will search for words that are spelled similarly to the original word.

d. Citator

HeinOnline does not have an associated citator, but it does let you find and read articles that cite to the article you are reading. [See Illustration 14-18.]

SECTION E. SUBSCRIPTION SERVICES—TAX FOCUS

The services included in this section provide access to a variety of primary and secondary source materials. Discussion in this chapter focuses on two of these services, IntelliConnect and Checkpoint.

1. IntelliConnect

Commerce Clearing House offers a web-based service, IntelliConnect. The materials below discuss using this service.

a. Database Screens and Contents

The opening screen for IntelliConnect is relatively spare as compared to those for LexisNexis, Westlaw, and Checkpoint.

Illustration 19-12. IntelliConnect Home Screen

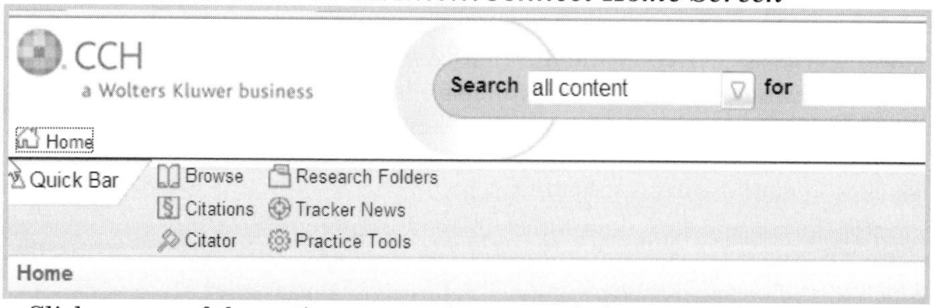

→Click on one of the options to receive more choices.

Illustration 19-13. Browse Screen Sections

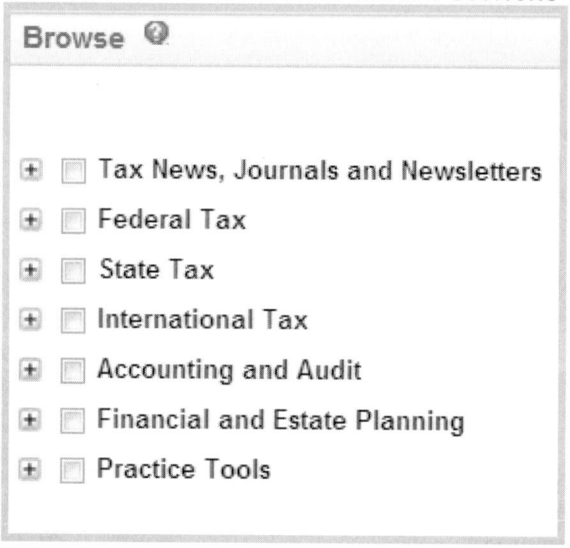

Illustration 19-14. Browse Screen: Tax News

Illustration 19-15.Browse Screen: Federal Tax

→Editorial Content includes Master Tax Guide and Standard Federal Tax Reporter.

→Primary Sources includes the Code, regulations, IRS material, and judicial decisions.

→Tax Legislation includes bills and acts, committee reports, and JCT and CRS reports.

IntelliConnect includes the Code, committee reports, regulations, treaties, IRS materials, and judicial decisions. The service includes Standard Federal Tax Reporter, CCH newsletters and journals, a citator, and various practice aids. It does not have an articles index.

b. Connectors, Wildcard Characters, and Synonyms

IntelliConnect uses several Boolean and proximity connectors:

Table 19-4. IntelliConnect Connectors

Term	Meaning
AND	both terms must appear
OR	either term must appear
NOT	only the first term may appear
w/n	the first term must appear within n words of the second (n cannot exceed 127)
f/n	the first term must follow within n words of the second (n cannot exceed 127)
p/n	the first term must precede the second within n words of the second (n cannot exceed 127)
w/sen	the first term must appear within 20 words of the second
w/par	the first term must appear within 80 words of the second

IntelliConnect lets you use one or more question marks (?) as a wildcard symbol to insert the requisite number of characters. You can use an asterisk (*) to add missing letters anywhere except the beginning of the word. The system will replace a single * with more than one character.

IntelliConnect lets you find synonyms for your search term. You can also use its Thesaurus function in your searches.

c. Date Restrictions

You can restrict your search by date. Options include any day, on, before, after, and from/to.

d. Search Method Options

You can use the Search bar at the top of the IntelliConnect home page or you can click on Search Options to add additional search features. Both methods allow you to select searching in the entire IntelliConnect database ("all content") or in selected files or content. The Search Options tool lets you add limitation based on date and to control the Thesaurus option.

Illustration 19-16. IntelliConnect Search Options Screen

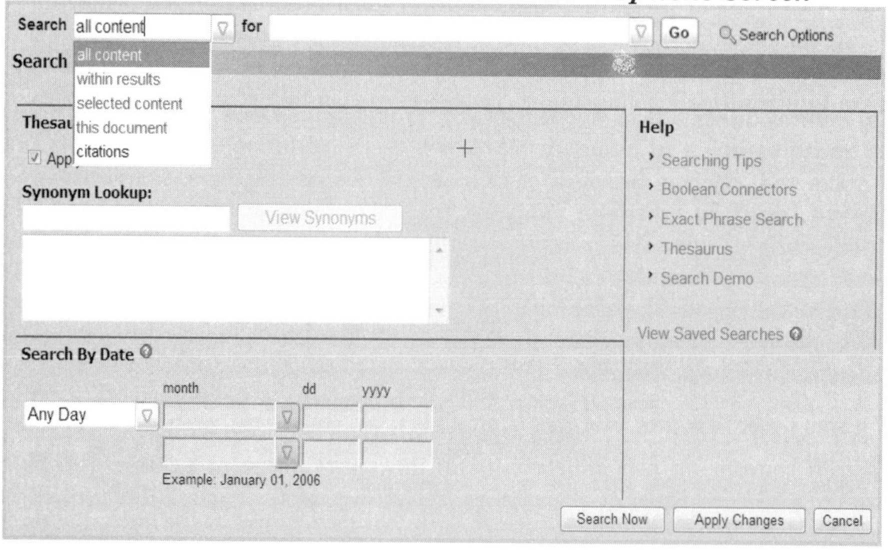

e. Citator

IntelliConnect includes the CCH Citator, which is discussed in Chapter 12. The looseleaf version of this citator is divided into three services, one for each of CCH's Code-based looseleaf services. The online version is not divided in this manner. For example, you can find both income and gift tax cases that cite to a particular tax case with a single search. The online citator does not have an alphabetical (judicial decisions) or numerical (IRS material) browse function. You can use the online citator only if you have a citation or are using the citator after finding a document some other way.

2. Checkpoint

This service was originally named RIA Checkpoint and many users still refer to it by that name. Its content includes several RIA looseleaf services in addition to other material.

a. Database Screens and Contents

Several sections of the Checkpoint Research Screen are relevant. One is the list of available databases, which is excerpted in Illustration 19-17. Discussion and illustrations that appear later in this section cover various search and browse options, including the Table of Contents feature.

Illustration 19-17. Checkpoint Research Screen: Contents

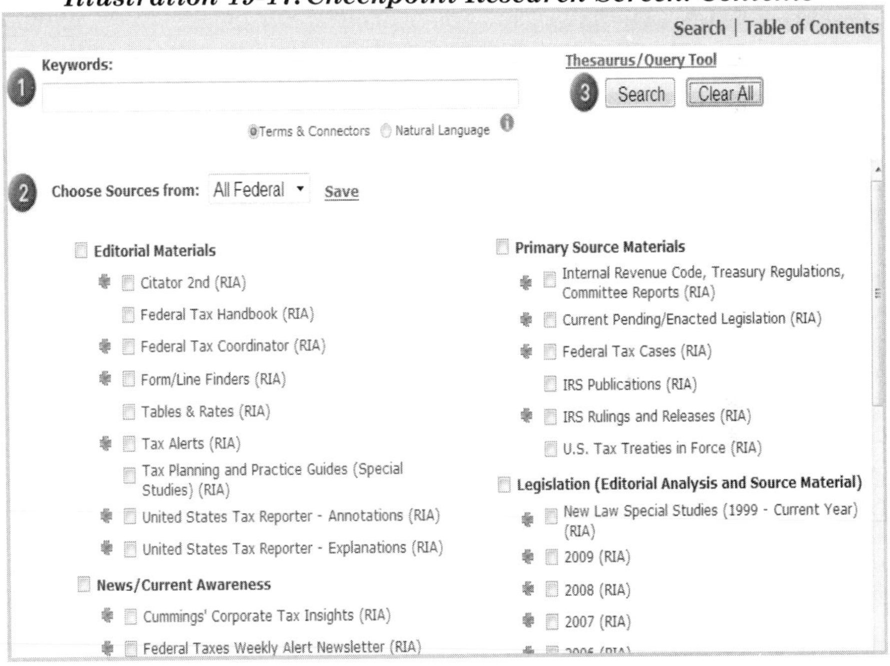

Checkpoint includes the Code, committee reports, regulations, treaties, IRS materials, and judicial decisions. The service includes United States Tax Reporter, Federal Tax Coordinator 2d, newsletters and journals, the RIA citator, and various practice aids.

b. Connectors, Wildcard Characters, and Synonyms

Checkpoint uses several Boolean and proximity connectors:

Table 19-5. Checkpoint Connectors

Term	Meaning
AND; &; space	both terms must appear
OR; |	either term must appear
NOT; ^	only the first term may appear
/#	the first term must appear within # words of the second (# can't exceed 255)
pre/#	the first term must precede the second within # words of the second (# can't exceed 255)
/s	the first term must appear within 20 words of the second
pre/s	the first term must precede the second within 20 words
/p	the first term must appear within 50 words of the second
pre/p	The first term must precede the second within 50 words
" "	terms must appear together in order (exact phrase)

Checkpoint uses an asterisk (*) as a placeholder for one or more characters; a question mark (?) is a placeholder for a single character. A pound sign (#) at the beginning of a word tells the system not to retrieve plural forms. The Thesaurus/Query tool option has a Connectors box; you can select the connectors you want to use in your search.

If you hyphenate a search word (-), Checkpoint retrieves variations that include a hyphen, a space, or neither.[317]

The Thesaurus/Query tool option includes both a Thesaurus and a spell-checker. You can use these to modify your search.

c. Date Restrictions

Checkpoint's date range search has from and to date options for searching in cases and rulings. You can use Terms & Connectors and Natural Language searches using a date restriction. The Thesaurus and Spelling options are also available.

d. Search Method Options

Checkpoint has two search options: Terms & Connectors and Natural Language. You can use the Thesaurus and spell-checking functions in both options. The Natural Language option includes a Restrictions link that lets you require or exclude particular words or phrases from your search; it also includes a Tools link that lets you add quotation marks to indicate an exact phrase within your search.

---

[317] Checkpoint indicates "e-mail" will also retrieve "e mail" and "email."

Before beginning a search, you can specify a practice area (Federal, International, Estate Planning, etc.) or search in "All" areas. You can also choose between Keyword (the default option), Date Range, and Legislation Searches. You can combine a Date Range Search with a Keyword Search if you click Date Range Search instead of Keyword Search. You can use this option to search in cases or rulings databases. The Legislation Search option is subdivided back to year, beginning in 1996, and includes committee reports.

If you already have a citation, you can retrieve the document using the Find by Citation option. "More" offers a list of additional document types for which you can use the Find by Citation option.

Illustration 19-18. Options for Limiting Search

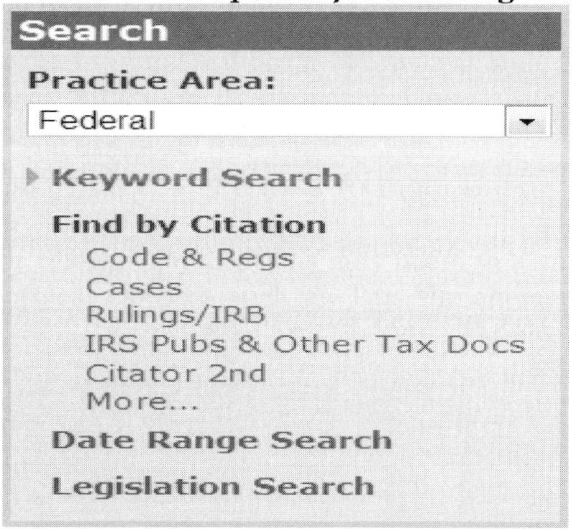

Illustration 19-19. Keyword Search in Federal Tax Coordinator 2d

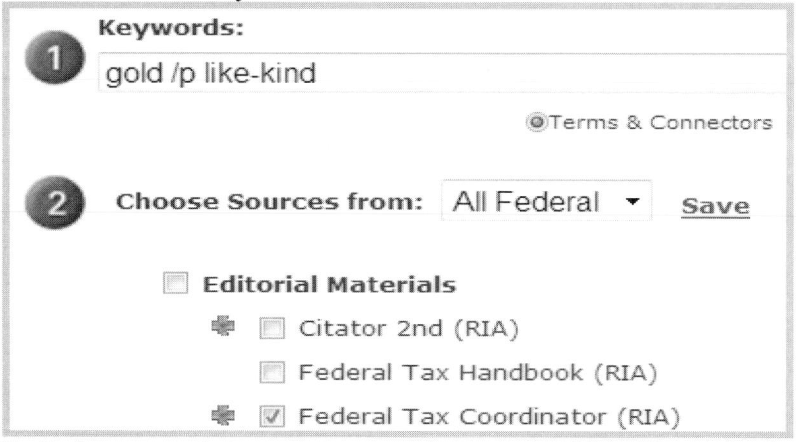

→I limited my search to one source and to terms within 50 words of each other.

Illustration 19-20. Checkpoint Thesaurus Option

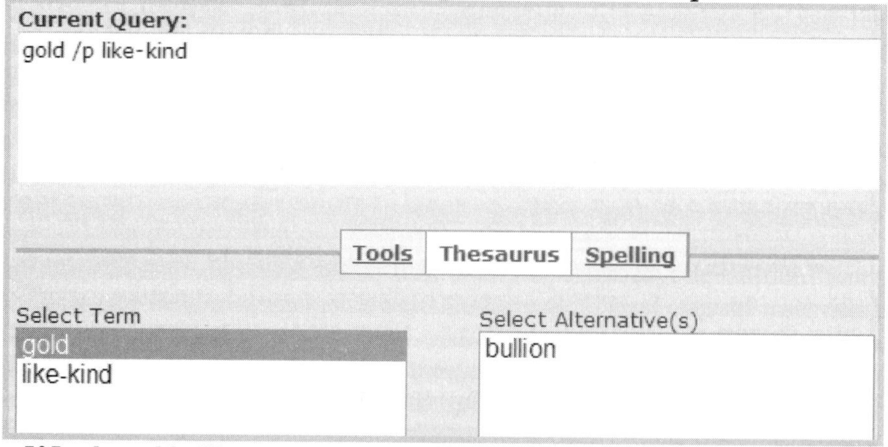

Current Query:

gold /p like-kind

Tools	Thesaurus	Spelling

Select Term

gold
like-kind

Select Alternative(s)

bullion

→If I selected bullion, my search would be displayed as (gold | bullion) /p like-kind. My results would include gold or bullion within 50 words of like-kind.

You can search in the entire database or limit your search to one or more of the sources shown on the opening screen [Illustration 19-17].

Instead of searching for documents by term, you can also browse a source's table of contents. Click on the Table of Contents link at the top right of the opening screen and then select the particular databases you want to browse.

Illustration 19-21. Checkpoint Table of Contents Option

Currently in: **Checkpoint Contents**

- ☐ **Tax News**
- ☐ **Federal Library**
  - ☐ **Tax Legislation**
  - ☐ **Federal Editorial Materials**
    - ☐ **Federal Tax Coordinator 2d**
    - ☐ **United States Tax Reporter**
      - ☐ **Income (USTR)**
      - ☐ **Estate & Gift (USTR)**
      - ☐ **Excise (USTR)**
    - ☐ **Code Arranged Annotations & Explanations (USTR)**

→Click on each successive plus sign until you reach the text you want to read. A printer icon indicates you can print the document.

e. Citator

Checkpoint includes the RIA Citator 2d. It does not include the earlier RIA (and Prentice-Hall) citator service. The Table of Contents option lets you browse the citator by taxpayer name or IRS document number. The RIA citator is discussed in Chapter 12.

3. Other Online Services

Subscribers to Daily Tax Report can access full-text primary source materials in BNA's TaxCore service. BNA also offers web-based versions of its Tax Management Portfolios, Daily Tax Report, and other products.[318]

Tax Analysts provides primary source documents in its web-based Federal Research Library. Tax Analysts also has a web-based Worldwide Tax Treaties service. It includes treaty history documents in addition to the treaty texts.

SECTION F. GOVERNMENT AND OTHER NONSUBSCRIPTION SITES

There are a variety of useful websites available. Some provide primary source material directly; some provide hypertext links to other websites; some perform both functions. Unfortunately, websites often change address or cease to exist altogether. You are likely to find that many of your searches lead you to at least a few nonexistent sites.

This section briefly discusses government and other free sites.

1. Government Sites[319]

This section lists a selected sample of government sites that you might use in conducting tax research. Table 19-6 lists government website illustrations appearing throughout this book.

a. Government Printing Office

GPO Access, which is migrating to FDsys, provides text of, or links to, documents generated by all branches of the federal government. It offers PDF format for many documents, thus allowing you to cite original pagi-

---

[318] The BNA Tax & Accounting Center replaced the BNA Tax Management Library as the web-based platform for the Portfolios.

[319] Online access to government documents is attributable to the Government Printing Office Electronic Information Access Enhancement Act of 1993, Pub. L. No. 103-40, 107 Stat. 112.

nation. It is particularly useful for statutes and legislative history.This site allows limited searching by terms; you do not need an exact citation to find many of the covered documents.

b. Library of Congress THOMAS

Users can find texts of bills, note the progress of bills in Congress, and gain access to the Congressional Record, committee reports, and hearings. You can use THOMAS to find various versions of a bill, trace its history, and read it as a Public Law.

c. Congressional Support Entities

Entities that provide reports and other analysis include Congressional Budget Office, Congressional Research Office, Government Accountability Office, and Joint Committee on Taxation.

d. Treasury Department

The most useful parts of this site are pages for the Office of Tax Policy page, which provides text for recent tax treaties and Treasury testimony at congressional hearings, and for the Office of Tax Analysis, which includes analytical reports on tax policy issues.

e. Internal Revenue Service

The IRS site includes text of tax forms and publications, Internal Revenue Bulletins, the Internal Revenue Manual, IRS releases that are not included in the I.R.B., and income tax treaties. There also links to other primary source materials.

f.White House Home Page

This site provides text of presidential speeches, including bill-signing messages. It also provides links to such support functions as the Office of Management and Budget.

g. Federal Judiciary and Supreme Court Home Pages[320]

The Federal Judiciary site provides links to individual courts. The Opinions page of the Supreme Court site (www.supremecourtus.gov) includes a Case Citation Finder. This service provides the preferred cita-

---

[320] The Federal Judiciary home page (www.uscourts.gov) includes a link to the Supreme Court site. Its Court Locator feature includes web page information for Courts of Appeals, District Courts, and Bankruptcy Courts.

tion, as determined by the Reporter of Decisions, for all Supreme Court decisions scheduled for publication in a bound volume since 1790.

h. United States Tax Court Home Page

This site provides text of Regular, Memorandum, and Summary Opinions. You can search the site by judge, date, taxpayer name, and opinion type. It currently includes Regular and Memorandum decisions since September 25, 1995, and Summary decisions since 2001.

Table 19-6. Illustrations of Government Websites

Source	Illustrations
Congressional Budget Office	7-15
e-CFR	9-8; 9-11
Government Accounta-bility Office	7-16
GPO Access; FDsys	6-19; 7-9; 9-6; 9-18; 9-19
House Ways and Means Committee	7-11
Internal Revenue Service	9-17; 10-1; 10-2; 10-3; 10-6; 10-7; 10-8; 10-9; 10-10; 10-15; 10-16; 10-17; 10-18; 10-19; 10-21; 10-22; 10-23; 10-26; 15-4; 15-5
Joint Committee on Taxation	7-14
Reginfo.gov	9-2; 9-3; 9-4; 9-12; 9-13; 9-14
Regulations.gov	9-26; 9-27; 9-28
Tax Court	3-5; 3-6
THOMAS	6-20; 6-21; 7-1; 7-3; 7-4; 7-5; 7-6; 7-7; 7-8; 7-17

→Table 8-3 lists government websites that include treaty materials.

2. Tax-Oriented Blogs

Several attorneys and academics maintain blogs focusing on taxation. In addition to commentary on current statutes, judicial decisions, or other matters, the blogs include a variety of links to primary sources, to professional and research organizations, and to other blogs. The sites below are a sample of those available.

• A Taxing Matter (http://ataxingmatter.blogs.com/tax/)

• Mauled Again (http://mauledagain.blogspot.com/)

• TaxProf
(http://taxprof.typepad.com/taxprof_blog/about_this_blog/index.html)

3. Other Sites

Chapter 14 includes a partial list of nongovernment entities that prepare reports on a wide array of tax and economic issues. In addition, several law school sites offer text of tax-oriented material, links to sources providing that information, or research guides for finding tax materials in their libraries.

SECTION G. SEARCH ENGINES

Online sites have Uniform Resource Locator (URL) addresses, most of which begin with http://www (or with http:// without www). This book provides URL locations for numerous websites relevant to tax research. Those sites represent only a small portion of what is available online.

Navigating online can be a daunting task if you lack a site's URL or if you don't know if a site exists. Fortunately, you can use search engines and related services to locate information based on key words.

Search engines are unlikely to lead you to as much primary source material as you can locate using the subscription services discussed in Sections D and E. But search engines may find articles and other analysis that aren't in a commercial service's database.

Search engines let you customize your searches to retrieve documents by date, language, type (e.g., PDF or html), or website or domain. Be sure you take advantage of your search engine's capabilities to maximize the chances you will find relevant information.[321]

No matter how you locate your material, remember to determine the last time it was updated. Materials posted to websites may be current, but there is no requirement that they be. Indeed, unlike government or subscription services, there is no guarantee that items posted to a particular website were ever accurate.

Although Google has become an everyday word, it is not the only search engine option. In addition to Google, you may decide to use Alta-Vista, Bing, Yahoo, or another search engine. You will get a better idea of what each can do if you conduct the same search in several search engines.

---

[321] See Thomas R. Keefe, *The Invisible Web: What You Can't See Might Hurt You*, RES. ADVISOR, May 2002, at 1.

Section H. Problems

You can solve many of the problems in earlier chapters using online services. For some of them, online or CD/DVD searches are your only viable option. Those problems lack sufficient identifying information to allow searches using print materials. To practice your online research skills, try the following tasks.

1. Find recently introduced legislation on a topic your instructor selects and follow its history.

2. Track the progress of a regulations project your instructor selects.

3. Find all IRS documents released this year that mention a Code section your instructor selects.

4. Download a presidential tax return.

5. Find articles posted on the web on a topic your instructor selects. Concentrate on websites for law and accounting firms.

6. Using a search engine, search for a phrase of your instructor's choice. First, conduct your search without treating the words as a phrase. Then redo the search using the search engine's advanced search options. What refinements did you need to produce more relevant results?

APPENDIX A. COMMONLY USED ABBREVIATIONS

NOTE: Abbreviations may appear with or without periods, depending on the service you use. The list below presents some items in both formats.

A	Acquiescence
ACI	Appeals Coordinated Issue
Acq.	Acquiescence
AF; AF2d	American Federal Tax Reports
A.F.T.R.; A.F.T.R.2d	American Federal Tax Reports
ALI	American Law Institute
AM	Legal Advice Issued by Associate Chief Counsel
Am. Jur.	American Jurisprudence
Ann.	Announcement
ANPRM	Advance Notice of Proposed Rulemaking
AOD	Action on Decision
APA	Advance Pricing Agreement; Administrative Procedure Act
App.	Appeals
A.R.M.	Committee on Appeals and Review Memorandum
A.R.R.	Committee on Appeals and Review Recommendation
Art.	Article
ASG	Appeals Settlement Guideline
A.T.	Alcohol Tax Unit; Alcohol and Tobacco Tax Division
Bankr.	Bankruptcy
BAP	Bankruptcy Appellate Panel
BATF	Bureau of Alcohol, Tobacco, and Firearms
BNA	Bureau of National Affairs
B.R.	Bankruptcy Reporter
BTA	Board of Tax Appeals
BTC	Treasury Office of Benefits Tax Counsel
Bull.	Bulletin
CA	Court of Appeals
CB; C.B.	Cumulative Bulletin
CBO	Congressional Budget Office
CBS	Collection, Bankruptcy and Summons Bulletin
CC	Chief Counsel
CCA	Chief Counsel Advice or Advisory
CCDM	Chief Counsel Directives Manual
CCH	Commerce Clearing House
CCM	Chief Counsel Memorandum
CCN	Chief Counsel Notice
CEA	Council of Economic Advisers

C.F.R.	Code of Federal Regulations
Ch.	Chapter
CIR	Commissioner of Internal Revenue
Cir.	Circuit; Circular
CIS	Congressional Information Service
CIT	Court of International Trade
C.J.S.	Corpus Juris Secundum
Cl.	Clause
Cl. Ct.	Claims Court Reporter
CLI	Current Law Index
C.L.T.	Child-Labor Tax Division
CO	IRS Corporate Division
Comm.	Commissioner; Commission; Committee
Comm'r	Commissioner
Comp.	Compilation; Compliance
Con.	Concurrent
Conf.	Conference
Cong.	Congress
Cong. Rec.	Congressional Record
Const.	Constitution
CPE	Continuing Professional Education
CRS	Congressional Research Service
C.S.T.	Capital-Stock Tax Division
C.T.	Carriers Taxing Act of 1937; Taxes on Employment by Carriers
Ct.	Court
CTB	Criminal Tax Bulletin
Ct. Cl.	Court of Claims
Ct. D.	Court Decision
Cum. Bull.	Cumulative Bulletin
D.	Decision; District
D.C.	Treasury Department Circular
Dec.	Decision
Del. Order	Delegation Order
Deleg. Order	Delegation Order
Dept. Cir.	Treasury Department Circular
Dist.	District
Dkt.	Docket
DLB	Disclosure Litigation Bulletin
D.O.	Delegation Order
Doc.	Document
E.A.S.	Executive Agreement Series
EE	IRS Employee Plans and Exempt Organization Division
Em. T.	Employment Taxes
E.O.	Executive Orders

EO	Exempt Organizations
E.P.C.	Excess Profits Tax Council Ruling or Memorandum
E.T.	Estate and Gift Tax Division or Ruling
Ex.	Executive
Exec. Order	Executive Order
FAA	Legal Advice Issued by Field Attorneys
F.; F.2d; F.3d	Federal Reporter
Fed.	Federal; Federal Reporter
Fed. Appx.	Federal Appendix
Fed. Cl.	Court of Federal Claims
Fed. Reg.	Federal Register
Fed. Supp.; Fed. Supp. 2d	Federal Supplement
FI	IRS Financial Institutions and Products Division
FOIA	Freedom of Information Act
FR	Federal Register
FSA	Field Service Advice; Field Service Advisory
F. Supp.; F. Supp.2d	Federal Supplement
FTC; FTC2d	Federal Tax Coordinator
GAO	General Accounting Office; Government Accountability Office
GATT	General Agreement on Tariffs and Trade
GCM	General Counsel Memorandum
G.C.M.	Chief Counsel's Memorandum; General Counsel's
Memorandum;	Assistant General Counsel's Memorandum
Gen. Couns. Mem.	General Counsel Memorandum
GL	IRS General Litigation Division
GPO	Government Printing Office
GSA	General Services Administration
H	House of Representatives
H.R.	House of Representatives
HRG	Hearing
IA	IRS Income Tax and Accounting Division
ICM	IRS Compliance Officer Memorandum
IIL	IRS Information Letter
IL	IRS International Division
ILM	IRS Legal Memoranda
ILP	Index to Legal Periodicals
INTL	IRS International Division
Int'l	International
IR	Information Release
IRB	Internal Revenue Bulletin
IRC	Internal Revenue Code
IRM	Internal Revenue Manual

IR-Mim.	Published Internal Revenue Mimeograph
IRS	Internal Revenue Service
ISP	Industry Specialization Program
I.T.	Income Tax Unit or Division
ITA	IRS Technical Assistance
ITC	Treasury Office of International Tax Counsel
JEC	Joint Economic Committee
JCT	Joint Committee on Taxation
Jt.	Joint
KC	KeyCite
L.	Law; Legal; Letter
L. Ed.	United States Supreme Court Reports, Lawyers' Edition
LGM	Litigation Guideline Memorandum
L.M.	Legal Memorandum
LMSB	IRS Large & Mid-Size Business Operating Division
L.O.	Solicitor's Law Opinion
LR; L & R	IRS Legislation and Regulations Division
LRI	Legal Resource Index
LSA	C.F.R. List of Sections Affected
LTR	Private Letter Ruling
Ltr. Rul.	Private Letter Ruling
M.A.	Miscellaneous Announcements
Mem.	Memorandum
Memo.	Memorandum
Mim.	Mimeographed Letter; Mimeograph
MS.	Miscellaneous Unit or Division or Branch
MSSP	Market Segment Specialization Paper
M.S.U.	Market Segment Understanding
M.T.	Miscellaneous Division or Branch
NA	Nonacquiescence
NARA	National Archives and Records Administration
NEC	National Economic Council
Nonacq.	Nonacquiescence
NPRM	Notice of Proposed Rulemaking
NSAR	Non Docketed Service Advice Review
NTA	IRS National Taxpayer Advocate
O.	Solicitor's Law Opinion
O.D.	Office Decision
OECD	Organisation for Economic Co-operation and Development
Off. Mem.	Office Memorandum
OMB	Office of Management and Budget
Op.	Opinion
Op. A.G.	Opinion of Attorney General

OTA	Treasury Office of Tax Analysis
OTP	Treasury Office of Tax Policy
Para.	Paragraph
PERAB	President's Economic Recovery Advisory Board
PH; P-H	Prentice-Hall
PLR	Private Letter Ruling
PMTA	Program Manager Technical Assistance
Priv. Ltr. Rul.	Private Letter Ruling
Prop.	Proposed
PS	IRS Passthroughs and Special Industries Division
P.T.	Processing Tax Decision or Division
Pt.	Part
P.T.E.	Prohibited Transaction Exemption
PTO	United States Patent and Trademark Office
Pub.	Public; Published
Rec.	Record
Reg.	Register; Registration; Regular; Regulation
Rep.	Report; Reports; Representatives; Reporter
Res.	Resolution
Rev. Proc.	Revenue Procedure
Rev. Rul.	Revenue Ruling
RIA	Research Institute of America
RIN	Regulation Identifier Number
RISC	Regulatory Information Service Center
RP	Revenue Procedure
RR	Revenue Ruling
S.	Senate; Solicitor's Memorandum
SAM	Strategic Advice Memorandum
SB/SE	IRS Small Business/Self-Employed Operating Division
SCA	Service Center Advice
S. Ct.	Supreme Court
Sec.	Section
Sess.	Session
SFTR	Standard Federal Tax Reporter
Sil.	Silver Tax Division
S.M.	Solicitor's Memorandum
Sol. Op.	Solicitor's Opinion
S.P.R.	Statement of Procedural Rules
S.R.	Solicitor's Recommendation
S.S.T.	Social Security Tax and Carriers' Tax; Social Security Tax; Taxes on Employment by Other than Carriers
S.T.	Sales Tax Unit or Division or Branch
Stat.	United States Statutes at Large
T.	Temporary; Tobacco Division; Treaty

TAM	Technical Advice Memorandum
TAS	IRS Taxpayer Advocate Service
T.B.M.	Advisory Tax Board Memorandum
T.B.R.	Advisory Tax Board Recommendation
T.C.	Tax Court Reports
TCM	Tax Court Memorandum Opinion
TC Memo	Tax Court Memorandum Opinion
T. Ct.	Tax Court
T.D.	Treasury Decision
TEAM	Technical Expedited Advice Memorandum
TECH	Assistant Commissioner, Technical
Tech. Adv. Mem.	Technical Advice Memorandum
Tech. Info. Rel.	Technical Information Release
Tech. Mem.	Technical Memorandum
TE/GE	IRS Tax Exempt/Government Entities Operating Division
Temp.	Temporary
T.I.A.S.	Treaties and International Acts Series
TIF	Treaties in Force
TIGTA	Treasury Inspector General for Tax Administration
T.I.R.	Technical Information Release
TLB	Tax Litigation Bulletin
TLC	Treasury Office of Tax Legislative Counsel
TM	Technical Memorandum
Tob.	Tobacco Branch
TRAC	Tip Reporting Alternative Commitment
Treas.	Treasury Department
Treas. Dep't Order	Treasury Department Order
Treas. Reg.	Treasury Regulation
T.S.	Treaty Series
UIL	Uniform Issue List
UN	United Nations
UNTS	United Nations Treaty Series
U.S.	United States Reports
U.S.C.	United States Code
U.S.C.A.	United States Code Annotated
USCCAN	United States Code Congressional & Administrative News
U.S.C.S.	United States Code Service
USPTO	United States Patent and Trademark Office
U.S.T.	United States Treaties and Other International Agreements
U.S. Tax Cas.	U.S. Tax Cases
USTC	U.S. Tax Cases

USTR	United States Tax Reporter;
	United States Trade Representative
UTC	U.S. Tax Cases
WG & L	Warren Gorham & Lamont
W & I	IRS Wage and Investment Operating Division
WL	Westlaw
WTO	World Trade Organization

APPENDIX B. ALTERNATE CITATION FORMS

This appendix does not cover all possible citation forms. It reflects formats I found in citation manuals and in several tax-oriented periodicals. Chapter 10 provides several abbreviation formats for IRS items.
Sources Used

> ALWD Citation Manual (3d ed. 2006)
> The Bluebook: A Uniform System of Citation (18th ed. 2005)
> TaxCite (1995 edition)
> Various periodical articles

1. Citations for Internal Revenue Code section 61
   I.R.C. § 61 (year of U.S.C.)
   I.R.C. § 61
   Section 61
   Code Sec. 61

2. Citations for Treasury Regulation section 1.61-1
   Treas. Reg. § 1.61-1 (promulgation/amendment year)
   Reg. § 1.61-1 (promulgation/amendment year)
   Reg. § 1.61-1
   Reg. §1.61-1
   Reg. section 1.61-1
   Teas. reg. section 1.61-1
   Treasury reg. section 1.61-1
   Reg. 1.61-1

3. Citations for Temporary Treasury Regulation section 1.71-1T
   Temp. Treas. Reg. § 1.71-1T (promulgation/amendment year)
   Temp. Reg. § 1.71-1T (promulgation/amendment year)
   Temp. Reg. § 1.71-1T
   Temporary Reg. §1.71-1T
   Treas. reg. section 1.71-1T
   Temp. Reg. 1.71-1T

4. Citations for Cumulative Bulletin
   C.B.
   CB

5. Citations for Private Letter Ruling 199929039
   Priv. Ltr. Rul. 1999-29-039 (Apr. 12, 1999)
   P.L.R. 1999-29-039 (Apr. 12, 1999)
   LTR 199929039 (Apr. 12, 1999)
   Ltr. Rul. 199929039
   PLR 199929039

APPENDIX C. POTENTIAL RESEARCH ERRORS

Statements in this section reflect comments made elsewhere in this book.

Don't assume that a library lacks a source because it is not available in its general print collection or online. Check the CD/DVD, microform, and government documents collections.

Check a service's coverage dates before you begin your research. An electronic service may omit a source's initial years. A print service may not have been updated recently enough to catch a very recent item.

Before using a service, determine how it treats revoked items. Some services delete these items; others include them but indicate they have been revoked.

If you check research results in a second publication, try to select a source from a different publishing group. Although corporate parents offer several imprints (Appendix E), there is no guarantee they will always use separate editors.

If you find a Code section on point, don't forget to check effective dates and special rules that may not be codified.

Never assume a definition in one section of the Code or regulations applies to all other sections.

Don't ignore potentially related Code provisions merely because they don't refer to each other.

Don't confuse an act section number with a Code section number.

Don't assume every relevant provision is actually codified.

Don't assume section numbers in a bill remain unchanged through the enactment process.

Don't confuse enactment date, effective date, and sunset date for statutes (or the comparable date limitations for treaties and regulations).

If you use cross-reference tables to trace a statute's history, remember that these tables may not reflect changes in a section's numbering.

Don't forget to compare the issue date of regulations and the decision date for cases against the revision date for relevant statutory amendments. Otherwise you risk citing sources whose authority has been weakened or overruled altogether. Online citators may indicate this information.

Remember to use the designation required by the source you are searching. For example, don't insert hyphens in IRS documents when searching online unless the service allows hyphens; remember that Tax Analysts frequently gives its own names to Chief Counsel advice documents.

Don't forget to check for pending items (legislation, regulations, appeals from judicial decisions) that may be relevant to your project.

Don't overestimate the degree of deference a court will accord legislative history and Treasury or IRS documents.

Don't assume the government conceded an issue merely because it didn't appeal after losing a case. Check to see if there is an AOD or other announcement regarding the case.

If you find a notice of acquiescence or nonacquiescence, check to make sure the IRS didn't reverse itself in a later AOD or Internal Revenue Bulletin.

When searching for cases using the taxpayer's name, remember that early cases are not captioned Taxpayer v. Commissioner or Taxpayer v. United States. Eisner and Helvering are government officials, not taxpayers. Likewise, remember that different services use different caption formats for bankruptcy cases.

Remember that U.S.T.C. is an abbreviation for U.S. Tax Cases; that case reporter service does not include United States Tax Court cases.

Don't confuse page and paragraph numbers. Make sure you know if a service cross-references by page, by paragraph, or by section number. Make sure you know whether new material is located in the same volume or a different volume (and where in the relevant volume it appears). Although online services avoid this problem, you must still use the appropriate format in any memorandum or brief you prepare.

Don't rely on a service's editor for a holding. Read the document yourself.

Remember that Index to Legal Periodicals only recently began indexing short articles.

Don't overlook free government websites, particularly if you need
access to a document and already have a citation.

When using electronic materials (CD/DVD or online), make sure you
understand the particular service's Boolean search rules and rules for
limiting searches to a particular range of dates. From date 1 to date 2 is
not the same as after date 1 and before date 2.

Make sure that s means sentence (and p means paragraph) in an electronic service. Some services define sentence and paragraph by a maximum number of words rather than by grammatical rules.

If a URL no longer yields the desired website, assume the site changed
its URL but still exists. Try using your service provider's search function
(or a search engine) to search for the new URL.

APPENDIX D. BIBLIOGRAPHY

CHAPTER 1. OVERVIEW

Steven M. Barkan, Roy M. Mersky & Donald J. Dunn, FUNDAMENTALS OF LEGAL RESEARCH (9th ed. 2009).

Katherine T. Pratt, *Federal Tax Sources Recommended for Law School Libraries*, 87 LAW LIBR. J. 387 (1995).

CHAPTER 2. SOURCES OF LAW

Michael L. Cook & Corby Brooks, *Determining Whether Substantial Authority Exists in Facts and Circumstances Cases*, J. TAX'N, Sept. 2009, at 173.

Franklin L. Green, *Exercising Judgment in the Wonderland Gymnasium*, TAX NOTES, Mar. 19, 2001, at 1691.

Kip Dellinger, *The Substantial Understatement, Negligence and Tax-Return Preparers' Penalties—An Overview*, TAXES, Nov. 1999, at 41.

OFFICE OF TAX POLICY, DEPARTMENT OF THE TREASURY, REPORT TO THE CONGRESS ON PENALTY AND INTEREST PROVISIONS OF THE INTERNAL REVENUE CODE (1999).

Shop Talk, *IRS FSA Gives Guidance on Substantial Authority in Penalty Situation*, 91 J. TAX'N 61 (1999).

STAFF OF THE JOINT COMMITTEE ON TAXATION, STUDY OF PRESENT-LAW PENALTY AND INTEREST PROVISIONS AS REQUIRED BY SECTION 3801 OF THE INTERNAL REVENUE SERVICE RESTRUCTURING AND REFORM ACT OF 1998 (INCLUDING PROVISIONS RELATING TO CORPORATE TAX SHELTERS), JCS 3-99 (106th Cong., 1st Sess.) (Jt. Comm. Print 1999).

George R. Goodman, *Tax Return Compliance*, TAX NOTES, Sept. 1, 1997, at 1201.

Shop Talk, *Courts Disagree on Substantial Authority*, 82 J. TAX'N 380 (1995).

CHAPTER 3. RESEARCH PROCESS

Heidi W. Heller, *The Twenty-First Century Law Library: A Law Firm Librarian's Thoughts,* 101 LAW LIBR. J. 517 (2009)

Patrick Meyer, *Law Firm Legal Research Requirements for New Attorneys*, 101 LAW LIBR. J. 297 (2009).

Jasper L. Cummings, Jr., *Legal Research in Federal Taxation*, TAX NOTES, Oct. 17, 2005, at 335.

Michelle M. Wu, *Why Print and Electronic Resources Are Essential to the Academic Law Library*, 97 LAW LIBR. J. 233 (2005).

John A. Barrick, *The Effect of Code Section Knowledge on Tax Research Performance*, J. AM. TAX. ASS'N, Fall 2001, at 20.

Gitelle Seer, *10 Things You Hate to Hear: Tips from Your Librarian*, LAW PRAC. Q., Aug. 2001, at 20.

CHAPTER 5. CONSTITUTION

Michael W. Evans, *'A Source of Frequent and Obstinate Altercations': The History and Application of the Origination Clause*, TAX NOTES, Nov. 29, 2004, at 1215.

Calvin H. Johnson, *Purging Out Pollock: The Constitutionality of Federal Wealth or Sales Taxes*, TAX NOTES, Dec. 30, 2002, at 1723.

Erik M. Jensen, *The Taxing Power, The Sixteenth Amendment, and the Meaning of Incomes*, TAX NOTES, Oct. 7, 2002, at 99.

Bruce Ackerman, *Taxation and the Constitution*, 99 COLUM. L. REV. 1 (1999).

Boris I. Bittker & Lawrence Lokken, FEDERAL TAXATION OF INCOME, ESTATES AND GIFTS ch. 1 (3d ed. 1999 & Cum. Supp.).

Calvin H. Johnson, *The Constitutional Meaning of 'Apportionment of Direct Taxes,'* TAX NOTES, Aug. 3, 1998, at 591.

Erik M. Jensen, *The Apportionment of "Direct Taxes": Are Consumption Taxes Constitutional?*, 97 COLUM. L. REV. 2334 (1997).

John O. McGinnis & Michael B. Rappaport, *The Rights of Legislators and the Wrongs of Interpretation: A Further Defense of the Constitutionality of Legislative Supermajority Rules*, 47 DUKE L.J. 327 (1997).

Richard Belas, *The Post-Carlton World: Just When Is a Retroactive Tax Unconstitutional?*, TAX NOTES, Oct. 30, 1995, at 633.

CHAPTER 6. STATUTES

Mary Whisner, The *United States Code, Prima Facie Evidence, and Positive Law*, 101 L. LIBR. J. 545 (2009).

David F. Shores, *Textualism and Intentionalism in Tax Litigation*, 61 TAX LAW. 53 (2007)

Christopher H. Hanna, *The Magic in the Tax Legislative Process*, 59 SMU L. REV. 649 (2006).

William D. Popkin, STATUTES IN COURT: THE HISTORY AND THEORY OF STATUTORY INTERPRETATION (1999).

John F. Coverdale, *Text as Limit: A Plea for a Decent Respect for the Tax Code*, 71 TUL. L. REV. 1501 (1997).

Edward A. Zelinsky, *Text, Purpose, Capacity and Albertson's: A Response to Professor Geier*, 2 FLA. TAX REV. 717 (1996).

Jasper L. Cummings, Jr., *Statutory Interpretation and Albertson's*, TAX NOTES, Jan. 23, 1995, at 559.

Myron Grauer, *A Case for Congressional Facilitation of a Collaborative Model of Statutory Interpretation in the Tax Area: Lessons to be Learned from the Corn Products and Arkansas Best Cases and the Historical Development of the Statutory Definition of "Capital Asset(s),"* 84 KY. L.J. 1 (1995).

Deborah A. Geier, *Commentary: Textualism and Tax Cases*, 66 TEMP. L. REV. 445 (1993).

CHAPTER 7. LEGISLATIVE HISTORIES

See also separate section on deference following Chapter 11.

Tax History Project (http://www.taxhistory.org) (Tax Analysts website for historical research, including such documents as policy papers from presidential libraries, posters, presidential tax returns, The Federalist Papers, and a "Tax History Museum").

Michael W. Evans, *The New Rules for Limited Tax Benefits in Tax Legislation*, TAX NOTES, May 12, 2008, at 597.

Marc J. Gerson, *Technically Speaking: The Art of Tax Technical Corrections*, TAX NOTES, Mar. 5, 2007, at 927

Michael Livingston, *What's Blue and White and Not Quite As Good As a Committee Report: General Explanations and the Role of "Subsequent" Tax Legislative History*, 11 AM J. TAX POL'Y 91 (1994).

CHAPTER 8. TREATIES

Edward K. Dennehy & Stephen E Ehrlich, *Tax Treaty Interpretation and Conflicts with U.S. Federal Law*, TAX NOTES, Mar. 2, 2009, at 1101.

Richard L. Reinhold & Catherine A. Harrington, *What NatWest Tells Us About Tax Treaty Interpretation*, TAX NOTES, Apr. 14, 2008, at 169.

William P. Streng, *U.S. Tax Treaties: Trends, Issues, & Policies in 2006 and Beyond*, 59 SMU L. REV. 853 (2006)

Anthony C. Infanti, *The Proposed Domestic Reverse Hybrid Entity Regulations: Can the Treasury Department Override Treaties?*, 30 TAX MGMT. INT'L J. 307 (2001).

John A. Townsend, *Tax Treaty Interpretation*, 55 TAX LAW. 221 (2001).

John F. Avery Jones, *The David R. Tillinghast Lecture: Are Tax Treaties Necessary?*, 53 TAX L. REV. 1 (1999).

Philip F. Postlewaite & David S. Makarski, *The A.L.I. Tax Treaty Study—A Critique and a Proposal*, 49 TAX LAW. 731 (1999).

Ernest R. Larkins, *U.S. Income Tax Treaties in Research and Planning: A Primer*, 18 VA. TAX REV. 133 (1998).

Robert Thornton Smith, *Tax Treaty Interpretation by the Judiciary*, 49 TAX LAW. 845 (1996).

CHAPTER 9. REGULATIONS

See also separate section on deference following Chapter 11.

Kristin E. Hickman, *Coloring Outside the Lines: Examining Treasury's (Lack of) Compliance with Administrative Procedure Act Rulemaking Requirements*, 82 NOTRE DAME L. REV. 1727 (2007).

Philip Gall, *Phantom Regulations: The Curse of Spurned Delegation*, 56 TAX LAW. 413 (2003).

Naftali Z. Dembitzer, *Beyond the IRS Restructuring and Reform Act of 1998: Perceived Abuses of the Treasury Department's Rulemaking Authority*, 52 TAX LAW. 501 (1999).

CHAPTER 10. INTERNAL REVENUE SERVICE DOCUMENTS

See also separate section on deference following Chapter 11.

Mitchell Rogovin & Donald L. Korb, *The Four R's Revisited: Regulations, Rulings, Reliance and Retroactivity in the 21st Century: A View from Within*, TAXES, Aug. 2009, at 21.

Jasper L. Cummings, Jr., *Chief Counsel Legal Advice: Questions and Answers*, TAX NOTES, Mar. 8, 2004, at 1291.

Marion Marshall, Sheryl Stratton & Christopher Bergin, *The Changing Landscape of IRS Guidance: A Downward Slope*, TAX NOTES, Jan. 29, 2001, at 673.

Inventory of IRS Guidance Documents—A Draft, TAX NOTES, July 17, 2000, at 305.

CHAPTER 11. JUDICIAL REPORTS

See also separate section on deference following Chapter 11.

Thomas D. Greenaway, *Choice of Forum in Federal Civil Tax Litigation*, 62 TAX LAW. 311 (2009).

James Bamberg, *A Different Point of Venue: The Plainer Meaning of Section 7482(b)(1)*, 61 TAX LAW. 445 (2008).

Daniel M. Schneider, *Assessing and Predicting Who Wins Federal Tax Trial Decisions*, 37 WAKE FOREST L. REV. 473 (2002).

Mark P. Altieri, Jerome E. Apple, Penny Marquette & Charles K. Moore, *Political Affiliation of Appointing President and Outcome of Tax Court Cases*, 84 JUDICATURE 310 (May/June 2001).

Cornish F. Hitchcock, *Public Access to Special Trial Judge Reports*, TAX NOTES, Oct. 15, 2001, at 403.

Robert A. Mead, *"Unpublished" Opinions as the Bulk of the Iceberg: Publication Patterns in the Eighth and Tenth Circuit United States Courts of Appeals*, 93 LAW LIBR. J. 589 (2001).

Daniel M. Schneider, *Empirical Research on Judicial Reasoning: Statutory Interpretation in Federal Tax Cases*, 31 N.M. L. REV. 325 (2001).

Kirk J. Stark, *The Unfulfilled Tax Legacy of Justice Robert H. Jackson*, 54 TAX L. REV. 171 (2001).

Paul E. Treusch, *What to Consider in Choosing a Forum to Resolve an Ordinary Tax Dispute*, 55 TAX LAW. 83 (2001).

James Edward Maule, *Instant Replay, Weak Teams, and Disputed Calls: An Empirical Study of Alleged Tax Court Bias*, 66 TENN. L. REV. 351 (1999).

Mark F. Sommer & Anne D. Waters, *Tax Court Memorandum Opinions—What Are They Worth?*, TAX NOTES, July 20, 1998, at 384.

CHAPTERS 7–11. DEFERENCE

Kristin E. Hickman, *IRB Guidance: The No Man's Land of Tax Code Interpretation*, 2009 MICH. ST. L. REV. 239.

Mark E. Berg, *Judicial Deference to Tax Regulations: A Reconsideration in Light of National Cable, Swallows Holding, and Other Developments*, 61 TAX LAW. 481 (2008).

Voris Blankenship, *Determining the Validity of Tax Regulations—Uncertainties Persist*, J. TAX'N, Oct. 2007, at 205.

Irving Salem, *Supreme Court Should Clarify Its Deference Standard*, TAX NOTES, Sept. 18, 2006, at 1063.

Andre L. Smith, *Deferential Review of Tax Court Decisions of Law: Promoting Expertise, Uniformity, and Impartiality*, 58 TAX LAW. 361 (2005).

Gregg D. Polsky, *Can Treasury Overrule the Supreme Court?*, 84 B.U. L. REV. 185 (2004).

Peter A. Lowy & Juan F. Vasquez, Jr., *How Revenue Rulings Are Made and the Implications of That Process for Judicial Deference*, J. TAX'N, Oct. 2004, at 230.

ABA Section of Taxation, *Report of the Task Force on Deference*, TAX NOTES, Sept. 13, 2004, at 1231 (reprinted from 57 TAX LAW. 717 (2004)).

Mitchell M. Gans, *Deference and the End of Tax Practice*, 36 REAL PROP., PROB. & TR. J. 731 (2002).

Edward J. Schnee & W. Eugene Seago, *Deference Issues in the Tax Law: Mead Clarifies the Chevron Rule—Or Does It?*, 96 J. TAX'N 366 (2002).

David F. Shores, *Deferential Review of Tax Court Decisions: Taking Institutional Choice Seriously*, 55 TAX LAW. 667 (2002).

Irving Salem & Richard Bress, *Agency Deference Under the Judicial Microscope of the Supreme Court*, TAX NOTES, Sept. 4, 2000, at 1257.

David F. Shores, *Rethinking Deferential Review of Tax Court Decisions*, 53 TAX LAW. 35 (1999).

Benjamin J. Cohen & Catherine A. Harrington, *Is the Internal Revenue Service Bound by Its Own Regulations and Rulings?*, 51 TAX LAW. 675 (1998).

Steve R. Johnson, *The Phoenix and the Perils of the Second Best: Why Heightened Appellate Deference to Tax Court Decisions Is Undesirable*, 77 OR. L. REV. 235 (1998).

David A. Brennen, Treasury Regulations and Judicial Deference in the Post-Chevron Era, 13 GA. ST. U. L. REV. 387 (1997).

Ellen P. Aprill, Muffled Chevron: Judicial Review of Tax Regulations, 3 FLA. TAX REV. 51 (1996).

Paul L. Caron, *Tax Myopia Meets Tax Hyperopia: The Unproven Case of Increased Judicial Deference to Revenue Rulings*, 57 OHIO ST. L.J. 637 (1996).

Beverly I. Moran & Daniel M. Schneider, *The Elephant and the Four Blind Men: The Burger Court and Its Federal Tax Decisions*, 39 HOW. L.J. 841 (1996).

John F. Coverdale, *Court Review of Tax Regulations and Revenue Rulings in the Chevron Era*, 64 GEO. WASH. L. REV. 35 (1995).

Linda Galler, *Judicial Deference to Revenue Rulings: Reconciling Divergent Standards*, 56 OHIO ST. L.J. 1037 (1995).

Paul L. Caron, *Tax Myopia, or Mamas Don't Let Your Babies Grow Up to be Tax Lawyers*, 13 VA. TAX REV. 517 (1994).

CHAPTER 14. LEGAL PERIODICALS AND NONGOVERNMENTAL REPORTS

Mary Rumsey, *Runaway Train: Problems of Permanence, Accessibility, and Stability in the Use of Web Sources in Law Review Citations*, 94 LAW LIBR. J. 27 (2002).

Richard A. Danner, Electronic Publication of Legal Scholarship: New Issues and New Models, 52 J. LEGAL EDUC. 347 (2002).

William J. Turnier, Tax (and Lots of Other) Scholars Need Not Apply: The Changing Venue for Scholarship, 50 J. LEGAL EDUC. 189 (2000).

CHAPTER 19. ONLINE LEGAL RESEARCH

Peggy Garvin, *Congressional Documents on FDsys: Advanced Techniques*, at http://www.llrx.com/columns/govdomain44.htm (Jan. 23, 2010).

David Tsai & Courtney Minick, *Google Scholar: A New Way to Search for Cases and Related Legal Publications*,
at http://www.llrx.com/features/googlescholar.htm (Dec. 30, 2009).

Marcus Zillman, *Deep Web Research 2010*,
at http://www.llrx.com/features/deepweb2010.htm (Dec. 13, 2009).

Peggy Garvin, *Congressional Documents on FDsys: the Basics*, at http://www.llrx.com/columns/govdomain41.htm (July 27, 2009).

Katherine Pratt, Jennifer Kowal & Daniel Martin, *The Virtual Tax Library: A Comparison of Five Electronic Research Platforms*, 8 FLA. TAX REV. 935 (2008).

Lisa Smith-Butler, *Cost-Effective Legal Research Redux: How to Avoid Becoming the Accidental Tourist, Lost in Cyberspace*, 9 FL. COASTAL L. REV. 293 (2008).

Gary W. White, *Internet Resources for Taxation: A Selective, Annotated Guide*, LEGAL REFERENCE SERVICES Q., vol. 18(4), at 49 (2001).

Lisa Smith-Butler, *Cost Effective Legal Research*, LEGAL REFERENCE SERVICES Q., vol. 18(2), at 61 (2000).

APPENDIX E. COMMONLY OWNED PUBLISHERS

Aspen	Wolters Kluwer
Bureau of National Affairs	Bureau of National Affairs
Butterworths	Reed Elsevier
Clark Boardman Callahan	Thomson
Commerce Clearing House	Wolters Kluwer
Congressional Information Service	Reed Elsevier
Dialog[322]	ProQuest
FindLaw	Thomson
Foundation Press	Thomson
Gale Group[323]	Cengage Learning
Hein	William S. Hein & Co., Inc.
Kleinrock	Wolters Kluwer
Kluwer	Wolters Kluwer
Lawyers Cooperative	Thomson
Lexis Publishing	Reed Elsevier
LexisNexis	Reed Elsevier
Little, Brown[324]	
Loislaw	Wolters Kluwer
Matthew Bender	Reed Elsevier
Michie	Reed Elsevier
Oceana online	Oxford University Press
Prentice-Hall[325]	
Research Institute of America	Thomson
Rothman	William S. Hein & Co., Inc.
Shepard's	Reed Elsevier
Tax Analysts	Tax Analysts
Tax Management	Bureau of National Affairs
Warren Gorham & Lamont	Thomson
West Group	Thomson
Westlaw	Thomson

→The information above reflects ownership groups in December 2009. Thomson and Reuters combined in 2008 to form Thomson Reuters.

---

[322] Part of Thomson until mid-2008.

[323] Part of Thomson until mid-2007.

[324] Still exists, but relevant titles purchased by Aspen.

[325] Still exists, but relevant titles acquired by Research Institute of America and Warren Gorham & Lamont.

INDEX (REFERENCES TO PAGE NUMBERS)